FRESH FROM FRANCE
VEGETABLE CREATIONS

ALSO BY FAYE LEVY

Faye Levy's Chocolate Sensations
Classic Cooking Techniques
La Cuisine du Poisson (in French, with Fernand Chambrette)
French Cooking Without Meat (in Hebrew)
French Desserts (in Hebrew)
French Cakes, Pastries and Cookies (in Hebrew)
The La Varenne Tour Book

Fresh From France
VEGETABLE CREATIONS

FAYE LEVY

ILLUSTRATIONS BY MAUREEN JENSEN
PHOTOGRAMS BY BILL WESTHEIMER

E. P. DUTTON   NEW YORK

Published in the United States by E. P. Dutton,
a division of NAL Penguin Inc.,
2 Park Avenue, New York, N.Y. 10016.

Published simultaneously in Canada by
Fitzhenry and Whiteside, Limited, Toronto.

Library of Congress Cataloging-in-Publication Data
Levy, Faye.
Vegetable creations.
(Fresh from France)

1. Cookery (Vegetables) 2. Cookery, French. I. Title.
II. Series.
TX801.L485   1987   641.6'5   87-483

ISBN: 0-525-24533-2

W

DESIGNED BY EARL TIDWELL

1 3 5 7 9 10 8 6 4 2

First Edition

TO CHEF FERNAND CHAMBRETTE

Contents

Acknowledgments   xv

Introduction   1

VEGETABLE TIMBALES, TERRINES, MOUSSES, AND SOUFFLÉS   8

VEGETABLE TIMBALES   8

Beet Timbales • Asparagus Timbales with Hollandaise Sauce • Carrot Timbales • Broccoli Timbales with Garlic Butter Sauce • Parsnip Timbales with Parsley Sauce • Spinach Timbales with Quick Cumin Hollandaise Sauce • Cauliflower Timbales with Tomato Butter Sauce • Turnip Timbales • Squash Timbales with Dill Sauce

VEGETABLE TERRINES AND MOLDS   29

Tricolored Vegetable Terrine with Creamy Basil-Garlic Sauce • Vegetable Terrine with Mushroom Mousse and Fresh Tomato Vinaigrette • Quick Spinach Pâté • Eggplant Savarin with Fresh Tomato Sauce • Spinach-Cauliflower Gâteau with Creamy Mushroom Sauce

VEGETABLE MOUSSES   41

Two-Tone Tomato Mousse • Avocado Mousse • Broccoli Bavarian • Cold Carrot Soufflé with Peas

CONTENTS

VEGETABLE SOUFFLÉS   48

Spinach and Goat Cheese Soufflé • Winter Squash Soufflé • Individual Onion Soufflés • Broccoli and Mushroom Soufflé with Chives • Cauliflower Soufflé Pudding with Gruyère Cheese

•

VEGETABLE TARTS, PASTRIES, AND CRÊPES   57

VEGETABLE QUICHES AND PIE-PASTRY TARTS   58

Bright Green Spinach Tart • Tomato and Goat Cheese Tartlets with Fresh Thyme • Cabbage Tart with Caraway Seeds • Creamy Mushroom Tart with Chives • Cauliflower Quiche with Onion and Gruyère Cheese • Chard and Tomato Tart

SAVORY VEGETABLE CREAM PUFFS AND QUENELLES   69

Cheese Puff Crown with Asparagus • Cream Puffs with Carrot Purée • Brie Beignets • Baked Broccoli Gnocci with Parmesan Cheese Sauce • Green Vegetable Quenelles with Mushroom Cream

VEGETABLE PIZZAS AND COUNTRY TARTS   79

Provençal Pizza • Ratatouille Pizza • Pipérade Pizza • Country Leek Tart • Festive Vegetable Tart • Alsatian Onion and Cream Cheese Tart

VEGETABLES IN PUFF PASTRY   90

Green Onion and Parmesan Croissants • Mushroom and Olive Pastry Rolls • Asparagus-Filled Pastry Cases with Watercress Sauce • Chanterelle Feuilletés with Vegetable Julienne • Layered Vegetable Tourte • Cèpe Turnovers

VEGETABLE CRÊPES   103

Buckwheat Crêpes with Creamy Vegetables • Spinach-Filled Crêpes with Crème Fraîche • Leek and Mushroom Crêpes • Crêpes with Peppers, Onions, and Peas in Curry Sauce • Eggplant Soufflé-Filled Crêpes with Red Pepper Sauce • Niçoise Baked Chick-Pea Pancake

VEGETABLES CANAPÉS   116

Asparagus and Roquefort Canapés • Cucumber and Herbed Goat Cheese Canapés • Radish Flower Canapés • Tomato and Egg Canapés • Roasted Pepper Canapés

GRATINS, PURÉES, AND STUFFED VEGETABLES 120

VEGETABLE GRATINS 121

Leek and Duxelles Gratin • Belgian Endive Gratin with Cream Sauce and Walnuts • Winter Squash Gratin with Fresh Tomato Sauce • Cauliflower Gratin with Light Cheese Sauce • Layered Cabbage and Mushroom Gratin • Quick Broccoli Gratin with Gruyère and Nuts • Brussels Sprouts Baked in Mornay Sauce • Swiss Chard and Pepper Gratin with Tomatoes • Turnip and Onion Gratin with Parmesan

VEGETABLE PURÉES 134

Zucchini Purée with Basil • Cauliflower and Potato Purée • Spinach Purée on Croûtes • Parsley Purée • Celery Root Purée • Creamy Carrot Purée • Green Pea Purée with Mint Butter

STUFFED VEGETABLES 141

Mushrooms Stuffed with Fresh Tomato Purée • Artichokes with Onion Compote • Artichokes Filled with Peas • Stuffed Eggplant with Pine Nut Pilaf and Tomato Curry Sauce • Eggplant with Tomatoes, Saffron, and Garlic • Eggplant Stuffed with Duxelles • Zucchini Stuffed with Red Pepper Purée • Tomatoes Filled with Artichoke and Rice Salad • Plum Tomatoes with Shallot Purée • Peppers Stuffed with Rice, Mushrooms, and Olives • Onions Stuffed with Spinach • Stuffed Pattypan Squash with Parmesan and Rice

•

GLAZED, BRAISED, STEAMED, AND POACHED VEGETABLES 158

GLAZED VEGETABLES 159

Ginger-Glazed Carrots and Turnips • Butter-Glazed Carrots • Glazed Baby Onions and Zucchini

BRAISED AND STEWED VEGETABLES 162

Braised Chestnuts • Cream-Braised Cabbage with Leeks • Cabbage with Apples and Cider • Butter-Braised Endives • Braised Fennel with Peppers and Olives • Asparagus and Carrots with Madeira • Flageolets with Green and Yellow Beans and Green Onion Butter • Colorful Vegetable Blanquette • Mixed Mushroom Ragoût

STEAMED VEGETABLES   172

Zucchini with Mint Butter • Pattypan Squash with Paprika Cream • Asparagus with Beurre Blanc • Steamed Carrots with Pistachio Butter • Beets with Orange Hollandaise

POACHED AND BOILED VEGETABLES   178

Provençal Vegetable and Garlic Feast • Baby Vegetables with Herb Butter Sauce • Cauliflower in Rosemary-Scented Tomato Sauce • French Curried Cauliflower • Broccoli with Roquefort Sauce • Zucchini with Capers and Hazelnut Butter • Lyonnaise Green Beans • Green Beans with Delicate Garlic Butter • Wax Beans with French Pesto Sauce • Brussels Sprouts with Creamy Mustard-Sage Sauce • Cabbage with Butter and Wine Vinegar • Artichokes with Tomato Béarnaise Sauce • Morels with Cream • White Beans with Tomatoes and Onions • Fava Beans in Garlic Cream

•

BAKED, GRILLED, SAUTÉED, AND FRIED VEGETABLES   196

BAKED AND GRILLED VEGETABLES   197

Zucchini, Eggplant, and Tomato Slices Baked with Herbs • Baked Mushrooms with Escargot Butter and Walnuts • Artichokes and Baby Onions Antiboise • Baked Onions with Dill Butter • Provençal Baked Tomatoes • Baked Beets with Lemon Cream • Grilled Peppers with Garlic and Olive Oil • Grilled Eggplant with Fresh Herbs • Grilled Mushrooms with Garlic Purée

SAUTÉED AND FRIED VEGETABLES   206

Medley of Vegetables with Fresh Thyme • Green Beans with Sautéed Walnuts • Carrots with Raspberry Vinegar • Sautéed Jerusalem Artichokes • Red and Green Cabbage Sauté with Goat Cheese • Sautéed Cucumbers with Dill • Garlic-Scented Zucchini with Celery • Sautéed Salsify with Fresh Herbs • Spinach, Leek, and Pumpkin Pancakes • Batter-Fried Vegetables with Rémoulade Sauce

POTATOES, RICE, AND PASTA 217

POTATOES 218

Potatoes with Vegetable Julienne Sauce • Potato and Cheese Gâteau • Steamed New Potatoes with Tarragon Butter • Light Potato Fritters with Pine Nuts • Potato Gratin with Cream • Potato Soufflé in Potato Skins • Baked Potato Cakes • Sautéed Potatoes with Peppers and Thyme • Creamy Potato Purée • Potato and Leek Pancakes • French Fried Sweet Potatoes

RICE 231

Rice with Peas and Basil • Rice with Sautéed Vegetables and Walnut Oil • Savory Rice Pilaf with Eggplant • Mediterranean Saffron Rice Pilaf with Vegetables • Creamy Rice Pilaf with Asparagus • Multicolored Pilaf with Sweet Red Peppers and Walnuts • Rice Pilaf with Artichoke Hearts, Carrots, and Toasted Almonds • Brown Rice Pilaf with Tarragon • Rice Ring with Curried Eggplant

PASTA 245

Tomato Pasta with Goat Cheese and Garlic • Pasta with Fresh Peas and Saffron Butter Sauce • Pasta with Creamy Broccoli Purée • Fettucine with Morels and Asparagus • Spaghetti with Fall Vegetables and Tomato-Tarragon Sauce • Pasta with Vegetable "Noodles" • Creamy Pasta Gratin with Cheese • Baked Pasta with Eggplant • Pasta with Broccoli, Cauliflower, and Roquefort Sauce • Couscous with Chanterelles • Couscous Pilaf with Carrots, Peas, and Sautéed Mushrooms

•

VEGETABLE SOUPS 260

HEARTY VEGETABLE SOUPS 261

Vegetable Bouillabaisse • Rich Onion Soup with Port • Creamy Onion Soup with Pasta • Country Spinach Soup • Provençal Vegetable Soup with Pasta and Pistou • Mushroom Cream Soup with Fresh Herbs • Vegetable Bourride with Aïoli • Southwestern Vegetable Soup with Vegetable Croutons

VEGETABLE PURÉE SOUPS 273

Fresh Pea Soup with Mint Cream • Touraine Chestnut Soup • Asparagus Soup with Olive Oil • Light Cauliflower Soup • Pumpkin and Pasta Soup • Pumpkin, Potato, and Leek Soup • Provençal Tomato Soup • Light Zucchini Soup with Curry Puffs • Norman Potato-Shallot Soup • Carrot Soup with Chives

VEGETABLE CREAM AND VELOUTÉ SOUPS 286

Swiss Chard Soup with Toasted Hazelnuts • Leek Cream Soup with Diced Tomatoes • Sorrel Velouté Soup • Watercress Velouté Soup with Cheese Puffs • Cauliflower Velouté Soup with Broccoli • Red Pepper Velouté Soup • Vegetable Stock • Chicken Stock

•

VEGETABLE SALADS 299

SIMPLE VEGETABLE SALADS 301

Watercress Salad with Goat Cheese and Walnuts • Green Salad with Pine Nuts and Sherry Vinaigrette • Celery Root Salad with Mustard Dressing • Fennel Salad with Herbed Crème Fraîche • Cucumber Salad with Yogurt Herb Dressing • Escarole Salad with Roquefort Cheese • Summer Tomato Salad with Fresh Herbs • Leeks Mimosa with Hazelnuts • Marinated Green Bean Salad with Green Onions • Warm Dandelion Salad with Mushrooms and Poached Eggs • Baby Artichokes with Hazelnut Oil Vinaigrette

COMPOSED VEGETABLE SALADS 313

Breton Vegetable Salad with Chive Mayonnaise • Corn Salad with Peppers • Tomatoes Stuffed with Mushroom Salad • Endive and Beet Salad • Chick-Pea and Bean Salad with Tomatoes and Basil • Avocado and Mushroom Salad with Swiss Chard • Cauliflower and Tomato Salad with Garlic and Walnut Dressing • Artichoke, Asparagus, Green Bean, and Fresh Pea Salad with Tarragon Mayonnaise • Provençal Marinated Vegetables

POTATO, RICE, AND PASTA SALADS 325

Potato and Beet Salad • Summer Potato and Green Bean Salad • Potato-Pepper Salad à la Provençale • Auvergne Potato Salad with Cantal Cheese • Potato Salad with Watercress • Potato, Asparagus, and Artichoke Salad • Rice Salad with Peas and Peppers • Rice Salad with Pyrenees Cheese, Mushrooms, and Tomatoes • Pasta Salad with Red Peppers, Broccoli, and Garlic Dressing • Mayonnaise • Crème Fraîche

Index   341

Eight pages of color plates follow page 174.

Acknowledgments

I would like to thank Anne Willan, president of La Varenne Cooking School in Paris, for enabling me to live in France for five wonderful years and giving me the most fabulous job any food lover could imagine—researching and drafting the recipes for such major books as *French Regional Cooking, The La Varenne Cooking Course,* and *Basic French Cookery.* During these years my beloved cooking teachers and associates at La Varenne—Master Chefs Fernand Chambrette, Albert Jorant, and Claude Vauguet—and Denis Ruffel of the excellent Parisian Patisserie Millet, shared with me their vast knowledge of the art of cooking, and I wish to convey my heartfelt appreciation to them.

I am also grateful to the people at *Bon Appétit* and *Gourmet* magazines for being open to my ideas. I originally developed some of the material here for these magazines. I learned so much from writing for them, and I feel that my work has benefited from the high standards they demand.

My sincere thanks to my editor, Carole DeSanti, for her support and encouragement, and for making the book clearer and easier to read; to Gregory Dinner for thinking of the series title, *Fresh from France;* and to Annie Horenn, Teri Appleton, Leona Fitzgerald, and Patsy Allen for their help in recipe testing.

Finally, a big thank-you to my husband and associate Yakir Levy for helping me write this book.

FRESH FROM FRANCE

VEGETABLE CREATIONS

Introduction

"In all of France, we are witnessing the triumph of vegetables." This is how the famous French gastronome, Christian Millau, summed up vegetables' recent stardom. Of course vegetables have been an important part of French cooking for centuries, but never before have they been used so lavishly throughout the meal. Vegetables are being used today in imaginative new ways to add color and excitement to contemporary menus.

Increasingly, vegetables are emphasized in the names of the most exquisite creations. Where a dish was once called, for example, "sole with white wine sauce," we might now say "sole with white wine sauce and baby vegetables." Some leading chefs will name the vegetable first, calling dishes "petits pois au homard" or "green peas with lobster," for example. Elegantly prepared vegetables have become symbolic of fresh, light, and natural cuisine.

Our own markets offer a growing selection of fresh native American produce and even many imported vegetables. Specialty produce farmers are now developing new varieties for us to enjoy. It would be difficult, perhaps impossible, to think of a food that comes to us in as many flavors, shapes, and colors as vegetables. It is not surprising, therefore, when people on both sides of the Atlantic are incorporating more and more vegetables into their diet, that everyone is looking for wonderful ways to prepare them.

People from all over the world travel to France to savor French food and to learn more about the greatest style of cooking in the Western world. If we take a look at the chefs who are considered to be at the forefront of the "new American cuisine," we will find that many of them studied in France, and this is obviously reflected in their cooking philosophy and their food. Even more than in fashion and the arts, in fine cuisine the French set the tone, style, and standards. Major French culinary trends are soon followed in other countries.

French cuisine is constantly evolving. Seasoning techniques and cooking methods are crossing international borders, and cooks in France are continuously experimenting with and searching for superb vegetable dishes. The French have been actively exploring, matching, and marrying the favorite flavorings of nearby Mediterranean and North African countries, as well as those of the Orient, into their own repertoire.

In fine kitchens, vegetables are treated with respect and are given the attention they deserve. French cooks have developed a set of rules for cooking the different types of vegetables so they retain maximum flavor and color and acquire a pleasing texture. This book teaches these principles and will enable home cooks to reproduce France's finest vegetable dishes. It includes updated versions of the best vegetable dishes from traditional family cooking, country cooking, and classic cuisine, as well as innovative vegetable dishes in the style of contemporary French cuisine.

The recipes in this book do not include meat, and thus perfectly complement meat or fish as side dishes or first courses. Many are ideal main courses for elegant light meals "à la française."

Following are several hints on vegetable preparation techniques you might find informative.

Artichoke Hearts

To shape in bottoms or "hearts": Squeeze juice of ½ lemon into bowl of cold water.

Break stem off of one fresh artichoke. Break off largest leaves at bottom. Put artichoke on its side on board.

Holding very sharp knife or small serrated knife against side of artichoke (parallel to leaves), cut lower circle of leaves off, up to edge of artichoke heart. Turn artichoke slightly after each cut. Rub exposed edges of artichoke heart with cut lemon.

Cut off central cone of leaves just above artichoke heart. Cut off leaves under base and trim base so it is round, removing all dark green areas.

Rub again with lemon. Put artichoke in bowl of lemon water. Repeat with remaining artichokes.

To cook artichoke hearts: Squeeze juice of ¼ to ½ lemon into a saucepan containing enough boiling salted water to generously cover artichokes.

Add artichoke hearts to water. Reduce heat to low, cover, and simmer about 15 minutes, or until tender when pierced with the point of a knife. Cool to lukewarm in liquid.

Using a teaspoon, scoop out hairlike choke from center of each fresh artichoke heart. Return artichokes to liquid until ready to use.

Asparagus

Very thin asparagus (about the thickness of a pencil) do not need to be peeled but other asparagus should be. Put an asparagus spear on a cutting board. Holding base of asparagus and beginning slightly below the tip, peel spear with a vegetable peeler all around. Cut off and discard about ½ inch from the bottom of the spear; this part is tough.

Garlic

To peel a garlic clove easily, put it on a board and hold the flat side of a large knife just above it. Hit the knife with your fist. The peel will be released and can be pulled off. If it remains partially attached at one end, cut it off at that end.

To chop or mince a peeled clove of garlic, hit it vigorously by holding the flat side of a large knife above the garlic and pounding the knife until the garlic is crushed. Cut it several times in one direction with a paring knife. Slice it against the direction of the first cuts. Chop it further with an up-and-down motion of a chopping knife. For minced garlic, continue chopping until it is in very tiny pieces.

Herbs

To chop herbs, rinse and dry thoroughly. Remove leaves from stems. Use a large, heavy chopping knife and a dry board. Holding the point of the knife down, move the handle up and down so that the knife blade goes through the herb several times, until it is chopped. For minced herbs, continue chopping until the herb is in very tiny pieces.

Chives can be held together and snipped with scissors or thinly sliced, instead of being chopped. Dill can also be snipped.

Leeks

To clean leeks, cut off the root ends, remove and discard the coarse outer leaves and about 1 inch of the leek tops. Split each leek lengthwise with a sharp knife, beginning about 1 inch from the root end and cutting toward the green end. Turn the leek around by about 90 degrees and split it again in the same way. Holding each leek by its root end, dip it repeatedly in a sinkful or large bowl of cold water. If dirt remains, soak the leeks in cold water for several minutes. Then separate the leaves under running water to rinse away any clinging dirt, and drain.

Mushrooms

To clean mushrooms, gently rinse one at a time under cold running water; do not soak them in water. Dry mushrooms upside down on paper towels.

To slice mushrooms, cut them in half, set each mushroom, cut side down, on board, and thinly slice.

Onions and Shallots

To peel an onion, cut off the root; do not cut off too much of the root end or the onion will begin to fall apart. Pull off the peel with the aid of a paring knife. Cut off the top.

To slice an onion, cut it lengthwise from stem end to root end. Put it, cut side down, on a cutting board. Holding a slicing knife in your right hand, slice the onion half crosswise, holding the knife against the curved fingers of your left hand and moving your left hand gradually back to guide the knife in cutting slices of an even thickness. The onion will be cut in half slices.

To chop or mince an onion, cut it lengthwise from stem end to root end. Put it, cut side down, on a cutting board. Using a slicing knife, cut the onion in vertical slices, starting nearly at the root end and slicing toward the stem end but leaving the onion joined at its root end. Next cut the onion in several horizontal slices, still leaving it attached at the root end.

Slice the onion crosswise, beginning at the stem end, and form small cubes. Chop onion cubes further with an up-and-down motion of a chopping knife. For minced onion, continue chopping until the onion is in very tiny pieces.

Onions and shallots can also be sliced or chopped in a food processor, according to the machine's instruction manual. If using a food processor, drain the chopped onion on paper towels before cooking so it will not be watery.

Spinach

To clean spinach, as fresh spinach is sandy and must be carefully cleaned before cooking, remove stems by pulling them off the leaves; discard. Wash the leaves thoroughly by placing them in a sinkful of cold water, lifting them out into a bowl, and changing the water. Repeat rinsing two or three times or until no sand remains.

To substitute frozen spinach for fresh: Frozen spinach can be substituted for fresh in recipes calling for cooked puréed spinach, although the flavor and texture will not be quite as good because frozen spinach also contains stems. Because frozen spinach is already blanched, it does not require cooking in water, but simply thawing;

to save time, however, it can be cooked in boiling water until it thaws, then drained and squeezed according to the recipes.

Both fresh and frozen spinach vary in the amounts of actual cooked spinach obtainable from a certain weight. From 1½ pounds of fresh spinach (weight including stems), I have most often obtained ¾ cup purée, but occasionally only ½ cup. In comparing 10-ounce packages of frozen spinach of different brands, I have also found they give between ½ cup and ¾ cup purée. To solve the problem, in recipes in which the exact quantity of purée is important, I have included it, even though in some cases part of the spinach will not be used.

Tomatoes

To peel: Before using tomatoes for cooking, they are often peeled, seeded, and chopped. Using a paring knife, cut the cores from the tomatoes. Turn the tomatoes over and slit the skin in an X-shaped cut. Fill a large bowl with cold water. Put the tomatoes in a pan containing enough boiling water to generously cover them and boil about 10 to 15 seconds, or until the skin begins to pull away from the flesh along the cut. Remove the tomatoes with a slotted spoon and put them in the bowl of cold water. Leave for a few seconds. Remove the tomatoes and pull off the skins with the aid of the paring knife.

To seed: With a large knife, cut the tomatoes in half horizontally. Hold each half over a bowl, cut side down, and squeeze to remove the seeds.

To chop: With a chopping knife, cut the tomatoes several times in one direction, then in the other direction. Chop them further with an up-and-down motion of the knife.

Other Ingredients

In this book, unless otherwise specified, instructions are predicated on using the following ingredients:

• Unsalted, or sweet, butter is of higher quality than salted, but salted butter can be used in recipes unless the unsalted type is specified.

• Use large eggs unless otherwise specified.

- Use whole milk.
- Heavy cream is called whipping cream in part of the country.
- For vegetable oil, use any neutral-flavored oil, such as corn oil, safflower oil, sunflower seed oil, or peanut oil.
- Always use dry wine for cooking unless otherwise specified. The best wine to choose is one that you also like to drink, but there is no need to use expensive wines for cooking.

Vegetable Timbales, Terrines, Mousses, and Soufflés

Timbales, terrines, mousses, and soufflés are the most glamorous types of vegetable dishes. Vegetable soufflés and timbales are traditional favorites that have reached new heights in popularity, while vegetable mousses and terrines are modern creations.

Vegetable Timbales

Vegetable timbales are round molds of baked creamy purées. They are sophisticated and elegant in appearance but at the same time quick and easy to prepare.

These versatile dishes can be prepared from a great variety of vegetables during all seasons of the year. Even humble vegetables such as parsnips or turnips acquire distinction and a delicious flavor when turned into timbales. Simply cooked foods, from poached fish fillets to sautéed chicken to broiled meats, become festive when accompanied by a bright green spinach timbale or a vivid orange timbale of carrot or squash.

The term *timbale* refers to both the molds and to the foods cooked in them. Vegetable timbales are baked in special cylindrical timbale molds, sometimes called *dariole* molds, or in ramekins. The word *dariole* is also occasionally used to refer to these vegetable dishes.

Traditional recipes for timbales often use flour or bread crumbs to bind the vegetable mixtures together, but contemporary cooks prefer to use another technique. They treat timbales as savory vegetable custards, in which the vegetable purée is the main ingredient, and the purée is thickened by reducing it with cream. Both classic and modern timbales make use of eggs to firm the mixture so it holds together when unmolded.

When served as a first course, timbales are generally accompanied by a sauce, which can be a tomato sauce, brown sauce, cream-based sauce, cheese sauce, or butter sauce. The color and flavor of the sauce should complement the vegetable; its consistency should be smooth and flowing so it can be poured easily around the base of the timbales.

Timbales served as side dishes can be accompanied by whatever sauce is planned for the main course; there is no need in this case to prepare a separate sauce for the timbale. The rule for matching timbales with entrées is simple: Select a timbale made of a vegetable that would ordinarily complement the main dish. Timbales of sweet vegetables such as carrots, beets, turnips, or parsnips can be paired with beef, lamb, pork, or poultry; delicate ones such as asparagus or squash are perfect with veal; spinach, cauliflower, and broccoli timbales go well with most foods.

With today's trend toward lighter eating, timbales can be the basis for unconventional main courses as well. Surround a broccoli timbale, for example, with garlic butter sauce topped by several steamed shrimp for an elegant entrée. For a change-of-pace luncheon menu, set a cool beet timbale on a bed of crisp greens and accompany it with a light rice salad dressed with dill vinaigrette.

Hints

• When preparing timbale mixtures, whisk the eggs only until smooth but not frothy. Whisking the eggs too vigorously creates foam that solidifies during baking and mars the smoothness of the timbales.

• Timbales, terrines, and molds are delicate and are therefore baked gently in a water bath to ensure a silky texture. The dishes are set in a large shallow pan in the oven. The pan is filled with hot water, and the molds are then covered with a sheet of foil to protect their tops. The water moderates the oven temperature so the molds bake slowly and evenly and provides moisture so they do not dry out.

• When preparing a water bath, pull out the oven rack slightly before adding water to the pan. After adding the water, very carefully slide the rack back into the oven to avoid spilling water into the molds.

• For proper cooking, the water in a water bath should remain hot but not boiling. If it begins to boil, the texture of the molds becomes marred by small holes.

• Careful checking is essential when baking timbales and other baked molds. Overcooking results in rubbery rather than soft, creamy timbales and may cause them to separate. Underbaked custards may stick or fall apart when unmolded. When a timbale is ready, its surface should be firm and springy to the touch. At this point, carefully insert a cake tester in the center of the mixture, which is the last part to set; if the tester comes out clean, the timbale is done. When making individual servings, check each timbale to see if it is done, because the temperature may not be uniform throughout the oven.

• Unmold timbales while they are hot; otherwise the butter congeals on the molds and makes the timbales stick. Hold the knife straight when running it around the sides of the timbale to unmold. If a timbale did not unmold neatly, use a metal spatula to smooth it; or spoon some sauce over it. Baked timbales can be unmolded and kept warm for 15 to 30 minutes by being covered carefully with the molds and set in a warm place. When serving a timbale on a plate with meat and sauce, it is easiest to first unmold the timbale onto the plate, and then to add the main course and sauce.

❧ BEET TIMBALES
Timbales de betteraves

Beets are an underutilized vegetable in the United States and deserve to be better known. Making them into beautiful bright-colored timbales might be the best way to introduce them to your table. These new timbales have a delicately sweet flavor and make a lovely first course or side dish for light meats and poultry. For a spectacular presentation they can be served surrounded by a sauce, such as the mustard sauce suggested below or with Dill Sauce (page 26) or Lemon Cream (page 202).   MAKES 4 OR 5 SERVINGS

BEET TIMBALES
*2¼ pounds small beets, 1½ to 2
    inches in diameter, without
    leaves*
*⅔ cup heavy cream, room
    temperature*

3 eggs
Salt and freshly ground pepper

MUSTARD SAUCE (OPTIONAL)
1 tablespoon unsalted butter
2 shallots, finely chopped
¼ cup dry white wine
*½ cup Chicken Stock (see recipe) or
    Vegetable Stock (see recipe)*

Salt and freshly ground pepper
1¼ cups heavy cream
*1½ to 2 tablespoons Dijon
    mustard*

BEET TIMBALES
Preheat oven to 375°F. Generously butter four 5-ounce ramekins or five 4- or 4½-ounce timbale molds, being careful to thoroughly butter bases of molds. Butter sheet of foil to cover ramekins or molds.

Put beets in medium or large saucepan, cover with water, add pinch of salt, and bring to boil. Cover, reduce heat to medium-low, and cook about 35 minutes, or until tender when pierced with a small sharp knife. Slip off skins while rinsing beets with cold water. Cut off root ends. Drain beets thoroughly in large strainer. Purée beets in food processor or hand food mill until very smooth. Measure 2 cups purée.

Cook purée in a heavy, medium-size wide saucepan over low heat, stirring often, for 5 minutes to evaporate excess moisture. Stir heavy cream into purée. Raise heat to high and bring to boil. Reduce heat to medium and cook, stirring often, until cream is absorbed and mixture is reduced to 2 cups. Transfer mixture to a bowl and cool 7 minutes.

Whisk eggs in a medium-size bowl until blended. Gradually whisk in beet mixture. Season to taste with salt and pepper; season well so timbales will not be bland.

Divide mixture among ramekins or molds, tapping each on counter to pack down mixture. Smooth tops, set ramekins in roasting pan, and transfer to oven. Add enough boiling water to roasting pan to come halfway up sides of ramekins. Set sheet of buttered foil atop ramekins.

Bake about 40 to 50 minutes or until timbales are firm to the touch and cake tester inserted into centers comes out dry. If necessary, add hot water occasionally to roasting pan so that it does not become dry. If water comes close to a boil, add a few tablespoons cold water.

MUSTARD SAUCE

Melt butter in a medium-size heavy saucepan over low heat. Add shallots and cook, stirring, about 2 minutes, or until softened. Add wine, stock, salt, and pepper, and simmer, stirring, until liquid is reduced to about 2 tablespoons.

Stir in cream and bring to a boil, stirring. Reduce heat to medium and cook, stirring often, until sauce is thick enough to coat a spoon, about 7 minutes. Set aside. (Sauce can be kept, covered, in refrigerator up to 1 day.)

To Finish Timbales and Sauce: When timbales are done, carefully remove molds from water bath and cool on rack 5 minutes. Run thin-bladed flexible knife around edge of each ramekin or mold. Set small plate atop one mold and invert. Holding them together, tap on towel-covered working surface. Gently lift off mold. Repeat with remaining molds. Serve timbales hot or at room temperature.

Reheat sauce, if necessary, over medium heat, whisking. Reduce heat to low and whisk in 1½ tablespoons mustard. Taste, and add salt, pepper, and mustard, if needed. Serve hot or at room temperature.

To serve, spoon 2 to 3 tablespoons sauce on plate around each timbale and tilt plate so sauce runs around it. Serve remaining sauce separately.

ASPARAGUS TIMBALES WITH HOLLANDAISE SAUCE
Timbales d'asperges, sauce hollandaise

In classic cuisine hollandaise sauce is a favorite accompaniment for poached asparagus. Here, a quick version of the sauce surrounds the pale green asparagus timbales. Bright green asparagus tips provide a decorative finishing touch.   MAKES 4 OR 5 SERVINGS

ASPARAGUS TIMBALES
*3 pounds medium-size asparagus
    spears*
*⅔ cup heavy cream, room
    temperature*

3 eggs
Salt and white pepper
Freshly grated nutmeg

QUICK HOLLANDAISE SAUCE
3 egg yolks, room temperature
Pinch of salt
*1 tablespoon strained fresh lemon
    juice*

*¾ cup unsalted butter, cut in
    pieces*
1 tablespoon hot water
Pinch of cayenne pepper

*16 to 20 asparagus tips, for
    garnish*

ASPARAGUS TIMBALES
Preheat oven to 375°F. Generously butter four 5-ounce ramekins or five 4- or 4½-ounce timbale molds, being careful to thoroughly butter bases of molds. Butter sheet of foil to cover ramekins.

Peel asparagus spears and cut into 2-inch pieces, discarding tough ends (about ½ inch from end). In a medium-size saucepan, boil asparagus pieces, uncovered, in boiling salted water, about 3 to 5 minutes, or until tender when pierced with small sharp knife. Drain thoroughly. Return asparagus to dry saucepan and cook over low heat, stirring and mashing with wooden spoon, until excess liquid evaporates, about 7 minutes. Place asparagus in large strainer. Press to remove excess liquid; do not push asparagus pulp through strainer. Purée asparagus in food processor until very smooth. Measure 2 cups.

Cook purée in heavy, medium-size wide saucepan over low heat, stirring often, for 5 minutes to evaporate excess moisture. Stir cream into purée. Raise heat to high and bring to boil. Reduce heat to medium and cook, stirring often, until cream is absorbed and mixture is reduced to 2 cups, about 5 minutes. Transfer mixture to bowl and cool 7 minutes.

Whisk eggs in medium-size bowl until blended. Gradually whisk in asparagus purée. Season to taste with salt, pepper, and nutmeg; season well so timbales will not be bland.

Divide mixture among ramekins. Tap each on counter to pack down. Smooth tops, set ramekins in roasting pan, and transfer to oven. Add enough boiling water to roasting pan to come halfway up sides of ramekins. Set sheet of buttered foil atop ramekins.

Bake about 35 minutes, or until timbales are firm to the touch and a cake tester inserted into centers comes out dry. If necessary, add hot water occasionally to roasting pan so that it does not become dry. If water comes close to a boil, add a few tablespoons cold water.

When timbales are done, remove molds from water bath. Cool on rack 5 minutes. Carefully run thin-bladed flexible knife around edge of each ramekin or mold. Set small plate atop one ramekin and invert. Holding them together, tap on towel-covered working surface. Gently lift off ramekin. Repeat with remaining ramekins. Cover each timbale gently with a ramekin or mold while preparing garnish and sauce.

In a large pan of boiling salted water, cook 16 to 20 asparagus tips about 2 minutes, or until barely tender and still bright green. Drain thoroughly.

QUICK HOLLANDAISE SAUCE

Prepare sauce a short time before serving. Combine egg yolks, salt, and 2 teaspoons lemon juice in blender or food processor, and process until lightened in color and very well blended. Remove pusher from processor.

Place butter in small heavy saucepan; if possible use one with a lip to facilitate pouring melted butter into blender or processor. Set over medium-low heat, and warm until butter melts and sizzles. With blade of machine turning (at high speed if using blender), gradually pour hot butter, drop by drop, through top. After 2 or 3 tablespoons of butter have been added, pour remaining butter through in thin, steady stream, with blade of machine still turning. Add hot water and process briefly to mix. Blend in cayenne pepper and remaining lemon juice. Taste and adjust seasoning. Serve sauce immediately. (It can be transferred to bowl and kept warm for about 15 minutes on a rack set above hot water, but it must be whisked frequently. It can also be kept warm in vacuum bottle. Sauce may thicken if it is kept warm and should be diluted with a little more hot water; whisk in water, 1 teaspoon at a time.)

To serve, remove ramekins, spoon 2 to 3 tablespoons sauce on plate around each timbale, and tilt plate so sauce runs evenly around it. Garnish with reserved asparagus tips, pointing outward. Serve remaining sauce separately.

CARROT TIMBALES
Timbales de carottes

Vivid orange carrot timbales make an impressive first course, especially when they are accompanied by a sauce of a contrasting color, such as Watercress Sauce (page 94), or surrounded by Glazed Baby Onions and Zucchini (see recipe). Another delicious and attractive way to present them is to surround each with Herb Butter Sauce (page 181) and to set a steamed baby carrot on the sauce on each plate. As a side dish, they are perfect with sautéed chicken or veal.

MAKES 4 SERVINGS

1 pound carrots, peeled and cut in medium-size slices	½ cup milk
	Salt and freshly ground pepper
1 tablespoon butter	Pinch of sugar
3 eggs	

Preheat oven to 400°F. Generously butter four 5-ounce ramekins.

Put carrots in a saucepan, cover them with water, and add a

pinch of salt. Bring to a boil, cover, and cook about 15 minutes, or until very tender. Drain thoroughly. Purée in a food processor until smooth.

Melt butter in saucepan used to cook carrots. Add carrot purée and cook over low heat, stirring often, about 3 minutes, or until butter is absorbed and excess moisture evaporates. Remove from heat.

Whisk eggs with milk in a medium-size bowl. Gradually whisk in carrot purée. Season to taste with salt, pepper, and sugar.

Divide carrot mixture among ramekins, tapping each to pack down mixture. Smooth top, and set ramekins in a roasting pan in oven. Add enough boiling water to pan to come halfway up sides of ramekins. Bake 35 to 40 minutes, or until firm to the touch; a cake tester inserted into centers should come out dry. Add water occasionally to roasting pan so that it does not become dry.

Remove molds from water bath and let cool 2 or 3 minutes. Carefully run a thin-bladed flexible knife around edge of each ramekin. Set small plate atop each mold and invert. Holding them together, tap on towel-covered working surface. Gently lift off mold. Repeat with each ramekin. Serve hot, room temperature, or cold.

BROCCOLI TIMBALES WITH GARLIC BUTTER SAUCE
Timbales de brocolis, beurre à l'ail

Tiny broccoli florets provide a bright green garnish for the light green timbales and their golden butter sauce.   MAKES 4 SERVINGS

BROCCOLI TIMBALES

2 pounds broccoli, divided into
     medium-size florets, stalks
     reserved
⅔ cup heavy cream, room
     temperature

3 eggs
Salt and white pepper
Freshly grated nutmeg (optional)

GARLIC BUTTER SAUCE

2 tablespoons minced garlic
3 tablespoons minced shallots
⅓ cup dry white wine
2 tablespoons mild white wine
 vinegar (5 percent acidity)

2 tablespoons heavy cream
Salt and white pepper
1 cup well-chilled unsalted butter,
 cut into 16 cubes

15 or 16 small broccoli florets, for
 garnish

BROCCOLI TIMBALES

Preheat oven to 375°F. Generously butter four 5-ounce rame-kins, being careful to thoroughly butter bases. Butter sheet of foil to cover ramekins.

Trim off bottom 2 inches of broccoli stalk. Peel remaining stalk and cut in ½-inch-thick slices. In a large saucepan of boiling salted water, cook broccoli florets and slices, uncovered, about 8 minutes, or until very tender. Drain, rinse with cold water, and drain thoroughly. Purée broccoli in food processor or blender until very smooth.

Cook purée in a medium-size shallow, heavy saucepan over low heat, stirring often, for 5 minutes to evaporate excess moisture. Stir heavy cream into purée. Raise heat to high and bring to boil. Reduce heat to medium and cook, stirring often, until cream is ab-sorbed and mixture is reduced to 2 cups. Transfer to a bowl and cool 7 minutes.

Whisk eggs in medium-size bowl until blended. Gradually add broccoli purée and season to taste with salt, pepper, and nutmeg; season well so timbales will not be bland.

Divide mixture among ramekins. Tap each on counter to pack down. Smooth tops and set ramekins in roasting pan in oven. Add enough boiling water to roasting pan to come halfway up sides of ramekins. Set sheet of buttered foil atop ramekins.

Bake about 38 minutes, or until timbales are firm to touch and cake tester inserted into centers comes out dry. If necessary, add hot water occasionally to roasting pan so that it does not become dry. If water comes close to a boil, add a few tablespoons cold water.

GARLIC BUTTER SAUCE

In small heavy saucepan, combine garlic, shallots, wine, and vine-gar and cook over medium heat until liquid is reduced to about 2 tablespoons.

Reduce heat to low, add cream, and simmer, whisking often, until mixture is reduced to about 3 tablespoons. Keep butter cubes in refrigerator until ready to use. (Reduction can be prepared several hours ahead and kept, covered, in refrigerator.)

To Finish Timbales and Sauce: When timbales are done, re-move from water bath. Cool on rack 5 minutes. Carefully run thin-bladed flexible knife around edge of each ramekin. Set small plate atop one ramekin and invert. Holding them together, tap on towel-covered working surface. Gently lift off ramekin. Repeat with remain-ing ramekins. Cover each timbale gently with a ramekin while finish-ing sauce and garnish.

In medium-size saucepan of boiling salted water, blanch broccoli florets, uncovered, over high heat about 2 minutes, or until just ten-der. Drain thoroughly.

To finish sauce, bring garlic mixture to a simmer in a small heavy saucepan. Reduce heat to low, and season lightly with salt and white pepper. Add 2 cubes of butter, whisking liquid constantly. When butter cubes are nearly blended into liquid, add another cube, still whisking. Continue adding butter cubes, 1 or 2 at a time, whisking constantly. Sauce should thicken and should be pleasantly warm to touch. (If at any time sauce becomes too hot and drops of melted butter appear, immediately remove from heat and add 2 butter cubes off heat, whisking constantly. When temperature of sauce drops again to warm, return to low heat and continue whisking in remaining butter cubes.) Remove from heat as soon as last butter cube is added.

Strain sauce into a bowl. Taste and adjust seasoning.

(Sauce can be kept warm for about 15 minutes in its bowl set on rack above hot water, but it must be whisked frequently to prevent separation. It can also be kept warm in a vacuum bottle.)

To serve, remove ramekins, spoon 2 to 3 tablespoons sauce on plate around timbale, and tilt plate so sauce runs evenly around it. Set a few broccoli florets on each plate. Serve remaining sauce separately.

❧ PARSNIP TIMBALES WITH PARSLEY SAUCE
Timbales de panais, sauce au persil

This is my favorite way to prepare parsnips. These timbales could change the minds of many people about this vegetable, even avowed parsnip haters. Serve the timbales with roasted or grilled lamb, beef, or chicken.   MAKES 4 OR 5 SERVINGS

PARSNIP TIMBALES

1½ pounds parsnips	*3 eggs*
⅔ cup heavy cream, room	*Salt and white pepper*
temperature	*Freshly grated nutmeg*

PARSLEY SAUCE

4 medium-size shallots, minced	*2 cups heavy cream*
1 bay leaf	*Salt and freshly ground pepper*
½ cup dry white wine	*Pinch of cayenne pepper*
1 cup Chicken Stock (see recipe) or	*½ cup well-packed fresh parsley*
Vegetable Stock (see recipe)	*sprigs without stems*

PARSNIP TIMBALES

Preheat oven to 375°F. Generously butter five 4- or 4½-ounce timbale molds or four 5-ounce ramekins, being careful to thoroughly butter bases of molds. Butter sheet of foil to cover ramekins.

Peel parsnips and cut crosswise into ½-inch slices. Put parsnips in medium-size saucepan, cover them with water, add pinch of salt, and bring to boil. Cover, reduce heat to medium, and cook about 20 minutes, or until very tender. Drain thoroughly. Purée in food processor until very smooth. Measure 2 cups purée.

Cook measured purée in a medium-size heavy, wide saucepan over low heat, stirring often, for 5 minutes to evaporate excess moisture. Stir cream into purée. Raise heat to high and bring to boil. Reduce heat to medium and cook, stirring often, until cream is absorbed and mixture is reduced to 2 cups. Transfer mixture to a bowl and cool 7 minutes.

Whisk eggs in medium-size bowl until blended. Gradually whisk in parsnip purée. Season to taste with salt, pepper, and nutmeg; season well so timbales will not be bland.

Divide mixture among molds. Tap each on counter to pack down. Smooth tops, set molds in roasting pan, and transfer to oven. Add enough boiling water to roasting pan to come halfway up sides of molds. Set sheet of buttered foil atop molds.

Bake about 40 minutes or until timbales are firm to touch and cake tester inserted into center comes out dry. If necessary, add hot water occasionally to roasting pan so that it does not become dry. If water comes close to a boil, add a few tablespoons cold water.

PARSLEY SAUCE

Combine shallots, bay leaf, and wine in a large heavy saucepan and bring to boil over high heat. Add stock and bring to boil. Reduce heat to medium-high and cook, stirring often, until liquid is reduced to about ½ cup. Stir in cream, add a pinch of salt and pepper, and bring to boil, stirring. Reduce heat to medium and cook, stirring often, until sauce is thick enough to coat spoon, about 7 minutes. Strain sauce, pressing seasonings against sides of strainer. (Sauce can be kept, covered, up to 1 day in refrigerator.)

Reheat sauce, if necessary, in a medium-size saucepan over low heat, whisking. Remove from heat and add cayenne pepper. Chop parsley in food processor, add sauce, and purée until well blended. Return to saucepan and heat, stirring, about 2 minutes, or until again thick enough to coat a spoon. Taste and adjust seasoning.

To Finish Timbales and Sauce: When timbales are done, remove molds from water bath. Cool on rack 5 minutes. Carefully run thin-bladed flexible knife around edge of each mold. Set small plate atop mold and invert. Holding them together, tap on towel-covered working surface. Gently lift off mold. Repeat with remaining molds. Cover each timbale gently with a mold while finishing sauce.

Remove molds from timbales, spoon 2 to 3 tablespoons sauce on plate around timbale, and tilt plate so sauce runs around it. Serve remaining sauce separately.

SPINACH TIMBALES WITH QUICK CUMIN HOLLANDAISE SAUCE
Timbales d'épinards, sauce hollandaise au cumin

These deep green timbales are served with cumin-flavored hollandaise sauce, typical of the current fashion of French cooks of incorporating seasonings from other cuisines (in this case, from nearby Morocco) into their own. For extra color, garnish the top of each timbale with a very small spoonful of diced raw or cooked tomato. The timbales are also good served alone or with Garlic Butter Sauce (page 16), Beurre Blanc (page 174), or Fresh Tomato Sauce (page 36).　　　　　　　　　　　　　　　　MAKES 4 OR 5 SERVINGS

SPINACH TIMBALES

4 pounds fresh spinach (leaves with
　　stems)
¾ cup heavy cream, room
　　temperature

3 eggs
Salt and white pepper
Freshly grated nutmeg

QUICK CUMIN HOLLANDAISE SAUCE

3 egg yolks, room temperature
1 teaspoon ground cumin,
　　preferably fresh
Salt
1 tablespoon strained fresh lemon
　　juice

¾ cup unsalted butter, cut in pieces
1 tablespoon hot water
Pinch of cayenne pepper

SPINACH TIMBALES

Preheat oven to 375°F. Generously butter four 5-ounce ramekins or five 4- or 4½-ounce timbale molds, being careful to thoroughly butter bases of molds. Butter sheet of foil to cover ramekins.

Remove stems of spinach and wash leaves thoroughly. In very large saucepan of boiling salted water over high heat, cook spinach, uncovered, pushing leaves down into water often, about 3 minutes, or until very tender. Rinse with cold water, and drain thoroughly. Squeeze by handfuls until dry. Purée in food processor until very smooth.

Cook purée in medium-size shallow, heavy saucepan over low heat, stirring often, for 5 minutes to evaporate excess moisture. Stir cream into purée. Raise heat to high and bring to boil. Reduce heat to medium and cook, stirring often, until cream is absorbed, and mixture is reduced to 2 cups. Transfer to bowl and cool 7 minutes.

Whisk eggs in medium-size bowl until blended. Gradually whisk in spinach purée. Season to taste with salt, pepper, and nutmeg; season well so timbales will not be bland.

Divide mixture among ramekins. Tap each on counter to pack down. Smooth tops, set ramekins in roasting pan, and transfer to oven. Add enough boiling water to roasting pan to come halfway up sides of ramekins. Set sheet of buttered foil atop ramekins.

Bake about 40 minutes, or until timbales are firm to touch and cake tester inserted into centers comes out dry. If necessary, add hot water occasionally to roasting pan so that it does not become dry. If water comes close to a boil, add a few tablespoons cold water.

When timbales are done, remove molds from water bath. Cool on rack 5 minutes. Carefully run thin-bladed flexible knife around edge of each ramekin or mold. Set small plate atop mold and invert. Holding them together, tap on towel-lined working surface. Gently lift off mold. Repeat with remaining molds. Cover each timbale gently with a ramekin or mold while preparing sauce.

QUICK CUMIN HOLLANDAISE SAUCE
Prepare sauce a short time before serving. Combine egg yolks, cumin, salt, and 2 teaspoons lemon juice in blender or food processor and process until lightened in color and very well blended. Remove pusher from processor.

Place butter in small heavy saucepan; if possible use one with a lip to facilitate pouring melted butter into blender or processor. Set over medium-low heat and warm until butter melts and sizzles. With blade of machine turning (at high speed if using blender), gradually pour hot butter, drop by drop, through top. After 2 or 3 tablespoons of butter have been added, pour remaining butter through in thin, steady stream, with blade of machine still turning. Add hot water and process briefly to mix. Blend in cayenne pepper and remaining lemon juice. Taste and adjust seasoning. Use immediately.

To serve, remove molds from timbales, spoon 2 to 3 tablespoons sauce on plate around timbale, and tilt plate so sauce runs around it. Serve remaining sauce separately.

NOTE: Three 10-ounce packages frozen spinach can be substituted for fresh. Thaw completely, squeeze dry, and purée. Measure 2 cups purée. Continue as above, with step of heating purée with cream.

❧ CAULIFLOWER TIMBALES WITH TOMATO BUTTER SAUCE
Timbales de chou-fleur, beurre à la tomate

These timbales, whether served hot or at room temperature, are also good with Fresh Tomato Vinaigrette (page 32) or with a green salad. For a different shape, bake them in 4- or 5-ounce oval molds. The tomato butter sauce here can be prepared ahead or while the timbales are baking, except for the final amount of butter, which should be added a short time before serving.

MAKES 4 OR 5 SERVINGS

CAULIFLOWER TIMBALES
One 2-pound head of cauliflower
⅔ cup heavy cream, room
    temperature

3 eggs
Salt and white pepper
Freshly grated nutmeg (optional)

TOMATO BUTTER SAUCE
1 sprig of fresh thyme
1 bay leaf
5 parsley stems
1 tablespoon unsalted butter
1 cup chopped onion
2 medium-size garlic cloves, minced
1½ pounds ripe tomatoes, peeled,
    seeded (juice reserved), and
    chopped

1 cup unsalted butter, well chilled,
    cut in ½-inch pieces
2 teaspoons tomato paste
Salt and freshly ground pepper

CAULIFLOWER TIMBALES

Preheat oven to 375°F. Generously butter four 5-ounce ramekins or five 4- or 4½-ounce timbale molds, being careful to thoroughly butter bases of molds. Butter sheet of foil to cover ramekins.

Discard leaves and large stalk from cauliflower and divide it into medium florets. In a large saucepan of boiling salted water over high heat, cook cauliflower, uncovered, about 8 minutes, or until very tender. Drain, rinse with cold water, and drain thoroughly. Purée in food processor until very smooth. Measure 2 cups purée.

Cook purée in medium-size heavy, wide saucepan over low heat, stirring often, for 5 minutes to evaporate excess moisture. Stir cream into purée. Raise heat to high and bring to boil. Reduce heat to medium and cook, stirring often, until cream is absorbed and mixture is reduced to 2 cups. Transfer to a bowl and cool 7 minutes.

In medium-size bowl, whisk eggs until blended. Gradually whisk in cauliflower purée. Season to taste with salt, pepper, and nutmeg; season well so timbales will not be bland.

Divide mixture among ramekins. Tap each on counter to pack down. Smooth tops, set ramekins in roasting pan, and transfer to oven. Add enough boiling water to roasting pan to come halfway up sides of ramekins. Set sheet of buttered foil atop ramekins.

Bake about 40 minutes, or until timbales are firm to touch and cake tester inserted into centers comes out dry. If necessary, add hot water occasionally to roasting pan so that it does not become dry. If water comes close to a boil, add a few tablespoons cold water.

TOMATO BUTTER SAUCE

Tie thyme, bay leaf, and parsley stems in a piece of cheesecloth to make a bouquet garni. Melt 1 tablespoon butter in medium saucepan over low heat. Stir in onion and cook over low heat, stirring, about 10 minutes, or until soft but not brown. Add garlic and cook 30 seconds. Stir in tomato and add bouquet garni. Raise heat to medium and cook, stirring often, about 25 minutes, or until mixture is thick and reduced to about 1⅓ cups. Discard bouquet garni. (Tomato mixture can be prepared 1 day ahead up to this point and refrigerated.)

To Finish Timbales and Sauce: When timbales are done, remove molds from water bath. Cool on rack 5 minutes. Carefully run thin-bladed flexible knife around edge of each ramekin or mold. Set small plate atop ramekin and invert. Holding them together, tap on towel-covered working surface. Gently lift off ramekin. Repeat with remaining ramekins. Cover each timbale gently with a ramekin while finishing sauce.

Transfer tomato mixture to small saucepan. Bring to a simmer. Reduce heat to low. Add 2 cubes of butter, whisking liquid constantly. When butter cubes are nearly blended into liquid, add another cube, still whisking. Continue adding butter cubes, 1 or 2 at a time, whisking constantly. Sauce should thicken and should be pleasantly warm to touch. Do not cook too long. Remove from heat as soon as last butter cube is added.

Strain 2 tablespoons reserved tomato juice into sauce. Strain sauce into another small saucepan, pressing on tomatoes with back of spoon to extract all liquid. Place over very low heat briefly just to rewarm, whisking constantly. Remove from heat. Whisk in tomato paste. Add salt and pepper to taste. Serve immediately.

To serve, remove ramekins, spoon 2 to 3 tablespoons sauce on plate around timbale, and tilt plate so sauce runs around it. Serve remaining sauce separately.

TURNIP TIMBALES
Timbales de navets

Turnips gain glamour when turned into timbales and go very well with roast duck, chicken, or lamb. If desired, serve the timbales with Dill Sauce (page 26) or Parsley Sauce (page 19). No sauce is needed if the timbales will be an accompaniment for a dish that already has its own sauce.   MAKES 4 OR 5 SERVINGS

1 ¾ pounds small turnips   *Salt and white pepper*
⅔ cup heavy cream, room   *Freshly grated nutmeg*
  temperature   *1 teaspoon snipped chives, for*
3 eggs   *garnish (optional)*

Preheat oven to 375°F. Generously butter four 5-ounce ramekins or five 4- or 4½-ounce timbale molds, being careful to thoroughly butter bases of molds. Butter sheet of foil to cover ramekins.

Peel turnips using paring knife and cut into quarters. Put in medium-size saucepan, cover with water, add pinch of salt, and bring to boil. Cover, reduce heat to medium-low, and cook about 12 minutes, or until very tender. Drain thoroughly. Purée in food processor until very smooth. Measure 2 cups purée.

Cook measured purée in medium-size heavy, wide saucepan over low heat, stirring often, for 5 minutes to evaporate excess moisture. Stir cream into purée. Raise heat to high and bring to boil. Reduce heat to medium and cook, stirring often, until cream is absorbed and mixture is reduced to 2 cups. Transfer to a bowl and cool 7 minutes.

Whisk eggs in medium-size bowl until blended. Gradually whisk in turnip purée. Season to taste with salt, pepper, and nutmeg; season well so timbales will not be bland.

Divide mixture among ramekins. Tap each on counter to pack down. Smooth tops, set ramekins in roasting pan, and transfer to oven. Add enough boiling water to roasting pan to come halfway up sides of ramekins. Set sheet of buttered foil atop ramekins.

Bake about 45 minutes or until timbales are firm to touch and a cake tester inserted into centers comes out dry. If necessary add hot water occasionally to roasting pan so that it does not become dry. If water comes close to a boil, add a few tablespoons cold water.

When timbales are done, remove molds from water bath. Cool on rack 5 minutes. Carefully run thin-bladed flexible knife around edge of each ramekin or mold. Set small plate atop mold and invert. Holding them together, tap on towel-covered working surface. Gently lift off mold. Repeat with remaining molds.

If desired, garnish each timbale with a small pinch of snipped chives.

SQUASH TIMBALES WITH DILL SAUCE
Timbales de courge, sauce à l'aneth

The delicate flavor of these bright orange squash timbales makes them a good accompaniment for poached chicken breasts.

MAKES 4 OR 5 SERVINGS

SQUASH TIMBALES

2 pounds banana or Hubbard squash	3 eggs
⅔ cup heavy cream, room temperature	Salt and white pepper
	Freshly grated nutmeg

DILL SAUCE

2 dill sprigs	1¼ cups heavy cream
2 medium-size shallots, minced (about 3 tablespoons)	Salt and freshly ground pepper
¼ cup dry white wine	2 tablespoons snipped fresh dill
½ cup Chicken Stock (see recipe) or Vegetable Stock (see recipe)	

4 dill sprigs, for garnish

SQUASH TIMBALES

Preheat oven to 375°F. Generously butter five 4- or 4½-ounce timbale molds or four 5-ounce ramekins, being careful to thoroughly butter bases of molds. Butter sheet of foil to cover molds.

Remove seeds and strings from squash. Cut squash into approximately 2-by-2-by-1-inch chunks. In a large saucepan of boiling salted water, boil squash, uncovered, about 10 minutes, or until very tender when pierced with a small sharp knife. Drain and rinse with cold water. Cut off skin and discard it. Return squash to dry saucepan and cook over low heat, stirring and mashing with wooden spoon, for 5 minutes. Drain in large strainer 15 minutes. Purée in food processor until very smooth.

Cook purée in a medium-size heavy, wide saucepan over low heat, stirring often, for 5 minutes to evaporate excess moisture. Stir cream into purée. Raise heat to high and bring to boil. Reduce heat to medium and cook, stirring often, until cream is absorbed and mixture is reduced to 2 cups. Transfer to bowl and cool 7 minutes.

Whisk eggs in medium-size bowl until blended. Gradually whisk in squash purée. Season to taste with salt, pepper, and nutmeg; season well so timbales will not be bland.

Divide mixture among molds. Tap each on counter to pack down. Smooth tops, set molds in roasting pan, and transfer to oven.

Add enough boiling water to roasting pan to come halfway up sides of molds. Set sheet of buttered foil atop molds.

Bake about 50 minutes, or until timbales are firm to touch and cake tester inserted into centers comes out dry. If necessary, add hot water occasionally to roasting pan so that it does not become dry. If water comes close to a boil, add a few tablespoons cold water.

DILL SAUCE

Combine dill sprigs, shallots, and wine in medium-size heavy saucepan and bring to boil over high heat. Add stock and bring to boil. Reduce heat to medium-high and cook, stirring often, until liquid is reduced to about 2 tablespoons.

Stir in cream, add a pinch of salt and pepper, and bring to boil, stirring. Reduce heat to medium, and cook, stirring often, until sauce is thick enough to coat a spoon, about 7 minutes. Strain sauce, pressing on solids. (Sauce can be kept, covered, up to 1 day in refrigerator.)

To Finish Timbales and Sauce: When timbales are done, remove molds from water bath. Cool on rack 5 minutes. Carefully run thin-bladed flexible knife around edge of each mold. Set small plate atop mold and invert. Holding them together, tap on towel-covered working surface. Gently lift off mold. Repeat with remaining molds. Cover each mold gently with a ramekin while finishing sauce.

Reheat sauce, if necessary, in small saucepan over low heat, whisking. Remove from heat and add snipped dill. Taste and adjust seasoning.

Remove molds from timbales. To serve, spoon 2 to 3 tablespoons sauce on plate around timbale, and tilt plate so sauce runs around it. Serve remaining sauce separately. Set small dill sprig on each timbale and serve.

Vegetable Terrines and Molds

Today, vegetable terrines, or vegetable pâtés, as they are often called, are displayed in the windows of the finest French charcuteries. There are several ways to prepare them. The terrines can be made from layers of vegetable purées held together by eggs and baked; or vegetables can be added in pieces to give a colorful confetti effect to the terrine. To hold the vegetable pieces together, French cooks use either a mousseline of chicken, veal, or ham; a vegetable aspic; or a vegetable mousse (as in Vegetable Terrine with Mushroom Mousse and Fresh Tomato Vinaigrette). Terrines bound with aspic or mousse do not require baking.

TRICOLORED VEGETABLE TERRINE WITH CREAMY BASIL-GARLIC SAUCE
Terrine tricolore de légumes, crème au basilic et à l'ail

Three vegetable purées—spinach, carrot, and turnip—make up this terrine, producing a striped pattern of green, orange, and white. The terrine is easiest to slice when cold. A platter of slices of this terrine, with the sauce served on the side, makes a lovely buffet dish.   MAKES 8 SERVINGS

TRICOLORED VEGETABLE TERRINE

Spinach Layer

3 pounds fresh spinach (leaves with
    stems)
⅔ cup heavy cream, room
    temperature

2 eggs
1 egg yolk
Salt and freshly ground pepper
Freshly grated nutmeg

Carrot Layer

1 pound carrots
½ cup heavy cream, room
    temperature

2 eggs
Salt and freshly ground pepper

Turnip Layer

1 pound small turnips
6 tablespoons heavy cream, room
    temperature

2 eggs
Salt and white pepper
Freshly grated nutmeg

CREAMY BASIL-GARLIC SAUCE

3 large garlic cloves, minced
⅓ cup dry white wine
1¾ cups heavy cream, plus a few
    teaspoons more if necessary

Salt and freshly ground pepper
5 tablespoons chopped fresh basil
A few drops fresh lemon juice

To Begin Spinach, Carrot, and Turnip Layers: Remove stems of fresh spinach and wash leaves thoroughly. In very large saucepan of boiling salted water, cook spinach, uncovered, over high heat, pushing leaves down into water often, about 3 minutes, or until very tender. Drain, rinse with cold water, and drain thoroughly. Squeeze by handfuls until dry. Purée in food processor until very smooth.

Peel carrots and cut in crosswise slices ½ inch thick. Put carrots in medium-size saucepan, cover with water, add pinch of salt, and bring to boil. Cover, reduce heat to medium, and cook about 35 minutes, or until very tender. Drain thoroughly. Purée in food processor until very smooth.

Peel turnips using paring knife and cut into quarters. Put in medium-size saucepan, cover with water, add pinch of salt, cover, and bring to boil. Reduce heat to medium-low and cook about 20 minutes, or until very tender. Drain thoroughly. Purée in food processor until very smooth.

Preheat oven to 375°F. Generously butter an 8-by-4-inch loaf pan. Line base and sides of pan with parchment paper, letting paper extend slightly above edge of pan, and butter paper. Butter a sheet of foil to cover terrine.

To Enrich Each Layer with Cream: Cook spinach purée in medium-size heavy, wide saucepan over low heat, stirring often, for 5 minutes to evaporate excess moisture. Stir ⅔ cup cream into purée. Raise heat to high and bring to boil. Reduce heat to medium and cook, stirring often, until cream is absorbed and mixture is reduced to 2 cups, about 5 minutes. Transfer to bowl.

Cook carrot purée in medium-size heavy, wide saucepan over low heat, stirring often, for 5 minutes to evaporate excess moisture. Stir ½ cup cream into purée. Raise heat to high and bring to boil. Reduce heat to medium and cook, stirring often, until cream is absorbed and mixture is reduced to 1⅔ cups, about 8 minutes. Transfer to bowl.

Cook turnip purée in medium-size heavy, wide saucepan over low heat, stirring often, for 5 minutes to evaporate excess moisture. Stir 6 tablespoons cream into purée. Raise heat to high and bring to boil. Reduce heat to medium and cook, stirring often, until cream is absorbed and mixture is reduced to 1½ cups, about 12 minutes. Transfer to bowl.

To Complete Each Layer and Assemble Terrine: For spinach, whisk 2 eggs with 1 yolk in large bowl until blended. Gradually whisk in spinach mixture. Season to taste with salt, pepper, and nutmeg. For carrot layer, whisk 2 eggs in a bowl; whisk in carrot mixture. Season to taste with salt and pepper. For turnip layer, whisk 2 eggs in a bowl; whisk in turnip mixture. Season to taste with salt, pepper, and nutmeg. Season each well so terrine will not be bland.

Spread spinach mixture evenly in terrine. Tap on counter to pack down. Spoon carrot mixture over spinach mixture and spread smooth. Last, spoon turnip mixture evenly on top. Smooth gently. Set terrine in roasting pan and transfer to oven. Add enough boiling water to roasting pan to come halfway up sides of terrine. Set sheet of buttered foil atop terrine.

Bake about 2½ hours or until terrine is firm to touch when pressed gently and cake tester inserted into center comes out dry. During baking, add hot water to roasting pan occasionally so that it does not become dry. If water comes close to a boil, add a few tablespoons cold water.

CREAMY BASIL-GARLIC SAUCE

Combine garlic and wine in a large, heavy saucepan and bring to a boil over high heat. Reduce heat to medium-high and cook, stirring often, until liquid is reduced to about 2 tablespoons.

Stir in cream, add a pinch of salt and pepper, and bring to a boil, stirring. Reduce heat to medium and cook, stirring often, until sauce is thick enough to coat a spoon, about 7 minutes. (Sauce can be kept, covered, up to 1 day in refrigerator.)

To Finish Terrine and Sauce: When terrine is done, carefully remove it from water bath. For serving warm, cool terrine on rack at least 30 minutes. If necessary, carefully run a metal spatula around edge of terrine. Set oval or rectangular platter atop loaf pan and invert both. Gently lift off pan. Carefully peel off paper. Slice very gently with point of a thin-bladed sharp knife in ¾-inch slices. Slices are fragile, especially when warm. With aid of a spatula, set each slice on a plate. Serve warm, at room temperature, or cold.

If sauce was prepared in advance, and will be served hot, reheat in a small saucepan over low heat, whisking.

Add basil. Flavor with a few drops of lemon juice and a little freshly ground pepper. If sauce is too thick, stir in a few teaspoons cream. Taste and adjust seasoning. Serve the sauce hot or at room temperature.

Spoon 2 to 3 tablespoons sauce on plate around slice of terrine and tilt plate so sauce runs around it. Serve remaining sauce separately.

NOTE: Two 10-ounce packages frozen spinach can be substituted for fresh. Thaw completely, squeeze dry, and purée. Measure 1½ cups purée. Continue as above, with step of heating purée with cream.

❧ VEGETABLE TERRINE WITH MUSHROOM MOUSSE AND FRESH TOMATO VINAIGRETTE
Terrine de légumes à la mousse de champignons, vinaigrette à la tomate

The Troisgros brothers started the fashion of serving vegetable terrines in fine restaurants and their terrine is indeed delicious. For this elegant, light terrine, a creamy white mushroom mousse flecked with herbs is layered with a variety of fresh vegetables. The vegetables are lined up in rows so they dot each slice. When the terrine is cut, you see the mosaic pattern of colorful vegetables—golden carrots, asparagus, green beans, and peas. I find this terrine tastier than other "vegetable" terrines bound by meat mixtures. Perfect for warm weather, the terrine requires no baking and is served cold or at room temperature.

The tomato vinaigrette is a favorite accompaniment for vegetable terrines in starred restaurants. It is also marvelous with simply cooked vegetables. MAKES 8 SERVINGS

VEGETABLE TERRINE

Vegetables

3 fairly thin carrots of even thickness, about 8 inches long (about 5 ounces)

5 medium asparagus spears, peeled

3 ounces wax beans or green beans, ends removed, broken in 3 pieces

1 cup shelled fresh peas (about 1 pound in pods)

Mushroom Mousse

2¼ cups heavy cream

6 ounces very white mushrooms, halved and sliced

Salt and freshly ground pepper

2 envelopes (¼ ounce each) plus ½ teaspoon unflavored gelatin

6 tablespoons water

1 tablespoon plus 1½ teaspoons minced fresh tarragon

1 tablespoon plus 1½ teaspoons minced fresh parsley

1 tablespoon snipped chives

FRESH TOMATO VINAIGRETTE

1½ pounds large ripe, very red tomatoes

1 tablespoon plus 1½ teaspoons white wine vinegar or herb vinegar

Salt and freshly ground pepper

¾ cup plus 2 or 3 tablespoons extra-virgin olive oil

1 tablespoon minced fresh tarragon

1 tablespoon minced fresh parsley

VEGETABLES

Cut off tapering ends of carrots so each carrot is of even thickness. Put carrots in a medium-size saucepan of salted water and bring to a simmer. Cover and cook about 30 minutes, or until carrots are very tender when pierced with sharp knife. Drain thoroughly.

In a sauté pan of boiling salted water to generously cover, cook asparagus, uncovered, about 3 minutes, or until just tender. Drain very thoroughly.

In a medium-size saucepan containing enough boiling salted water to generously cover, put wax beans or green beans and cook, uncovered, over high heat about 5 minutes, or until just tender. Rinse with cold water and drain very thoroughly.

In a medium-size saucepan of boiling salted water, cook peas about 5 minutes, or until just tender. Rinse with cold water and drain very thoroughly.

MUSHROOM MOUSSE

Bring 1½ cups cream to a simmer in a large, heavy saucepan. Refrigerate remaining cream and chill a medium bowl for whipping it. Add mushrooms, salt, and pepper to simmering cream. Reduce heat to low and cook, uncovered, stirring often, about 30 minutes, or until mushrooms are very tender and cream is well flavored.

Transfer mushrooms to a food processor using slotted spoon. Process with short bursts of food processor until mushrooms are coarsely chopped. Return to pan of cream. (If using blender, process mushrooms together with cream.)

Sprinkle gelatin over 6 tablespoons water in a small cup and let stand 5 minutes to soften. Bring mushrooms in cream to a boil and remove from heat. Add gelatin and stir thoroughly to dissolve completely. Transfer to a bowl. Cool to room temperature. Stir in herbs.

Whip remaining ¾ cup cream in chilled bowl until soft peaks form. Fold into mushroom mixture. (Mixture should be thick enough so mushrooms do not fall to bottom; if it is not thick enough, refrigerate a few minutes, stirring often so it does not set.) Taste and adjust seasoning; mixture should be well seasoned so it will not be bland after chilling.

To Assemble Terrine: Lightly oil an 8-by-4-inch loaf pan. When layering vegetables with mousse, do not let pieces of vegetables touch side of pan; vegetable pieces should be surrounded by mousse.

To layer vegetables with mousse, spoon ¾ cup mushroom mousse into loaf pan. Arrange carrots in pan lengthwise, with thicker end of center carrot in opposite direction from other two. Spoon ¾ cup mushroom mousse over carrots. Arrange peas on top in one layer. Carefully spoon ½ cup mushroom mousse over peas. Arrange wax beans on top in one layer, in four lengthwise rows. Carefully spoon ½ cup mushroom mousse over beans. Arrange asparagus on top, with tips of alternating spears pointing in opposite directions. Spoon remaining mousse over asparagus. Cover and refrigerate 4 hours. (Terrine can be kept up to 2 days in refrigerator.)

FRESH TOMATO VINAIGRETTE

Peel, cut into halves, and seed tomatoes. Then cut each half into quarters, salt lightly, and leave in strainer 15 minutes to drain well.

Finely chop tomato pieces, transfer to a medium-size bowl, add vinegar, salt, and pepper, and whisk until smooth. Gradually whisk in all but 1 tablespoon olive oil, drop by drop. The sauce should remain thick and emulsified. Taste and add remaining tablespoon oil, if desired. Add herbs, taste, and adjust seasoning. Serve at room temperature.

To Finish and Serve: To unmold terrine, run a thin-bladed flexible knife around its edge, gently pushing mixture slightly from edge of mold to let in air. Dip mold, nearly to depth of contents, in warm, not hot, water about 10 seconds. Dry outside of mold, and set a long platter on top. Holding platter and mold firmly together, flip quickly so terrine is upside down. Shake mold gently downward; terrine should slip from mold onto platter. If terrine remains in mold, repeat dipping procedure. Carefully remove mold by lifting it straight up. Refrigerate terrine until ready to serve.

To serve, cut in ¾-inch slices using a sharp, heavy knife, cutting cleanly through vegetables. Set on plates. Spoon a little tomato vinaigrette next to each slice.

QUICK SPINACH PÂTÉ
Pâté d'épinards minute

The French term *pâté* is now used interchangeably with *terrine,* but this recipe illustrates the other type of pâté—a flavorful spread. Serve this bright green pâté with fresh or toasted French bread or with lightly salted crackers.

MAKES ABOUT 1 CUP, 4 SERVINGS

1 ½ pounds spinach (leaves with
    stems)
2 tablespoons butter
Salt and freshly ground pepper
Freshly grated nutmeg

½ cup plus 2 tablespoons Crème
    Fraîche (see recipe) or
    purchased crème fraîche
1 tablespoon minced fresh parsley
    (optional)

Remove spinach stems and wash leaves thoroughly. In a large saucepan of boiling salted water, cook spinach, uncovered, over high heat, pushing leaves down into water often, until very tender, about 3 minutes. Rinse with cold water and squeeze dry by handfuls.

Melt butter in medium-size saucepan. Add spinach, salt, pepper, and nutmeg, and cook over medium heat, stirring, about 2 minutes, or until spinach absorbs butter and any excess liquid has evaporated. Remove from heat and cool to room temperature.

Purée spinach in food processor with 3 tablespoons crème fraîche. Stir in remaining crème fraîche. Add parsley, if desired. Taste for seasoning; the spread should be generously seasoned with nutmeg. (Pâté can be kept, covered, 1 day in refrigerator.) Serve in a bowl or a ramekin at room temperature.

NOTE: Instead of crème fraîche, you can use ½ cup sour cream mixed with 2 tablespoons heavy cream.

EGGPLANT SAVARIN WITH FRESH TOMATO SAUCE
Savarin d'aubergines, sauce tomate

This ring-shaped eggplant dish is named for the familiar cake of the same form. In France it's popular to make use of eggplant slices with their skin on to line a mold and form an attractive pattern. Small Japanese eggplants are ideal because they can be cut in thin slices and their peels are not tough. Choose straight rather than curved Japanese eggplants for this savarin so it will be easy to slice them lengthwise. The dried mushrooms used in the filling are available at specialty food shops.

MAKES 6 FIRST-COURSE SERVINGS,
OR 2 TO 3 MAIN-COURSE SERVINGS

FRESH TOMATO SAUCE

2 large sprigs fresh thyme, or
   ½ teaspoon dried thyme,
   crumbled
1 bay leaf
2 tablespoons extra-virgin olive
   oil

2 medium-size garlic cloves, minced
1 ½ pounds ripe tomatoes, peeled,
   seeded, and chopped
Salt and freshly ground pepper
1 tablespoon tomato paste

EGGPLANT SAVARIN

⅓ ounce dried cèpes *or* porcini
   mushrooms (about ⅓ cup
   packed)
6 Japanese eggplants (about 1 ¼ to
   1 ⅓ pounds)
About ¾ cup olive oil

Salt and freshly ground pepper
2 medium-size garlic cloves, minced
3 tablespoons chopped fresh parsley
4 eggs
5 tablespoons freshly grated
   Parmesan cheese

FRESH TOMATO SAUCE

Wind a piece of kitchen string around fresh thyme and bay leaf several times and tie them together to make a bouquet garni; if using dried thyme, wrap it and bay leaf in a piece of cheesecloth and tie tightly. Heat oil in a medium-size heavy saucepan over low heat. Add garlic and cook, stirring occasionally, 30 seconds. Add tomatoes, bouquet garni, salt, and pepper. Combine well and bring mixture to a boil. Reduce heat to low and cook, uncovered, stirring occasionally, about 40 minutes, or until tomatoes are very soft and sauce is thick. Discard bouquet garni. Stir tomato paste into sauce.

Purée sauce in a food processor or blender until smooth. Taste and adjust seasoning. (The sauce may be kept, covered, up to 3 days in refrigerator.)

EGGPLANT SAVARIN

Soak mushrooms in a bowl of hot water, covered, for 30 minutes or until softened. Drain, rinse, and pat them dry. Chop them in very small pieces and reserve.

Cut caps off 4 eggplants. Cut off a lengthwise slice at one side and cut eggplants in ¼-inch lengthwise slices so that each slice has a rim of eggplant peel.

Heat 3 tablespoons oil in a large skillet over medium-high heat until it is very hot. Add enough eggplant slices to make one layer and sauté them for 1 minute on each side, or until they are just tender. Drain them and pat them dry on paper towels. Add 3 tablespoons oil to skillet, heat oil until it is hot, and sauté remaining eggplant in batches the same way, adding more oil between batches as necessary so that skillet is never dry; you will need about 4 tablespoons more oil.

Lightly oil a 4- to 5-cup ring mold. Line it with about 20 sautéed eggplant slices, placing them crosswise in mold with their more attractive side facing down and wider end of each slice resting on outer edge of mold; overlap slices slightly so there are no holes.

Preheat oven to 350°F. Cut remaining eggplants and any remaining pieces of first eggplants in ½-inch dice. You will need 3 cups of diced eggplant. Measure any oil left from sautéing eggplant slices and add enough oil to make 2 tablespoons. Heat it in a medium-size skillet, add diced eggplant and a small pinch of salt and pepper, and sauté eggplant over medium heat for 2 minutes. Reduce heat to low, cover, and cook eggplant, stirring often, for 15 minutes or until very tender. Stir in reserved mushrooms, add garlic, and cook, stirring, for 1 minute. Transfer to a bowl and let cool to lukewarm. Stir parsley, eggs, and cheese into eggplant mixture, taste, and add salt and pepper, if needed.

Spoon mixture into prepared ring mold. Cover mold with a sheet of foil, set it in a roasting pan, and add enough very hot water to come halfway up sides of mold. Bake 45 minutes, or until a cake tester inserted in several places comes out clean. Remove mold from pan of water and let it cool on a rack for 10 minutes.

Cut off any eggplant ends sticking up above filling in mold and place them on filling. Run a thin-bladed flexible knife around outer and inner edges of ring. Unmold eggplant ring onto a round platter. Spoon hot tomato sauce into center of ring. Serve savarin hot; leftovers are also good cold.

✣ SPINACH-CAULIFLOWER GÂTEAU WITH CREAMY MUSHROOM SAUCE
Gâteau d'épinards et chou-fleur, sauce aux champignons

This festive layered vegetable cake, decorated with carrot "coins," can be assembled at leisure and served hot or at room temperature.

To feature it as the star of a menu highlighting vegetables, accompany it by fresh bread and serve a light salad, such as Marinated Green Bean Salad with Green Onions (see receipe) or Endive and Beet Salad (see receipe), followed by a simple fruit dessert.

MAKES 3 TO 5 MAIN-COURSE SERVINGS,
OR 6 TO 8 APPETIZER SERVINGS

SPINACH-CAULIFLOWER GÂTEAU

2 medium-size carrots of uniform thickness, trimmed, peeled, and cut in ⅛-inch-thick slices

2½ pounds cauliflower (about 2 small heads), trimmed of leaves and large stalk, divided into medium-size florets

3 tablespoons butter

3 tablespoons heavy cream

2 pounds fresh spinach (leaves with stems)

4 eggs

2 tablespoons plus 1 teaspoon minced fresh dill

5 tablespoons fine, dry bread crumbs

Salt and white pepper

Freshly grated nutmeg

CREAMY MUSHROOM SAUCE

1½ tablespoons butter

¼ pound white mushrooms, halved and cut in thin slices

Salt and freshly ground pepper

1 cup heavy cream

1 tablespoon minced fresh parsley

SPINACH-CAULIFLOWER GÂTEAU

Put carrots in medium-size saucepan; add enough water to cover and a pinch of salt. Bring to boil. Reduce heat to low, cover, and simmer until very tender, about 7 minutes. Drain.

In large saucepan of boiling salted water, boil cauliflower, uncovered, about 7 minutes, or until very tender. Drain, rinse with cold water, and drain. Purée in food processor or blender until very smooth. Melt 2 tablespoons butter in large heavy saucepan. Add cauliflower purée and cook over medium heat, stirring very often, about 10 minutes, or until butter is absorbed and purée is dry. Add 2 tablespoons cream and cook, stirring, 2 minutes. Transfer to bowl and cool to room temperature.

Remove spinach stems and wash leaves thoroughly. In very large saucepan of boiling salted water, cook spinach, uncovered, over high heat, pushing leaves down into water often, until very tender, about 3 minutes. Rinse with cold water and squeeze dry by handfuls. Purée in food processor until very smooth. Melt 1 tablespoon butter in large heavy saucepan. Add spinach purée and cook over low heat, stirring, about 3 minutes, or until butter is absorbed and purée is dry. Add 1 tablespoon cream and cook, stirring, 30 seconds. Transfer to second bowl and cool to room temperature. (Carrots, cauliflower purée, and spinach purée can be prepared up to 8 hours ahead and kept covered in refrigerator.)

Beat 2 eggs and add to bowl of cauliflower. Add dill and 4 tablespoons bread crumbs, and season to taste with salt and white pepper. Beat remaining 2 eggs and add to spinach. Add 1 tablespoon bread crumbs and season to taste with salt, white pepper, and nutmeg.

Preheat oven to 375°F. Heavily butter a 5-cup soufflé dish. Line base with foil, press in foil smoothly, and butter. Arrange carrot slices of uniform size, side by side, in two concentric rings on base of dish. Set one carrot slice in center. (Reserve remaining carrot slices for other uses.)

Spoon 1½ cups cauliflower purée carefully over carrots. Spread smooth with rubber spatula. Tap dish on work surface so contents settle. Spoon spinach purée by tablespoons over cauliflower and spread to smooth layer. Spoon remaining cauliflower purée by tablespoons over spinach purée and spread to smooth layer. (Layers must be added carefully so each remains distinct.)

Set soufflé dish in roasting pan and add enough boiling water to come to one-third of height of dish. Set piece of buttered foil on top. Bake, adding more boiling water to water bath if it evaporates, about 2 hours, or until gâteau is set and a cake tester inserted into center comes out clean. (Mixture should not stick to your fingers when pressed on top.) Remove from oven. (Gâteau can be kept warm in water bath for 30 minutes.) Remove from water bath and let stand 10 minutes. If desired, let cool to room temperature.

CREAMY MUSHROOM SAUCE

In a medium-size skillet, melt butter over medium-high heat. Add mushrooms, salt, and pepper. Sauté, tossing often, about 4 minutes, or until mushrooms are tender and lightly browned and any liquid that escapes from them has evaporated. Add cream, reduce heat to medium-low, and simmer, stirring often, until sauce is thick enough to coat a spoon, about 5 minutes. (Sauce can be prepared up to 8 hours ahead and kept covered in refrigerator. Reheat in saucepan over low heat; thin if necessary with 1 or 2 tablespoons cream.) Stir in parsley. Taste and adjust seasoning.

To serve, carefully run a thin-bladed flexible knife around sides of vegetable gâteau and unmold onto round platter. Carefully peel off foil. Serve sauce separately. When cutting, place a metal spatula or pie server underneath the gâteau so wedges stay whole.

NOTE: If a 5-cup soufflé dish is not available, a 6-cup dish can be used.

Vegetable Mousses

Mousses made of purées of colorful cooked vegetables make creamy, fresh-tasting appetizers. Like fruit mousses, they are held together with a little gelatin and enriched with whipped cream. They can be formed into an impressive soufflé, as in Cold Carrot Soufflé with Peas, or can be unmolded from a ring mold, as in Two-Tone Tomato Mousse. Vegetable Bavarians are a special type of mousse, modeled on the pattern of dessert Bavarian creams.

TWO-TONE TOMATO MOUSSE
Mousse de tomates

The two layers of this mousse—one of deep red color and the other creamy—are both made from the same fresh tomato mixture.   MAKES 4 TO 6 SERVINGS

1 tablespoon vegetable oil
1 medium-size garlic clove, minced
2 ½ pounds ripe tomatoes, peeled, seeded (juice reserved), and finely chopped
1 ½ teaspoons fresh thyme, or ½ teaspoon dried thyme, crumbled
1 bay leaf
Salt and freshly ground pepper

1 tablespoon chopped fresh basil, or 1 teaspoon dried basil, crumbled (optional)
1 to 2 teaspoons tomato paste (optional)
1 envelope unflavored gelatin (¼ ounce)
3 hard-boiled eggs, cut in half
¾ cup heavy cream, well chilled
Fresh French or sourdough bread or toast, for serving

Heat oil in a large skillet or sauté pan over medium heat. Add garlic and sauté, stirring, 30 seconds. Add tomatoes, thyme, bay leaf, salt, and pepper. Cook over medium heat, stirring often, about 20 minutes, or until tomatoes are soft and mixture is thick and smooth. Discard bay leaf. Stir in basil. If a deeper color is desired, stir in tomato paste.

Put about 1 cup of mixture into a medium-size bowl (for red tomato layer) and remaining mixture into a larger bowl (for creamy layer).

Pour ⅓ cup reserved tomato juice into a small heatproof bowl, and sprinkle with gelatin. Leave 5 minutes to soften. Set bowl of softened gelatin in a saucepan of hot water over very low heat, and stir, about 5 minutes, or until dissolved.

Stir 2 tablespoons of gelatin into cup of tomato mixture reserved for red layer. Combine thoroughly to be sure gelatin is evenly distributed. Taste and adjust seasoning. Overseason slightly to avoid blandness after chilling. Stir remaining gelatin into second tomato mixture in large bowl; combine thoroughly.

Refrigerate the medium-size bowl of red tomato mixture 5 minutes, or set in a bowl of ice cubes and water to chill, stirring often to prevent it from setting at sides and bottom. Lightly oil a 4- to 5-cup ring mold or other decorative mold.

Spoon chilled red tomato mixture into mold. Arrange egg halves on top at regular intervals, being careful not to let them touch sides of mold. Chill mold 10 minutes, leaving second bowl of tomato mixture at room temperature. Chill bowl for whipping cream.

Whip cream in chilled bowl until soft peaks form. Fold it into remaining tomato mixture. If mixture sets before cream is added, whisk it first until smooth, and whisk in cream. Taste for seasoning; overseason slightly. Carefully spoon it into mold, without moving eggs. Smooth with a rubber spatula, making sure to push mixture into cracks between mold and eggs. Refrigerate at least 2 hours, or until set. (The mousse can be kept, covered, up to 8 hours in refrigerator.)

To unmold mousse, run a thin-bladed flexible knife around its edge, gently pushing mixture slightly from edge of mold to let in air. If using a ring mold, run knife around central part of ring. Dip mold, nearly to depth of contents, in warm, not hot, water about 10 seconds. Dry mold. Set a round platter on top of mold. Holding them firmly together, flip quickly so mold is upside down. Shake mold gently downward; mousse should slip from mold onto platter. If mousse remains in mold, repeat dipping procedure. Carefully remove mold by lifting it straight up. Refrigerate mousse until ready to serve.

Serve with fresh French bread or toast.

❧ AVOCADO MOUSSE
Mousse d'avocats

Avocado halves are often used in France as attractive containers for a variety of luxurious salads or for mousses, as in this recipe. If desired, set each avocado half on a bed of lettuce and decorate with a few Niçoise olives. MAKES 4 SERVINGS

2 large ripe avocados	¼ cup water
1 tablespoon strained fresh lemon juice, or to taste	1 teaspoon unflavored gelatin
	⅓ cup heavy cream, well chilled
2 teaspoons minced fresh parsley	3 small cherry tomatoes, or 2 small
1 tablespoon snipped fresh chives	plum tomatoes, for garnish
Salt	French bread or toast, for an
Pinch of cayenne pepper	accompaniment

Cut avocados in half carefully. Remove each pit by hitting it with heel of a sharp knife so that it sticks in pit; then lift pit up. Carefully remove avocado pulp with a spoon, reserving shells to use as serving containers.

In a food processor, purée avocado pulp with lemon juice. Transfer to a medium-size bowl and stir in parsley, 2 teaspoons chives, salt, and cayenne pepper to taste.

Pour water into a small cup and sprinkle gelatin over it. Let stand 5 minutes. Set cup in a pan of hot water over low heat, and stir until gelatin is dissolved. Whisk into avocado purée. Cool to room temperature. Chill small bowl for whipping cream.

Whip cream in chilled bowl until soft peaks form. Fold it into avocado mixture. Cover by setting plastic wrap directly on surface of mousse. Refrigerate 1 hour or until thick. (The mousse can be prepared up to 4 hours ahead but no longer because it will discolor.)

To serve, cut tomatoes in crosswise slices. Spoon mousse into avocado halves. Smooth tops.

Arrange row of tomato slices lengthwise down middle of each avocado half. Sprinkle tomatoes with remaining chives. Serve with French bread or toast.

BROCCOLI BAVARIAN
Bavarois de brocolis

Although Bavarian creams are traditionally sweet, French chefs now make savory Bavarians as well, using vegetables. This pale green Bavarian is prepared in the same way as a dessert Bavarian but, of course, without sugar and with vegetable purée as the flavoring.

Small, briefly cooked broccoli florets provide a bright garnish and pleasantly textured accompaniment.   MAKES 8 SERVINGS

2 pounds broccoli

⅓ cup water

1 envelope (¼ ounce) plus 1½
  teaspoons unflavored gelatin

3 egg yolks, room temperature

1 cup milk

Salt and white pepper

Freshly grated nutmeg

1 cup heavy cream, well chilled

Remove about 25 small florets from broccoli, refrigerate and reserve for garnish. Divide remaining broccoli into medium-size florets. Peel thick stalk with paring knife and cut in slices about ¼ inch thick.

In a large saucepan of boiling salted water, cook broccoli florets (except those reserved for garnish) and slices, uncovered, over high heat about 7 minutes, or until very tender. Drain, rinse gently with cold water until completely cooled, and drain thoroughly.

Purée in food processor until very smooth. Return purée to saucepan and cook over low heat, stirring, 5 minutes to dry it slightly.

Pour water in small bowl and sprinkle gelatin over it. Let stand 5 minutes.

Whisk egg yolks in medium bowl. Bring milk to a simmer in a small heavy saucepan. Gradually pour milk into yolks, whisking. Return to saucepan and cook over low heat, stirring constantly, until slightly thickened so it just begins to coat a spoon; on an instant-read thermometer, it should reach 150°F. (It will not be as thick as sweet *crème anglaise.*) Remove from heat and immediately whisk in gelatin. Pour into large bowl. Whisk in broccoli purée. Season to taste with salt, white pepper, and nutmeg.

Cool broccoli mixture to room temperature. Lightly oil a 5- to 6-cup ring mold. Chill a large bowl for whipping cream.

Whip cream in chilled bowl until soft peaks form. Fold cream into broccoli purée. Taste and add more salt, pepper, and nutmeg, if needed. Overseason slightly to avoid blandness after chilling. Fold in seasoning thoroughly. Spoon mixture into prepared mold.

Refrigerate about 4 hours or until set. Cover after top sets. (Mold can be kept up to 1 day in refrigerator.)

In a medium-size saucepan of boiling salted water, boil florets reserved for garnish, uncovered, over high heat about 2 minutes, or until barely tender and still bright green. Drain, rinse gently with cold water until well cooled, and drain thoroughly.

To unmold Bavarian, run a thin-bladed flexible knife around edge of mold, gently pushing mixture slightly from edge to let in air. Run knife around central part of ring as well. Dip mold, nearly to depth of contents, in warm, not hot, water about 10 seconds. Dry mold. Set a round platter on top. Holding them firmly together, flip quickly so mold is upside down. Shake mold gently downward; mixture should slip from mold onto platter. If mixture remains in mold, repeat dipping procedure. Carefully remove mold by lifting it straight up. Spread if necessary to smooth. Refrigerate Bavarian until ready to serve.

To serve, garnish center or outer edge with blanched broccoli florets. If placing them in center, arrange one layer in center of ring and put remaining florets on top, with their flower ends pointing outward.

COLD CARROT SOUFFLÉ WITH PEAS
Soufflé froid aux carottes et aux petits pois

This soufflé resembles a dessert soufflé in appearance but is actually a festive first course in disguise. The creamy carrot mousse is layered with a green pea mousse for a ribboned effect.

MAKES 8 SERVINGS

1 tablespoon butter
White part of 1 medium-size leek, chopped
2 pounds carrots, peeled and cut into 1-inch chunks
3½ cups water

1 bay leaf
Salt and freshly ground pepper
2 cups shelled fresh or frozen peas
1 envelope (¼ ounce) plus 1 teaspoon unflavored gelatin
1½ cups heavy cream, well chilled

GARNISH
Reserved carrots and peas
⅓ cup heavy cream, well chilled

Pinch of salt

Melt butter in a large saucepan, add leek, and cook over low heat, stirring, about 7 minutes, or until softened. Add carrots, water, bay leaf, salt, and pepper. Bring to a boil. Cover, reduce heat to low, and cook about 25 minutes, or until carrots are very tender. Do not drain.

Cut a 25-inch sheet of wax paper and fold it in half. Wrap paper around a 5-cup glass soufflé dish so that it extends about 2 inches above rim to make a collar. Fasten tightly with tape.

In a large saucepan of boiling salted water, cook peas about 5 minutes for fresh or 2 minutes for frozen peas, or until just tender. Remove about ½ cup peas with slotted spoon; these will be left whole. Continue cooking remaining peas about 2 more minutes, or until tender enough to purée. Meanwhile, drain reserved peas and rinse well; set aside. Drain remaining peas and rinse well. Purée with 2 tablespoons carrot cooking liquid and transfer to a bowl.

Discard bay leaf from carrots. Set aside 3 pieces carrot for garnish. Remove carrot and leek pieces with slotted spoon, reserving liquid. Pour ⅓ cup cooking liquid into a small bowl and cool to room temperature. Pour 1 cup remaining liquid into a medium-size saucepan.

Purée carrot and leek pieces until smooth. Return to dry saucepan and dry purée over low heat, stirring constantly, about 5 minutes. Transfer to a large bowl.

Chill a large bowl for whipping cream. Sprinkle gelatin over the ⅓ cup carrot liquid in the small bowl. Let stand 5 minutes to soften. Bring reserved 1 cup carrot liquid to boil and remove from heat. Add softened gelatin and whisk until gelatin is completely dissolved.

Pour ¼ cup gelatin mixture into pea purée, stirring vigorously. Pour remaining gelatin into carrot purée, stirring vigorously.

Set bowl of carrot mixture in a bowl of ice cubes and water, stirring often to prevent mixture from setting at sides and bottom of bowl, until completely cool but not set.

Whip cream in chilled bowl until soft peaks form. Fold 2 cups whipped cream into carrot purée and remaining cream into pea purée. Fold all but 1 tablespoon of peas into pea mixture. Taste each and adjust seasoning; mixtures should be slightly overseasoned so soufflé will not be bland after chilling. Fold in seasoning thoroughly.

Spoon 2½ cups of carrot mousse into prepared dish. Spoon all of pea mousse carefully over carrot layer. Refrigerate 20 minutes, keeping remaining carrot mixture at room temperature. Spoon remaining carrot mousse carefully on top of pea layer. Smooth top. Refrigerate about 5 hours, or until set. (Mousse can be kept overnight; keep remaining carrot pieces and peas separately, covered.)

For Garnish: Chill a small bowl for whipping cream. Cut reserved carrot pieces into small dice about size of peas. Whip ⅓ cup cream with pinch of salt in chilled bowl until stiff.

To serve, carefully peel off and discard paper from soufflé dish. Using a pastry bag and small star tip, pipe an even number of rosettes of whipped cream on top of soufflé near edge. Decorate with small pieces of carrot and peas by setting them on top of alternating rosettes. Serve cold.

Vegetable Soufflés

To many, soufflés are the symbol of French cooking because they are delicate, rich yet light, and have the reputation of being difficult to prepare. Actually they are quite simple to make and do not involve techniques different from those required for making many cakes.

Vegetable soufflés are made basically of vegetable purée mixed with cream sauce, enriched with egg yolks, and lightened with beaten egg whites. Although they can be made without the sauce, the soufflés taste moister and more creamy when it is included. Vegetable soufflés are delicious when flavored with cheeses, as in Spinach and Goat Cheese Soufflé.

Although soufflés are generally baked in a soufflé dish, they can be baked in individual dishes or even inside crêpes, as in Eggplant Soufflé-Filled Crêpes with Red Pepper Sauce (see recipe).

When prepared to the French taste, soufflés should be soft and moist inside, so that the inner part acts almost as a sauce for the outer, firmer section. Still, baking is to taste, and the soufflé can be baked a bit longer if desired.

It is well known that soufflés do not wait for the guests, but the soufflé base can be made ahead, so that only the whipping of the egg whites and baking must be done at the last minute.

❦ SPINACH AND GOAT CHEESE SOUFFLÉ
Soufflé aux épinards au fromage de chèvre

The wonderful French goat cheese blends beautifully with vegetables, which balance its richness. In this savory soufflé it provides a creamy and tangy complement to the spinach.   MAKES 4 SERVINGS

1 pound fresh spinach (leaves with stems)	1 cup milk
¼ pound creamy goat cheese, such as Montrachet	Salt and freshly ground pepper
	Freshly grated nutmeg
3 tablespoons unsalted butter	3 egg yolks, room temperature
3 tablespoons all-purpose flour	4 egg whites, room temperature
	Pinch of cream of tartar

Butter a 5-cup soufflé dish, making sure to butter rim well. Position rack in lower third of oven and preheat to 425°F.

Remove spinach stems and wash leaves thoroughly. In a large saucepan of boiling salted water, cook spinach, uncovered, over high heat, pushing leaves down into water often, about 3 minutes, or until very tender. Drain, rinse thoroughly with cold water, and drain. Squeeze by handfuls until dry. Purée in food processor until finely chopped.

If goat cheese has a dark rind, remove it. Crumble cheese or cut in small pieces.

In a small heavy saucepan, melt butter over low heat, add flour, and cook, whisking constantly, about 2 minutes, or until foaming but not browned. Remove from heat. Gradually whisk in milk, bring to a boil over medium-high heat, whisking, reduce heat to low, and cook, whisking often, 2 minutes. Remove from heat and add small pinches of salt, pepper, and nutmeg. Whisk in spinach purée and goat cheese. Bring to a boil.

Remove from heat and vigorously whisk in egg yolks, one by one. Heat yolk mixture over low heat, whisking constantly, about 2 minutes or until slightly thickened; do not overcook or let mixture boil or yolks may curdle. Taste and add more salt, pepper, and nutmeg, if needed. (Mixture can be kept, covered, up to 8 hours in refrigerator.)

Have a round heatproof platter ready near oven. If soufflé mixture was cold, heat it in a small saucepan over low heat, whisking, until just warm. Remove from heat.

In a large bowl, beat egg whites with cream of tartar at medium speed until soft peaks form. Continue beating at high speed until whites are stiff but not dry.

Quickly fold about one-quarter of whites into spinach mixture. Spoon this mixture over remaining whites and fold in lightly but quickly, just until mixture is blended.

Transfer mixture to prepared soufflé dish and smooth top. Bake about 20 minutes, or until puffed and browned; when you gently move oven rack, soufflé should shake very slightly in center. Do not overbake or soufflé may burn on top and may shrink. Set soufflé dish on prepared platter and serve immediately.

NOTE: About one 10-ounce package frozen spinach can be substituted for fresh. Thaw spinach completely, squeeze it dry, and purée it in a food processor. Measure ½ cup purée and use it for soufflé.

❧ WINTER SQUASH SOUFFLÉ
Soufflé à la courge rouge

A beautiful bright orange color and delicate flavor and texture make this soufflé a favorite starter to a dinner. Whole garlic cloves are steamed alongside the squash to provide a pleasant background taste.

MAKES 4 SERVINGS

1 ½ to 2 pounds winter squash,   *½ cup plus 1 tablespoon milk*
    such as banana or Hubbard   *White pepper*
    squash   *Freshly grated nutmeg*
Pinch of salt   *4 egg yolks, room temperature*
5 large garlic cloves, unpeeled   *5 egg whites, room temperature*
3 tablespoons butter   *Pinch of cream of tartar*
¼ cup all-purpose flour

Remove seeds and strings from squash. Cut squash into approximately 2-by-2-by-1-inch chunks.

Bring at least 1 inch of water to a boil in base of pan with a steamer. Boiling water should not reach holes in bottom part of steamer. Put squash in 1 layer in steamer above boiling water and sprinkle lightly with salt. Add garlic cloves. Cover, and steam about 14 minutes, or until squash is tender. Remove squash, and reserve garlic. Cut off squash skin and discard it. Purée squash in food processor until very smooth.

Butter a 5-cup soufflé dish, making sure to butter rim well. Position rack in lower third of oven and preheat to 425°F.

Put squash purée in a very heavy medium-size saucepan, preferably one that is lined with enamel. Bring to a boil, reduce heat to medium, and cook, stirring often, about 12 minutes, or until purée is reduced to 1½ cups. Be careful; mixture spatters and burns easily. Set aside.

In a medium-size shallow, heavy saucepan, melt butter over low heat, add flour, and cook, whisking constantly, about 2 minutes, or until foaming but not browned. Remove from heat. Whisk in milk and reduced purée, and bring nearly to a boil, whisking. (Mixture will barely bubble and will be too thick to come to a full boil.) Reduce heat to low and cook, whisking constantly, 5 minutes. Peel and mash garlic; stir into mixture. Add a small pinch of salt, white pepper, and nutmeg.

Remove from heat and vigorously whisk in egg yolks, one by one. Return to low heat and cook, whisking, 3 minutes, or until mixture thickens; do not overcook or let mixture boil or yolks may curdle. Taste and adjust seasoning. (Mixture can be kept, covered, up to 8 hours in refrigerator.)

Have a round heatproof platter ready near oven.

If soufflé mixture is cold, heat it in a small saucepan over low heat, whisking, until just warm. Remove from heat.

In a large bowl, beat egg whites with cream of tartar at medium speed until soft peaks form. Continue beating at high speed until whites are stiff but not dry.

Quickly fold about one-quarter of whites into squash mixture. Spoon this mixture over remaining whites, and fold in lightly but quickly, until just blended.

Transfer to prepared soufflé dish and smooth top. Bake about 18 minutes or until puffed and browned; when you gently move oven rack, soufflé should shake very slightly in center. Do not overbake or soufflé may burn on top and may shrink. Set soufflé dish on prepared platter and serve immediately.

❧ INDIVIDUAL ONION SOUFFLÉS
Petits soufflés à l'oignon

When onions cook very slowly and gently in butter, they acquire a wonderful slightly sweet flavor. They are used as the base for these savory soufflés.   MAKES 4 SERVINGS

¼ cup butter

1 ¼ pounds onions, halved and
     thinly sliced

2 sprigs fresh thyme, or ½ teaspoon
     dried thyme, crumbled

Pinch of salt and freshly ground
     pepper

2 tablespoons plus 1 teaspoon
     all-purpose flour

¾ cup milk

4 egg yolks, room temperature

5 egg whites, room temperature

Pinch of cream of tartar

Melt 2 tablespoons butter in a medium sauté pan over very low heat. Add onions, thyme, salt, and pepper, and mix well. Cover with a round of buttered foil or parchment paper and a cover. Cook, stirring occasionally, about 45 minutes, or until onions are soft enough to be easily crushed with a spoon. If you used fresh thyme, remove sprigs. If there is liquid in pan, uncover and cook over medium heat, stirring, until dry.

Butter four 1- to 1¼-cup soufflé dishes, making sure to butter rims well. Position rack in lower third of oven and preheat to 425°F.

In a small heavy saucepan, melt remaining 2 tablespoons butter over low heat, add flour, and cook, whisking constantly, about 2 minutes, or until foaming but not browned. Remove from heat. Gradually whisk in milk and bring to a boil over medium-high heat, whisking. Add a small pinch of salt and pepper, reduce heat to low, and cook, whisking often, for 5 minutes. Remove from heat, and stir in onions. Bring to a boil, stirring.

Remove from heat and vigorously whisk in egg yolks, one by one. Cook over low heat, whisking constantly, about 3 minutes or until thickened. Do not overcook or let boil or yolks may curdle.

Taste and adjust seasoning. (Mixture can be kept, covered, up to 8 hours in refrigerator.)

Have four heatproof plates ready near oven. Put soufflé dishes on a baking sheet.

If soufflé mixture is cold, heat it in a small saucepan over low heat, whisking, until just warm. Remove from heat.

In a large bowl, beat egg whites with cream of tartar at medium speed until soft peaks form. Continue beating at high speed until whites are stiff but not dry.

Quickly fold about one-quarter of whites into onion mixture. Spoon this over remaining whites and fold in lightly but quickly, until just blended.

Transfer to prepared soufflé dishes and smooth tops. Bake about 12 minutes, or until puffed and browned; when you gently move oven rack, soufflés should shake very slightly in center. Do not overbake or soufflés may burn on top and may shrink. Set soufflé dishes on plates and serve immediately.

❧ BROCCOLI AND MUSHROOM SOUFFLÉ WITH CHIVES
Soufflé de brocolis et champignons à la ciboulette

Broccoli was not common in France until it began appearing on the tables of fine restaurants with the beginning of nouvelle cuisine in the early seventies. This soufflé is flavored with broccoli purée and dotted with sautéed mushrooms for a contrasting texture.

MAKES ABOUT 4 SERVINGS

1 pound broccoli, divided into medium-size florets, stalk reserved	*3 tablespoons all-purpose flour*
	¾ cup plus 2 tablespoons milk
	Freshly grated nutmeg
3 tablespoons plus 2 teaspoons butter	*4 egg yolks, room temperature*
¼ pound mushrooms, halved and thinly sliced	*2 tablespoons snipped chives*
	5 egg whites, room temperature
Salt and freshly ground pepper	*Pinch of cream of tartar*

Butter a 5-cup soufflé dish, making sure to butter rim well. Position rack on bottom third of oven and preheat to 425°F.

Trim off 2 inches of broccoli stalk. Peel remaining stalk and cut into ½-inch slices. In a large saucepan of boiling salted water, cook broccoli florets and slices, uncovered, over high heat about 7 minutes, or until very tender. Drain, rinse with cold water, and drain thoroughly. Purée broccoli in a food processor or blender until very smooth. Measure 1 cup purée. Return purée to saucepan and cook over medium heat, stirring, about 3 minutes to dry.

Melt 1 tablespoon butter in a medium-size skillet over medium-high heat. Add mushrooms, salt, and pepper, and sauté for 2 or 3 minutes, or until lightly browned and any liquid that comes out of mushrooms evaporates.

In a small heavy saucepan over low heat, melt 2 tablespoons plus 2 teaspoons butter, add flour, and cook, whisking constantly, about 2 minutes or until foaming but not browned. Remove from heat. Gradually whisk in milk. Bring to a boil over medium-high heat, whisking. Reduce heat to low, and cook, whisking constantly, for 2 minutes. Remove from heat and whisk in broccoli purée and a small pinch of salt, pepper, and nutmeg. Bring to a boil, stirring.

Remove from heat and vigorously whisk in egg yolks, one by one. Return to low heat and cook, whisking, 2 to 3 minutes or until slightly thickened. Do not overcook or let mixture boil or yolks may curdle. Taste and adjust seasoning. Stir in mushrooms. (Mixture can be kept, covered, up to 8 hours in refrigerator.)

Have a round heatproof platter ready near oven. If soufflé mixture is cold, heat it in a small saucepan over low heat, stirring, until just warm. Remove from heat and stir in chives.

In a large bowl, beat egg whites with cream of tartar at medium speed until soft peaks form. Continue beating at high speed until whites are stiff but not dry.

Quickly fold about one-quarter of whites into broccoli mixture. Spoon over remaining whites, and fold in lightly but quickly, until just blended.

Transfer mixture to prepared soufflé dish and smooth top. Bake about 18 minutes, or until soufflé is puffed and lightly browned; when you gently move oven rack, soufflé should shake very slightly in center. Do not overbake or soufflé may burn on top and may shrink. Set soufflé dish on prepared platter and serve immediately.

❧ CAULIFLOWER SOUFFLÉ PUDDING WITH GRUYÈRE CHEESE
Pudding soufflé de chou-fleur au fromage de Gruyère

A soufflé pudding is not quite as fragile as a soufflé because it is baked slowly in a water bath and thus does not fall as much as it cools. This soufflé pudding can be served with Fresh Tomato Sauce (page 36).   MAKES 4 TO 6 SERVINGS

1 large cauliflower, trimmed of leaves and large stalk, and divided into medium-size florets	*Salt and freshly ground white pepper*
2 cups milk	*Freshly grated nutmeg*
¼ onion, sliced	*¾ cup Crème Fraîche (see recipe) or purchased crème fraîche (see p. 274) or heavy cream*
10 black peppercorns	*4 eggs, separated, room temperature*
1 bay leaf	*Pinch of cream of tartar*
3 tablespoons butter	*1 cup grated Gruyère cheese*
¼ cup all-purpose flour	

Preheat oven to 375°F. Butter a 6-cup soufflé dish or other deep baking dish.

In large saucepan of boiling salted water, cook cauliflower, uncovered, about 7 minutes, or until very tender. Drain, rinse with cold water, and drain thoroughly. Purée in food processor or blender until very smooth.

In a medium-size saucepan, bring milk to a boil, add onion, peppercorns, and bay leaf, and remove from heat. Cover and let stand about 10 minutes so that milk can absorb flavor from seasonings. Strain.

In a medium-size heavy saucepan over low heat, melt butter, add flour, and cook, whisking constantly, about 2 minutes, or until foaming but not browned. Remove from heat and gradually whisk in milk. Bring to a boil over medium-high heat, whisking. Add small pinch of salt, pepper, and nutmeg. Reduce heat to low and cook, whisking often, for 5 minutes. Add crème fraîche or heavy cream and bring to a boil, whisking. Remove from heat.

Stir in cauliflower purée. Beat in egg yolks. Taste and add more salt, pepper, and nutmeg, if needed. (Mixture can be prepared 4 hours ahead; dab top with a small piece of butter to prevent a skin from forming and keep covered in refrigerator.)

In a large bowl, beat egg whites with cream of tartar at medium speed until soft peaks form. Continue beating at high speed until whites are stiff but not dry.

Quickly fold about one-quarter of whites into onion mixture. Spoon this over remaining whites, add Gruyère cheese, and fold in lightly but quickly, just until blended.

Transfer mixture to prepared soufflé dish and smooth top. Set dish in roasting pan and transfer to oven. Add enough boiling water to roasting pan to come halfway up sides of soufflé dish.

Bake about 30 to 40 minutes, or until a thin-bladed knife inserted into center comes out dry. Serve hot, from the dish.

NOTE: If desired, mixture can be baked and served in individual ramekins instead of a large dish; it will require 20 to 25 minutes of baking time.

Vegetable Tarts,
Pastries,
and Crêpes

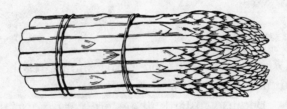

Presenting vegetables in pastry is a good way to make them the stars of any meal or party. Vegetables are perfect partners for pastry as they provide a light complement to rich crusts. Whether they are paired with elaborate puff pastry feuilletés for special occasions or with simple crêpes for everyday dinners, vegetables can always serve as a colorful, elegant filling.

In France, pastry is usually made with white flour, but if you prefer to use whole-wheat tart or pie shells, the fillings in this chapter will be fine with your favorite whole-wheat pastry recipes.

Vegetable Quiches and Pie-Pastry Tarts

Vegetables baked in pie pastry as quiches or tarts are favorite items of pâtisseries and charcuteries in France. The most popular fillings are made of mushrooms, spinach, onions, and leeks, but the vegetables used vary with the seasons. Cheeses add a zesty touch to Tomato and Goat Cheese Tartlets with Fresh Thyme and to numerous other vegetable tarts. At Androuet, the most famous Parisian cheese shop and restaurant specializing in cheese, I feasted on a savory onion and Roquefort tart.

Hints

- For best results, pie pastry should rest both before being rolled out and again before baking.
- Because custard fillings are very moist, the pastry for tarts and quiches is often prebaked so it will not become soggy once the filling is added.

BRIGHT GREEN SPINACH TART
Tarte aux épinards

Puréed spinach gives this tart a vivid green filling with a firmer texture than that of a quiche. To ensure the delicate flakiness of the *pâte brisée,* or French pie pastry, the tart shell is baked briefly before the filling is added.

MAKES 6 SERVINGS

PASTRY SHELL
2 egg yolks
2 tablespoons ice water
1½ cups all-purpose flour

⅜ teaspoon salt
½ cup cold unsalted butter, cut into bits

SPINACH FILLING

2½ pounds fresh spinach (leaves   *Salt and freshly ground pepper*
    with stems)   *Freshly grated nutmeg*
3 eggs   *1¼ cups heavy cream*
2 egg yolks

PASTRY SHELL

To make dough in processor: Beat egg yolks with ice water. Combine flour and salt in a food processor fitted with a metal blade. Process briefly to blend. Scatter butter pieces over mixture. Mix, using on/off turns, until mixture resembles coarse meal. Pour egg yolks and water evenly over mixture in processor. Process with on/off turns, scraping down occasionally, until dough forms sticky crumbs that can easily be pressed together but do not come together in a ball. If crumbs are dry, sprinkle ½ teaspoon water, and process with on/off turns until dough forms sticky crumbs. Add more water in same way, ½ teaspoon at a time, if crumbs are still dry. Using a rubber spatula, transfer dough to a sheet of plastic wrap, wrap it, and push it together. Shape dough in a flat disk.

To make dough by hand: Beat egg yolks with ice water. In a large bowl combine flour and salt, add butter, and cut butter through until it forms fine crumbs. Add egg yolks and water and toss until liquid is incorporated, adding more ice water by half teaspoons, if necessary, to form dough into a ball. Knead dough lightly with heel of hand against a smooth surface for just a few seconds and press it gently into a ball. Dust dough with flour and wrap it in plastic wrap. Shape dough in a flat disk.

Refrigerate dough 1 or 2 hours. (Dough can be kept up to 2 days in refrigerator.)

Butter a 9½- to 10-inch fluted tart pan with a removable base. Let dough soften 1 minute at room temperature. Set dough on a cool, lightly floured surface. Tap it firmly several times with a heavy rolling pin to flatten it. Roll it out, flouring often and working as quickly as possible, to a circle about ⅛ inch thick. Roll up dough loosely around rolling pin and unroll it over pan. Gently ease dough into pan. (If dough tears, use a piece of dough hanging over rim of pan to patch it up.)

Using your thumb, gently push down dough a little bit at top edge of tart pan, making top edge of dough thicker than remaining dough. Roll the rolling pin across pan to cut off dough at edges. With your finger and thumb, push up top edge of dough all around pan so it is about ¼ inch higher than rim of pan. Prick bottom of shell lightly with a fork and refrigerate shell 30 minutes. (Tart shell can be kept, covered, up to 2 days in refrigerator; or it can be frozen.)

Position rack in lower third of oven and preheat to 425°F. Line pastry shell with parchment paper or foil and fill with rice, beans or pie crust weights. Set shell on a baking sheet and bake 10 minutes. Carefully remove rice, beans, or weights and paper, and bake shell 8 to 10 more minutes or until it is lightly browned. Transfer tart pan to a rack and let shell cool. Move baking sheet to center of oven. Reduce oven temperature to 350°F.

SPINACH FILLING

Remove stems of spinach and wash leaves thoroughly. In a large saucepan of boiling salted water, cook spinach, uncovered, over high heat, pushing leaves down into water often, about 3 minutes, or until very tender. Rinse with cold water and drain thoroughly. Squeeze by handfuls until dry. Purée in food processor until very finely chopped.

In a bowl, whisk eggs with yolks and pinches of salt, pepper, and nutmeg. Stir in cream and chopped spinach. Taste and add more salt, pepper, and nutmeg, if needed.

Return pastry shell to baking sheet in oven. Ladle spinach mixture slowly into tart. Bake for 30 minutes, or until filling is set. Let cool on a rack for 10 minutes. Set tart on an upside-down flat-bottomed bowl and remove pan rim. (The tart can be kept, covered, 1 day in refrigerator; before serving, heat it in a 300°F. oven.) Serve warm or at room temperature.

NOTES

• Three 10-ounce packages frozen spinach can be substituted for fresh. Thaw spinach completely, squeeze it dry, and purée it in a food processor. Measure 1¼ cups purée. (With some brands of frozen spinach, two packages will be enough.)

• Tart can also be baked in a pie pan.

❧ TOMATO AND GOAT CHEESE TARTLETS WITH FRESH THYME
Tartelettes aux tomates et au fromage de chèvre

Freshly cooked tomatoes and cubes of creamy goat cheese make a colorful, luscious filling for these small pastries. Tartlets make a lovely individual portion but the filling can also be baked in a large tart shell.　　　　　　　　　　　MAKES 12 SMALL TARTLETS

PASTRY SHELLS
2 egg yolks

3 tablespoons plus ½ teaspoon ice water

2 cups all-purpose flour

⅜ teaspoon salt

¾ cup cold unsalted butter, cut into bits

TOMATO AND GOAT CHEESE FILLING
3 sprigs fresh thyme

1 bay leaf

2 tablespoons unsalted butter

1 small onion, minced (about ⅓ cup)

1½ pounds ripe tomatoes, peeled, seeded, and chopped

Salt and freshly ground pepper

3 ounces creamy goat cheese, such as Montrachet

1½ teaspoons fresh thyme leaves, or ½ teaspoon dried thyme, crumbled

1 egg

¼ cup heavy cream

PASTRY SHELLS
To make pastry in processor, whisk egg yolks with 3 tablespoons ice water. Combine flour and salt in a food processor fitted with a metal blade. Process briefly to blend. Scatter butter pieces over mixture. Mix using on/off turns until mixture resembles coarse meal. Pour egg yolks evenly over mixture in processor. Process with on/off turns, scraping down occasionally, until dough forms sticky crumbs that can easily be pressed together but does not come together in a ball. If crumbs are dry, sprinkle ½ teaspoon water and process with on/off turns until dough forms sticky crumbs. Add more water in same way, ½ teaspoon at a time, if crumbs are still dry.

To make pastry by hand, see Bright Green Spinach Tart, page 58.

Using a rubber spatula, transfer dough to a sheet of plastic wrap, wrap it, and push it together. Shape dough in a flat disk. Refrigerate dough 1 or 2 hours. (Dough can be kept up to 2 days in refrigerator.)

Butter twelve fluted 3-inch round tartlet pans. Let dough soften 1 minute at room temperature before rolling it. Set dough on a cold, lightly floured surface. Tap it firmly with a heavy rolling pin several times to flatten it. Roll it out, flouring often and working as quickly as possible, until it is slightly less than ¼ inch thick. Set eight tartlet pans next to each other. Roll up dough loosely around rolling pin and unroll it over pans. With a small ball of dough (from edge of sheet of dough) dipped in flour, gently press dough into tartlet pans.

Using your thumb, gently push down dough a little bit at top edge of each pan, making top edge of dough thicker than remaining dough. Roll the rolling pin across pans to cut off dough at edges. With your finger and thumb, press up edge of dough around each pan so it extends slightly above rim. Prick dough all over with a fork. Cover lined pans and refrigerate at least 30 minutes. Refrigerate scraps. Roll out remaining dough and scraps, and line remaining tartlet pans. (Tartlet shells can be kept, covered, up to 2 days in refrigerator; or they can be frozen for several weeks.)

TOMATO AND GOAT CHEESE FILLING

Position rack in lower third of oven and preheat to 400°F. Wrap thyme sprigs and bay leaf in a piece of cheesecloth and tie tightly to make a bouquet garni. In a large skillet, melt butter over low heat. Add onion and cook, stirring, about 10 minutes, or until soft but not brown. Add tomatoes, bouquet garni, and small pinches of salt and pepper. Raise heat to medium and cook, stirring often, about 20 minutes, or until mixture is very thick and most of moisture has evaporated. Remove bouquet garni.

If goat cheese has a dark rind, remove it. Cut cheese in ¼-inch dice.

Set tartlets on a baking sheet. Spoon 1 tablespoon tomato mixture into tartlet pans. Spread smooth. Put 4 cheese cubes in center. Sprinkle with a few thyme leaves.

Whisk egg with cream and salt and pepper to taste until blended. Ladle 1½ to 2 teaspoons egg and cream mixture over tomatoes, using enough to just cover tomatoes without running over side of tartlet.

Bake 15 minutes. Reduce oven temperature to 350°F. and bake about 18 minutes longer, or until filling sets and puffs and pastry is golden brown. Serve warm or at room temperature. (The tartlets can be kept, covered, up to 1 day in refrigerator. Warm them in a 300°F. oven before serving.)

NOTE: For small hors d'oeuvres, the pastry and filling can be baked in 2-inch tartlet pans; for a more substantial first course, large tartlet pans of 4 inches in diameter can be used.

CÈPE TARTLETS
For each tartlet, use 1 tablespoon cèpe duxelles filling, as in Cèpe Turnovers (see recipe), instead of Tomato and Goat Cheese Filling. Top cèpe filling with 1½ to 2 teaspoons egg and cream mixture, as above. Bake as above.

CABBAGE TART WITH CARAWAY SEEDS
Tarte aux choux au grains de carvi

The cabbage in this tart is surprisingly delicate in taste because it is boiled only briefly and then heated in butter. It is topped with a savory mixture of sour cream and heavy cream, which give a flavor reminiscent of that of crème fraîche.   MAKES 6 SERVINGS

One 10-inch Pastry Shell (page 58)

CABBAGE FILLING

½ medium-size head green cabbage (about 1 pound), cored, rinsed, and cut in thin strips
1 tablespoon butter
Salt and freshly ground pepper
2 eggs

1 egg yolk
¼ cup sour cream
Freshly grated nutmeg
¾ cup heavy cream
1 teaspoon caraway seeds
¼ cup grated Gruyère cheese

Prepare dough and prebake crust according to the instructions given in recipe for Bright Green Spinach Tart. Reduce oven temperature to 350°F.

CABBAGE FILLING

In a large pan of boiling salted water, boil cabbage, uncovered, over high heat for 5 minutes, or until tender. Rinse under cold running water, and drain. Squeeze out excess liquid.

In a large skillet, melt butter over low heat, add cabbage, and cook, stirring often, for 2 minutes, or until butter is absorbed. Add salt and pepper to taste. Transfer cabbage to a bowl and let it cool to room temperature.

In a bowl, whisk eggs with yolk, sour cream, ½ teaspoon salt, ⅛ teaspoon pepper, and nutmeg. Beat in heavy cream. Taste mixture and add salt, pepper, and nutmeg, if needed.

Spoon cabbage into shell. Sprinkle evenly with caraway seeds. Return shell to baking sheet in oven. Ladle egg mixture slowly over cabbage and sprinkle with Gruyère. Bake tart for 30 minutes, or until it is puffed, golden, and set. Let cool on a rack 10 minutes. Set tart on an upside-down flat-bottomed bowl and remove tart pan rim. (The tart can be kept, covered, 1 day in refrigerator; warm it before serving in a 300°F. oven.) Serve warm or at room temperature.

CREAMY MUSHROOM TART WITH CHIVES
Tarte aux champignons à la ciboulette

This pastry is inspired by a favorite tart at La Varenne in Paris. Unlike other mushroom tarts, which make use of sautéed sliced mushrooms, the chopped mushrooms used in this version flavor the creamy filling much more intensely.   MAKES 4 TO 6 SERVINGS

One 8-inch Pastry Shell (page 58)

MUSHROOM FILLING WITH CHIVES

2 tablespoons butter

1 medium-size onion, finely chopped

½ pound mushrooms, finely chopped

2 tablespoons all-purpose flour

1 cup heavy cream

¼ cup milk

Salt and freshly ground pepper

Freshly grated nutmeg

3 egg yolks

2 tablespoons thinly sliced chives

1 egg, beaten with a pinch of salt, for glaze

Prepare dough according to the instructions given in recipe for Bright Green Spinach Tart. Reserve one-fourth of dough in refrigerator to make a lattice; roll out the remainder and line a buttered 8-inch fluted tart pan. Prick bottom of shell lightly with a fork and refrigerate for 30 minutes, or freeze for 15 minutes. Cut any long scraps of dough in strips about ¼ inch wide and 9 inches long. Roll out remaining dough into a thin sheet and cut in strips of same size. Refrigerate strips side by side on a plate, about 15 minutes. (Tart shell can be kept, covered, up to 1 day in refrigerator; if chilled strips become too stiff to handle, remove them briefly so they soften slightly before using.)

MUSHROOM FILLING WITH CHIVES

In a large sauté pan or deep skillet, melt butter over low heat. Add onion and cook, stirring often, about 7 minutes, or until soft but not brown. Add mushrooms, increase heat to high, and cook, stirring often, until liquid has evaporated.

Remove mushroom mixture from heat, sprinkle in flour, and stir well. Reduce heat to low and cook, stirring, for 1 minute. Stir in cream and milk and season with salt, pepper, and nutmeg. Raise heat to medium and cook, stirring, until mixture comes to a boil and thickens. Reduce heat to low and continue cooking for 2 minutes. Remove from heat and let cool.

When filling is lukewarm, stir in egg yolks and chives. Taste, and add more salt, pepper, and nutmeg, if needed. Let cool completely.

To Assemble Pastry Shell and Filling: Position rack in lower third of oven, set a baking sheet on rack, and preheat oven to 425°F. Spoon cool filling into tart shell. Brush rim of shell lightly with egg glaze. Arrange 5 or 6 parallel strips at equal intervals above filling. Press gently to stick each strip to dough lining pan. Arrange 5 or 6 more strips intersecting first group at an angle so they form diamond shapes. Also stick these to dough lining pan. Remove excess from ends of strips by pressing against edge of tart pan. Gently brush strips with egg glaze.

Put tart on hot baking sheet and bake 10 minutes. Reduce oven temperature to 400°F. and bake 20 to 25 minutes more, or until pastry browns and filling sets. Let cool on a rack for 10 minutes. Set tart on an upside-down flat-bottomed bowl and remove tart pan rim. (The tart can be kept, covered, 1 day in refrigerator; warm it before serving in a 300°F. oven.) Serve warm or room temperature.

CAULIFLOWER QUICHE WITH ONION AND GRUYÈRE CHEESE
Quiche au chou-fleur

The classic quiche originated in Lorraine, a region in eastern France, and was topped with bacon and onions. Quiche now is part of the repertoire of many cuisines and appears in countless versions. In this one the cauliflower florets show through the creamy, cheesy topping.   MAKES 6 TO 8 SERVINGS

One 9- or 10-inch Pastry Shell
    (page 58)

CAULIFLOWER, ONION, AND GRUYÈRE FILLING

2 tablespoons butter	3 eggs
2 medium-size onions, halved and thinly sliced	½ cup milk
	1 cup heavy cream
Salt and freshly ground pepper	Freshly grated nutmeg
1½ pounds cauliflower, divided into large florets	1 cup grated Gruyère cheese

Prepare dough and line a 9- or 10-inch fluted tart pan with a removable rim or a pie pan as in Bright Green Spinach Tart. Prebake crust and reduce oven temperature to 350°F.

CAULIFLOWER, ONION, AND GRUYÈRE FILLING

In a medium-size skillet, melt butter over low heat. Add onions and a pinch of salt and pepper, and cook, stirring often, about 10 minutes, or until soft but not brown.

Meanwhile, in a large saucepan of boiling salted water, cook cauliflower florets, uncovered, over high heat for 3 minutes. Remove gently to a colander and rinse with cold water. Remove stalks and divide large florets into very small ones.

In a bowl, whisk eggs with milk, cream, and salt, pepper, and nutmeg to taste.

Spoon onions into cooled pastry shell. Arrange a ring of cauliflower florets near edge of shell, with flower end of each one facing outward. Arrange another circle of florets, with flower ends resting on stalk ends of first circle. Continue arranging rings of florets until pie shell is covered. Put a few florets in center. Sprinkle cauliflower with ½ cup grated cheese.

Return shell to baking sheet in oven. Ladle egg and cream mixture slowly over cauliflower and sprinkle with remaining cheese. Bake tart for 30 minutes, or until it is puffed, golden, and set; when you touch filling gently, it should not stick to your finger. Do not overbake or filling may separate. Let cool on a rack for 10 minutes. Set tart on an upside-down flat-bottomed bowl and remove tart pan rim. (The quiche can be kept, covered, 1 day in refrigerator. Warm it in a 300°F. oven before serving.) Serve warm or at room temperature.

CHARD AND TOMATO TART
Tarte aux blettes et aux tomates

Two fillings—one of Swiss chard and one of tomato and onion —are layered in this vegetable tart. It is filled entirely with vegetables and does not contain custard. There is no need to prebake the crust because the vegetables are cooked until thick and do not soak into the pastry.   MAKES 6 TO 8 SERVINGS

PASTRY SHELL

1 egg yolk
2 to 3 tablespoons ice water
1⅓ cups all-purpose flour

¼ teaspoon salt
7 tablespoons cold unsalted butter, cut into bits

SWISS CHARD, TOMATO, AND ONION FILLING

1 pound Swiss chard
3 tablespoons unsalted butter
Salt and freshly ground pepper
2 tablespoons olive oil
1 medium-size onion, halved and sliced
10 ounces ripe tomatoes, peeled, seeded, and chopped

1 teaspoon fresh thyme, or ¼ teaspoon dried thyme, crumbled
1 large garlic clove, minced
2 ounces Gruyère cheese, cut into 1¼-by-⅜-by-⅛ inch strips
¼ cup freshly grated Parmesan cheese

PASTRY SHELL

To make pastry shell, follow instructions in recipe for Bright Green Spinach Tart (page 58). Use a buttered 8-inch fluted tart pan. Prick bottom of shell lightly with a fork and refrigerate shell 30 minutes. (Tart shell can be kept, covered, up to 2 days in refrigerator; or it can be frozen.)

SWISS CHARD, TOMATO, AND ONION FILLING

Remove chard leaves from stalks, and discard stalks or reserve for other uses. Rinse leaves thoroughly. Pile chard leaves and cut in half lengthwise, then crosswise, into ½-inch-wide strips.

In a large skillet, melt 2 tablespoons butter over low heat. Add about half of chard and a pinch of salt and pepper. Cook, stirring often, about 6 minutes, or until tender. Remove with tongs, add remaining chard and a little salt and pepper and cook it also until tender. Return all of chard to pan and heat, stirring, 1 minute. Transfer to a plate and cool to room temperature.

In a medium-size skillet, heat oil and 1 tablespoon butter over low heat. Add onion and a pinch of salt and pepper and cook, stirring often, about 15 minutes, or until very tender but not browned. Add tomatoes and thyme. Raise heat to medium-high and cook, stirring often, about 15 minutes, or until juice from tomatoes has evaporated and mixture is dry. Stir in garlic. Taste and adjust seasoning. Cool to room temperature.

Preheat oven to 400°F. Heat a baking sheet in oven. Spread chard evenly in tart shell. Scatter Gruyère cheese strips evenly over mixture. Cover chard with tomato mixture. Sprinkle with Parmesan cheese.

Set tart on baking sheet in oven. Bake about 40 minutes, or until pastry is brown at sides and filling browns on top. Let cool on a rack for 10 minutes. Set tart on an upside-down flat-bottomed bowl and remove tart pan rim. (The tart can be kept, covered, 1 day in refrigerator. Warm it in a 300°F. oven before serving.) Serve hot or warm.

Savory Vegetable Cream Puffs and Quenelles

Cream puffs and quenelles are made of choux pastry, which is extremely versatile and can be baked, poached, or fried. The dough puffs when baked and leaves a hollow for filling. Fillings can be hot, cooked vegetables in a sauce, vegetable purées, or even cool vegetable salads with a rich mayonnaise-type dressing.

For vegetable quenelles, or light dumplings, the pastry itself is flavored with the vegetables and poached or baked, then served with a creamy sauce. When a mixture of this type is deep-fried instead, it creates a totally different effect. The result is little round beignets, which puff and become lightly crisp on the outside and soft inside, as in Brie Beignets flavored with celery.

CHEESE PUFF CROWN WITH ASPARAGUS
Gougère aux asperges

Gougère originated in the Burgundy region and these cheese puffs traditionally accompanied tastings of the great red wines. Small *gougères* are often served at fine restaurants as a treat while diners are looking over the menu. This vegetable version makes a festive first course or luncheon main course.　　　MAKES 4 TO 6 SERVINGS

CHOUX PASTRY WITH CHEESE

½ cup plus 1 tablespoon
    all-purpose flour
½ cup water
¼ teaspoon salt
¼ cup unsalted butter, cut in 8
    pieces

About 3 eggs
Pinch of freshly ground pepper
2 ounces Gruyère cheese, cut in tiny
    cubes about ¼ inch square
    (1⅓ cup cubes)

ASPARAGUS CREAM FILLING

1½ cups water
½ pound medium-size asparagus
    spears (about 9 spears), peeled
    and cut in 1-inch pieces
1 tablespoon minced shallots
3 tablespoons butter

3 tablespoons all-purpose flour
½ cup milk
Salt and white pepper
Freshly grated nutmeg
½ cup heavy cream
¼ cup grated Gruyère cheese

CHOUX PASTRY WITH CHEESE

Position rack in lower third of oven and preheat to 400°F. Lightly butter a 9- or 10-inch round gratin dish or other heavy shallow baking dish. Sift flour onto a piece of wax paper.

In a small, heavy saucepan, combine water, salt, and butter and cook over low heat, stirring constantly, until butter melts. Raise heat to medium-high and bring to a boil. Remove from heat. Immediately add flour all at once and stir quickly with a wooden spoon until mixture is smooth. Set pan over low heat and beat mixture for about 30 seconds.

Remove from heat and cool about 3 minutes. Add 1 egg and beat it thoroughly into mixture. Add second egg and beat mixture until it is smooth. Beat third egg in a small bowl. Gradually beat 1 or 2 tablespoons of this egg into dough, adding enough so that dough becomes very shiny and is soft enough to just fall from spoon.

Add a pinch of salt to remaining egg and beat until blended; reserve for glaze.

Beat pepper and cubes of cheese into dough.

Using two tablespoons, shape mounds of dough of about 1½-inch diameter, spacing them at edge of gratin dish so they nearly touch each other. Brush them with egg glaze.

While puffs bake, prepare filling as directed below. Bake puffs about 35 minutes, or until dough is puffed and browned; cracks that form during baking should be golden. Mounds will join and form a crown.

ASPARAGUS CREAM FILLING

In a medium-size saucepan, bring 1½ cups water to a boil, and add a pinch of salt. Add asparagus and cook, uncovered, over high heat about 5 minutes, or until just tender. Remove asparagus with a slotted spoon, reserving liquid. Rinse with cold water and drain well.

Measure ½ cup asparagus cooking liquid. Boil measured liquid with minced shallots until reduced to ¼ cup. Cover and reserve.

In a small heavy saucepan, melt butter over low heat, stir in flour, and cook, whisking constantly, about 2 minutes, or until foaming but not browned. Remove from heat. Gradually add reduced asparagus cooking liquid and milk. Bring to a boil over medium-high heat, whisking. Add a small pinch of salt, pepper, and nutmeg. Stir in cream and bring to boil, reduce heat to low, and cook, whisking often, until mixture is thick enough to coat a spoon, about 5 minutes.

Reserve 8 asparagus tips for garnish. Add remaining asparagus pieces to sauce, bring to a simmer, and remove from heat. Stir in Gruyère. Taste, and add more salt, pepper, and nutmeg if needed. Spoon filling into baking dish, in center of baked crown.

Garnish with asparagus spears pointing from center outward like spokes of a wheel. Serve immediately by separating puffs with a knife and serving filling with a spoon.

❧ CREAM PUFFS WITH CARROT PURÉE
Choux à la purée de carottes

Cream puffs filled with a vegetable purée make a delicious first course. Besides carrot, other colorful purées such as spinach or broccoli make flavorful fillings. MAKES 6 SERVINGS, ABOUT 18 PUFFS

CARROT PURÉE

1 ¼ pounds carrots, peeled and cut   *Salt*
   in ½-inch slices

CHOUX PASTRY

½ cup all-purpose flour   *3 tablespoons unsalted butter, cut*
½ cup cooking liquid from carrots   *in pieces*
¼ teaspoon salt   *2 to 3 eggs*
Freshly ground pepper

TO FINISH CARROT PURÉE

½ teaspoon sugar   *¼ cup unsalted butter, softened*

CARROT PURÉE

Put carrots in a medium-size saucepan with enough water to cover and a pinch of salt and bring to boil. Reduce heat to medium-low, cover, and simmer 25 to 30 minutes, or until carrots are very tender and can be easily pierced with sharp knife.

Remove carrots from liquid with slotted spoon, reserving cooking liquid. Purée carrots in a food processor, food mill, or blender until smooth. (If using blender, purée in small amounts and use a little liquid with each batch.)

CHOUX PASTRY

Position rack in lower third of oven and preheat to 425°F. Lightly butter baking sheet. Sift flour onto a piece of wax paper.

Combine ½ cup reserved carrot cooking liquid, salt, pepper, and butter in a small heavy saucepan. Cook over low heat, stirring constantly, until butter melts. Raise heat to medium-high and bring to a boil. Remove from heat. Immediately add flour all at once and stir quickly with a wooden spoon until mixture is smooth. Set pan over low heat and beat mixture for about 30 seconds.

Remove from heat and cool about 3 minutes. Add 1 egg and beat it thoroughly into mixture. Using a fork, beat second egg in a small bowl. Gradually beat 1 or 2 tablespoons of this egg into dough, adding enough so that dough becomes very shiny and is soft enough to just fall from spoon. To check, scoop up about one-third of dough on wooden spoon, hold spoon sideways and wait for dough to fall; if it falls into pan in 10 to 15 seconds, it is ready; if it takes longer or does not fall, add a little more egg.

Reserve remaining egg for glaze. (If no egg remains, beat a third egg with a pinch of salt and set aside to use for glaze.)

Using a pastry bag and ½-inch plain tip, shape mounds of dough about 1¼ inches in diameter, spacing them about 2 inches apart on baking sheet. Alternatively, take 1 tablespoon dough and, with another tablespoon, push it onto baking sheet; continue with remaining dough. Using a pastry brush, coat each mound of dough with beaten egg, gently pushing down any points.

Bake puffs in preheated oven about 25 minutes, or until golden brown and firm; cracks that form during baking should also turn golden brown. To test for doneness, remove one from oven and cut open. Interior should be slightly moist.

To Finish: Put carrot purée in a saucepan and stir constantly over low heat for 5 minutes, or until dry. Add sugar and salt to taste, and stir until dissolved. Remove from heat and stir in butter until it is absorbed.

When puffs are baked, cut them in half horizontally with a serrated knife. Let cool 5 minutes. Fill bottom half of each puff generously with carrot purée, so that purée shows when top half is put back in place. Serve warm as a first course.

BRIE BEIGNETS
Beignets de Brie

Beignets of vegetables and cheese are great appetizers. These pair celery with Brie and are held together by choux pastry, which makes them puff when they are fried.   MAKES 4 TO 6 SERVINGS

1 large celery stalk	About 2 eggs
1 cup water	2 ounces Brie cheese, cut in
½ cup plus 1 tablespoon	¼-inch cubes (½ cup cubes)
all-purpose flour	Freshly ground black pepper
¼ teaspoon salt	Pinch of cayenne pepper
3 tablespoons unsalted butter, cut	Oil or shortening for deep-frying (at
in pieces	least 6 cups)

Review the hints on deep-frying on page 206 before proceeding.

Peel celery with vegetable peeler to remove strings. Cut in very fine dice. Measure ½ cup.

In a small saucepan, bring water to a boil, add celery, and boil, uncovered, over high heat about 3 minutes, or until tender. Drain well, reserving cooking liquid and celery separately.

Sift flour onto a piece of wax paper.

Combine ½ cup reserved celery cooking liquid, salt, and butter in a small heavy saucepan. Cook over low heat, stirring constantly, until butter melts. Raise heat to medium-high and bring to a boil. Remove from heat. Immediately add flour all at once and stir quickly with a wooden spoon until mixture is smooth. Set pan over low heat and beat mixture for about 30 seconds.

Remove from heat and cool about 3 minutes. Add 1 egg and beat it thoroughly into mixture. Beat second egg in a small bowl. Gradually beat this egg by tablespoons into dough, adding enough so that dough becomes very shiny and is soft enough to just fall from spoon. To check, scoop up about one-third of dough on wooden spoon, hold spoon sideways and wait for dough to fall; if it falls into pan in 10 to 15 seconds, it is ready; if it takes longer or does not fall, add a little more egg.

Beat in Brie cubes and celery. Add black pepper and cayenne, taste, and adjust seasoning.

In a deep fryer or large deep, heavy saucepan, heat oil or shortening to 360°F. on a thermometer for deep-frying. Preheat oven to 250°F. Take about 1 teaspoon dough. Dip second teaspoon in hot oil and use it to push dough from spoon into oil. Continue making more beignets in same way. Do not crowd.

Fry about 3 to 4 minutes, or until they are golden brown. Remove with slotted skimmer to paper towels on heatproof tray. Put in preheated oven while frying rest.

Transfer beignets to platter lined with doily. Serve immediately.

❧ BAKED BROCCOLI GNOCCHI WITH PARMESAN CHEESE SAUCE
Gnocchis parisienne aux brocolis

This is a new vegetable version of the familiar Parisian gnocchi. Here they are enriched with a colorful purée of fresh broccoli. Classic Parisian gnocchi, which are small balls of poached choux pastry coated with a creamy cheese sauce, have always been associated in my mind with the fabulous food shop Fauchon in Paris, where I tasted them for the first time. The gnocchi in this recipe are baked instead of being poached because the broccoli purée makes them softer than the classic ones. **MAKES 3 MAIN COURSE OR 6 APPETIZER SERVINGS**

BROCCOLI GNOCCHI

1 ¾ pounds (about 1 medium-size bunch) broccoli
½ cup plus 2 tablespoons all-purpose flour
½ cup milk
¼ teaspoon salt

¼ cup unsalted butter, cut in 4 pieces
2 eggs
Freshly ground pepper
Freshly grated nutmeg

PARMESAN CHEESE SAUCE

2 tablespoons unsalted butter
2 tablespoons all-purpose flour
1 ½ cups milk
Salt and white pepper
Freshly grated nutmeg

¼ cup heavy cream
¼ cup freshly grated Parmesan cheese
Pinch of cayenne pepper

3 tablespoons freshly grated Parmesan cheese, for topping

BROCCOLI GNOCCHI

Peel central stalk of broccoli by cutting off tough outer layer and discarding small stems. Cut peeled stalk into ½-inch slices. Cut remaining broccoli in medium-size florets. Reserve 1 cup small broccoli florets, each with about ¾ inch of stem, for garnish. In a large saucepan of boiling salted water, cook broccoli slices and florets, uncovered, over high heat until very tender, about 7 minutes. Drain thoroughly. Purée in food processor or in blender until very smooth. Return to saucepan and cook over medium heat, stirring, until dry, about 3 minutes.

Sift flour onto piece of wax paper. Combine milk, ¼ teaspoon salt, and butter in small heavy saucepan, and cook over low heat until butter melts. Increase heat, bring to boil, and remove from heat. Add flour immediately and stir quickly with wooden spoon until mixture is smooth. Beat mixture over low heat 30 seconds. Remove from heat and let cool 2 minutes. Using wooden spoon, beat 1 egg thoroughly into flour mixture. Repeat with other egg; at first mixture will seem separated but keep beating and it will come together.

Beat broccoli purée into choux pastry in four portions. Scrape mixture carefully from sides and bottom of pan to make sure there is no unmixed dough. Add pepper and nutmeg, taste, and adjust seasoning. Cover tightly with plastic wrap and refrigerate 30 minutes.

Butter two 5-cup gratin dishes or heavy shallow baking dishes. Preheat oven to 375°F. Using two teaspoons, shape broccoli mixture into egg-shaped dumplings by taking heaping teaspoon of mixture on one spoon and using second spoon to push it onto dish, leaving ½ inch between dumplings. Cover dish tightly with buttered foil. Bake until surface of dumplings is firm, about 15 minutes. Let cool. Release gnocchi gently from dish using metal spatula but leave in baking dish.

PARMESAN CHEESE SAUCE
In small heavy saucepan, melt butter over low heat, add flour and cook, whisking constantly, until foaming but not browned, about 2 minutes. Remove from heat. Gradually stir in milk. Bring to boil over medium-high heat, whisking. Add a small pinch of salt, white pepper, and nutmeg. Reduce heat to low and cook, whisking often, 5 minutes. Add cream and bring to boil, reduce heat to low, and cook, whisking often, 5 minutes.

Remove from heat and stir in ¼ cup Parmesan cheese. Add cayenne pepper. Taste and add more salt, pepper, and nutmeg, if needed.

Spoon sauce carefully over each gnocchi to coat it completely. Sprinkle with 3 tablespoons Parmesan cheese. (Dish can be prepared ahead and kept 1 day in refrigerator. Let reach room temperature before continuing.)

Bake at 375°F. until sauce is bubbling, about 10 minutes. Remove from oven; preheat broiler. Meanwhile, in medium-size saucepan of boiling salted water, blanch reserved broccoli florets over high heat until crisp-tender and drain thoroughly.

Broil baked gnocchi just until sauce is light golden. Garnish with blanched florets. Serve hot, from baking dishes.

GREEN VEGETABLE QUENELLES WITH MUSHROOM CREAM
Quenelles de legumes vertes à la crème de champignons

Quenelles are light French dumplings. I made these based on the classic formula for fish quenelles. The blend of vegetables and herbs gives these quenelles an intriguing pale-green color and a delicate flavor.   MAKES 6 SERVINGS

GREEN VEGETABLE QUENELLES

Vegetable-Herb Mixture
One 5-ounce bunch watercress
1 pound fresh spinach (leaves with stems)
¼ cup parsley sprigs
1 tablespoon chopped fresh tarragon

1 medium-size zucchini, coarsely grated (5 ounces)
1 tablespoon butter
1 medium-size onion, minced
Salt

Choux Pastry
½ cup plus 2 tablespoons all-purpose flour
½ cup milk
¼ teaspoon salt

¼ cup unsalted butter, cut in 4 pieces
2 large eggs
Freshly ground pepper

MUSHROOM CREAM
2 tablespoons butter
¼ pound mushrooms, halved and thinly sliced
Salt and freshly ground pepper

1½ cups heavy cream
Pinch of cayenne pepper
1 tablespoon chopped fresh tarragon

GREEN VEGETABLE QUENELLES

Vegetable-Herb Mixture

Remove leaves from watercress, discarding stems. Remove and discard spinach stems and wash leaves thoroughly. In a large saucepan of boiling salted water, cook spinach, uncovered, over high heat, pushing leaves down into water often, about 1 minute. Add watercress and boil 1 minute. Drain, rinse with cold water, and drain. Squeeze by handfuls until dry. Put in food processor and add parsley sprigs. Purée in food processor until finely chopped. Transfer to bowl and add tarragon.

Squeeze excess juice from grated zucchini. In medium-size skillet over low heat, melt butter, add onion, and cook about 10 minutes, or until soft but not brown. Add zucchini and cook over medium heat, stirring, about 3 minutes or until liquid evaporates. Add to spinach mixture.

Choux Pastry

Sift flour onto piece of wax paper. Combine milk, salt, and butter in small heavy saucepan and cook over low heat until butter melts. Increase heat, bring to boil, and remove from heat. Add flour immediately and stir quickly with wooden spoon until mixture is smooth. Beat mixture over low heat 30 seconds. Remove from heat and let cool 2 minutes. Using wooden spoon, beat 1 egg thoroughly into flour mixture. Repeat with second egg; at first mixture will seem separated but keep beating and it will come together.

Beat vegetable mixture into choux pastry in four portions. Scrape mixture carefully from sides and bottom of pan to make sure there is no unmixed dough. Add pepper, taste, and adjust seasoning.

Bring about 1½ inches salted water to a simmer in sauté pan or other shallow pan. Using two teaspoons, shape vegetable mixture into egg-shaped dumplings by taking heaping teaspoon of mixture on one spoon and using second teaspoon to give it a neat round shape. Tap spoon on edge of pan to drop dumpling into water. Continue adding dumplings but not enough to crowd. Adjust heat so water just moves but does not simmer. Poach, uncovered, for 20 minutes. With slotted spoon, remove carefully and transfer to tray lined with paper towels. Repeat with remaining dumpling mixture.

Butter two 5-cup (8-inch) gratin dishes or heavy, shallow baking dishes. Preheat oven to 375°F.

MUSHROOM CREAM

In large heavy skillet, melt butter over medium-high heat. Add mushrooms, salt, and pepper, and sauté until lightly browned. Add cream and bring to boil. Cook, stirring often, until sauce is thick enough to coat a spoon, about 6 minutes. Add cayenne pepper and tarragon. Taste and adjust seasoning.

Put quenelles in prepared dishes. (Dish can be prepared ahead and kept, covered, 1 day in refrigerator. Keep sauce separately. Let quenelles reach room temperature and reheat sauce before continuing.)

Spoon sauce carefully over each quenelle. Bake about 10 minutes, or until sauce begins to bubble. Serve hot, from baking dishes.

Vegetable Pizzas and Country Tarts

Pizzalike tarts have long been popular in French regional cooking. These are among the easiest of pastries to make. The base can vary from a simple oil-enriched dough similar to that of Italian pizza, to a rich brioche-type dough, as in Festive Vegetable Tart. They can be baked in a tart pan, like Provençal Pizza, or on a baking sheet, like Alsatian Onion and Cream Cheese Tart.

Fillings can vary enormously and can include many vegetables, but do not necessarily contain tomatoes or cheese. Actually, yeast dough can be used as a base for custardy, quiche-type vegetable fillings just as easily as pie pastry can.

PROVENÇAL PIZZA
Pissaladière

The original version of this French pizza was prepared without tomatoes, but many cooks add them when they are in season for their bright color and delicious flavor. MAKES 4 TO 6 SERVINGS

PIZZA DOUGH

1 envelope dry yeast, or 1 cake
    fresh yeast
6 tablespoons warm water (105°F.
    to 115°F.)

1 ½ cups all-purpose flour
¾ teaspoon salt
1 extra-large egg

ONION AND TOMATO TOPPING

5 tablespoons extra-virgin olive oil
5 medium-size onions, thinly sliced
Salt and freshly ground pepper
2 pounds ripe tomatoes, peeled,
    seeded, and chopped
1 bay leaf
1 ½ teaspoons fresh thyme, or
    ½ teaspoon dried thyme,
    crumbled

1 tablespoon chopped fresh basil
    (optional)
1 small can anchovy fillets, drained
    (optional)
⅓ cup pitted black olives, preferably
    Niçoise or other oil-cured olives

PIZZA DOUGH

To make dough in a food processor: Sprinkle dry yeast or crumble fresh yeast over 4 tablespoons water in a cup or small bowl and let stand for 10 minutes. Stir until smooth. In food processor fitted with dough blade or metal blade, process flour and salt briefly to mix them. Add remaining water and egg to yeast mixture. With blades of processor turning, pour in yeast-liquid mixture. If dough is too dry to come together, add 1 tablespoon water and process again. Process for 1 minute to knead dough.

To make dough by hand: Sift flour into a bowl and make a well in center. Sprinkle dry yeast or crumble fresh yeast into well. Pour 4 tablespoons water over yeast and let stand for 10 minutes. Stir until smooth. Add remaining water, egg, and salt, and mix with ingredients in middle of well. Stir in flour and mix thoroughly to obtain a fairly soft dough. If dough is dry, add 1 tablespoon water. Knead dough vigorously, slapping it on working surface, until it is smooth and elastic. If it is very sticky, flour it occasionally while kneading.

Lightly oil a medium-size bowl. Add dough, turning to coat entire surface. Cover with plastic wrap or with lightly dampened towel. Let dough rise in a warm, draft-free area about 1 hour, or until doubled in volume.

ONION AND TOMATO TOPPING

In a skillet, heat 3 tablespoons oil over low heat and add onions and a pinch of salt and pepper. Cover, and cook over low heat, stirring occasionally, about 30 minutes, or until very tender. Taste and adjust seasoning.

In another skillet or sauté pan, heat 1 tablespoon olive oil over medium heat. Stir in tomatoes, bay leaf, thyme, and a pinch of salt and pepper. Cook, stirring occasionally, about 20 minutes, or until mixture is dry. Discard bay leaf; stir in basil. Taste and adjust seasoning.

Oil a 10- or 11-inch tart pan. Roll out dough on a floured surface, or with oiled hands pat it out in pan. Line pan with dough.

Fill dough with onion mixture. Spread tomato mixture on top. Arrange anchovy fillets in a lattice and set olives in spaces. Let rise in a warm place for 15 minutes. Preheat oven to 375°F.

Bake pizza for about 30 minutes, or until dough is golden brown and firm but not hard. Serve hot.

RATATOUILLE PIZZA
Pizza à la ratatouille

Ratatouille is a traditional vegetable stew that has remained one of the most popular French vegetable dishes. There are many versions, some sautéed, some stewed, and some including potatoes. Recently, chefs have been using ratatouille as a filling for pastries. In this recipe it is paired with pizza. The vegetables are cooked separately before being briefly simmered together so that they keep their form and color and make an attractive topping for the pizza. The ratatouille can also be served on its own, hot or cold.

MAKES 6 TO 8 SERVINGS

PIZZA DOUGH

1 envelope dry yeast
1 cup plus 2 tablespoons warm
  water (105°F. to 115°F.)

3 cups all-purpose flour
1 ½ teaspoons salt
2 tablespoons olive oil

RATATOUILLE

3 sprigs fresh thyme, or ¾ teaspoon
  dried thyme, crumbled
2 sprigs fresh rosemary, or ½
  teaspoon dried rosemary,
  crumbled
1 bay leaf
½ cup plus 1 tablespoon olive oil
1 ¼ pounds ripe tomatoes, peeled,
  seeded, and chopped
Salt and freshly ground pepper
1 large onion, halved and thinly
  sliced (about ½ pound)

1 small green bell pepper, cut in
  strips about ½ inch wide
1 small red bell pepper, cut in
  strips about ½ inch wide
½ pound zucchini (3 small), cut
  in approximately ⅜-inch slices
¾ pound thin eggplant (1 small
  eggplant)
3 large garlic cloves, minced
2 tablespoons chopped fresh basil

Basil leaves, for garnish (optional)

PIZZA DOUGH

To make dough in a food processor: Sprinkle yeast over ⅓ cup water in a cup or small bowl and let stand for 10 minutes. Stir until smooth. In food processor fitted with dough blade or metal blade, process flour and salt briefly to mix them. Add remaining water and oil to yeast mixture. With blades of processor turning, pour in yeast-liquid mixture. If dough is too dry to come together, add 1 tablespoon water and process again. Process for 1 minute to knead dough.

To make dough by hand: Sift flour into a bowl and make a well in center. Sprinkle dry yeast or crumble fresh yeast into well. Pour ⅓ cup water over yeast and let stand for 10 minutes. Stir until smooth. Add remaining water, oil, and salt, and mix with ingredients in middle of well. Stir in flour and mix well, to obtain a fairly soft dough. If dough is dry, add 1 tablespoon water. Knead dough vigorously, slapping it on working surface, until it is smooth and elastic. If it is very sticky, flour it occasionally while kneading.

Lightly oil a medium-size bowl. Add dough, turning to coat entire surface. Cover with plastic wrap or with lightly dampened towel. Let dough rise in a warm, draft-free area about 1 hour, or until doubled in volume.

RATATOUILLE

Wrap thyme, rosemary, and bay leaf in a piece of cheesecloth to make a bouquet garni. In a medium-size heavy saucepan or stew pan, heat 1 tablespoon oil over medium-high heat. Add tomatoes, salt, pepper, and bouquet garni, and cook, stirring often, 20 minutes. Remove bouquet garni.

In a large sauté pan, heat 2 tablespoons oil over low heat. Add onion and cook 5 minutes. Add peppers and cook over medium-low heat, stirring often, about 10 minutes. Add zucchini, reduce heat to low, and cook about 5 minutes, or until barely tender.

Peel eggplant and cut in ¼-inch-thick slices. Cut any large slices in half. In a skillet, heat 2 tablespoons oil over medium-high heat. Add half of eggplant slices and sauté about 2 minutes per side, or until just tender. Repeat with another 2 tablespoons oil and remaining eggplant slices.

Stir garlic into tomato mixture and transfer it to zucchini and pepper mixture, then add eggplant slices. Mix very gently. Bring to a boil, cover, reduce heat to low, and simmer 5 minutes to blend flavors. Uncover, raise heat to medium-high, and cook about 5 minutes to evaporate excess liquid. Mixture should be thick. All vegetables should be tender; a few eggplant slices may be falling apart. Stir in chopped basil. Taste and adjust seasoning. Cool in pan, not in a bowl, so mixture stays dry.

Oil two baking sheets. Knead dough again briefly, divide it in two parts, and put each on a baking sheet. With oiled hands, pat each portion of dough into a 10-inch circle, with rims slightly higher than centers.

Spread half of ratatouille over each circle of dough, setting some of pepper and zucchini pieces on top and leaving about ½ inch of dough at edge uncovered. Brush edge of dough with olive oil and sprinkle remaining olive oil over topping.

Preheat oven to 400°F. Let pizzas rise for about 15 minutes.

Bake in preheated oven for 20 minutes, or until dough is golden brown and firm but not hard. Serve hot. Garnish, if desired, with small leaves of basil.

❧ PIPÉRADE PIZZA
Pizza à la pipérade

Pipérade is a pepper mixture from the Basque area of southern France. Generally it is used as a flavoring for omelets and scrambled eggs. Here it makes a wonderful, bright-red topping for a new pizza.

MAKES 6 TO 8 SERVINGS

Pizza Dough (page 82), using
    vegetable oil in place of olive
    oil

PIPÉRADE TOPPING

1 fresh jalapeño pepper or other hot	2 garlic cloves, chopped
pepper	1½ pounds ripe tomatoes, peeled,
¼ cup vegetable oil	seeded, and chopped
1 large onion, chopped	Salt and freshly ground pepper
2 red bell peppers (about ¾	
pound), cut in ¼-inch dice	

Prepare pizza dough following instructions in recipe for Ratatouille Pizza.

Lightly oil a medium-size bowl. Add dough, turning to coat entire surface. Cover with plastic wrap or with lightly dampened towel. Let dough rise in a warm draft-free area about 1 hour, or until doubled in volume.

PIPÉRADE TOPPING

Wear rubber gloves if you are sensitive to hot peppers. Discard seeds and ribs from hot pepper and finely chop. Wash your hands, cutting board, and knife immediately.

In a deep skillet, heat 3 tablespoons oil over low heat, add onion, and cook, stirring often, about 5 minutes, or until soft but not brown. Add bell peppers, garlic, and hot pepper, and cook, stirring often, about 7 minutes, or until peppers soften.

Add tomatoes and a pinch of salt and pepper and raise heat to medium. Cook, uncovered, stirring often, about 30 minutes, or until mixture is thick. Taste and adjust seasoning.

Oil two baking sheets. Knead the dough again briefly, divide in two, and put each part on baking sheet. With oiled hands, pat dough into two 10-inch circles, with rims slightly higher than centers.

Spread pipérade over dough, using about 1 cup for each pizza, and leaving about ½ inch of dough uncovered. Again push up dough so rim is higher than center. Brush edge of dough with oil and sprinkle remaining oil over topping.

Preheat oven to 400°F. Let pizzas rise about 15 minutes.

Bake about 20 minutes, or until dough is golden brown and firm but not hard. Serve hot.

COUNTRY LEEK TART
Tarte campagnarde aux poireaux

Leek tarts are favorites in Champagne and northern France. This one is enriched with cèpes and baked in a buttery crust, which is an easy version of brioche. If serving the tart as a main course, a good appetizer is Endive and Beet Salad, which originated in the same area of France.   MAKES 4 MAIN-COURSE OR 6 APPETIZER SERVINGS

BUTTERY YEAST DOUGH

1 envelope dry yeast	*2 eggs, room temperature*
¼ cup warm water (105°F. to 115°F.)	*¾ teaspoon salt*
1¾ cups all-purpose flour, preferably unbleached	*¼ cup unsalted butter, room temperature, cut in 8 pieces*

LEEK FILLING

1 ounce dried cèpes	*1 egg yolk*
2 pounds leeks	*¾ cup plus 2 tablespoons heavy cream*
3 tablespoons butter	
Salt and freshly ground pepper	*Freshly grated nutmeg*
2 eggs	*¼ cup grated Gruyère cheese*

BUTTERY YEAST DOUGH

To make dough in mixer with dough hook: Combine yeast and warm water in small bowl and leave 10 minutes. Stir well with fork. Sift 1½ cups flour into bowl of heavy-duty mixer fitted with dough hook. Add yeast mixture, eggs, and salt and mix at medium-low speed, scraping dough down occasionally from bowl and hook, about 7 minutes, or until dough is well blended and just begins to cling to hook. Dough will be soft. (If dough seems too wet, beat in remaining flour 1 tablespoon at a time.) Knead by mixing at medium speed, scraping down twice, about 5 minutes or until dough is smooth, clings to hook, and almost cleans sides of bowl. Scrape down from hook. Add half of butter pieces and mix at medium-low speed until dough is thoroughly blended, about 3 minutes. Add remaining butter and mix again until blended, 3 more minutes. Dough will be soft and sticky.

To make dough in food processor: Sprinkle yeast over warm water in a small bowl and let stand 10 minutes. Combine flour and salt in a food processor fitted with dough blade or metal blade. Process briefly to blend. Add eggs. With blades of processor turning, quickly pour in yeast mixture. Process 1 minute to knead dough. Add butter and process just until it is absorbed. Dough will be soft and sticky.

Lightly oil a medium bowl. Add dough, turning to coat entire surface. Cover with plastic wrap or with lightly dampened towel. Let dough rise in a warm, draft-free area about 1 hour, or until doubled in volume.

LEEK FILLING

Soak cèpes in hot water to cover until tender, about 20 minutes. Lift into strainer, rinse, and drain well. Cut cèpes into ¼-inch pieces.

Use white and light green parts of leeks for filling. Cut leeks in half lengthwise, rinse well, and cut into ¼-inch slices crosswise. Soak sliced leeks in cold water to cover for 5 minutes to remove any sand. Lift into colander or large strainer, rinse, and drain well.

In a large heavy skillet, melt butter over low heat, add leeks and salt and pepper to taste, cover, and cook, stirring often, for 15 minutes. Add cèpes, cover, and cook, stirring occasionally, until leeks are very soft but not brown, about 5 more minutes. If any liquid remains in pan, uncover and cook over medium-high heat, stirring, until mixture is dry. Transfer leek and mushroom mixture to large bowl and let cool to room temperature.

Combine eggs, egg yolk, cream, and nutmeg in medium-size bowl and whisk until blended. Mix with leek mixture, taste, and adjust seasoning.

Position rack in center of oven and preheat to 425°F. Butter 9-inch round fluted tart pan with removable bottom. Lift dough and let it fall lightly into bowl a few times to knock out air. Transfer dough to tart pan with aid of rubber spatula. With oiled knuckles, push dough outward from center toward rim, to line pan. Push dough against rim of pan with oiled fingers, so tart has border about ½ inch thick at top edge. Set tart pan on baking sheet. Ladle leek mixture carefully into tart shell. With side of finger, gently push up edge of dough again so it is slightly higher than rim of pan. Sprinkle filling with grated cheese. Let tart rise in warm draft-free area 10 minutes.

Bake tart for 15 minutes. Reduce oven temperature to 350°F. and bake about 25 minutes longer, or until filling is set and lightly browned. Let cool on rack for 15 minutes and remove tart pan rim by setting pan on an overturned bowl. (Tart can be baked up to 4 hours ahead and kept at room temperature.) Serve tart warm or at room temperature.

❧ FESTIVE VEGETABLE TART
Tarte aux légumes

This tart is filled mainly with vegetables, with just a little custard topping. Peas, yellow zucchini, asparagus, and other colorful vegetables can be added when in season.   MAKES ABOUT 6 SERVINGS

Buttery Yeast Dough (page 85)

VEGETABLE FILLING

2 medium-size carrots, peeled	*1 small red bell pepper*
White and light green part of 2 large leeks, cleaned	*6 ounces mushrooms, halved and cut in thin slices*
2 small zucchini	*2 eggs*
1 medium-size celery stalk, peeled	*½ cup heavy cream or milk*
¼ cup butter	*White pepper*
Salt and freshly ground pepper	*Freshly grated nutmeg*

Prepare dough and let rise as in Country Leek Tart.

VEGETABLE FILLING

Cut carrots, leeks, and zucchini in pieces about 1½ inches long. Cut these pieces in thin lengthwise slices, and each slice in thin lengthwise strips. Cut celery in thin strips also.

In a large skillet, melt 2 tablespoons butter over low heat. Add carrots, leeks, celery, salt, and pepper. Cover and cook, stirring often, 15 minutes. Add zucchini and cook, uncovered, about 3 minutes, or until all vegetables are tender.

Preheat broiler. Broil pepper about 2 inches from heat source, turning often with tongs, about 15 to 20 minutes or until blistered and charred. Transfer to plastic bag and close bag. Let stand 10 minutes and then peel. Cut pepper in half and remove core. Drain well in colander. Pat dry. Cut in thin strips. Add to vegetable mixture. Taste and adjust seasoning.

In a medium-size skillet, melt remaining 2 tablespoons butter over medium heat. Add mushrooms, salt, and pepper to taste, and sauté, stirring often, about 3 minutes, or until tender.

Combine eggs, cream, and salt, white pepper, and nutmeg to taste in a medium-size bowl and whisk until blended.

Position rack in center of oven and preheat to 400°F. Butter a 9-inch round fluted tart pan with removable bottom. Lift dough and let it fall lightly into bowl a few times to knock out air. Transfer dough to tart pan with aid of rubber spatula. With oiled knuckles, push dough outward from center toward rim, to line pan. Push dough against rim of pan with oiled fingers, so tart has border about ½ inch thick at top edge. Set tart pan on a baking sheet.

Scatter mushrooms over dough and top evenly with vegetable mixture. Ladle cream mixture carefully over vegetables. Let tart rise in warm draft-free area 10 minutes.

Bake about 40 to 45 minutes, or until dough browns and filling sets. Let cool on a rack for 15 minutes and remove tart pan rim by setting pan on an overturned bowl. (Tart can be baked up to 4 hours ahead and kept at room temperature; it can also be frozen. Heat in 300°F. oven before serving.) Serve tart warm or at room temperature.

❦ ALSATIAN ONION AND CREAM CHEESE TART
Tarte alsacienne à l'oignon et au fromage frais

This is a northern French "pizza." A soft creamy cheese is used in Alsace, but cream cheese softened with sour cream and heavy cream is a fine substitute. In some traditional versions, thin strips (lardons) of bacon are scattered on top before baking, but the tart has plenty of flavor without them.   MAKES 8 SERVINGS

Pizza Dough (page 81), using
    melted unsalted butter in place
    of olive oil

ONION AND CREAM CHEESE TOPPING

3 tablespoons butter	½ cup sour cream
2 medium-size onions, finely chopped (about 10 ounces)	½ cup heavy cream
	2 egg yolks
¼ pound cream cheese, room temperature	Salt and white pepper
	Freshly grated nutmeg

Prepare pizza dough following instruction in recipe for Ratatouille Pizza.

ONION AND CREAM CHEESE TOPPING

In a medium-size skillet, melt butter over low heat, add onions, and cook about 7 minutes, or until soft but not brown. Cool to room temperature.

Whisk cheese until smooth. Gradually beat in sour cream and heavy cream. Add egg yolks, and salt, pepper, and nutmeg to taste. Stir in onions, taste, and add more seasonings if needed.

Position rack in center of oven and preheat to 400°F. Oil a 17-by-11-inch baking sheet. Knead dough again briefly and put it on baking sheet. With oiled hands, pat dough out to cover, giving it a rim slightly higher than the center. It will make a thin layer. When dough is nearly patted out, let it rest 2 or 3 minutes before continuing.

Spread topping over dough, leaving a rim of about ½ inch at sides uncovered by filling. Let tart rise about 15 minutes.

Bake tart in preheated oven about 22 to 25 minutes, or until topping is golden brown and dough is firm but not hard. Serve hot.

Vegetables in Puff Pastry

A rich vegetable filling served in a puff pastry case may be today's most popular first course at the finest restaurants. Generally, the noble vegetables, such as asparagus or wild mushrooms, are the favorites, and they are moistened with a rich butter or cream-based sauce.

Puff pastry is rather time-consuming to prepare, but fortunately, good-quality puff pastry can now be purchased from many bakeries, making it easier to prepare a variety of delectable savory pastries at home. You can match the quality of the pastry hors d'oeuvres that are prominently displayed in fine food shops in France, and make the lovely first courses served at good restaurants.

Puff pastry can be baked in a multitude of shapes, from round bouchées, to square, rectangular, or diamond-shaped feuilletés to crescent-shaped turnovers. It can also be used to make impressive tourtes, such as Layered Vegetable Tourte, filled with roasted red peppers, spinach, and sautéed mushrooms.

GREEN ONION AND PARMESAN CROISSANTS
Croissants au parmesan et aux oignons nouveaux

Savory croissants have become popular in recent years, and so has purchased puff pastry, which simplifies the making of these croissants. Serve these small pastries as an hors d'oeuvre, as part of a buffet, or as an accompaniment for soups.   MAKES ABOUT 24 PASTRIES

2 tablespoons unsalted butter

1 cup sliced green onions (white
    and green parts)

¾ cup freshly grated Parmesan
    cheese

Pinch of cayenne pepper

Pinch of freshly grated nutmeg

1 pound good-quality puff pastry
    (either homemade or purchased
    from a bakery), well chilled

1 egg, beaten with a pinch of salt

In a medium-size skillet, melt butter over low heat, add green onions, and cook, stirring, about 4 minutes, or until soft but not brown. Cool completely.

Mix grated cheese with cayenne pepper and nutmeg. Sprinkle two baking sheets very lightly with water. Keep puff pastry refrigerated until ready to use.

Work with half of pastry, keeping rest refrigerated. On a cold, lightly floured surface, roll pastry out into a 7-by-13½-inch rectangle about ⅛ inch thick. Work quickly so pastry does not soften, moving it often and flouring it occasionally to prevent sticking. Brush pastry lightly with beaten egg and sprinkle with half of cheese mixture. Press cheese so it will adhere.

Using heel of a large knife, cut pastry lengthwise into two strips, each about 3½ inches wide. Cut each strip into triangles in which two sides are approximately equal, making each cut across width of strip; first triangle will be pointing up, second one will be touching it and pointing down, and so on, so that all of strip is cut into triangles and there are no scraps. Flour knife occasionally if it begins to stick to pastry. Spoon about ½ teaspoon green onions near one side of one triangle. Roll up tightly in direction of point opposite it. Press to attach to point. Repeat with remaining triangles.

Transfer pastries to one of prepared baking sheets and curve both ends to form a croissant. Refrigerate for at least 30 and preferably 60 minutes, or keep pastries in freezer until ready to bake. Continue shaping croissants from remaining pastry.

Preheat oven to 425°F. Brush pastries with beaten egg. Bake pastries about 12 minutes, or until puffed and brown. (The pastries can be kept for 2 days in an airtight container, or they can be frozen.) Serve warm or at room temperature.

MUSHROOM AND OLIVE PASTRY ROLLS
Roulés aux champignons et aux olives

Cylinders of filled puff pastry, with both ends dipped in a generous quantity of grated Gruyère cheese, are a common attraction in the windows of charcuteries throughout France. Generally a meat filling is used, but I am certain that many will find this luscious vegetable filling even tastier. These make delightful hors d'oeuvres at parties.

MAKES ABOUT 24 SMALL PASTRIES

MUSHROOM-OLIVE FILLING

½ cup Niçoise or other black olives, pitted and cut into quarters
5 tablespoons unsalted butter
¼ pound small mushrooms, halved and thinly sliced
Salt and freshly ground pepper

5 tablespoons all-purpose flour
2 cups milk
Freshly grated nutmeg
Pinch of cayenne pepper
1 egg
1 cup finely grated Gruyère cheese

1¼ pounds good-quality puff pastry (either homemade or purchased from a bakery), well chilled
1 egg, beaten with pinch of salt, for glaze

2 tablespoons heavy cream
1⅓ cups finely grated Gruyère cheese

MUSHROOM-OLIVE FILLING

If using Niçoise or other oil-cured black olives (but not olives in brine), put them in a small saucepan, cover with water, and bring to a boil. Drain thoroughly.

In a medium-size skillet, melt 1 tablespoon butter over medium heat, add mushrooms and salt and pepper to taste, and sauté about 5 minutes, or until tender.

In a medium-size heavy saucepan, melt remaining 4 tablespoons butter over low heat, stir in flour, and cook, whisking constantly, about 2 minutes, or until foaming but not browned. Remove from heat. Gradually whisk in milk, and bring to a boil over medium-high heat, whisking. Add a small pinch of salt, pepper, and nutmeg. Reduce heat to low and cook, whisking often, about 5 minutes, or until very thick. Add cayenne pepper. Set aside ½ cup of sauce for spreading on finished pastries and dab top with a small piece of butter to prevent a skin from forming. Let cool completely.

Remove remaining sauce from heat and let cool slightly. Add egg and whisk it in vigorously. Return to very low heat and cook, whisking constantly, a few seconds. Do not overcook or egg will scramble. Add olives and mushrooms. Dab top of mixture with a small piece of butter. Let cool completely. Add 1 cup grated Gruyère to filling. Taste and adjust seasoning.

To Assemble and Bake Pastry Rolls: Sprinkle water on two baking sheets, preferably having a nonstick coating. Roll out half of dough on a cool, lightly floured surface until just under ¼ inch thick. Trim edges so that dough forms an even rectangle. Spoon a row of filling mixture along edge of one long side of rectangle. Carefully roll dough over once from long side so that filling is enclosed. Using a pastry brush, apply water on dough in a thin line alongside rolled section. Roll filled section over slightly in order to stick it to dough brushed with water. Using heel of a heavy knife, cut this roll off from rest of dough.

Cut roll into smaller pieces about 1½ inches long, and transfer to prepared baking sheets. Refrigerate. Continue making rolled pieces with remaining dough and filling. Refrigerate about 30 minutes, or freeze 15 minutes, or until firm.

Position rack in center of oven and preheat to 425°F. Brush all pastry rolls with beaten egg. Bake about 15 minutes, or until puffed and browned; do not worry if some of filling begins to come out, but reduce heat to 375°F. if it begins to burn. (The pastries can be kept for 12 hours at room temperature, or they can be frozen. Reheat in a 300°F. oven before serving.)

To finish, whisk 2 tablespoons cream into reserved ½ cup sauce. Adjust seasoning. Spread both open ends of cylinders with a thin layer of reserved sauce and dip each side in grated cheese. Serve hot, warm, or at room temperature.

~ ASPARAGUS-FILLED PASTRY CASES WITH WATERCRESS SAUCE
Bouchées aux asperges, sauce au cresson

Bouchées, or round puff pastry cases, have long been a popular pastry in France, both in tiny cocktail size for hors d'oeuvres and larger sizes for a first course. Their charm lies in the variety of textures presented —the flaky pastry, tender filling, and creamy sauce. Asparagus is regarded as a "noble" vegetable and therefore makes an ideal choice for a luxurious filling. By using purchased pastry, shaping the bouchées ahead, and preparing the sauce in advance as well, the total amount of work and last-minute fuss are kept to a minimum.

MAKES 6 SERVINGS

1¼ pounds good-quality puff pastry (either homemade or purchased from a bakery), well chilled
1 egg, beaten with a pinch of salt

12 medium-size asparagus spears, peeled
Salt

WATERCRESS SAUCE
About 8 ounces watercress
1½ cups heavy cream
1 tablespoon butter
3 medium-size shallots, minced
¾ cup dry white wine

¾ cup asparagus cooking liquid or Vegetable Stock (see recipe)
Salt and freshly ground pepper
A few drops fresh lemon juice

Sprinkle baking sheet with water. Roll out half of pastry dough on a cool, lightly floured surface until about ¼ inch thick. Using a 3- or 3½-inch fluted round cutter, cut six rounds of dough. Turn over three rounds and transfer to baking sheet. Brush these rounds with beaten egg. Using a 2-inch cutter (if you used a 3-inch cutter for the first rounds) or a 2½-inch cutter (if you used a 3½-inch cutter for first rounds), cut out centers of three of the rounds. (Save these centers for scraps.) Turn resulting rings over and set them on top of rounds on baking sheet. Press gently so they adhere. Refrigerate 1 hour, or freeze 30 minutes. Repeat with remaining dough and refrigerate. (Cases can be kept 1 day in refrigerator. Scraps can be refrigerated or frozen and used for lining tart pans or for other recipes.)

Preheat oven to 425°F. Brush rings carefully with beaten egg without letting it drip into center or onto baking sheet. Using a small sharp knife, mark crisscross lines on rings. Bake about 20 minutes, or until pastry cases puff and brown. Using a sharp knife, carefully remove small "hat" that forms in center of case and reserve it. If uncooked dough remains inside, remove it with a spoon. Transfer pastries to a rack. (They can be kept overnight in an airtight container or can be frozen.)

Cut 2½-inch-long asparagus tips from stems. Cut stems in about ½-inch pieces, discarding tough ends.

Put asparagus pieces into medium-size saucepan containing enough boiling salted water to cover them generously. Return to boil, cook, uncovered, about 2 minutes, or until asparagus is just tender when pierced with a small sharp knife. Drain, reserving ¾ cup cooking liquid for sauce. Rinse with cold running water until cool and drain thoroughly.

WATERCRESS SAUCE

Cut off leafy section of watercress; discard thick stems. Put leafy section into a large saucepan of boiling salted water. Return to a boil and cook 1 minute. After rinsing well with cold water, drain, pressing hard to extract excess liquid. Purée cooked watercress in a food processor or blender with ½ cup cream, scraping down often and continuing to purée until mixture turns a fairly uniform green. Push watercress purée through a strainer, pressing firmly to make sure it goes through and using a rubber spatula to scrape it from underside of strainer.

Melt butter in a medium-size saucepan over low heat. Add shallots and cook, stirring, 1 minute. Add wine and bring to boil. Cook, stirring often, until wine is reduced to about ⅓ cup. Add asparagus liquid and boil until mixture is again reduced to about ⅓ cup. Stir in remaining 1 cup cream and pinch of salt and pepper. Reduce heat to medium and simmer, stirring often, until sauce is thick enough to coat a spoon, about 7 minutes. Stir in watercress purée and simmer 1 minute. Strain sauce, pressing firmly on solids. Taste and adjust seasoning.

Before serving, reheat bouchées in 300°F. oven. Reheat asparagus by steaming above boiling water or by plunging into a medium-size saucepan of boiling salted water about 30 seconds. Drain well. Reserve asparagus tips for garnish. Reheat sauce, add a few drops lemon juice, and taste again.

To serve, set bouchées on small rimmed plates or individual gratin dishes. Fill bouchées with asparagus stem pieces. Spoon in a little sauce. Garnish with asparagus tips and set pastry "hat" on at an angle. Spoon a little sauce on each plate around bouchée. Serve immediately.

❧ CHANTERELLE FEUILLETÉS WITH VEGETABLE JULIENNE
Feuilletés aux chanterelles et a la julienne de legumes

Diamond-shaped or square feuilletés, today's favorite type of puff pastry cases, are often served with a fine vegetable filling. For this recipe, oyster mushrooms or other wild mushrooms can be substituted for the chanterelles, which can also be served separately. On its own, the vegetable julienne makes a delightful vegetable accompaniment for fish and white meats.   MAKES 6 SERVINGS

1 pound good-quality puff pastry
  (either homemade or purchased
  from a bakery), well chilled

1 egg, beaten with a pinch of salt

VEGETABLE JULIENNE
4 large carrots
4 large leeks, white and light green
  parts only

6 medium-size celery stalks
Salt and freshly ground pepper
¼ cup unsalted butter

CHANTERELLES
1 pound fresh chanterelles
2 tablespoons vegetable oil
3 tablespoons unsalted butter

1 large shallot, finely chopped
Salt and freshly ground pepper

Beurre Blanc (page 174)

Sprinkle a large baking sheet lightly with water. Roll puff pastry on a cold, lightly floured surface until ¼ inch thick. Work as quickly as possible. Keep edges of dough as straight as possible and flour often. Cut it in six 4-inch squares or diamonds.

Turn each one over and transfer to prepared baking sheet. Refrigerate 30 minutes, or freeze 15 minutes, or until pastry is firm. (Cases can be kept 1 day in refrigerator.) Position rack in center of oven and preheat to 450°F.

Brush pastries with egg glaze. Using point of a sharp knife, mark a crisscross design on top, cutting through only top few layers of pastry.

Bake pastries 5 minutes. Reduce oven temperature to 400°F. and bake about 15 minutes or until pastries are puffed and browned. Transfer to racks. (Baked cases can be kept 1 day in an airtight container or can be frozen.)

VEGETABLE JULIENNE

Leave oven at 400°F. Cut carrots in pieces about 1½ inches long. Slice pieces lengthwise. Stack slices and cut in thin lengthwise strips.

Slit leeks twice lengthwise, from center of white part upward. Cut leeks in pieces about 1½ inches long. Flatten each piece and cut in thin strips, using a large, sharp, heavy knife. Put strips in a bowl of cold water to rid them of any remaining sand. Remove them from bowl; sand will sink to bottom.

Peel celery with a vegetable peeler to remove strings. Cut in thin strips, about 1½ inches long.

Spread vegetables on a tray and toss well to mix. Sprinkle with salt and pepper and toss to distribute seasoning.

Spread 2 tablespoons butter on sides and base of a medium-size heavy ovenproof saucepan. Pack vegetables in saucepan. Dot them with 2 tablespoons butter. Cover them with buttered parchment paper, with buttered side of paper pressed onto vegetables. Cover tightly with a lid. Bake 30 minutes, stirring frequently with a fork, until tender; be careful because vegetables burn easily. Taste and adjust seasoning. (Vegetable julienne can be kept 1 day in refrigerator.)

CHANTERELLES

Gently rinse chanterelles and dry on paper towels. Cut in pieces if they are large. Heat oil and butter in a large heavy skillet over medium-high heat. Add shallot, stir, and add mushrooms and salt and pepper to taste. Sauté mushrooms, stirring. When mushrooms render their liquid, raise heat to high, and toss often, until mushrooms are browned and tender and liquid has evaporated; total cooking time is about 6 or 7 minutes.

Reheat pastry cases, if necessary, in a 300°F. oven. Reheat vegetable julienne, if necessary, in a covered saucepan over very low heat. Reheat chanterelles if necessary, uncovered.

Prepare Beurre Blanc following instructions in recipe for Asparagus with Beurre Blanc.

Carefully cut each pastry case in half horizontally, using a serrated knife. Put bottom half of each case on a plate. Spoon vegetable julienne onto each case and top with some chanterelles. Set top half on at an angle, allowing filling to show. Spoon sauce on plates around pastry. Serve immediately.

₰ LAYERED VEGETABLE TOURTE
Tourte feuilletée aux légumes

The French often prepare tourtes of vegetables, which have a double crust and thus are different from "tarts," which are open-faced. This tourte is a tall, glamorous puff pastry pie with colorful vegetable layers baked in a springform pan. Under the name "tourte milanaise" or "tourte de Paris," versions of this pastry can be found at the finer charcuteries in France. Although it includes several components, they can be prepared ahead; it is best to assemble and bake the tourte on the day it will be served.   MAKES 6 TO 8 SERVINGS

2¼ pounds good-quality puff pastry
   (either homemade or purchased
   from a bakery), well chilled

BÉCHAMEL SAUCE
2 tablespoons unsalted butter   *Salt and freshly ground white*
2 tablespoons all-purpose flour   *pepper*
1 cup milk   *Freshly grated nutmeg*

LAYERED VEGETABLE FILLING

4 eggs
Salt and freshly ground pepper
5 tablespoons butter
*3 pounds fresh spinach (leaves with
    stems)*

Freshly grated nutmeg
3 red bell peppers
½ pound mushrooms, thinly sliced
*1 teaspoon fresh thyme, or ¼
    teaspoon dried thyme, crumbled*

1 cup grated Gruyère cheese
*3 ounces thinly sliced Gruyère
    cheese*

1 egg, beaten with salt, for glaze

To make pastry shell, lightly butter the sides of an 8-inch spring-form pan. On a cool, floured surface, roll out two-thirds of puff pastry about ¼ inch thick, and cut a circle about 13 inches in diameter. Line prepared pan with pastry round. Smooth sides with your fingers. Using a sharp knife, cut off excess pastry at sides, leaving about 1 inch of excess. Prick bottom of shell lightly with a fork and refrigerate 30 minutes. Roll out remaining puff pastry about ¼ inch thick and cut in a 9-inch-diameter circle. Place circle on a lightly floured baking sheet and refrigerate.

BÉCHAMEL SAUCE

In a small heavy saucepan, melt butter over low heat. Add flour and cook, whisking constantly, about 2 minutes, or until foaming but not browned. Remove from heat. Gradually whisk in milk. Bring to boil over medium-high heat, whisking. Add a small pinch of salt, white pepper, and nutmeg. Reduce heat to low and cook, whisking often, about 5 minutes, or until thick. Taste and adjust seasoning.

Transfer sauce to a bowl, dab top with a small piece of butter, and cool completely.

LAYERED VEGETABLE FILLING

Beat eggs with a pinch of salt and pepper. Melt 1 tablespoon butter in an 8-inch skillet, preferably nonstick, over medium-high heat. Add half of egg mixture and stir briefly. Stop stirring and let mixture set to make a flat omelet. Remove from skillet. Wipe clean. Melt another tablespoon butter in skillet. Add remaining egg mixture and make another omelet.

Remove spinach stems and wash leaves thoroughly. In a large saucepan of boiling salted water, cook spinach, uncovered, over high heat, pushing leaves down into water often, about 3 minutes, or until tender. Drain, rinse with cold water, and drain thoroughly.

Squeeze spinach by handfuls until dry, then press between paper towels to be sure it is dry. Finely chop. In a large sauté pan, melt 1 tablespoon butter over medium heat. Add spinach and salt, pepper, and nutmeg to taste. Sauté, stirring, about 5 minutes. Adjust seasoning.

Preheat broiler. Broil peppers about 2 inches from heat source, turning often with tongs, for 15 to 20 minutes, or until they are blistered and charred. Transfer to plastic bag and close bag. Let stand 10 minutes. Peel, cut in half, and remove cores. Drain well in colander. Pat dry with paper towels. Cut each half in 4 pieces.

In a medium-size skillet, melt 2 tablespoons butter over medium heat. Add mushrooms, salt and pepper to taste, and thyme, and sauté, stirring often, about 3 minutes, or until tender. (Tourte components can be prepared 1 day ahead and each covered and refrigerated separately; pastry should also be covered.)

To Assemble the Tourte: Sprinkle ¼ cup grated Gruyère cheese on pastry base. Put 1 omelet on top of grated cheese. Whisk béchamel sauce until smooth. Gently spread ½ cup over omelet. Top with half of spinach. Sprinkle with ½ cup grated Gruyère. Arrange half of peppers on top and spoon all of mushrooms over peppers. Top with second omelet. Gently spread another ½ cup béchamel over omelet. Top with remaining spinach, then with all of Gruyère slices, followed by remaining peppers. Sprinkle with ¼ cup grated cheese.

Position rack in lower third of oven and preheat to 400°F. Brush edge of tourte thoroughly with egg glaze. Set pastry round on top, pressing firmly to stick it to sides. Cut off excess pastry with knife. Crimp edge decoratively. Brush top with egg glaze. Using point of a small sharp knife, score top in curved lines from center outward, cutting through only a few pastry layers. Make three small slits in top, this time cutting through to filling, so steam can escape.

Refrigerate tourte 15 minutes. Set tourte on a baking sheet. Bake tourte about 45 minutes. Reduce oven temperature to 350°F. and bake 15 minutes more, until pastry is well browned.

Let tourte rest about 30 minutes. Remove sides of springform pan. (Tourte can be kept 1 day in refrigerator but is best on day it is baked.) Serve at room temperature.

NOTES

• Cooked fresh spinach can be replaced by two 10-ounce packages frozen spinach. Thaw spinach and squeeze dry. Purée and continue as above.

• Puff pastry scraps can be used to make small pastries such as Green Onion Croissants (see recipe).

CÈPE TURNOVERS
Chaussons aux cèpes

Duxelles, a flavorful mixture of chopped sautéed mushrooms, can be made not only with plain mushrooms, but with wild ones as well. Here a duxelles made of cèpes is used as a filling for puff pastry turnovers. As with all filled pastries, avoid the temptation to put too generous an amount of filling in the turnovers or they will burst open. These are small turnovers that are good as an hors d'oeuvre, but they can be made larger and served as a first course.

MAKES ABOUT 40 PASTRIES

CÈPE DUXELLES FILLING

½ pound fresh cèpes, or 2 ounces dried cèpes
1 tablespoon butter
2 shallots, finely chopped
Salt and freshly ground pepper
¼ cup heavy cream for fresh cèpes, or ½ cup for dried cèpes

2 tablespoons minced fresh parsley
1 tablespoon unseasoned bread crumbs
1 egg yolk

2 pounds good-quality puff pastry (either homemade or purchased from a bakery), well chilled

1 egg, beaten with a pinch of salt

CÈPE DUXELLES FILLING

Thoroughly rinse fresh cèpes and cut off sandy ends of stems; pat dry. Soak dried cèpes in hot water to cover about 20 minutes, or until tender. Lift into strainer, rinse, and drain well. Finely chop fresh or dried cèpes.

In a medium-size skillet, melt butter over low heat, add shallots, and cook, stirring, 1 minute. Add cèpes and a small pinch of salt and pepper. Raise heat to medium-high and cook, stirring often, 5 minutes for fresh cèpes, or until liquid they render evaporates; cook only 1 minute for dried. Stir in cream and bring to a boil. Simmer, stirring often, about 2 minutes, or until mixture is thick and cream has been absorbed.

Transfer mixture to a bowl. Stir in parsley and bread crumbs. Cool to lukewarm. Add egg yolk and beat until mixture is blended. Taste and adjust seasoning. Cover and refrigerate 30 minutes. (Mixture can be kept up to 1 day in refrigerator).

To Assemble Turnovers: Sprinkle two baking sheets with water. Roll out half of dough on a cool, lightly floured surface until about ⅛ inch thick. Using a 3-inch-diameter cutter, cut circles of dough, reserving scraps. Roll each circle to elongate it slightly into an oval. Put 1 teaspoon filling in center of each. Brush half of oval, around a narrow end, with beaten egg. Fold in half to enclose filling, joining second side to egg-brushed side. Press to seal well. Set turnovers on the prepared baking sheets. Refrigerate at least 30 minutes; or wrap and keep pastries in freezer until ready to bake. Continue shaping turnovers from remaining pastry. Make turnovers from scraps too, after refrigerating them at least 30 minutes.

Preheat oven to 425°F. Defrost frozen turnovers briefly. Brush turnovers with beaten egg. With point of a sharp knife, mark a few decorative lines in a half-sunburst pattern on each turnover, cutting through a few layers of pastry but not all the way to the filling.

Bake pastries about 10 minutes. Reduce oven temperature to 375°F. and bake about 12 minutes, or until puffed and brown. (The pastries can be kept for 2 days in an airtight container, or they can be frozen.) Serve warm or at room temperature.

Vegetable Crêpes

One of the joys of strolling in Paris is purchasing a crêpe from an outdoor vendor. The crêpe is first quickly heated on a griddle with a pat of butter. Next it is topped with a selection of ingredients— grated Gruyère cheese, cooked vegetables, strips of ham, beaten egg, or a combination of these, for example—and heated until the filling is warm. Finally the crêpe is folded in quarters and wrapped in paper in a cone shape for easy holding. My own favorite at some Parisian crêperies is a filling of Roquefort cheese mixed with chopped walnuts and butter. The result is the finest fast food imaginable.

Crêpes are available throughout France as snacks but are a specialty of the region of Brittany, where they are still more popular than anywhere else. They make delicious and convenient wrappings for almost any vegetable. The batter for these thin French pancakes takes only a minute to make, whether it is done in a food processor, a blender, or in a bowl with a whisk. With a stack of crêpes on hand in the refrigerator or the freezer, the busy cook can easily prepare a festive treat for a light meal or a snack. Crêpes can be turned into an elegant first course or luncheon entrée or can be enjoyed in a more casual setting right out of the pan. They can enclose a great variety of vegetable fillings, from classic spinach with crème fraîche to elegant eggplant soufflé.

For a savory snack, many people are fond of the hearty taste of buckwheat crêpes, whereas white-flour crêpes are preferred for pairing with delicate fillings. For most purposes, they are interchangeable.

One of the most delicious ways to dress up leftovers is to turn them into crêpe fillings. Basically, any cooked vegetable and any flavoring can be used, according to what is available and your imagination. The only rule for fillings is that all the ingredients should be tender and in small pieces, and their flavors should harmonize well. The filling should be moistened with melted butter, a fragrant oil such as olive oil or hazelnut oil, or a little sauce, whether tomato sauce, cream sauce, or cheese sauce. The sauce can also accompany the filled crêpes, as in Crêpes with Peppers, Onions, and Peas in Curry Sauce.

Rolling is the most common way to wrap the crêpes around a filling, but some chefs put the filling in the center of the crêpe, then gather up the edges around it to form a little bundle, which they tie with a ribbon of blanched leek greens or green onion.

Crêpe batter can be cooked in a skillet, but the low sides of a crêpe pan make turning them easy. Traditional crêpe pans made of cast iron or rolled steel produce crêpes that are lacier, moister, and more attractively browned than those cooked in other pans. These heavy pans need to be seasoned with oil before they are used the first time, so the crêpes will not stick. Crêpe pans with a nonstick surface are lighter and do not require buttering before the batter is added. There also are crêpe pans that are dipped in the batter and cook the crêpes on the bottom of the pan. Which type of pan to select is a matter of personal choice.

The technique for cooking crêpes perfectly can be mastered quite easily after making just a few. The key is regulating the heat and the thickness of the batter so that the crêpes will be thin and lacy.

Hints

- To season a cast-iron or rolled-steel crêpe pan, brush it with vegetable oil and bake it at 200°F. for 2 to 4 hours.
- Do not wash cast-iron or rolled-steel crêpe pans after use; to clean them, rub them well with paper towels while they are still warm.
- Before cooking the crêpe batter, have all the utensils ready near the crêpe pan and burner: a plate for stacking them, a spatula for turning them, and a ¼-cup measure.
- A few small holes in a crêpe give a lacy effect and are fine; but if the crêpes have many large holes, the pan is probably too hot and the heat should be reduced slightly.
- Gratin dishes are ideal for baking crêpes. Either large or individual dishes can be used.

ꙮ BUCKWHEAT CRÊPES WITH CREAMY VEGETABLES
Galettes de sarrasin aux légumes

Buckwheat crêpes are a specialty of Brittany, a region bordering the Atlantic. If you have these crêpes on hand, it is easy to whip up a delicious light main course. That is part of the reason they have long been so popular, both as street snacks and at home, throughout France. The vegetables can be varied according to the season and stirred into the cream sauce, which can then be enclosed inside any unsweetened crêpe.   MAKES 10 TO 12 CRÊPES, 4 TO 6 SERVINGS

BUCKWHEAT CRÊPES
½ cup buckwheat flour
¼ cup all-purpose flour
3 eggs
1¼ cups milk, or a little more if
  needed

¾ teaspoon salt
3 to 5 tablespoons unsalted butter

CREAMY VEGETABLE FILLING
2 tablespoons butter
2 tablespoons all-purpose flour
1¼ cups milk
Salt and freshly ground white
  pepper
Freshly grated nutmeg
⅓ cup heavy cream or Crème
  Fraîche (see recipe)

Pinch of cayenne pepper
3 to 3½ cups diced or coarsely
  chopped cooked vegetables, one
  or a mixture of the following:
  cauliflower, broccoli, spinach,
  Swiss chard, or mushrooms

2 tablespoons butter, melted, for
  brushing crêpes

BUCKWHEAT CRÊPES
To prepare crêpe batter and cook crêpes, follow directions in Spinach-Filled Crêpes with Crème Fraîche (see recipe), substituting flour mixture for flour in recipe. Sift buckwheat flour with all-purpose flour. Reserve 12 crêpes for this recipe.

CREAMY VEGETABLE FILLING

In a medium-size heavy saucepan, melt 2 tablespoons butter over low heat. Add flour and cook, whisking constantly, about 2 minutes, or until foaming but not browned. Remove from heat. Gradually stir in milk. Bring to boil over medium-high heat, whisking. Add a small pinch of salt, white pepper, and nutmeg. Reduce heat to low and cook, whisking often, 3 minutes. Add cream and bring to a boil. Reduce heat to low and cook, whisking often, about 5 minutes, or until thick. Add cayenne pepper, stir in diced or chopped cooked vegetables, taste and adjust seasoning.

Preheat oven to 425°F. Butter one large shallow baking dish or two 8-inch gratin dishes or other shallow baking dishes. On lower third of the less attractive side of each crêpe, spoon 3 tablespoons filling and roll up in cigar shape, beginning at edge with filling. Arrange crêpes in single layer in buttered dish and brush with melted butter. (Crêpes can be prepared up to this point and kept, covered, up to 1 day in refrigerator. Bring crêpes to room temperature and preheat oven before continuing.)

Bake in preheated oven about 10 minutes, or until hot and sauce is bubbling. Serve immediately.

SPINACH-FILLED CRÊPES WITH CRÈME FRAÎCHE
Crêpes aux épinards à la crème

The spinach filling gives these crêpes an interesting appearance; its green color can be seen through the thin, lacy crêpes. Be sure to season the filling generously with nutmeg; spinach and nutmeg are a favorite French flavor combination.   MAKES 4 TO 6 SERVINGS

CRÊPES

¾ cup all-purpose flour   ¾ teaspoon salt
3 eggs   3 to 5 tablespoons unsalted butter
1¼ cups milk, or a little more if
    needed

SPINACH FILLING AND CHEESE TOPPING

1¾ pounds fresh spinach (leaves with stems)	*¾ cup grated Gruyère cheese*
¼ cup unsalted butter	*Salt and freshly ground pepper*
½ to ¾ cup Crème Fraîche (see recipe) or purchased crème fraîche or heavy cream	*Freshly grated nutmeg*

CRÊPES

To prepare batter in food processor: Combine eggs, ¼ cup milk, flour, and salt in work bowl and mix, using several on / off turns; batter will be lumpy. Scrape down sides and bottom of work bowl. With machine running, pour remaining 1 cup milk through feed tube and process batter about 15 seconds. Scrape down sides and bottom of work bowl thoroughly. Blend batter about 15 seconds.

To prepare batter in blender: Combine eggs, 1¼ cups milk, flour, and salt in blender. Mix on high speed about 1 minute or until batter is smooth.

To prepare batter in bowl: Sift flour into medium-size bowl. Push flour to sides of bowl, leaving large well in center. Add eggs, salt, and ¼ cup milk and whisk ingredients in well briefly until blended. Using whisk, stir flour gently and gradually into egg mixture until smooth. Gradually add remaining 1 cup milk.

Strain batter if it is lumpy. Cover and let stand at room temperature about 1 hour. (Batter can be refrigerated, covered, up to 1 day. Bring to room temperature before continuing.)

In small saucepan, melt butter over low heat. Gradually add 3 tablespoons melted butter to crêpe batter, stirring constantly with a whisk. Pour remaining butter into a small cup. Skim off foam to clarify. (Batter should have consistency of heavy cream. If it is too thick, gradually add more milk, about 1 teaspoon at a time. If too much liquid was added and crêpe batter is too thin, sift 2 or 3 tablespoons all-purpose flour into another bowl and gradually stir batter into it.

Heat crêpe pan or skillet with 6- to 6½-inch base over medium-high heat. Sprinkle with few drops of water. If water immediately sizzles, pan is hot enough. Brush pan lightly with some clarified butter; if using nonstick crêpe pan, no butter is needed. Remove pan from heat and hold it near bowl of batter. Working quickly, fill a ¼-cup measure half full of batter (to easily measure 2 tablespoons) and add batter to one edge of pan, tilting and swirling pan until its base is covered with thin layer of batter. Immediately pour any excess batter back into bowl.

Return pan to medium-high heat. Loosen edges of crêpe with metal spatula, discarding any pieces of crêpe clinging to sides of pan. Cook until bottom browns lightly. Slide spatula under it and turn carefully. Cook until second side browns lightly in spots. Slide crêpe onto plate. Top with sheet of wax paper or foil, if desired. Reheat pan a few seconds. Continue making crêpes with remaining batter, stirring it occasionally. If the first crêpes are too thick, whisk a teaspoon of milk or water into the batter. Adjust heat and add more clarified butter to pan if necessary. If batter thickens on standing, very gradually add a little more milk, about 1 teaspoon at a time. Pile crêpes on plate as they are done. Reserve 10 or 12 crepes for this recipe. (Crêpes can be kept, wrapped tightly, up to 3 days in refrigerator, or they can be frozen. Bring them to room temperature before using to avoid tearing them.)

SPINACH FILLING AND CHEESE TOPPING

Remove spinach stems and wash leaves thoroughly. In a very large saucepan of boiling salted water, cook spinach, uncovered, over high heat, pushing leaves down into water often, about 3 minutes, or until very tender. Rinse with cold water and drain. Squeeze by handfuls until dry and chop coarsely.

In a medium-size saucepan, melt 2 tablespoons butter over medium heat, add spinach, and cook, stirring, until most of spinach liquid evaporates. Remove from heat and stir in ½ cup cream. If mixture is thick, stir in ¼ cup more cream. Add 6 tablespoons cheese. Season to taste with salt, pepper, and nutmeg.

Lightly butter a large shallow baking dish or 2 medium-size baking dishes. On lower third of less attractive side of each crêpe, spoon about 3 tablespoons filling and roll up in cigar shape, beginning at edge with filling. Arrange crêpes in one layer in buttered dish. Sprinkle with remaining 6 tablespoons cheese. Cut remaining 2 tablespoons butter in small bits and scatter them over crêpes. (Crêpes can be prepared up to this point and kept, covered, up to 1 day in refrigerator. Bring to room temperature and preheat oven before continuing.)

Preheat oven to 350°F. Bake crêpes about 15 minutes, or until cheese melts and filling is hot.

LEEK AND MUSHROOM CRÊPES
Crêpes aux poireaux et aux champignons

Sautéed vegetables make a rich, juicy filling for crêpes that is easy to prepare. This mixture of sautéed mushrooms and leeks is flavored with olive oil, white wine, and garlic. MAKES ABOUT 6 SERVINGS

12 Crêpes (page 106), using vegetable oil in place of butter

LEEK AND MUSHROOM FILLING

1 ½ pounds leeks
2 tablespoons unsalted butter
Salt and freshly ground pepper
2 teaspoons fresh thyme, or ½ teaspoon dried thyme, crumbled
3 tablespoons plus 1 teaspoon extra-virgin olive oil
½ pound mushrooms, halved and cut in ⅛-inch slices
1 tablespoon minced garlic
¼ cup dry white wine

1 tablespoon extra-virgin olive oil, for brushing crêpes

Prepare crêpes according to the instructions in Spinach-Filled Crêpes with Crème Fraîche. Reserve 12 crêpes for this recipe.

LEEK AND MUSHROOM FILLING

Use only white and light green parts of leeks for filling; reserve dark green parts for stock if desired. Cut leeks in half lengthwise, rinse well, and slice into ¼-inch pieces. Soak sliced leeks in cold water to cover for 5 minutes to remove any sand. Lift into colander or large strainer, rinse, and drain well.

Preheat oven to 400°F. if planning to serve crêpes as soon as they are ready. In a medium-size heavy skillet, melt butter over medium heat, add leeks, pinch of salt and pepper, and thyme. Cook, stirring often, until leeks are very soft but not brown, about 15 minutes. If any liquid remains in pan, cook over medium-high heat, stirring, until it evaporates. Transfer leek mixture to a large bowl.

Wipe skillet clean. Add 2 tablespoons olive oil and heat over medium-high heat. Add mushrooms, salt and pepper to taste, and sauté, stirring often, about 6 minutes, or until any liquid that escapes from mushrooms has evaporated and they begin to brown. Add 1 teaspoon olive oil, quickly stir in garlic, and sauté 30 seconds. Add white wine and bring to boil, stirring. Cook over high heat until wine is completely absorbed by mushroom mixture. Remove from heat and transfer to leek mixture. Mix very well. Stir in 1 tablespoon olive oil and a pinch of pepper. Taste and adjust seasoning.

Lightly oil a large shallow baking dish or 2 medium-sized baking dishes. On lower third of less attractive side of each crêpe, spoon about 3 tablespoons filling, and roll up in cigar shape, beginning at edge with filling. Arrange crêpes in one layer in oiled dish and brush with 1 tablespoon olive oil. (Crêpes can be prepared up to this point and kept, covered, up to 1 day in refrigerator. Bring to room temperature and preheat oven before continuing.)

Bake crêpes in preheated oven about 12 minutes, to heat filling. Serve immediately.

⚜ CRÊPES WITH PEPPERS, ONIONS, AND PEAS IN CURRY SAUCE
Crêpes aux poivrons, oignons, et petits pois, sauce curry

A colorful garnish of peas and peppers in a spicy but creamy French curry sauce is spooned over the rolled crêpes and hints at the vegetable filling inside. Other vegetables that are good with curry, such as cauliflower, carrots, sautéed eggplant, and zucchini, can also be used.   MAKES 6 SERVINGS

12 crêpes (page 106), 7 inches in
    diameter

PEPPER, ONION, AND PEA MIXTURE

2 tablespoons butter
*2 medium-size onions (about 12
    ounces), halved and cut in
    thin slices*
Salt and freshly ground pepper
*1 red bell pepper, cored, seeded, and
    cut in thin strips*

2 cups water
*1½ pounds fresh peas, shelled
    (about 1½ cups), or 1½ cups
    frozen peas*

CURRY SAUCE

2 tablespoons butter
2 tablespoons all-purpose flour
1½ teaspoons curry powder
*½ cup cooking liquid (from
    vegetables above)*

1 cup milk
Salt and freshly ground pepper
Pinch of cayenne pepper
*6 tablespoons heavy cream, to finish
    sauce*

*1 tablespoon unsalted butter,
    melted, for brushing crêpes*

Prepare crêpes according to the instructions in Spinach-Filled Crêpes with Crème Fraîche, using a 7-inch crêpe pan and about 3 tablespoons batter to make each crêpe. Reserve 12 crêpes for this recipe.

PEPPER, ONION, AND PEA MIXTURE

In a medium-size sauté pan, melt butter over low heat, add onions and salt and pepper to taste, and mix well. Cover with a circle of buttered foil or parchment paper and a lid. Cook, stirring occasionally, about 10 minutes. Add strips of bell pepper, cover, and continue cooking, stirring occasionally, about 20 minutes, or until onions and pepper are very soft but not brown. Remove from pan to bowl with slotted spoon.

Add water to pan and bring to a boil. Add a dash of salt and peas, and boil, uncovered, until just tender, about 8 minutes for fresh peas or 4 minutes for frozen peas. Drain, reserving ½ cup liquid for sauce. Reserve 2 tablespoons peas and 3 pepper strips for garnish. Cut pepper strips in small dice.

CURRY SAUCE

In a small heavy saucepan, melt butter over low heat. Add flour and curry powder, and cook, whisking constantly, about 2 minutes, or until foaming. Remove from heat and gradually whisk in reserved vegetable cooking liquid and milk. Bring to a boil over medium-high heat, whisking. Add small pinches of salt, pepper, and cayenne pepper. Reduce heat to low and cook, whisking often, for 5 minutes.

Drain any liquid that the vegetables may have rendered while sauce was being prepared. Stir ½ cup of sauce into vegetables. Reserve remaining sauce separately.

To Assemble Crêpes: Preheat oven to 425°F. Butter a 14-by-8-inch oval baking dish or other shallow baking dish. On lower third of less attractive side of each crêpe, spoon ¼ cup filling, and roll up in cigar shape, beginning at edge with filling. Arrange crêpes in single layer in buttered dish and brush with melted butter. (Crêpes can be prepared up to this point and kept, covered, up to 1 day in refrigerator; sauce and garnish vegetables should be reserved, covered, in separate bowls. Bring crêpes and garnish vegetables to room temperature and preheat oven before continuing.)

Bake crêpes in preheated oven about 10 minutes, or until hot and sauce begins to bubble.

In a small saucepan, bring reserved sauce just to a boil. Remove from heat and whisk in cream. Return to boil. Reduce heat and simmer, whisking, about 1 minute, or until sauce thickens slightly. Taste and adjust seasoning.

To serve, transfer crêpes to plates and spoon a little sauce over center of each. Sprinkle reserved vegetables over sauce.

❧ EGGPLANT SOUFFLÉ–FILLED CRÊPES WITH RED PEPPER SAUCE
Crêpes soufflées à l'aubergine, sauce aux poivrons rouges

Crêpes with soufflé fillings make elegant vegetable first or main courses. As with any soufflé, these should be baked just before serving. Fortunately, their baking time is very brief. If desired, serve these with Fresh Tomato Sauce (page 36) instead of Red Pepper Sauce, or on their own, without sauce.   MAKES 6 SERVINGS

12 crêpes (page 106)

RED PEPPER SAUCE
2 medium-size red bell peppers
½ cup dry white wine
6 tablespoons white wine vinegar
   (5 percent acidity)
4 sprigs fresh thyme, or ¾ teaspoon
   dried thyme, crumbled

Salt and freshly ground pepper
1 cup well-chilled unsalted butter,
   cut into ½-inch pieces

EGGPLANT SOUFFLÉ
1 pound eggplant
¼ cup vegetable or olive oil
1 ½ tablespoons butter
2 tablespoons all-purpose flour
½ cup milk
Salt and freshly ground pepper

Pinch of freshly grated nutmeg
2 egg yolks, room temperature
4 egg whites, room temperature
Pinch of cream of tartar
3 tablespoons freshly grated
   Parmesan cheese

Prepare crêpes according to the instructions in Spinach-Filled Crêpes with Crème Fraîche. Reserve 12 crêpes for this recipe.

RED PEPPER SAUCE
Preheat broiler. Broil peppers about 2 inches from heat source, turning often with tongs, about 15 to 20 minutes, or until they are blistered and charred. Transfer to plastic bag and close. Let stand 10 minutes. Peel, cut in half, and remove cores. Drain well in colander. Pat dry. Purée in food processor until very fine.

   In medium-size saucepan, combine wine, vinegar, and thyme and bring to boil. Cook over medium-high heat until liquid is reduced to 3 tablespoons. Strain into small heavy saucepan. Add pepper purée and bring to boil. Keep butter pieces in refrigerator until ready to finish sauce. (Sauce can be prepared up to 1 day ahead to this point and kept, covered, in refrigerator.)

EGGPLANT SOUFFLÉ

Preheat oven to 425°F. Cut eggplant in half and score flesh lightly with sharp knife. Pour 2 tablespoons oil into heavy baking dish. Put eggplant in dish, cut side up, and spoon remaining oil over it. Bake 5 minutes. Turn eggplant halves over and bake another 30 minutes, or until flesh is tender when pierced with a knife.

In small heavy saucepan, melt butter over low heat, add flour, and cook, whisking constantly, about 2 minutes, or until foaming but not browned. Remove from heat and gradually whisk in milk. Bring to a boil over medium-high heat, whisking. Add small pinches of salt, pepper, and nutmeg. Reduce heat to low and cook, whisking often, 2 minutes. Sauce will be very thick.

When eggplant is tender, scoop flesh from skin and put in strainer to drain well. Finely chop with a knife and whisk into sauce.

Heat eggplant mixture briefly. Remove from heat and whisk in egg yolks, one by one. Return to low heat and cook, whisking constantly, until mixture thickens slightly. Add pepper and adjust seasoning. (Mixture can be prepared ahead; dot with butter to prevent skin from forming, cover, and refrigerate up to 1 day. Warm over low heat briefly, whisking, then remove from heat and proceed.)

Before serving, preheat oven to 425°F. Oil two heatproof platters or shallow baking dishes.

In a large bowl, beat egg whites with cream of tartar at medium speed until soft peaks form. Continue beating at high speed until whites are stiff but not dry.

Quickly fold about one-quarter of whites into eggplant mixture. Spoon this mixture over remaining whites, add cheese, and fold in lightly but quickly, just until mixture is blended.

Working quickly, spoon 2 tablespoons mixture onto less attractive side of each crêpe, fold in half without pressing on filling, and transfer to prepared dishes in a single layer. (Crêpes can be kept up to 30 minutes in refrigerator but are best if baked as soon as possible.) Bake about 10 minutes, or until filling puffs; do not overbake or filling will dry out.

To Assemble and Serve: Set pan of pepper sauce over low heat and bring to simmer, whisking. Season lightly with salt and pepper. Add 2 pieces of chilled butter and whisk quickly until just incorporated. Whisk in remaining butter 1 piece at a time without stopping, adding each only after previous piece is just nearly incorporated.

Remove from heat as soon as last butter piece is incorporated. Taste and adjust seasoning. Keep sauce warm by placing saucepan on a rack above hot but not boiling water, or put in a Thermos.

To serve, set two crêpes on each plate and spoon a little sauce next to them. Serve immediately. Serve any remaining sauce separately.

NIÇOISE BAKED CHICK-PEA PANCAKE
Socca

This pancake is made of a crêpelike batter containing chick-pea flour. A specialty of Nice, it is served as a snack at markets and informal restaurants that resemble pizzerias. Chick-pea flour is available at Indian markets and at specialty food shops.

MAKES 4 SERVINGS

1 cup chick-pea flour (also called garbanzo flour)
1 cup water
½ teaspoon salt
¼ cup olive oil
Freshly ground black pepper

Preheat oven to 475°F. Pour chick-pea flour into a medium-size bowl and make a well in center. Add water to well and whisk chick-pea flour into it. Add salt and 2 tablespoons of olive oil. Strain to remove any lumps, pressing on mixture.

Pour remaining 2 tablespoons olive oil into a heavy gratin dish 8 to 9 inches in diameter. Heat in oven for 5 minutes, open oven door, and carefully pour batter into dish, standing back because hot oil can splatter. Bake for 10 minutes. Transfer to broiler and broil until surface browns in a few places. Cut in wedges, sprinkle with freshly ground black pepper, and serve.

Vegetable Canapés

Although canapés are not usually made with pastry, some chefs do prepare them on thin bases of puff pastry. These dainty open-face sandwiches make it possible to enjoy tasty combinations without the need to prepare or roll pastry and play a role similar to an hors d'oeuvre. Vegetables make perfect toppings for light and colorful canapés. Any type of bread can be used, so long as it is not sweet.

Butter, whether plain or flavored with herbs, is the most common spread for the bread base, but for a change try homemade cheese spreads or mayonnaise. Either fresh, marinated, or cooked vegetables can serve as the topping. Generally, the vegetable acts as garnish as well so that there is no need for further decoration.

ASPARAGUS AND ROQUEFORT CANAPÉS
Canapés aux asperges et au roquefort

The asparagus sits on a spread made of a traditional pair—Roquefort cheese and walnuts—with a little butter to soften the flavor.

MAKES 6 CANAPÉS

12 very thin asparagus spears
Salt
12 walnut halves
2 tablespoons Roquefort cheese, room temperature

2 tablespoons unsalted butter, softened
6 thin slices good-quality white bread, crusts discarded

Cut asparagus spears so they are slightly shorter than bread slices. In a medium-size saucepan of boiling salted water to generously cover, cook asparagus tips over high heat about 2 minutes, or until just tender. Drain carefully, rinse with cold water until chilled, and drain. Set on paper towels to dry.

Finely chop 6 walnut halves. Mash Roquefort cheese and beat it thoroughly with softened butter. Stir in chopped walnuts. Spread Roquefort mixture on bread slices.

To arrange asparagus decoratively on canapés, cut each spear in two pieces and arrange them in an **X** on bread. At center of **X** put a walnut half. (The canapés can be kept, covered with plastic wrap, up to 8 hours in refrigerator.) Serve at room temperature.

CUCUMBER AND HERBED GOAT CHEESE CANAPÉS
Canapés aux concombres et au fromage de chèvre

These canapés make use of a popular cheese spread from Burgundy. Cream cheese can be substituted for the goat cheese. To make a simple vegetable hors d'oeuvre, the cheese mixture can be spread on cucumber slices instead of being spread on bread.

MAKES 8 TO 10 CANAPÉS

¼ pound creamy goat cheese, such as Montrachet, room temperature

3 to 4 tablespoons Crème Fraîche (see recipe), heavy cream, or sour cream

3 tablespoons minced fresh parsley

2 tablespoons snipped chives

2 teaspoons chopped fresh tarragon, or ¾ teaspoon dried tarragon, crumbled

Salt (optional) and freshly ground pepper

½ seedless cucumber

8 to 10 thin slices French bread or good-quality white bread

Remove any dark rind from goat cheese by scraping gently with a knife. Using a wooden spoon, beat cheese with 2 tablespoons cream until smooth. Stir in enough remaining cream to obtain a spreading consistency.

Stir in parsley, 1 tablespoon chives, and tarragon. Add a pinch of pepper. Goat cheese is often salty, so taste spread before adding salt. Cover and refrigerate overnight so that flavors blend.

Peel cucumber and remove center with a corer. Cut cucumber in thin slices—they will be ring-shaped. Spread on paper towels to remove excess moisture.

Using a round cutter of same diameter as cucumber slices, cut bread into circles. Spread with goat cheese mixture and set cucumber slice on top. Sprinkle remaining tablespoon chives in center of rings.

❧ RADISH FLOWER CANAPÉS
Canapés aux fleurs de radis

Slices of baby radishes arranged like a flower, with a stem of green onion, complete this easy and attractive canapé. It has a very fresh vegetable taste.   MAKES 6 CANAPÉS

6 thin slices French bread or
    good-quality white bread
2 tablespoons lightly salted butter

6 small radishes, thinly sliced
2 green onions, green part only

Use an oval cutter to cut bread or use a knife to cut off corners, giving slice of bread an oval shape. Spread with butter.

At one end of bread arrange 5 radish slices, slightly overlapping each other, in a flower shape.

Cut strips of green onion for stems and diagonal pieces of onion for leaves. Arrange a stem with 3 leaves on each bread slice. (The canapés can be kept, covered with plastic wrap, up to 8 hours in refrigerator.) Serve at room temperature.

❧ TOMATO AND EGG CANAPÉS
Canapés aux tomates et aux oeufs

Half the round of bread is covered with a tomato wedge and the other with a wedge of egg, both facing each other. These simple canapés will add color to any buffet.   MAKES 8 CANAPÉS

8 thin slices good-quality white
    bread, crusts removed
3 tablespoons Mayonnaise (see
    recipe) or commercial
    mayonnaise

1 teaspoon snipped or thinly sliced
    chives
2 hard-boiled eggs
2 small ripe tomatoes, about same
    size as eggs

Cut bread into 2½- or 3-inch circles with a round cutter. Mix mayonnaise with chives and spread on bread.

Cut eggs in lengthwise quarters. Cut tomatoes in lengthwise quarters also.

On one side of each bread slice, set a quarter egg with cut side facing inward. On other side of slice, set a quarter tomato, with cut side facing inward. Serve as soon as possible; if these are made ahead, juice from tomatoes will begin to soak into bread.

ROASTED PEPPER CANAPÉS
Canapés aux poivrons grillés

These canapés feature the vibrant flavors of Provence—peppers, Niçoise olives, and fine olive oil. MAKES 8 CANAPÉS

1 medium-size red bell pepper
2 teaspoons extra-virgin olive oil
3 tablespoons unsalted butter
1½ teaspoons minced fresh parsley
Salt and freshly ground pepper

8 thin slices good-quality white bread, crusts removed
4 black olives, preferably Niçoise, cut in half and pitted

Preheat broiler. Broil pepper about 2 inches from heat source, turning often with tongs, for 15 to 20 minutes, or until blistered and charred. Transfer to plastic bag and close bag. Let stand 10 minutes. Peel, cut in half, and remove cores. Drain well in colander. Pat dry.

Cut pepper in strips about ½ inch wide and cut off uneven ends on the diagonal. Put in a bowl, sprinkle with olive oil, and toss until coated. Let stand about 30 minutes.

Soften butter and stir in parsley and salt and pepper to taste. Spread on bread. Set 2 pepper strips on each bread slice, crossing them to make an X. Set an olive half at point where strips cross. (The canapés can be kept, covered with plastic wrap, up to 8 hours in refrigerator.) Serve at room temperature.

Gratins, Purées, and Stuffed Vegetables

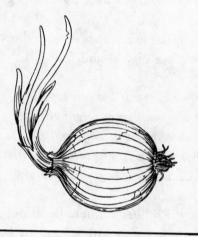

Gratins, purées, and stuffed vegetables are festive and proudly served both at home and in all types of restaurants. While gratins and stuffed vegetables are special forms of baked vegetables, purées are usually prepared from boiled or steamed vegetables.

The role of these types of vegetable dishes in the menu is versatile. All are perfect accompaniments for simply prepared foods, such as sautéed, grilled, or roasted poultry, fish, or meat. Gratins and stuffed vegetables also make an inviting main dish for a lunch, brunch, or a light dinner.

Vegetable Gratins

Coating a cooked vegetable with a flavorful sauce, sprinkling it with a simple topping, and browning it in the oven transforms it into a tempting gratin that is both attractive and elegant. A staple of French home cooking, gratins have long played a role similar to our casseroles. Since they can be assembled ahead and are baked and served in the same dish, gratins make menu planning easy. Many time-conscious cooks prepare a double quantity of vegetables in order to serve half with butter on one day, and the rest as a gratin on the next.

It is the crust that forms during baking that gives the gratin its name. The French *gratiner* means to bake until crusty. *Gratin* has been extended to mean any dish, most often of vegetables and usually sprinkled with a topping, that obtains a crusty surface after being baked or broiled. Depending on the topping used, the crust can be delicate or crunchy. The traditional topping is grated Parmesan or Gruyère cheese or bread crumbs. Other flavorful grating cheeses, such as French Cantal or Pyrénées, add a new touch. Chopped nuts give a crunchier topping.

Even the humblest of vegetables becomes enticing when transformed into a gratin. Green leafy vegetables and members of the onion, cabbage, and squash families all make delicious gratins; so do artichoke hearts, asparagus, eggplant, and mushrooms. Although gratins are usually made with one vegetable, they can also be composed of multicolored layers of vegetables, as in Swiss Chard and Pepper Gratin with Tomatoes.

In traditional recipes Mornay sauce, a thick cheese sauce enriched with egg yolks, was used most often for gratins. It is still quite popular, but today many cooks prefer lighter cheese sauces and cream sauces or, for a Mediterranean touch, fresh tomato sauce. Instead of a sauce, olive oil, melted butter, or cream can be sprinkled on the vegetables so they remain moist, as in Quick Broccoli Gratin with Gruyère and Nuts.

After the vegetables are cooked, they are drained thoroughly in a strainer or colander. If vegetables are not well drained, liquid adhering to them dilutes the sauce or moistening ingredient.

Gratins have given their name to a special baking dish, called a *gratin dish* or sometimes an *au gratin dish.* It is round or oval and is usually made of enamel-coated cast iron or earthenware. The dish is shallow so that the vegetable mixture can be spread in a relatively thin layer, which permits it to heat quickly and to have plenty of crust. Because gratin dishes are designed for both baking and serving, they are handsome and colorful. Other heavy, shallow, broilerproof baking dishes can be substituted.

LEEK AND DUXELLES GRATIN
Gratin de poireaux et duxelles

I learned to prepare this dish when I was training in the kitchen of a Parisian restaurant called La Ciboulette, or Chives. The chef would put his "signature" on each savory dish, including vegetable gratins like this, by sprinkling a little chives over it.

MAKES 4 TO 6 SERVINGS

CREAM SAUCE
2 tablespoons butter
2 tablespoons all-purpose flour
1 1/2 cups milk
Salt and white pepper

Freshly grated nutmeg
1/4 cup heavy cream
Pinch of cayenne pepper

1 1/2 pounds leeks
2 tablespoons unsalted butter
2 tablespoons minced shallots
3/4 pound mushrooms, finely
    chopped

1/2 cup coarsely grated Gruyère
    cheese

CREAM SAUCE
In a medium-size heavy saucepan, melt butter over low heat, add flour, and cook, whisking constantly, about 2 minutes or until foaming but not browned. Remove from heat. Gradually whisk in milk. Bring

to boil over medium-high heat, whisking. Add small pinches of salt, white pepper, and nutmeg. Reduce heat to low and cook, whisking often, for 5 minutes. Whisk in cream and bring to boil. Cook over low heat, whisking often, until sauce thickens and coats a spoon heavily, about 7 minutes. Remove from heat and add cayenne pepper. Taste and adjust seasoning. If not using immediately, dab surface of sauce with a small piece of butter to prevent a skin from forming.

To Prepare Vegetables and Assemble Gratin: Use white and light green parts of leeks only. Starting about 1 inch from root end of leeks, cut them in quarters lengthwise, leaving them still joined at root end and cutting toward top. Soak leeks in cold water to cover for 5 minutes. Rinse well to remove any remaining sand.

Preheat oven to 425°F. Put leeks into a large saucepan containing enough boiling salted water to cover them generously. Return to boil. Cook, uncovered, until leeks are just tender when pierced with a small sharp knife, about 7 minutes for small leeks or 10 minutes for large. Drain leeks gently, rinse with cold running water until cool, and drain thoroughly.

In a large skillet, melt butter over low heat. Add shallots and cook, stirring, about 1½ minutes, or until tender. Add mushrooms, a little salt, and pepper to taste, raise heat to medium-high, and cook, stirring often, about 8 minutes, or until most of liquid that mushrooms render has evaporated and mixture is very dry. Butter a heavy 5- or 6-cup gratin dish or other shallow baking dish. Spread mushroom mixture in even layer in dish.

If leeks are small or medium-size, cut them in half lengthwise; if they are large, cut them in quarters by continuing cuts made previously to clean them. Cut in 3-inch lengths, pat them dry, and arrange them in dish in one layer on top of mushrooms.

Spoon sauce carefully over leeks to coat completely. Sprinkle evenly with cheese. (Gratin can be prepared ahead and kept 1 day in refrigerator; bring to room temperature before continuing.)

Bake until sauce is beginning to bubble, about 7 minutes if sauce was still hot, or about 10 minutes if ingredients were at room temperature. Heat broiler and broil with broiler door partly open just until cheese is lightly browned, about 1 minute, turning dish if necessary so cheese browns evenly. Serve hot, from baking dish.

❦ BELGIAN ENDIVE GRATIN WITH CREAM SAUCE AND WALNUTS
Gratin d'endives aux noix

A versatile vegetable, Belgian endive is delicious raw in salads, braised with butter, or poached and baked in cream sauce, as in this gratin.

MAKES 4 SERVINGS

1 pound Belgian endive
1⅓ cups hot Cream Sauce (page 122)
2 tablespoons freshly grated Parmesan cheese, or ¼ cup grated Gruyère cheese

¼ cup coarsely chopped walnuts (optional)

Preheat oven to 425°F. Remove any damaged leaves from endive and trim bases very slightly, removing any brown parts.

Put endive into a large saucepan containing enough boiling salted water to cover it generously. Return to boil. Cook, uncovered, about 8 minutes, or until endive is just tender when pierced with a small sharp knife. Rinse with cold running water until cool and drain thoroughly. Press gently to remove excess water. Cut each endive in half lengthwise.

Butter a heavy 5-cup gratin dish or other shallow baking dish. In prepared dish, arrange endive halves, cut side down, in one layer. Spoon sauce carefully over them to coat completely. Sprinkle evenly with cheese and walnuts. (Gratin can be kept, covered, 1 day in refrigerator; bring to room temperature before continuing.)

Bake until sauce begins to bubble, about 7 minutes if sauce was still hot, or about 10 minutes if ingredients were at room temperature. If top is not brown, transfer dish to broiler and broil with door partly open just until cheese is lightly browned, about 1 minute, checking often and turning dish if necessary so cheese browns evenly. Serve hot, from baking dish.

SPINACH GRATIN WITH CREAM SAUCE
Omit walnuts. Substitute 1½ pounds fresh spinach (leaves with stems) or one 10-ounce package frozen spinach for endive. If using fresh

spinach, pull off and discard stems. Put leaves in a large saucepan containing enough boiling salted water to cover them generously. Return to boil. Cook, uncovered, about 2 minutes, or until just tender and wilted. Drain, rinse with cold running water until cool and drain. Squeeze spinach by handfuls to remove as much water as possible. Coarsely chop with a knife. If using frozen spinach, let it thaw, squeeze as above, and chop coarsely.

WINTER SQUASH GRATIN WITH FRESH TOMATO SAUCE
Gratin de courge à la sauce tomate

Fresh tomato sauce adds a lively Mediterranean flavor and bright color to gratins and turns the humble squash into a delightful dish. If you like, substitute fragrant oregano or marjoram for the thyme in the sauce.   MAKES 4 SERVINGS

FRESH TOMATO SAUCE

2 tablespoons olive oil

2 medium-size garlic cloves, minced

2 pounds ripe tomatoes, peeled, seeded, and chopped

Salt and freshly ground pepper

¾ teaspoon fresh thyme, or ¼ teaspoon dried thyme, crumbled

1 bay leaf

1 tablespoon tomato paste

Pinch of sugar (optional)

1½ pounds banana or Hubbard squash

2 tablespoons freshly grated Parmesan cheese

FRESH TOMATO SAUCE

Heat olive oil in a heavy large saucepan over low heat. Add garlic and cook, stirring, about 30 seconds, without letting it brown. Add tomatoes, salt, pepper, thyme, and bay leaf and stir well to combine with garlic mixture. Bring to a boil over high heat. Reduce heat to low and cook, uncovered, stirring occasionally, about 1 hour, or until tomatoes are very soft and sauce is thick.

Discard bay leaf. Purée sauce in a food processor until smooth. Return sauce to saucepan and whisk in tomato paste. Bring to a boil. Reduce heat to low and cook, stirring occasionally, until sauce is very thick and is reduced to 1⅓ cups, about 10 minutes. Taste and add sugar if sauce is too tart. Taste and adjust seasoning.

Preheat oven to 425°F. Remove seeds and strings from squash and cut into chunks approximately 2 by 2 by 1 inches. Put them into a large saucepan containing enough boiling salted water to cover generously. Return to boil. Cook, uncovered, about 10 minutes, or until just tender when pierced with a small sharp knife. Put in colander and rinse with cold running water until cool. Cut off skin, return to colander, and drain thoroughly.

Butter a heavy 5-cup gratin dish or other shallow baking dish. Arrange squash pieces in one layer in prepared dish. Spoon sauce carefully over squash pieces to coat them completely. (Gratin can be kept, covered, 1 day in refrigerator; bring to room temperature before continuing.)

Sprinkle with cheese. Bake until sauce begins to bubble, about 7 minutes if sauce was still hot, or about 10 minutes if ingredients were at room temperature. If top is not brown, transfer dish to broiler and broil with door partly open about 1 minute, or just until cheese is lightly browned, checking often and turning dish if necessary so cheese browns evenly. Serve hot, from baking dish.

CELERY GRATIN WITH TOMATO SAUCE

Substitute ¾ pound celery for squash. Peel to remove strings. Cut crosswise in 2-inch pieces. Cook in water for only 4 minutes.

CAULIFLOWER GRATIN WITH LIGHT CHEESE SAUCE
Gratin de chou-fleur au fromage

A classic combination, cauliflower with cheese sauce is a good accompaniment for roast beef or veal. This gratin can be instead the focus of a meal by being paired with a rice dish, such as Rice with Peas and Basil (see recipe), and a fresh vegetable salad.

MAKES 4 SERVINGS

LIGHT CHEESE SAUCE

2 tablespoons butter

2 tablespoons all-purpose flour

1 ½ cups milk

Salt and white pepper

Freshly grated nutmeg

¼ cup heavy cream

Pinch of cayenne pepper

¼ cup freshly grated Parmesan cheese

1 head cauliflower (about 1 ½ pounds)

2 tablespoons freshly grated Parmesan cheese

LIGHT CHEESE SAUCE

In medium-size heavy saucepan, melt butter over low heat, add flour, and cook, whisking constantly, about 2 minutes, or until foaming but not browned. Remove from heat. Gradually whisk in milk. Bring to boil over medium-high heat, whisking. Add a small pinch of salt, white pepper, and nutmeg. Reduce heat to low and cook, whisking often, for 5 minutes. Whisk in cream and bring to boil. Cook over low heat, whisking often, until sauce thickens and coats a spoon heavily, about 7 minutes. Remove from heat and add cayenne pepper. Taste and adjust seasoning. Dab surface of sauce with butter if not using immediately.

Before using, bring sauce to boil. Remove from heat. Whisk in ¼ cup Parmesan.

Preheat oven to 425°F. Divide cauliflower into medium-size florets, discarding stalk and green leaves. Put florets into a large saucepan containing enough boiling salted water to cover generously. Return to boil. Cook, uncovered, about 7 minutes, or until florets are just tender when pierced with a small sharp knife. Drain, rinse with cold running water until cool, and drain thoroughly.

Butter a heavy 5-cup gratin dish or other shallow baking dish. Arrange florets in one layer in prepared dish. Spoon sauce carefully over them to coat completely. Sprinkle evenly with 2 tablespoons cheese. (Gratin can be kept, covered, 1 day in refrigerator; bring to room temperature before continuing.)

Bake until sauce begins to bubble, about 7 minutes if sauce was still hot, or about 10 minutes if ingredients were at room temperature. If top is not brown, transfer dish to broiler and broil with door partly open just until cheese is lightly browned, about 1 minute, checking often and turning dish if necessary so cheese browns evenly. Serve hot, from baking dish.

BROCCOLI GRATIN WITH LIGHT CHEESE SAUCE
Substitute 1½ pounds broccoli for cauliflower. Boil only about 4 minutes.

CABBAGE GRATIN WITH LIGHT CHEESE SAUCE
Substitute 1¼ pounds cabbage (1 very small or ½ large head) for cauliflower. Cut out and discard core. Shred cabbage leaves coarsely with knife. Boil only about 5 minutes. After draining, squeeze gently to remove excess water.

NOTE: Both cauliflower and broccoli are fragile vegetables. To avoid crushing their florets, they should be drained as gently as possible after cooking and rinsed under a thin stream of water so they will not fall apart.

LAYERED CABBAGE AND MUSHROOM GRATIN
Gratin de choux et champignons

This gratin is made with cream rather than with sauce. Serve it with grilled chicken breasts or other light meats.

MAKES 4 TO 6 SERVINGS

½ medium-size head of green cabbage (about 1¼ pounds), cored, rinsed, finely shredded
1¼ cups heavy cream
Salt and freshly ground pepper
¼ teaspoon freshly grated nutmeg, or to taste

2 tablespoons unsalted butter
½ pound mushrooms, halved and thinly sliced
2 tablespoons freshly grated Parmesan cheese

In a large pan of boiling salted water, cook cabbage for 3 minutes. Drain thoroughly and return cabbage to pan. Stir in 1 cup cream and salt and pepper to taste. Cover and simmer over low heat for 5 minutes. Uncover and simmer over medium heat for 10 minutes. Reduce heat to low and simmer, stirring often, for 10 minutes, or until cream is completely absorbed and mixture appears dry. Add nutmeg and adjust seasoning. Preheat oven to 425°F.

In a medium-size skillet, melt butter over medium-high heat, add mushrooms with salt and pepper to taste, and sauté, stirring, about 4 minutes, or until browned and tender. Add remaining ¼ cup cream and simmer over medium-high heat, stirring, for 3 minutes, or until cream is completely absorbed and mushrooms appear quite dry. Taste and adjust seasoning. (Mixtures can be kept, covered, 1 day in refrigerator; reheat each over low heat before continuing.)

Butter a heavy 5-cup gratin dish or other shallow baking dish. Spread mushroom mixture in an even layer in prepared dish. Spoon cabbage mixture carefully on top to avoid moving mushrooms, and spread until smooth. Sprinkle with grated cheese.

Bake about 5 minutes, or until heated through. Broil for 1 or 2 minutes, or until cheese is golden.

QUICK BROCCOLI GRATIN WITH GRUYÈRE AND NUTS
Gratin de brocolis au gruyère et aux noix

This gratin has a crunchy topping and is ready in minutes. Serve it with roast or grilled chicken, or to accompany Eggplant Stuffed with Duxelles.   MAKES 4 SERVINGS

1 ½ pounds broccoli
¼ cup unsalted butter, melted
Salt and freshly ground pepper
½ cup coarsely grated Gruyère
cheese

¼ cup coarsely chopped walnuts or
toasted hazelnuts
2 tablespoons unseasoned bread
crumbs

Preheat oven to 425°F. Divide broccoli into medium florets, discarding stalks and leaves. Put florets into large saucepan containing enough boiling salted water to cover them generously. Return to boil. Cook, uncovered, about 4 minutes, or until just tender. Gently rinse with cold running water until cool and drain thoroughly.

Butter a shallow 5-cup gratin dish or other heavy baking dish. In prepared dish, arrange broccoli in one layer, stems pointing inward.

Sprinkle with 2 tablespoons melted butter and with a pinch of salt and pepper. Mix cheese, nuts, and bread crumbs and sprinkle evenly on top. Sprinkle with remaining 2 tablespoons melted butter.

Bake about 8 minutes, or until cheese melts. If topping is not brown, broil with broiler door partly open about 1 minute, or just until lightly browned, checking often and turning dish if necessary so topping browns evenly. Serve hot, from baking dish.

BRUSSELS SPROUTS BAKED IN MORNAY SAUCE
Choux de bruxelles Mornay

If you think you don't like Brussels sprouts, try them this way. They taste best when served with creamy sauces, which tame their assertive flavor. Egg yolks in the sauce give the gratin a golden color.

MAKES 4 SERVINGS

¾ pound Brussels sprouts

MORNAY SAUCE

1 ½ tablespoons butter
1 ½ tablespoons all-purpose flour
1 cup milk
Salt and white pepper

Freshly grated nutmeg
¼ cup freshly grated Parmesan
   cheese
2 egg yolks

2 tablespoons freshly grated
   Parmesan cheese for topping

Preheat oven to 425°F. Trim sprouts, removing tough bases and any yellow leaves. Put sprouts into a large saucepan containing enough boiling salted water to cover them generously. Return to boil. Cook, uncovered, about 10 minutes, or until they are just tender when pierced with a small sharp knife. Drain, rinse with cold running water until cool and drain thoroughly.

MORNAY SAUCE

In a small heavy saucepan, melt butter over low heat, add flour, and cook, whisking constantly, about 2 minutes, or until foaming but not browned. Remove from heat. Gradually whisk in milk. Bring to boil over medium-high heat, whisking. Add a small pinch of salt, white pepper, and nutmeg. Reduce heat to low and cook, whisking often, for 5 minutes.

Remove from heat and whisk in ¼ cup cheese. Quickly whisk in egg yolks. Taste and adjust seasoning.

Butter a heavy 5-cup gratin dish or other shallow baking dish. In prepared dish, arrange Brussels sprouts in one layer. Spoon sauce carefully over them to coat completely. Sprinkle evenly with 2 table-spoons cheese. (Gratin can be kept, covered, 1 day in refrigerator; bring to room temperature before continuing.)

Bake until sauce begins to bubble, about 7 minutes if sauce was still hot, or about 10 minutes if ingredients were at room temperature. If top is not brown, transfer dish to broiler and broil with door partly open just until cheese is lightly browned, about 1 minute, checking often and turning dish if necessary so cheese browns evenly. Serve hot, from baking dish.

ZUCCHINI BAKED IN MORNAY SAUCE
Substitute 12 to 14 ounces small zucchini for Brussels sprouts. Cut them in half lengthwise. Cut each half crosswise in 2- to 2½-inch pieces. Boil 4 minutes. Drain thoroughly.

🌿 SWISS CHARD AND PEPPER GRATIN WITH TOMATOES
Gratin de blettes et poivrons aux tomates

A favorite in southern France, Swiss chard is often cooked with olive oil and tomatoes, as in this gratin. Chard can be cooked like spinach and is a quicker substitute because chard has much larger leaves and takes little time to clean.   MAKES 6 SERVINGS

1 ½ pounds Swiss chard, rinsed
thoroughly

½ cup olive oil

½ cup finely chopped onion

1 ¾ pounds ripe tomatoes, peeled,
seeded, and finely chopped

4 anchovy fillets, rinsed and
chopped (optional)

3 small garlic cloves, minced

Salt and freshly ground pepper

2 small red bell peppers (about ½
pound)

1 medium-size green bell pepper
(about 5 ounces)

3 tablespoons unseasoned bread
crumbs

3 tablespoons coarsely chopped
blanched almonds, or 2
tablespoons freshly grated
Parmesan cheese

Preheat oven to 400°F. Cut chard leaves from stems, discarding stems. Pile chard leaves, cut them in half lengthwise and then crosswise in strips ½ inch wide. In medium-size saucepan of boiling salted water, cook, uncovered, about 3 minutes, or until just tender. Drain thoroughly. Squeeze by handfuls to remove excess moisture.

In a large skillet, heat 3 tablespoons olive oil over medium heat, stir in onion, and cook about 7 minutes, or until soft but not brown. Stir in tomatoes and anchovies. Raise heat to high and cook, stirring constantly, about 12 minutes, or until mixture becomes dry. Stir in garlic, add ground pepper, and adjust seasoning.

Cut bell peppers in half lengthwise, core, and remove ribs. Cut them crosswise and cut each piece into strips ¼ inch wide. In large skillet, heat 3 tablespoons of olive oil over medium-low heat, add peppers, salt and pepper to taste, and cook, tossing often, about 7 minutes, or until tender.

Lightly coat a heavy 5-cup gratin dish or other shallow baking dish with olive oil. Spread chard in dish. Spoon tomato mixture over chard and smooth. Spoon pepper mixture evenly over tomatoes. (Gratin can be kept, covered, 1 day in refrigerator; bring to room temperature before continuing.)

Scatter bread crumbs, then almonds or cheese, evenly over vegetables. Sprinkle with remaining 2 tablespoons olive oil. Bake about 15 minutes, or until vegetables are heated through and beginning to bubble at bottom. If topping is not brown, broil with broiler door partly open about 1 minute, or just until lightly browned, checking often and turning dish if necessary so topping browns evenly. Serve hot, from baking dish.

❧ TURNIP AND ONION GRATIN WITH PARMESAN
Gratin de navets et oignons au parmesan

In this unusual dish, the sweetness of turnips and onions is balanced by the sharpness of the Parmesan cheese. Serve it with roast chicken or grilled steak.   MAKES 4 SERVINGS

1 ½ pounds small turnips
5 tablespoons mild olive oil
2 medium-size onions, thinly sliced
Salt and freshly ground pepper
1 ½ teaspoons fresh thyme, or
*   ½ teaspoon dried thyme,*
*   crumbled*

2 large garlic cloves, minced
10 tablespoons freshly grated
*   Parmesan cheese*

Peel turnips using paring knife, cut them in half, then in ¼-inch-thick slices. Put in large saucepan, cover with water, add salt, and bring to boil. Reduce heat to low, cover, and simmer about 7 minutes, or until just tender.

Preheat oven to 425°F. In a large skillet, heat 3 tablespoons oil over low heat, and add onions, salt, pepper, and thyme. Cover and cook, stirring often, about 25 minutes, or until tender. Stir in garlic, then gently stir in turnip slices. Cook over low heat 2 minutes. Adjust seasoning, taking into account that Parmesan cheese will add a salty flavor.

Coat a heavy 5-cup gratin dish or shallow baking dish with olive oil. Transfer half of vegetable mixture to dish. Sprinkle with 5 tablespoons cheese, then with 1 tablespoon of oil. Spoon remaining vegetable mixture on top. Sprinkle with remaining 5 tablespoons cheese, then with remaining 1 tablespoon oil.

Bake about 15 minutes, or until hot. If cheese is not brown, broil with broiler door partly open about 1 minute, or just until lightly browned, checking often and turning dish if necessary so cheese browns evenly. Serve hot, from baking dish.

Vegetable Purées

⁓

Vegetable purées add style and color to any plate and are loved not only at simple restaurants but at the most sumptuous of tables. At Taillevent, the renowned Parisian restaurant, I enjoyed a stunning dish of Carré d'Agneau Rôti aux Trois Purées (roast rack of lamb with three purées). The silky-smooth texture of purées enables us to somehow perceive the taste of the vegetable even more intensely. Depending on how they're seasoned and served, purées can take on a character all their own or dramatically alter an otherwise straightforward dish.

Simply cooked foods, from poached fish fillets to hard-boiled eggs to broiled meats, look especially festive and appetizing served on a bed of colorful vegetable purée. Lightly steamed scallops or shrimp set on bright green spinach purée or fresh tomato purée make an elegant main course. The French like to serve roasted or broiled meats and game dishes such as venison with a selection of different-colored purées, so that each plate looks like an artist's palette.

The versatility of purées is apparent in the many roles they can play in a meal. Although their obvious function is as side dishes, they can also be eaten as appetizers if served in pastry, as in Cream Puffs with Carrot Purée, on toast, as a stuffing for vegetables, or even as part of a sauce for pasta. They can also be turned into mousses, timbales, and soufflés.

Purées can be made quickly and easily. They can be reheated and therefore make meal planning simple. Because they can be made from cooked vegetables left from the day before, they are also economical.

To be made into purées, green vegetables such as spinach, asparagus, and broccoli are cooked quickly, uncovered, in a large amount of boiling salted water so they conserve as much as possible of their color and fresh taste. Root vegetables are not in danger of losing their color and sometimes need to tame their strong flavors and so are started off in cold water. Some vegetables, such as eggplant or bell peppers, are baked or broiled instead. Steamed vegetables can also be made into purées.

When the vegetable can be pierced very easily with the tip of a sharp knife, it is soft enough to be puréed. It should be more tender than for serving whole or in pieces and not at all crunchy. It should not, however, be cooked beyond this point or its flavor will be watery and, in the case of a green vegetable, its color will be less vivid.

In France purées used to be made by pushing cooked vegetables through a sturdy sieve, but today most home cooks use a food processor, blender, or hand-operated food mill.

The easiest way to purée vegetables is in the food processor. If a blender is used, the vegetable should be processed in small batches with a few tablespoons of the cooking liquid or the cream in the recipe and should be pushed down the sides of the blender often to be sure it becomes smoothly puréed.

Many vegetable purées are heated until the excess water in the vegetable evaporates so they thicken. This method intensifies the flavor of the vegetable. If a purée will be tossed with pasta, it should be thinned with a generous amount of milk, cream, or stock so that it becomes saucelike and coats the pasta, as in Pasta with Creamy Broccoli Purée. A very thick purée is best for stuffing vegetables or filling pastry so the filling will not run out. For serving as a side dish, a purée of medium thickness is best.

Butter and cream give purées a wonderful taste, but olive oil adds a distinct flavor that is a pleasant change. Spices and herbs can also be added, but it is good to add them with a light hand so the character of the vegetable predominates.

ZUCCHINI PURÉE WITH BASIL
Purée de courgettes au basilic

Resembling pesto, this zesty purée is enriched with a little olive oil and has a deep green color. It can be served topped with hard-boiled or fried eggs or with sautéed croutons. Zucchini purée also makes a lovely accompaniment for grilled fish or chicken.

MAKES 4 SERVINGS

1 ½ pounds small zucchini
3 tablespoons extra-virgin olive oil
2 medium-size garlic cloves, minced

⅓ cup fresh basil leaves
Salt and freshly ground pepper
Pinch of cayenne pepper

In a large saucepan of boiling salted water to generously cover, cook whole zucchini about 10 minutes, or until tender enough to be easily puréed. Cut in 1-inch pieces, crush very lightly with spoon, and drain very thoroughly in colander about 15 minutes.

In a medium-size skillet, heat 2 tablespoons olive oil over low heat, add garlic, and sauté for 30 seconds. Add zucchini and cook over medium heat, stirring, about 5 minutes.

Purée mixture in food processor together with basil. With motor running, add remaining olive oil. (Purée can be kept, covered, 1 day in refrigerator.)

Reheat purée gently in saucepan. If mixture is too thin, cook over medium heat, stirring, until thickened. Add salt, pepper, and cayenne pepper to taste. Serve hot.

CAULIFLOWER AND POTATO PURÉE
Purée de chou-fleur

Potatoes harmonize well with most vegetables and are often combined with one or even several vegetables to make delicately flavored purées, as in this recipe. Besides cauliflower, other favorite partners are turnips, celery root, onions, and fennel. Serve this purée with light meats, especially veal, turkey, or chicken.

MAKES 4 SERVINGS

½ pound white boiling potatoes
1 medium-size cauliflower (about
   1 ½ pounds), divided into
   medium-size florets
½ to ¾ cup heavy cream or milk

3 to 5 tablespoons unsalted butter
Salt and white pepper
Freshly grated nutmeg
1 tablespoon finely sliced or snipped
   chives (optional)

Peel potatoes and cut each in two or three pieces. Put in a nonaluminum saucepan and add water to just cover and a pinch of salt.

Cover, bring to a boil, and simmer over medium heat 20 to 25 minutes, or until potatoes are very tender.

Meanwhile, in a large pan of boiling salted water, boil cauliflower, uncovered, over high heat about 10 minutes, or until very tender.

Drain both vegetables thoroughly. Purée potatoes and cauliflower in a food mill; if using a food processor, add a few tablespoons cream or milk and purée as briefly as possible.

Return purée to saucepan used to cook potatoes. Add 3 tablespoons butter and 2 tablespoons cream or milk to purée and season to taste with salt, pepper, and nutmeg. Heat over low heat, stirring vigorously with a wooden spoon, until purée is light and smooth. (Purée can be kept, covered, 1 day in refrigerator. Reheat over low heat before continuing.)

Gradually beat in enough of remaining cream or milk so purée is soft but not soupy. If using milk, beat in remaining butter. Taste and adjust seasoning. Sprinkle with chopped chives, if desired. Serve hot.

❧ SPINACH PURÉE ON CROÛTES
Croûtes à la purée d'épinards

The flavor of fresh spinach is vital for the taste of this appetizer or accompaniment. Not too much time need be spent washing large quantities of spinach leaves, though, because the spinach purée is spread on toasted *croûtes* of bread so that a little goes a long way.

MAKES 4 SERVINGS

1 ¼ pounds fresh spinach (leaves with stems)
7 tablespoons butter
3 tablespoons heavy cream
Salt and freshly ground pepper
Freshly grated nutmeg

8 slices, about ¼ to ½ inch thick, French or Italian bread, or 16 slices very thin French bread (baguette)
3 tablespoons shredded Gruyère cheese

Remove spinach stems and wash leaves thoroughly. In large saucepan of boiling salted water, cook spinach, uncovered, over high heat, pushing leaves down into water often, until very tender, about 2 minutes. Rinse with cold water and squeeze by handfuls until dry. Purée in food processor or chop with large knife until very fine.

In a medium-size saucepan, heat 1 tablespoon butter over low heat until very hot, add spinach, and stir until heated through. Stir in cream and heat until it is absorbed by spinach. Stir in 2 tablespoons butter and continue cooking just until absorbed. Season to taste with salt, pepper, and nutmeg. (Spinach purée can be kept, covered, 1 day in refrigerator; reheat gently before continuing.)

Preheat oven to 425°F. Put bread slices on a baking sheet. Soften remaining butter and spread on both sides of slices. Bake in preheated oven 5 minutes. Turn slices over and bake 3 more minutes.

Divide spinach purée among bread slices and spread evenly over them. Sprinkle with shredded cheese. Return to oven and bake 7 minutes, or until cheese melts and mixture is very hot. Serve immediately.

PARSLEY PURÉE
Purée de persil

Parsley is used here as a vegetable. It is really amazing how flavorful it is. Blanching keeps the parsley's color a bright green. Serve this purée as a part of a selection of purées, or to accompany fish or seafood.   MAKES 4 TO 6 SERVINGS

¾ pound parsley
¾ cup plus 2 tablespoons heavy
cream

¼ cup butter
Salt and freshly ground pepper

Remove small parsley sprigs, discarding large stems. In a large saucepan of boiling salted water, cook sprigs, uncovered, over high heat 1 minute. Drain, rinse under cold running water until cold, and drain thoroughly. Squeeze by handfuls until dry.

Purée parsley in a food processor or blender until very finely chopped. Add ½ cup cream and purée until smooth.

In a small saucepan, melt butter over low heat, add parsley mixture and heat until hot. Stir in remaining 6 tablespoons cream and salt and pepper to taste, and heat gently, stirring, about 2 minutes, or until cream is absorbed. Taste and adjust seasoning. (Purée can be kept up to 2 hours at room temperature and reheated.) Serve a spoonful of purée for each serving.

❧ CELERY ROOT PURÉE
Purée de céleri-rave

Celery root is excellent not only raw in salad, but cooked and made into a creamy purée. Serve it with warm hard-boiled or poached eggs, or with roast or grilled chicken, duck, or lamb.

MAKES 6 SERVINGS

½ lemon
2 pounds celery root
2 medium-size boiling potatoes

About ¾ cup milk
3 tablespoons butter
Salt and freshly ground pepper

Squeeze lemon juice into a bowl of water. Peel celery root, removing all brown parts. Cut in half, then in slices about ½ inch thick. Put each slice into lemon water as it is cut.

Remove celery root slices from lemon water and put in a large saucepan. Add enough water to cover generously, taking into account that potatoes will also be added to saucepan. Add a pinch of salt and bring to a boil. Cook over medium heat about 10 minutes.

Meanwhile, peel potatoes and cut each in two or three pieces. Add to saucepan containing celery root and cook about 20 minutes, or until potatoes and celery root are very tender. Drain thoroughly.

Purée potatoes and celery root in a food mill; if using a food processor, add a few tablespoons of milk and purée as briefly as possible.

Return purée to saucepan. Add butter, salt, pepper, and ¼ cup milk and stir over medium heat 2 or 3 minutes. Gradually add enough of remaining milk so that purée is soft but not runny. Taste and adjust seasoning. (Purée can be kept warm about 30 minutes by setting saucepan of purée in another saucepan of warm water over low heat; pour a little milk over purée to prevent a skin from forming and stir it into purée just before serving.) Serve hot.

✤ CREAMY CARROT PURÉE
Purée de carottes

Beautiful color and concentrated carrot flavor make this purée one of the most popular. It adds liveliness to any plate, and makes a delicious accompaniment for sautéed or roasted poultry or for poached or baked fish, alone or in combination with other purées.

MAKES 6 SERVINGS

2 pounds carrots
1 tablespoon butter
¼ to ⅓ cup heavy cream, or 2 to
  3 tablespoons milk, room
  temperature

Salt and freshly ground pepper
Pinch of sugar (optional)

Peel carrots and cut in ½-inch slices. In medium-size saucepan, cover carrots with water, add pinch of salt, and bring to boil. Cover, reduce heat to medium, and cook about 35 minutes, or until very tender when pierced with a sharp knife. Drain thoroughly in large strainer. Purée in a food processor until very smooth.

In a medium-size saucepan, melt butter over low heat, add purée, and heat thoroughly. Gradually stir in cream and cook until it is absorbed. Season to taste with salt, pepper, and sugar. (Purée can be kept, covered, 2 days in refrigerator.) Serve hot.

✤ GREEN PEA PURÉE WITH MINT BUTTER
Purée de petits pois au beurre de menthe

This purée takes a little time to prepare with fresh peas but can be made very quickly if frozen peas are used. It is delicious with grilled or broiled lamb or chicken.

MAKES 4 SERVINGS

1½ tablespoons chopped fresh mint
  leaves

¼ cup butter, softened
Salt and freshly ground pepper

3 pounds fresh peas in pods, or   ¼ cup heavy cream
    about 3 cups shelled peas, or   Pinch of sugar
    two 10-ounce packages frozen
    peas

To make mint butter, thoroughly mix mint leaves with butter and season to taste with salt and pepper. (Mint butter can be kept 1 day in refrigerator.)

In a saucepan of boiling salted water, cook fresh peas for 7 minutes, or frozen peas for 3 minutes, or until they are just tender. Rinse under cold running water and drain thoroughly.

Purée peas in a food processor in two batches, adding 2 table-spoons cream to each batch. (Purée can be kept, covered, up to 1 day in refrigerator.)

In a medium-size saucepan, heat purée, stirring, until hot. Stir in mint butter and remove from heat as soon as butter is absorbed. Add sugar, taste and adjust seasoning.

Stuffed Vegetables

Stuffed vegetables can be served as first courses, side dishes, or, according to a custom in Provence, a selection of them can become the main course. Many stuffed vegetables are good hot or cold.

Some vegetables seem to have been created to be stuffed. For many people, stuffing is the preferred way to prepare eggplant, zucchini, and peppers. Unlike cooks in the eastern end of the Mediterranean area, who like to stuff their vegetables whole, French chefs cut eggplants and zucchini in half lengthwise and scoop out the pulp, leaving boat-shaped shells.

The French acknowledge the Middle Eastern and Italian origins of some of their favorite stuffed vegetable recipes by qualifying them, for example, as *à l'orientale,* as in Eggplant with Tomatoes, Saffron, and Garlic, *à l'égyptienne,* or *à la napolitaine.*

Popular stuffings for vegetables are those based on rice or of vegetables mixed with bread crumbs, often with the addition of the pulp of the vegetable that is being stuffed. A classic duxelles mixture of chopped mushrooms cooked in butter remains a modern favorite. These types of mixtures are being substituted more and more for meat stuffings. Provençal cooks like to flavor their stuffings with their three favorite ingredients, labeled by some French food writers the "holy Mediterranean trio" of onions, garlic, and tomatoes. Saffron, fragrant herbs, and grated Parmesan or Gruyère cheese are also well-liked seasonings for vegetable fillings.

MUSHROOMS STUFFED WITH FRESH TOMATO PURÉE
Champignons à la tomate concassée

Spinach purée (see recipe for Spinach Purée on Croûtes, page 137) is another fabulous filling for mushrooms. The two versions of stuffed mushrooms can be presented alternating on a platter around a roast chicken as a colorful garnish.   MAKES 4 TO 6 SERVINGS

FRESH TOMATO PURÉE

2 tablespoons butter or olive oil	1 bay leaf
1 small onion or 2 shallots, minced	5 parsley stems
1 ½ pounds ripe tomatoes, peeled, seeded, and chopped	1 tablespoon chopped fresh basil, or 1 teaspoon dried basil
Salt and freshly ground pepper	(optional)
1 sprig of fresh thyme, or ¼ teaspoon dried thyme	

1 pound large mushrooms	2 tablespoons butter

FRESH TOMATO PURÉE

In a sauté pan, heat butter or olive oil over low heat. Add minced onion or shallots and cook, stirring often, until softened. Add tomatoes and salt and pepper to taste. Tie thyme, bay leaf, and parsley stems together with string or in a piece of cheesecloth to make a bouquet garni and add it to tomatoes. Cook over medium heat, stirring often, about 20 minutes, or until mixture is very thick. Discard bouquet garni. (Purée can be kept, covered, 2 days in refrigerator; reheat before continuing.) Add basil and adjust seasoning.

Meanwhile, preheat oven to 375°F. Remove mushroom stems and clean caps. Put them, rounded side down, in a lightly oiled shallow baking dish. Sprinkle them lightly with salt and pepper. Fill with tomato purée. Dot with butter.

Bake stuffed mushrooms for 10 to 15 minutes, or until mushrooms are tender and filling is hot. Serve hot.

NOTE: An equal weight of canned (a 16-ounce and an 8-ounce can) tomatoes can be substituted for fresh ones. Drain them, remove as many seeds as possible, and chop.

ARTICHOKES WITH ONION COMPOTE
Artichauts à la compote d'oignons

"Compotes" are vegetables that are cooked for a long time over very low heat so they become delicate and meltingly tender. Most often they are made from vegetables in the onion family. Here the sweetness of the white onions is balanced by the cream and flavored with a touch of wine vinegar. The onion compote can be served as a separate vegetable dish to accompany roast or sautéed chicken, veal or beef.
MAKES 6 SERVINGS

1 lemon   *6 artichokes*

ONION COMPOTE
¼ cup butter   *2 tablespoons heavy cream*
1½ pounds white onions, halved   *1 to 2 teaspoons white wine vinegar*
*   and thinly sliced*   *   (optional)*
Salt and freshly ground pepper

Squeeze juice of ½ lemon into medium-size bowl of cold water. Break off stems and largest leaves of artichoke bottoms. Cut off lower circle of leaves, up to edge of artichoke heart. Rub exposed edges of artichoke heart with cut lemon. Cut off central cone of leaves just above artichoke heart. Cut off leaves under base and trim so it is round, removing all dark green areas. Rub again with lemon. Put each artichoke in bowl of lemon water as it is finished.

Squeeze any juice remaining in lemon into medium-size saucepan of boiling salted water, add artichoke hearts, cover, and simmer over low heat about 15 minutes, or until tender when pierced with a knife. Cool to lukewarm in liquid. Using a teaspoon, scoop out choke from center of each artichoke heart. Return artichokes to liquid until ready to use.

ONION COMPOTE

In a heavy Dutch oven, heatproof casserole, or stew pan, heat butter over low heat, and add onions, a pinch of salt, and pepper. Cover and cook, stirring often, 45 minutes. Uncover and cook, stirring very often, about 25 minutes longer, or until onions are tender enough to crush easily with a wooden spoon and are golden; be careful not to let them burn.

Preheat oven to 400°F. Stir in cream, raise heat to high, and cook until bubbling. Reduce heat to very low and simmer, stirring often, about 5 minutes, or until cream is completely absorbed. (Compote can be kept, covered, 1 day in refrigerator; reheat in saucepan over low heat.)

Stir in vinegar, if desired, and heat until absorbed. Taste and adjust seasoning.

Butter a baking dish and set artichoke hearts in it. Spoon onion compote into each artichoke. Bake in preheated oven 10 minutes to heat through.

ARTICHOKES FILLED WITH PEAS
Fonds d'artichauts farcis Clamart

This classic garnish for roast meat is named for Clamart, a suburb of Paris once famous for its delicious peas. Artichokes and peas are a well-loved combination in other dishes as well. Sometimes they are cooked together and served as a stew.   MAKES 4 SERVINGS

1 lemon
4 artichokes
2 cups fresh shelled peas, or one
  10-ounce package frozen peas

1 to 2 tablespoons butter
1 teaspoon sugar
Salt

Prepare and cook artichokes as in Artichokes with Onion Compote (see recipe).

In a large pan of boiling salted water, cook fresh peas about 5 minutes, or until just tender. Cook frozen peas only about 1 or 2 minutes. Drain well. Melt the butter in a sauté pan, add peas, sugar, and salt to taste, and heat gently.

Reheat artichokes in their liquid. Drain thoroughly. To serve, carefully spoon peas into artichokes.

STUFFED EGGPLANT WITH PINE NUT PILAF AND TOMATO CURRY SAUCE
Aubergine farcie pilaf aux pignons, sauce tomate au curry

Eggplant is most delicious when it is thoroughly cooked and fork-tender. Unlike many other vegetables, it should not be undercooked with the aim of leaving it al dente.   MAKES 4 SERVINGS

TOMATO CURRY SAUCE

2 tablespoons olive oil

2 garlic cloves, minced

1 ½ teaspoons curry powder

1 ½ pounds ripe tomatoes, peeled, seeded, and chopped

Salt and freshly ground pepper

2 teaspoons tomato paste

RICE PILAF WITH PINE NUTS

2 tablespoons vegetable oil

½ medium-size onion, minced

½ cup long-grain white rice

1 cup hot water

Salt and freshly ground pepper

⅓ cup pine nuts or slivered almonds

2 tablespoons chopped flat-leaf parsley (optional)

2 medium-size eggplants (1 pound each), unpeeled

3 tablespoons olive oil

TOMATO CURRY SAUCE

In a large saucepan, heat olive oil over low heat, add garlic, and cook, stirring occasionally, about 30 seconds, or until soft but not browned. Add curry powder and cook, stirring, 30 seconds. Add tomatoes and salt and pepper to taste, and stir well to combine with curry mixture. Bring to boil, reduce heat to low, and cook, uncovered, stirring occasionally, about 30 minutes, or until tomatoes are very soft. Add tomato paste.

Purée sauce in food processor or blender until smooth. Taste and adjust seasoning. (Sauce can be prepared up to 2 days ahead and kept, covered, in refrigerator.)

RICE PILAF WITH PINE NUTS

In a medium-size skillet, heat 1 tablespoon plus 1 teaspoon vegetable oil over low heat, add onion, and cook, stirring, about 10 minutes, or until soft but not brown. Add rice and sauté, stirring, about 2 minutes, or until grains turn milky white. Add water and salt and pepper to taste. Bring to a boil, stir once, and cover. Reduce heat to low and cook, without stirring, 18 minutes. Taste rice; if not yet tender, simmer 2 more minutes. Remove from heat. Let stand, covered, 10 minutes. (Pilaf can be prepared up to 1 day ahead and kept, covered, in refrigerator.)

In a small heavy skillet, heat remaining 2 teaspoons vegetable oil over medium-low heat, add pine nuts or almonds and pinch of salt and sauté, tossing them often with slotted spoon, about 2 minutes or until lightly browned. Set aside and reserve at room temperature. Add nuts and parsley to rice and gently stir with a fork.

To Finish: Preheat oven to 450°F. Remove green caps of eggplants and cut in half lengthwise. Score flesh of each half lightly to make a border about ⅜ inch from skin, using point of sharp knife. Score lightly 3 times in center of eggplant half. (This enables heat to penetrate more evenly.) Place in a lightly oiled roasting pan or shallow baking dish, cut side up. Sprinkle cut surface with salt and 2 tablespoons olive oil. Bake about 25 minutes, or until flesh is tender when pierced with knife. Let cool slightly. Reduce oven temperature to 350°F.

Cut eggplant gently along scored border and remove pulp carefully with spoon, taking care not to pierce skin. Drain shells 5 minutes in colander. Transfer eggplant shells to oiled shallow baking dish, so they touch each other, or to four individual baking dishes. Chop eggplant flesh and add to pilaf. Taste and adjust seasoning. Spoon mixture into eggplant shells. Sprinkle with remaining tablespoon olive oil.

Bake about 15 minutes, or until eggplant is very tender and hot. Reheat sauce. If using individual baking dishes, spoon sauce around base of eggplant. If using large dish, divide sauce among four plates and set eggplant halves on top.

EGGPLANT WITH TOMATOES, SAFFRON, AND GARLIC
Aubergines farcies à l'orientale

Saffron is the reason this dish is called in French *à l'orientale.* In classic cuisine the spice is associated with the flavors of the East. Try making this part of a Mediterranean vegetable feast by serving it with Onions Stuffed with Spinach, Zucchini Stuffed with Red Pepper Purée, and Rice Salad with Pyrenees Cheese, Mushrooms, and Tomatoes. MAKES 4 SERVINGS

2 small eggplants (1 pound each),
    unpeeled
Salt
¼ cup extra-virgin olive oil
1 pound ripe tomatoes, peeled,
    seeded, and chopped
Freshly ground pepper

Large pinch of saffron threads,
    crushed (about ¼ teaspoon)
2 garlic cloves, minced
1 tablespoon unseasoned bread
    crumbs
¼ cup chopped fresh parsley

GARNISH (OPTIONAL)

8 black olives, cut in half
    lengthwise
¼ cup finely diced fresh
    tomato

4 small sprigs parsley

Preheat oven to 450°F. Remove green caps of eggplants and cut in half lengthwise. Score flesh of each half lightly to make a border about ⅜ inch from skin, using point of sharp knife. Score lightly 3 times in center of eggplant half. (This enables heat to penetrate more evenly.) Place in a lightly oiled roasting pan or shallow baking dish, cut side up. Sprinkle cut surface with salt and 2 tablespoons olive oil. Bake about 25 minutes, or until flesh is tender when pierced with knife.

Meanwhile, in medium-size skillet, heat 1 tablespoon olive oil over medium-high heat. Add tomatoes, salt, and pepper. Cook, stirring occasionally, about 15 minutes, or until mixture is dry. Reduce heat to low, stir in saffron, and cook 1 minute.

Let eggplant cool slightly. Cut gently along scored border and remove pulp carefully with spoon, taking care not to pierce skin. Drain pulp 5 minutes in colander. If shells are watery, drain them also. Return eggplant shells to oiled shallow baking dish.

Chop removed eggplant flesh and add to tomato mixture. Add garlic, bread crumbs, and parsley. Adjust seasoning; mixture should be well seasoned with salt and pepper.

Spoon mixture into eggplant shells. Sprinkle with remaining 1 tablespoon olive oil. Bake about 15 minutes, or until eggplant is very tender and hot. Serve hot, warm, or at room temperature.

Garnish: Make a row of 4 olive halves, rounded side down, along center of each eggplant half. Put a spoonful of diced tomato at one end and top tomato with a parsley sprig.

EGGPLANT STUFFED WITH DUXELLES
Aubergines farcies à la duxelles

For this simple dish, both the eggplant and the mushroom stuffing are precooked. The purpose of the final baking is just to warm them and lightly brown the topping. The duxelles mixture also makes an excellent filling for zucchini.   MAKES 4 SERVINGS

2½ pounds small or medium-size   Salt
   eggplants

DUXELLES
1 tablespoon butter   Salt and freshly ground pepper
2 shallots, minced   2 tablespoons chopped fresh parsley
10 ounces mushrooms, very finely
   chopped

3 tablespoons fresh bread crumbs   3 tablespoons melted butter or
                                       vegetable oil

Preheat oven to 450°F. Leave eggplants unpeeled; cut them in half lengthwise. Score flesh of each half lightly to make a border about ⅜ inch from skin, using a sharp knife. Score lightly 3 times in center of eggplant half. (This enables heat to penetrate more evenly.) Sprinkle cut surface with salt. Place in a lightly oiled roasting pan or shallow baking dish, cut side up. Bake about 20 to 25 minutes, or until flesh is tender when pierced with a knife. Let cool slightly.

Cut eggplant gently along scored border and remove pulp carefully with a spoon, taking care not to pierce skin. Put eggplant shells in a buttered gratin dish. Chop eggplant flesh.

DUXELLES
In a medium-size skillet, melt butter over low heat, add shallots, and cook until soft but not brown. Stir in mushrooms and sprinkle with salt and pepper. Raise heat and cook, stirring constantly, about 7 minutes, or until mixture is dry. Stir in parsley. Add chopped eggplant to mushroom mixture. Taste and adjust seasoning.

Spoon stuffing into eggplant shells. Sprinkle with bread crumbs, then with melted butter or oil. Bake 10 to 15 minutes, or until eggplant is hot. If bread crumbs have not browned in that time, place under broiler for a few seconds to brown. Serve hot.

ZUCCHINI STUFFED WITH RED PEPPER PURÉE
Courgettes à la purée de poivrons rouges

Zucchini boats make an attractive container for serving vegetable purées and are also good stuffed with carrot, spinach, or tomato purée. The striking red pepper purée can be served on its own, especially as a zesty accompaniment for chicken, turkey, or lamb.

MAKES 6 SERVINGS

4 red bell peppers
4 to 5 tablespoons extra-virgin
    olive oil
¼ teaspoon dried thyme

Salt and freshly ground pepper
6 small zucchini (about 1½
    pounds), trimmed

Preheat broiler. Broil peppers about 2 inches from heat, turning them slightly every few minutes, until their skin blisters on all sides and turns black, about 15 to 20 minutes. Put peppers in a plastic bag, close bag, and let stand 10 minutes. Peel peppers, remove seeds and ribs, and cut each pepper into 3 or 4 pieces.

In a skillet, heat 2 tablespoons olive oil over medium heat. Add peppers, thyme, and pinch of salt and pepper. Sauté peppers for 1 minute on each side.

Remove mixture from skillet and purée peppers until very smooth in a food processor or blender. Taste and adjust seasoning. (Purée can be kept, covered, 1 day in refrigerator; reheat before continuing.)

Preheat oven to 400°F. In a large saucepan of boiling salted water, cook zucchini for 2 minutes. Rinse under cold running water and drain thoroughly. Cut each zucchini in half lengthwise. With a small sharp knife, carefully scoop seeds out of each half, leaving a boat-shaped shell; be careful not to pierce the sides.

Put zucchini in an oiled shallow baking dish. Rub cut surfaces with remaining oil, and sprinkle with salt and pepper. Bake 5 minutes.

Spoon pepper purée evenly into zucchini shells. Bake 10 more minutes, or until ends of zucchini are tender when pierced with a sharp knife. Serve hot or at room temperature as a first course or side dish.

TOMATOES FILLED WITH ARTICHOKE AND RICE SALAD
Tomates farcies salade de riz aux artichauts

For this cool, colorful dish, a variety of vegetables, such as small broccoli florets or sautéed sliced mushrooms, can be added to the rice filling.

MAKES 6 SERVINGS

6 large tomatoes, ripe but firm   *4 to 6 artichokes*

RICE PILAF
1 tablespoon vegetable oil   *½ teaspoon curry powder*
1 tablespoon unsalted butter   *2 cups hot water*
1 small onion, finely chopped   *Salt and freshly ground pepper*
1 cup long-grain rice

VINAIGRETTE
2 tablespoons white wine vinegar   *Salt and freshly ground pepper*
6 tablespoons vegetable oil

1 cup cooked fresh or frozen peas   *6 basil leaves (optional), cut in*
1 small celery stalk, peeled and   *thin strips*
    finely diced   *½ green bell pepper, diced*

Cut tomatoes in half horizontally. Remove interior with a teaspoon, but leave a layer of pulp attached to skin to form a shell. Turn tomatoes over on a plate and leave to drain about 30 minutes. Prepare and cook artichoke hearts according to the instructions in Artichokes with Onion Compote (see recipe) and dice them.

RICE PILAF

In a medium-size skillet, heat oil and butter over low heat, add onion, and cook, stirring, about 10 minutes, or until soft but not brown. Add rice and sauté, stirring, about 2 minutes, or until grains turn milky white. Add curry powder, water, and salt and pepper. Bring to a boil, stir once, and cover. Reduce heat to low and cook, without stirring, for 18 minutes. Taste rice; if not yet tender, simmer 2 more minutes. Remove from heat. Let stand, covered, 10 minutes. Fluff with fork.

VINAIGRETTE

In a small bowl, stir vinegar, salt, and pepper with a whisk; whisk in oil. Taste and adjust seasoning.

In a bowl, combine rice with diced artichoke hearts, peas, celery, basil, and green pepper. Mix gently. Add vinaigrette and mix thoroughly. Taste and adjust seasoning. Refrigerate until ready to serve. Just before serving, fill tomato halves with rice salad.

PLUM TOMATOES WITH SHALLOT PURÉE
Olivettes au four à la purée d'échalotes

Velvety smooth shallot purée has a superb rich flavor that is perfectly complemented by the slight tartness of the baked tomato. These tomatoes make an elegant accompaniment for lamb or veal.

MAKES 4 SERVINGS

½ pound shallots, peeled and cut in half
3 tablespoons butter
Salt and freshly ground pepper
8 ripe plum tomatoes (about 12 ounces)

1 teaspoon vegetable oil
¼ cup heavy cream
About 1 teaspoon thinly sliced chives, or a few small parsley sprigs (optional), for garnish

Preheat oven to 400°F. In a medium-size saucepan, cover shallots with water, bring to a boil, and cook 2 minutes. Drain thoroughly.

In a medium-size heavy sauté pan, melt butter over low heat, add shallots, a pinch of salt, and pepper, and cover. Cook, stirring often, about 20 minutes, or until shallots are very tender; be careful not to let them burn.

Meanwhile, cut tomatoes in half lengthwise and scoop out interior with small melon-ball cutter. Oil shallow baking dish in which tomatoes can fit in one layer. Put tomato halves in baking dish. Sprinkle with salt and pepper. Sprinkle lightly with oil. Bake about 10 minutes, or until just tender. Carefully pour out juices from inside tomato halves. Pat insides dry with paper towel.

Purée shallots in a food processor. Put purée in a small heavy saucepan and stir over low heat. Add cream and continue to stir until absorbed. Taste and adjust seasoning.

Spoon shallot purée carefully into tomatoes, using 2 or 3 teaspoons purée for each tomato half, according to its size.

Return tomatoes to oven. Bake about 7 minutes, or until tomatoes are very tender. If desired, garnish each with chives or parsley sprig. Serve hot or warm. If any shallot purée remains, reheat it and serve it separately.

NOTE: Tomatoes can also be served standing on their ends. Instead of cutting them in half, cut a thin slice off wider end so it will balance. Then cut off top fourth of tomato, leaving it partially attached to be a "hat." They will hold less purée, so allow about 1 pound tomatoes.

PEPPERS STUFFED WITH RICE, MUSHROOMS, AND OLIVES
Poivrons farcis à la basquaise

Full of the flavors and colors of southern France, these peppers are roasted before being stuffed and therefore need to be baked only briefly with the stuffing.   MAKES 8 SERVINGS

8 bell peppers, red or green, or 4 of each
¾ cup long-grain white rice
Salt and freshly ground pepper
¼ cup vegetable or olive oil
¼ pound mushrooms, halved and cut in thin slices
1 medium-size onion, minced

1 pound ripe tomatoes, peeled, seeded, and chopped
2 teaspoons fresh thyme, or ¾ teaspoon dried thyme, crumbled
1 tablespoon chopped fresh basil leaves
½ cup pitted black olives, diced

Preheat broiler. Broil peppers about 2 inches from heat, turning them slightly every few minutes, until their skin blisters on all sides and turns black, about 15 to 20 minutes. Put peppers in a plastic bag, close bag, and let stand 10 minutes. Peel peppers, leaving them whole. Carefully cut out cores. With a teaspoon, carefully remove seeds, leaving pepper intact, if possible. Pour out any liquid. Preheat oven to 400°F.

In a large saucepan, bring about 6 cups water to a boil and add a pinch of salt. Add rice, stir once, and boil, uncovered, about 12 to 14 minutes, or until tender; check by tasting. Rinse with cold water and leave in a strainer to drain for 5 minutes.

In a medium-size skillet, heat 1 tablespoon oil over high heat, add mushrooms and salt and pepper to taste, and sauté, stirring, about 3 minutes, or until lightly browned. Set aside.

Add another tablespoon oil to skillet and lower heat. Add onion and cook, stirring, about 10 minutes, or until soft but not brown. Add tomatoes and thyme and cook over medium-high heat, stirring often, about 12 minutes, or until dry.

Gently mix tomatoes, mushrooms, basil, and diced olives with rice. Add 1 tablespoon oil. Taste and adjust seasoning. Spoon carefully into peppers, packing lightly.

Oil two 8-inch-square shallow baking dishes or a large gratin dish. Put peppers on their sides in prepared dishes. Sprinkle with remaining oil. Bake about 15 minutes, or until very tender. Serve hot, warm, or at room temperature.

ONIONS STUFFED WITH SPINACH
Oignons farcis aux épinards

Onions are amusing to stuff; after being briefly precooked, they can be easily separated into layers and each one can enclose a little stuffing. Long baking gives the stuffed onions a delicate flavor.

MAKES 4 SERVINGS

4 medium-size onions (about
    1 ½ pounds), peeled
1 ½ pounds fresh spinach (leaves
    with stems)
¼ cup butter
1 egg

2 tablespoons heavy cream
2 tablespoons unseasoned bread
    crumbs
Salt and freshly ground pepper
Freshly grated nutmeg
1 tablespoon vegetable oil

Preheat oven to 350°F. In a large pan of boiling salted water, cook onions about 15 minutes, or until somewhat tender when pierced with a small sharp knife. Drain and leave until cool enough to handle.

Cut off about one-quarter of onion at stem end. Carefully cut off root end. Beginning at stem end, scoop out center of onion with a paring knife and spoon, leaving a fairly thick shell of at least 4 layers of onion. Carefully separate shell into cases, each of 1 or 2 layers of onion; those with 1 layer will be more delicate and tender, but those with 2 layers keep their shape better. Put cases in a lightly oiled large gratin dish or other heavy shallow baking dish. Chop onion centers and tops.

Discard spinach stems. Wash leaves, put in a large pan of boiling salted water, and cook 1 minute, until just tender. Rinse under cold running water and drain thoroughly. Squeeze out as much liquid as possible and coarsely chop.

In a medium-size skillet or sauté pan, melt 3 tablespoons butter over low heat, add chopped onion, and cook about 10 minutes, or until tender. Add spinach and cook, stirring often, about 2 minutes. Transfer to a bowl and let cool slightly. Add egg, cream, and bread crumbs. Season to taste with salt, pepper, and nutmeg.

Spoon stuffing into onion cases without packing. Discard any extra cases. Sprinkle onions with 1 tablespoon oil, cover with foil, and bake 45 minutes. Uncover, dot stuffing with remaining butter, and bake about 30 minutes, or until onions are very tender when pierced with a sharp knife. Serve hot or warm.

NOTE: If desired, substitute one 10-ounce package frozen spinach for fresh. Thaw completely, then squeeze as above.

STUFFED PATTYPAN SQUASH WITH PARMESAN AND RICE
Pâtisson farci au riz et au parmesan

Pattypan squash have a pretty flowerlike shape, making them perfect for use as containers for savory stuffings.

MAKES 4 GENEROUS OR 8 SMALL SERVINGS

8 medium-size pattypan squash
Salt
¼ cup long-grain rice
3 tablespoons extra-virgin olive oil
1 medium-size onion, minced
3 tablespoons chopped fresh basil
    leaves, or 1 tablespoon dried
    basil, crumbled

Freshly ground pepper
1 garlic clove, chopped
2 eggs
⅓ cup freshly grated Parmesan
    cheese

Cut thin slice off bottom of each squash so it will sit squarely. Cut off stem, if desired. In a large pan of boiling salted water, cook squash 5 minutes. Drain, rinse with cold water and drain well.

Cut thin slice off stem end of squash and reserve as a "hat." Use sharp knife and spoon to carefully hollow out squash, taking care not to pierce shell; a small melon-ball cutter is useful for hollowing out sides. Try to leave a shell that is as thin as possible, at most ¼ inch thick. Pour out any water from inside squash. Chop squash pulp.

In a medium-size saucepan, boil about 2 cups water and add a pinch of salt. Add rice, stir once, and boil, uncovered, about 12 minutes, or until barely tender; check by tasting. Drain, rinse with cold water, and leave in a strainer for 5 minutes.

Preheat oven to 350°F. In medium-size skillet, heat 2 tablespoons olive oil over low heat, add onion, and cook, stirring, about 10 minutes. Add chopped squash pulp and cook over medium heat about 5 minutes, or until tender.

Transfer to bowl; mix with basil, pepper, garlic, rice, eggs, and Parmesan. Taste and adjust seasoning.

Oil a large shallow baking dish and a 1-cup ramekin. Put squash shells in oiled baking dish. Spoon filling inside, adding enough to fill but without packing. Set hats on top. Sprinkle evenly with remaining tablespoon olive oil. Spoon extra filling into ramekin. Bake about 45 minutes, or until squash is tender and filling is firm. Serve hot.

Glazed, Braised, Steamed, and Poached Vegetables

Very fresh vegetables are one of the best assurances of delicious vegetable dishes. In some of the finest restaurants, the owners are proud of having their own vegetable gardens. Of course this is not practical for most people, but the sooner a vegetable is cooked after purchase, the better.

Careful cooking is the other key to enjoying vegetables at their best. Vegetables should be cooked so that they are slightly crisp yet tender, with just a little bite. They should not be undercooked so that their texture is hard and their flavor still raw; neither should they be overcooked so that they become flavorless and flabby.

Although there are countless French vegetable recipes, the most frequently used method for cooking vegetables as an accompaniment is the simplest and quickest: they are boiled, poached, or steamed, then drained and tossed with a little salt, freshly ground pepper, and fine-quality butter.

Another quick way to season cooked vegetables, which is used in southern France, is to sprinkle a small amount of extra-virgin olive oil over them. Sometimes the olive oil, or a flavored oil with thyme, garlic, rosemary, or even hot peppers, is provided in a cruet so that each person can pour his own. The vegetable might then be served with a wedge of lemon. The versatile vinaigrette is another simple but popular seasoning for freshly cooked hot vegetables.

For the purpose of cooking, the French often divide vegetables into green vegetables, which are most often boiled, and root vegetables, which are poached or glazed. The category of "green" vegetables includes not only the leafy ones but also asparagus, green beans, leeks, and even cauliflower. Other vegetables, such as zucchini, eggplant, peppers, tomatoes, and mushrooms, which we will call "Mediterranean vegetables," are most often cooked by other methods and are discussed in the next chapter.

Glazed Vegetables

Glazing is a special cooking technique somewhere between poaching and sautéing. The vegetable is cooked with water, butter, and often a little sugar until it softens, the water evaporates, and the butter and sugar form a delicious glaze. It is best suited to root vegetables, especially carrots, turnips, and baby onions.

GINGER-GLAZED CARROTS AND TURNIPS
Carottes et navets glacés au gingembre

"Turned" vegetables, or vegetables that are carved in oval shapes, are popular in French restaurants because they cook evenly and look beautiful. Serve these vegetables with roast duck or chicken.

MAKES 3 TO 4 SERVINGS

*2½ cups Chicken Stock (see recipe)
or Vegetable Stock (see recipe)*
*5 tablespoons minced peeled fresh
ginger*
*4 medium-size thin carrots, of
uniform size and shape (about
10 ounces)*

*3 small turnips, of uniform size
and shape (about 10 ounces)*
Pinch of salt
1½ teaspoons sugar
3 tablespoons unsalted butter
Freshly ground pepper

Bring stock to boil with 3 tablespoons ginger. Simmer, uncovered, over medium-low heat for 30 minutes. Strain, pressing ginger.

Cut carrots in 1½-inch lengths. Trim each piece to oval, rounding off corners. Cut turnips in quarters from top to bottom and trim each piece to oval shape. (Trimmings of carrots, but not of turnips, can be saved for use in stock.)

Put carrots in small saucepan in which they fit in one layer and add about 1¼ cups ginger-flavored stock, or enough to barely cover them. Add salt, 1 teaspoon sugar, 2 tablespoons butter, and remaining 2 tablespoons ginger. Bring to boil, reduce heat to medium, and simmer, uncovered, about 15 minutes, or until carrots are tender. Leave until cool enough to handle. Remove carrots, leaving ginger in liquid. Boil liquid until reduced to ⅓ cup. Strain liquid, pressing ginger. Return liquid and carrots to saucepan.

Put turnips in another small saucepan in which they fit in one layer and add the remaining 1¼ cups ginger-flavored stock, or enough to barely cover turnips. Add salt, remaining ½ teaspoon sugar, and remaining 1 tablespoon butter. Bring to a boil, reduce heat to medium, and simmer, uncovered, about 7 minutes, or until turnips are barely tender. Remove gently with slotted spoon. Boil liquid until reduced to ¼ cup. Add liquid and turnips to saucepan of carrots.

Reheat vegetables in their liquid, uncovered, over medium-high heat, tossing often. Serve hot.

BUTTER-GLAZED CARROTS
Carottes Vichy

This classic carrot recipe remains the favorite French way to prepare the vegetable. The sugar gives just a touch of sweetness and does not produce candied carrots.   MAKES 4 SERVINGS

8 medium-size carrots, peeled
Pinch of salt
1 ½ teaspoons sugar

3 tablespoons unsalted butter
1 tablespoon chopped fresh parsley
(optional)

To turn carrots to an olive shape, cut into 1½- to 2-inch lengths. If carrots are wide, cut each piece into quarters lengthwise. Using a paring knife, shape each piece in an oval or olive shape, rounding off corners.

Put carrots in a medium-size sauté pan and cover with water. Add salt, sugar, and butter. Bring to a boil, reduce heat to medium, and simmer, uncovered, about 20 minutes, or until carrots are tender. If liquid has not evaporated by this time, continue to cook over medium-low heat, shaking pan often, until liquid evaporates and carrots become coated with a buttery glaze. Transfer to a serving dish and sprinkle with parsley, if desired.

GLAZED BABY ONIONS AND ZUCCHINI
Petits oignons et courgettes glacés

These glazed vegetables can be served with any poultry or meat, or can be spooned around Carrot Timbales (see recipe) for a delicious and attractive accompaniment.

MAKES 2 GENEROUS OR 4 SMALL SERVINGS

12 small boiling onions of uniform
   size (about ½ pound)
Salt and freshly ground pepper
2 tablespoons unsalted butter

¼ cup water
1 small zucchini (about ¼ pound)
1 teaspoon sugar

Put unpeeled onions in a heavy saucepan in which they can fit in one layer. Cover with water and bring just to a boil. Drain, rinse with cold water until they cool completely, and peel.

Return onions to saucepan with a pinch of salt and pepper, butter, and ¼ cup water. Cover and cook over low heat, shaking pan occasionally, 15 to 20 minutes, or until tender.

Cut zucchini into quarters lengthwise, then into 1-inch pieces.

Sprinkle onions with sugar and cook, uncovered, over medium heat, shaking pan often, until liquid is reduced to a buttery glaze of a syrupy consistency. Reduce heat to medium-low. Add zucchini, cover, and cook about 5 minutes, or until barely tender.

Braised and Stewed Vegetables

For these techniques, vegetables are cooked in a relatively small amount of liquid or sometimes, as in the case of Butter-Braised Endives, without any liquid at all. They are generally cooked until very tender, rather than crisp-tender as when boiled or steamed.

Often stewing and braising involve a flavor exchange between the vegetable and its cooking liquid, which can then be made into a sauce for the vegetable. Unlike braised or stewed meats, the vegetables are not usually browned before the liquid is added.

Vegetables can also enhance one another. Combining several in a stew can produce a delightful creation with contrasting tastes, textures, and colors. Dried beans, for example, seem lighter when they are matched with fresh vegetables, as in Flageolets with Green and Yellow Beans and Green Onion Butter. To ensure that each vegetable in a stew is perfectly cooked, fragile ones are often precooked separately until nearly tender and then all are heated together briefly so their flavors blend.

BRAISED CHESTNUTS
Marrons braisés

Peeling fresh chestnuts is time-consuming, but they are a real treat and in France are holiday fare. Braised chestnuts are usually served with turkey, duck, or chicken.   MAKES 2 TO 3 SERVINGS

¾ *pound large fresh chestnuts*
1½ *cups Chicken Stock (see recipe)*
  or Vegetable Stock (see recipe)
1 *small celery stalk, broken in two*
  pieces

Salt and freshly ground pepper
1 *to 2 tablespoons unsalted butter*

Put chestnuts in a medium-size saucepan and add enough water to cover them by about 1 inch. Bring to full boil and cook 1 minute. Remove one nut with slotted spoon and peel by first cutting base and pulling off outer skin, and then pulling and scraping off inner skin. Continue with remaining nuts, removing from water one by one.

Put chestnuts in a medium-size saucepan with stock, celery, salt, and pepper. Bring to a boil, reduce heat to low, cover, and simmer about 15 minutes, or until chestnuts are just tender when pierced with point of a knife; do not overcook, or chestnuts will fall apart. Uncover and leave in liquid until ready to use. (Chestnuts can be kept in their liquid, covered, up to 2 days in refrigerator.)

To serve, reheat chestnuts in their cooking liquid in covered saucepan over low heat. Discard celery and chestnut-cooking liquid. Add butter to chestnuts and shake over low heat until blended. Taste and adjust seasoning. Serve hot.

CREAM-BRAISED CABBAGE WITH LEEKS
Choux braisés à la crème et aux poireaux

Among many people, cabbage has a bad reputation. Yet cabbage is such a great favorite of the French that they even use the word for it as a term of endearment, calling loved ones *"mon petit chou"* or *"my little cabbage."* Combining cabbage with mild ingredients, especially butter and cream, is a popular way to moderate its nature, as in this recipe, in which it becomes extremely rich and delicate. Serve this dish as a base for baked or poached eggs or to accompany poultry or fish.

MAKES 4 TO 6 SERVINGS

1 medium-size head of green
     cabbage (about 2 pounds),
     cored and rinsed
3 tablespoons butter
Salt and freshly ground white
     pepper

3 cups milk
White and light green parts of 2
     large leeks, halved lengthwise,
     washed well, and thinly sliced
     crosswise (2 cups slices)
1 cup heavy cream

Cut cabbage in thin strips. In a large heavy casserole of boiling salted water, cook cabbage, uncovered, over high heat for 5 minutes. Rinse under cold water and drain thoroughly. Gently squeeze dry.

In a casserole, over low heat, melt 2 tablespoons butter. Stir in cabbage and salt and pepper to taste. Add milk, cover, and cook, stirring occasionally, about 20 minutes, or until very tender.

In a heavy skillet, melt remaining 1 tablespoon butter over low heat. Add leeks, salt and pepper to taste, and cook, stirring occasionally, about 10 minutes, or until soft but not brown.

When cabbage is tender, uncover and cook over high heat, stirring often, until it absorbs milk. Stir in cream and simmer for 5 minutes, or until thickened. Stir in leeks. Taste and adjust seasoning.

CABBAGE WITH APPLES AND CIDER
Choux à la normande

In this rich country dish from Normandy, the cabbage becomes slightly sweet and olive green in color. Serve it with sausages or roasted or braised meats.   MAKES 4 TO 6 SERVINGS

1 medium-size head of green
     cabbage (about 2 pounds),
     cored and rinsed
1 cup apple cider
¼ cup water
1 whole clove

Salt and freshly ground pepper
Freshly grated nutmeg
2 Golden Delicious apples, peeled,
     cut in half, and cored
½ cup unsalted butter, cut in
     pieces, room temperature

Cut cabbage in thin strips. In a large heavy casserole of boiling salted water, cook cabbage, uncovered, over high heat for 5 minutes. Rinse under cold water and drain thoroughly. Gently squeeze dry.

Return cabbage to casserole and add cider, ¼ cup water, clove, and salt, pepper, and nutmeg to taste.

Cut each apple half in 4 wedges, add to casserole, and bring liquid to a boil. Reduce heat to low, cover, and simmer about 20 minutes, or until cabbage and apples are tender. Uncover and cook over high heat, stirring gently, until nearly all liquid is evaporated. Try not to let apples fall apart. Remove from heat and discard clove. Stir butter into cabbage mixture. Taste and adjust seasoning. To serve, spoon cabbage onto a heated platter or plates and set apple wedges on top.

BUTTER-BRAISED ENDIVES
Endives braisées

Belgian endive is good not only in salads but also cooked. Braising, the most popular technique in France for cooking the vegetable, gives it a flavor completely different from raw. It is slightly bitter and somewhat of an acquired taste, but delightful. This dish makes a good partner for roast chicken. In fact, the endives can be braised in the oven while the chicken is roasting. MAKES 3 TO 4 SERVINGS

1 pound Belgian endives　　　　　*Salt and freshly ground pepper*
2 or 3 tablespoons unsalted butter

Preheat oven to 400°F. Trim any brown spots from endive leaves and from bases. Spread butter in a heavy ovenproof saucepan just large enough to contain endive in one layer. Set endive in saucepan and sprinkle with salt and pepper.

Cover very tightly and cook over medium heat until butter begins to sizzle. Transfer to oven and bake about 30 minutes. Turn endives over, cover tightly, and continue baking 20 to 30 minutes more, or until endives are very tender when pierced with a small sharp knife near base; cooking time varies with size of endives. Check occasionally to be sure they do not burn. Serve hot.

❧ BRAISED FENNEL WITH PEPPERS AND OLIVES
Fenouil braisé aux poivrons et aux olives

Fennel is generally braised whole but this way is quicker and enables the fennel to gain more flavor from the olive oil and peppers. Serve the fennel with chicken, veal, or lamb.   MAKES 4 SERVINGS

2 medium-size fennel bulbs (about
    1 ¼ pounds)
2 medium-size red bell peppers

2 tablespoons olive oil
Salt and freshly ground pepper
½ cup pitted black olives

Remove stalks and any browned outer leaves and cut each fennel bulb into quarters. Cut off and discard core from each piece. Holding layers together, cut each fennel piece in ¼-inch slices lengthwise, to obtain long strips. Cut peppers in half lengthwise and remove core and ribs. Cut in half crosswise and cut each half into lengthwise strips about ¼ inch wide.

Heat olive oil in large skillet over low heat. Add fennel, salt and pepper to taste, and stir well. Cover and cook, stirring occasionally, for 15 minutes. Add peppers, cover, and continue cooking about 10 minutes, or until vegetables are tender. Taste and adjust seasoning. Remove to platter. Top with olives and serve.

❧ ASPARAGUS AND CARROTS WITH MADEIRA
Asperges et carottes au madère

This colorful stew is wonderful served over rice or alongside sautéed or roast poultry.   MAKES 4 SERVINGS

3 medium-size carrots (about 10
    ounces), peeled, cut in 2-inch
    pieces
1 ¼ pounds asparagus
Pinch of salt

1 tablespoon unsalted butter
2 medium-size shallots, minced
⅓ cup Madeira
½ cup heavy cream

Cut thick carrot pieces in quarters lengthwise and thin pieces in half lengthwise. Put carrot pieces in medium-size saucepan, cover with water, and add pinch of salt. Bring to a boil, cover, and simmer about 15 minutes, or until barely tender.

Trim and peel asparagus and cut off tough ends. Remove asparagus tips, cut stems in half crosswise, then lengthwise, if necessary, so they will be of same thickness of carrots.

Add asparagus stem pieces to barely tender carrots and simmer 7 minutes longer, or until tender. Drain cooking liquid into a measuring cup. Reserve 1 cup. Cover saucepan to keep vegetables warm.

In a medium-size skillet, melt butter over low heat, add shallots, and cook, stirring, about 1 minute. Add reserved vegetable-cooking liquid and boil, stirring, until reduced to about ¼ cup. Add Madeira and bring to a boil, add cream, and simmer over medium heat, stirring often, until thick enough to coat a spoon.

At same time, put asparagus tips in a pan of boiling salted water and cook, uncovered, over high heat about 5 minutes, or until just tender. Drain thoroughly and reserve 8 tips for garnish. Add carrots, asparagus stems, and remaining asparagus tips to sauce and heat 2 or 3 minutes over low heat. Taste and adjust seasoning.

Spoon into a serving dish and garnish with reserved tips.

FLAGEOLETS WITH GREEN AND YELLOW BEANS AND GREEN ONION BUTTER
Flageolets aux haricots verts et au beurre d'oignons nouveaux

Pale green flageolets are aristocrats in the dried bean family and have a more delicate flavor than other types of dried beans. They are imported from France and are available in specialty shops. This is a new version of the traditional French recipe for "haricots panachés," made of equal amounts of flageolet beans and green beans and used to accompany roast or grilled lamb. Serve it according to this custom or on its own as a first course or light main course.

MAKES 4 SERVINGS

1 cup dried flageolets (about 7 ounces)
1 bay leaf

¼ teaspoon dried thyme
1 quart water

GREEN ONION BUTTER

1½ to 2 medium-size green onions, trimmed, cut into 1-inch pieces, and patted dry

½ cup unsalted butter, room temperature

6 ounces green beans, ends removed, broken in half
6 ounces wax beans, ends removed, broken in half

1 small garlic clove, minced
Salt and freshly ground pepper

Soak flageolets in 3 cups cold water in a cool place for 8 hours, or overnight. Drain and rinse.

Combine flageolets with bay leaf, thyme, and 1 quart water in a medium-size saucepan. Bring to a boil, reduce heat to low, cover, and cook about 1½ hours, or until just tender. (Flageolets can be kept in their cooking liquid for 1 day in refrigerator. Reheat before continuing.) Drain thoroughly, reserving 2 tablespoons cooking liquid. Discard bay leaf.

GREEN ONION BUTTER

In food processor fitted with steel knife, finely mince green onions. (The amount of green onions you use in green onion butter depends on how strong a flavor you like. For a strong onion flavor, use 2 green onions. For a more delicate flavor, use only 1½.) Add butter and process until blended; color will be light green with dots of deeper green. Do not overprocess or butter will melt. Refrigerate about 30 minutes, or until firm.

Meanwhile, cook green and wax beans, uncovered, separately, each in a medium-size saucepan of boiling salted water over high heat about 7 minutes, or until barely tender. Drain thoroughly.

In a skillet, combine flageolets with the reserved 2 tablespoons of their liquid, garlic, and salt and pepper to taste. Cook over low heat, stirring gently, 2 minutes. Add green and wax beans and mix.

Reserve 1 tablespoon green onion butter and cut in 2 pieces. With skillet of beans over low heat, gently stir in remaining green onion butter, about 2 tablespoons at a time, heating just until butter is absorbed. Taste and adjust seasoning. Transfer to serving dish and place remaining green onion butter on top. Toss when serving.

❧ COLORFUL VEGETABLE BLANQUETTE
Blanquette de légumes

In classic cuisine "blanquette" refers to a creamy veal or lamb stew. I find this formula excellent for preparing a sumptuous vegetable dish as well.   MAKES 4 SERVINGS

½ pound small mushrooms

2 cups Chicken Stock (see recipe) or
   Vegetable Stock (see recipe)

½ cup dry white wine

1 large lemon, cut in half (if using
   fresh artichokes)

2 medium-size artichokes, or 8
   frozen artichoke heart pieces,
   thawed

8 ounces Swiss chard, leaves only,
   rinsed thoroughly

¼ pound pearl onions

3 ounces snow peas

½ pound baby carrots, peeled,
   larger ones halved crosswise

½ pound small zucchini, quartered
   lengthwise and cut in 1½- to
   2-inch pieces

1¼ cups heavy cream

1 tablespoon minced fresh tarragon

1 tablespoon thinly sliced chives

1 tablespoon minced fresh parsley

Salt and freshly ground pepper

A few drops fresh lemon juice

Remove stems from mushrooms. Combine stems with stock and wine in a medium-size saucepan. Bring to a boil, reduce heat to low, and simmer, uncovered, for 15 minutes. Strain stock and reserve; discard mushroom stems.

If using fresh artichokes, squeeze juice of ½ lemon into medium-size bowl of cold water. Break off stems and largest leaves of artichoke bottom. Put artichoke on its side on board. Holding very sharp knife or small serrated knife against side of artichoke (parallel to leaves), cut lower circle of leaves off, up to edge of artichoke heart. Turn artichoke slightly after each cut. Rub exposed edges of artichoke heart with cut lemon. Cut off central cone of leaves just above artichoke heart. Cut off leaves under base and trim so it is round, removing all dark green areas. Rub again with lemon. Put each artichoke in bowl of lemon water as it is finished.

Squeeze any juice remaining in lemon into medium-size saucepan of boiling salted water, add artichoke hearts, cover, and simmer over low heat until tender when pierced with knife, about 15 minutes for fresh and about 7 minutes for frozen. Cool to lukewarm in liquid. Using a teaspoon, scoop out choke from center of each fresh artichoke heart. Return artichokes to liquid until ready to use. Cut each fresh artichoke into 4 pieces. (Stock mixture and artichokes in their liquid can be kept 1 day in refrigerator. Reheat artichokes in their liquid and drain them.)

Pile chard leaves, cut them in half lengthwise and then crosswise into ½-inch strips. In a large saucepan of boiling salted water, cook chard, uncovered, over high heat about 3 minutes, or until just tender. Rinse under cold water, drain well, and press gently to remove excess liquid.

Put pearl onions in a medium-size saucepan, cover with water, and bring to a boil. Boil 1 minute, rinse under cold water, drain well, then peel.

Remove ends and strings from snow peas. In a large saucepan of boiling salted water to generously cover, cook snow peas, uncovered, over high heat until they turn bright green, no more than 1 minute; snow peas should remain crisp. Rinse under cold water and drain well.

Bring strained stock to a boil in a medium-size shallow saucepan. Add baby carrots and simmer, covered, over medium heat about 15 minutes, or until they are just tender. Remove with a slotted spoon. Add mushroom caps and onions, cover, and simmer over medium heat about 10 minutes, or until onions are just tender. Remove with slotted spoon. Add zucchini, cover, and simmer about 4 minutes, or until just tender. Remove with slotted spoon.

Bring vegetable cooking liquid to a boil in a sauté pan. Whisk cream into cooking liquid and bring to a boil over medium-high heat, whisking. Boil, stirring often, until sauce is thick enough to coat spoon, about 6 minutes. Stir in chard, using a fork. Stir in remaining vegetables and reheat just to simmer. Cook over low heat 1 minute, stirring gently. Remove from heat. Add tarragon, chives, parsley, and salt, pepper, and lemon juice to taste. Toss gently, taste and adjust seasoning. Serve in gratin dishes or shallow bowls.

MIXED MUSHROOM RAGOÛT
Ragoût de champignons

Make use of any wild or cultivated mushrooms available for this richly flavored ragoût. Chanterelles, for example, can be used instead of the cèpes or shiitake mushrooms. The dish makes a wonderful topping for white rice, grilled steaks, or poached eggs.

MAKES 4 SERVINGS

¼ pound fresh cèpes or shiitake
*   mushrooms*
1 tablespoon vegetable oil
4 tablespoons butter
1 large shallot, minced

Salt and freshly ground pepper
¼ pound button mushrooms, halved
*   and thinly sliced*
⅓ cup Madeira
1 tablespoon minced fresh parsley

Gently rinse mushrooms and dry on paper towels. If using cèpes, cut in thin slices. If using shiitake mushrooms, use caps only; thinly slice.

In a large heavy skillet, heat oil and 2 tablespoons butter over medium heat. Stir in shallot, then cèpes or shiitake mushrooms, and salt and pepper to taste. Sauté, tossing often, about 4 minutes, or until mushrooms are just tender. Remove from pan.

Add remaining 2 tablespoons butter to skillet and melt over medium-high heat. Add button mushrooms and salt and pepper to taste, and sauté about 3 minutes, or until light brown. Return cèpes or shiitake mushrooms to skillet and reheat mushroom mixture until sizzling. Add Madeira and simmer over medium heat, stirring, about 3 minutes, or until it is absorbed by mushrooms. Taste and adjust seasoning, transfer to a serving dish, sprinkle with parsley, and serve.

Steamed Vegetables

Cooking vegetables by the moist heat of steam is favored by many cooks because it preserves more of their nutrients. In France steaming was not very much a part of classic restaurant cuisine, except for a few dishes like "pommes vapeur" or steamed new potatoes. Home cooks, however, have long valued steaming. The folding steamer is a standard piece of equipment even in the simplest of French home kitchens.

Most vegetables can be successfully steamed. Because steaming locks in flavors, it is better for mild-tasting rather than strong-flavored vegetables. Steaming usually requires a little more time than boiling.

Fresh steamed vegetables are delicious on their own but can be enhanced with a little plain butter or flavored butter, as in Steamed Carrots with Pistachio Butter, or with a sauce, as in Beets with Orange Hollandaise.

In all steamers the food is placed on a rack above boiling liquid and is not in direct contact with the liquid. The pan is covered to keep in the steam. Several types of steamers are available. The French folding steamer rack can be set in any deep saucepan with a tight cover to turn it into a steamer. Chinese bamboo or metal steamers are convenient because the trays can be stacked and several different vegetables can be steamed at once and each removed according to its cooking time. A couscous pot can also be used. For cooking small amounts of vegetables, steamers can be improvised by setting a colander or strainer in a large saucepan and covering it tightly.

Hints

• It is essential to drain steamed or boiled vegetables well so they will not be watery, especially if they will be served with a sauce, because excess liquid would dilute it.

• Vegetables can be boiled or steamed a day ahead, refrigerated, and reheated in a little butter in a sauté pan or skillet. They taste best, however, when freshly cooked.

• For the most even cooking, use a large steamer, in which the food can fit in one layer. If the vegetables are piled up, the steam cannot reach those in the center. If using a small steamer, steam the vegetables in several batches if possible, so that each forms one layer.

• When steaming vegetables, be sure they are at least one inch above the surface of the boiling water, so that when the water bubbles vigorously, it will not boil them. Be sure the water is boiling before the vegetables are added. Steam vegetables over high heat so the water continues to boil and to provide a constant flow of steam. Cover the vegetables in the steamer tightly so that the steam is kept in. When checking them, uncover as briefly as possible. Steam is very hot. When uncovering the steamer, hold the cover away from you in order to avoid the steam.

• During steaming, check occasionally to be sure most of the water has not evaporated. If the level of the water is low, add boiling water. Have ready a kettle of hot water for this purpose.

ZUCCHINI WITH MINT BUTTER
Courgettes au beurre de menthe

Be sure to use zucchini that are fresh—they should be firm and smooth. Although zucchini do not appear to spoil quickly in the refrigerator, they acquire bitterness after a few days. This very quick, simple vegetable dish can be spooned over rice or served with fish, chicken, or lamb.　　　　　　　　　　MAKES 4 TO 6 SERVINGS

1 tablespoon chopped fresh mint　　*Salt and freshly ground pepper*
　　leaves　　　　　　　　　　　　*1 ½ pounds zucchini, cut into*
3 tablespoons unsalted butter,　　　　*quarters lengthwise*
　　softened

Thoroughly mix mint leaves with butter and season to taste with salt and pepper. Let stand at room temperature.

Bring at least 1 inch of water to a boil in base of steamer. Boiling water should not reach holes in top part of steamer. Place zucchini on steamer rack in one layer or in a colander above boiling water. Sprinkle with salt, cover tightly, and steam about 5 minutes, or until just tender.

Transfer briefly to paper towels to drain, then to a serving plate. Top with spoonfuls of mint butter and serve.

PATTYPAN SQUASH WITH PAPRIKA CREAM
Pâtissons à la crème de paprika

Steaming is an ideal method for preserving the delicate taste of the squash. Serve this quick, easy-to-prepare vegetable dish with poached fish or chicken breasts, or with Brown Rice Pilaf with Tarragon.   MAKES 4 SERVINGS

1 tablespoon butter   *1 cup heavy cream*
1 tablespoon paprika   *Salt and freshly ground pepper*
¼ cup dry white wine   *6 medium-size pattypan squash*
1 bay leaf

Melt butter in a medium-size saucepan over low heat. Add paprika and sauté lightly for a few seconds. Stir in wine, add bay leaf, and cook over medium heat until liquid is reduced to about 2 tablespoons. Stir in cream and salt and pepper to taste and bring to a boil. Reduce heat to medium and cook, stirring, until sauce is thick enough to coat a spoon. Taste and adjust seasoning.

Cut tops and bottoms off squash, then cut into quarters.

Bring at least 1 inch of water to a boil in base of steamer. Put squash in steamer top in one layer or on a rack or in a colander above boiling water. Sprinkle with salt and pepper, cover, and steam about 10 minutes, or until just tender. Serve hot. Serve sauce separately.

ASPARAGUS WITH BEURRE BLANC
Asperges au beurre blanc

This is a favorite first course in fine restaurants when asparagus is in season. White asparagus is more available in France than green, but both types are well liked. If you have an asparagus cooker, in which the asparagus spears cook standing up so that the bases are

CARROT TIMBALES
Timbales de carottes

PLUM TOMATOES WITH SHALLOT PURÉE

Olivettes au four à la purée d'échalotes

BRIGHT GREEN SPINACH TART

Tarte aux épinards

FETTUCINE WITH MORELS AND ASPARAGUS
Fettucine aux morilles et aux asperges

GREEN VEGETABLE QUENELLES
WITH MUSHROOM CREAM
Quenelles de legumes vertes à la crème de champignons

GREEN SALAD

Salade verte

RED PEPPER VELOUTÉ SOUP

Velouté de poivrons rouges

PROVENÇAL VEGETABLE AND GARLIC FEAST
Le grand aïoli

boiled and the more tender tips steamed, use it rather than a steamer for this dish.   MAKES 6 SERVINGS

BEURRE BLANC
2 large shallots, minced   *Salt and freshly ground white*
2 tablespoons white wine vinegar   *pepper*
3 tablespoons dry white wine   *1 cup cold unsalted butter, cut into*
2 tablespoons heavy cream   *16 pieces*

3 pounds asparagus   *Salt*

BEURRE BLANC

In a small heavy nonaluminum saucepan, simmer shallots in vinegar and wine over medium heat until liquid is reduced to about 2 tablespoons. Reduce heat to low, stir in cream, and simmer, whisking occasionally, until mixture is reduced to about 3 tablespoons. Season lightly with salt and white pepper. Cover and reserve. (The mixture can be kept, covered, for 1 hour at room temperature.) Keep butter in refrigerator until ready to use.

Peel asparagus stems thoroughly and cut off about ½ inch of bases. Rinse well.

Bring at least 1 inch of water to boil in base of steamer. Put asparagus in steamer above boiling water. Sprinkle with salt, cover, and steam about 5 minutes, or until just tender when pierced with a sharp knife. With a slotted spatula, transfer asparagus carefully to a plate lined with paper towels.

Bring shallot mixture to simmer in a saucepan. Reduce heat to low and add one piece of butter, whisking liquid constantly. When butter piece is nearly blended into liquid, add another piece, still whisking. Continue adding butter pieces one or two at a time, whisking constantly. The sauce should be pleasantly warm to the touch. If it becomes too hot and drops of melted butter appear, remove pan immediately from heat and whisk well; add next butter pieces off heat, whisking constantly. When temperature of sauce drops again to warm, return to low heat to continue adding remaining butter pieces. Remove from heat as soon as last butter piece is added. Strain sauce if desired. Taste and adjust seasoning.

Serve sauce as soon as possible. (Sauce can be kept warm for about 15 minutes in its saucepan set on a rack above warm water, but it must be whisked frequently to prevent separation. It can also be kept warm in a Thermos.)

To serve, divide asparagus among 6 plates. Serve sauce separately.

STEAMED CARROTS WITH PISTACHIO BUTTER
Carottes à la vapeur au beurre de pistaches

Pistachios add a festive touch to carrots in this quick, easy dish. Serve it with chicken, rice, or couscous.   MAKES 6 SERVINGS

1 pound baby carrots, scraped or peeled
½ cup shelled roasted green pistachios

6 tablespoons unsalted butter, slightly softened
Salt and freshly ground pepper

Bring at least 1 inch of water to a boil in base of steamer. Boiling water should not reach holes in top part of steamer. Place carrots in steamer top in one layer or on a rack or in a colander above boiling water. Cover tightly and steam about 15 minutes, or until just tender.

Grind pistachios to fine powder in food processor. Set aside 2 teaspoons.

Cream butter until soft. Stir in remaining pistachios and salt and pepper to taste. Leave at room temperature.

Transfer carrots to serving dish. Toss with pistachio butter. Sprinkle with reserved ground pistachios.

BEETS WITH ORANGE HOLLANDAISE
Betteraves, sauce maltaise

Beets become very tender and keep in their good flavor when steamed. Although orange hollandaise is traditionally served with asparagus, it is also delicious in this appetizer. MAKES 6 SERVINGS

12 small beets (about 1½ inches in diameter)

½ medium-size orange

¾ cup unsalted butter

3 egg yolks

3 tablespoons water

Pinch of salt

Pinch of white pepper or cayenne pepper

½ teaspoon strained fresh lemon juice, or to taste

Rinse beets. Bring at least 1 inch of water to a boil in base of steamer. Boiling water should not reach holes in top part of steamer.

Place beets in steamer or on a rack or in a colander above boiling water. Cover tightly and steam 50 to 60 minutes, or until tender, adding boiling water occasionally if water evaporates.

Meanwhile, use a vegetable peeler to pare orange peel without including bitter white pith underneath. Cut peel in very thin strips. Squeeze juice of half orange and strain and set aside.

Put orange strips in a small saucepan, cover generously with water, and bring to a boil. Cook 2 minutes and drain thoroughly.

In a small heavy saucepan, melt butter over low heat. Skim white foam from surface and pour remaining clear butter into a bowl, leaving white sediment behind in saucepan. Let cool to lukewarm.

When beets are tender, let cool slightly. Run them briefly under water and slip off skins. Cut beets in half, cover, and keep warm while preparing sauce.

In a small heavy-bottomed nonaluminum saucepan, combine egg yolks, water, salt, and pepper, and whisk briefly. Set pan over low heat and cook, whisking vigorously and constantly, until mixture is creamy and thick enough so whisk leaves a trail on base of pan. Remove pan occasionally from heat; it should not become so hot that you can't touch sides of pan with your hands. Be careful not to let mixture become too hot or egg yolks will curdle. When yolk mixture becomes thick enough, remove it immediately from heat. Continue to whisk for about 30 seconds.

Gradually whisk in clarified butter, drop by drop. After sauce has absorbed about 2 or 3 tablespoons butter, add rest of butter in a very thin stream, whisking vigorously and constantly. Gradually whisk in lemon juice and orange juice. Stir in orange peel strips. Taste and adjust seasoning.

Serve sauce as soon as possible. (It can be kept warm for about 15 minutes in its saucepan set on a rack above warm water, but it must be stirred frequently. It can also be kept warm in a Thermos.)

Spoon a little orange sauce on each of 6 appetizer plates and top with beets. Serve any remaining sauce separately.

Poached and Boiled Vegetables

The most popular method for cooking green vegetables in France is to plunge them into a large saucepan of boiling salted water and cook them uncovered. A generous amount of water enables them to cook very quickly so that they keep their color and flavor. The vegetable must have plenty of room to cook evenly rather than being crowded.

Root vegetables and dried beans, on the other hand, are started from cold water so that any undesirable strong flavors they contain can gradually escape into the water as it heats. After they are brought to a boil, they are poached or simmered until tender.

After cooking by either method, the vegetables are well drained in a colander, seasoned with salt and pepper, and finished with butter or a flavorful oil; or, for a more festive dish, they are accompanied by a sauce, as in Wax Beans with French Pesto Sauce or Artichokes with Tomato Béarnaise.

If the cooking liquid of the vegetable tastes good, as in the case of carrots, zucchini, mushrooms, or asparagus, it can be used for soups or sauces.

If a green vegetable is being cooked for serving later (by being reheated in butter, for example) or for turning into a salad or a more elaborate dish, immediately after cooking it is rinsed in a colander with cold running water until completely cold. This rinsing, sometimes called "refreshing," preserves the vegetable's color and prevents it from overcooking and becoming mushy from its own heat.

❧ PROVENÇAL VEGETABLE AND GARLIC FEAST
Le grand aïoli

Aïoli, a versatile garlic sauce, has been important to the cuisine of southern France for hundreds of years. Recently it has gained favor in America as well. Not only does it suit our growing fondness for strong, assertive flavors; it also has the advantage of being quick to prepare and requiring no cooking. It makes a wonderful dipping sauce for vegetables, whether they are cooked or raw, hot or cold.

A traditional Provençal serving custom that is perfect for modern entertaining is called *"Le grand aïoli."* An assortment of vegetables in season, and sometimes eggs and seafood, are presented on separate plates and are accompanied by a bowl of aïoli. Each diner helps himself to the ingredients he likes and to a spoonful of the sauce. Because each spoonful packs quite a punch, a little goes a long way.

The spinach and red pepper variations of aïoli are new vegetable interpretations of the famous sauce. I have also flavored aïoli with chopped fresh basil and even with cilantro and jalapeño peppers and found these versions delicious as well. MAKES 6 SERVINGS

3 medium-size or 6 small
  artichokes, trimmed
6 small carrots, peeled and left
  whole or cut in half crosswise
6 medium-size potatoes, peeled and
  cut into quarters

1 pound green beans, ends removed
1 cauliflower, divided into
  medium-size florets

AÏOLI
6 medium-size garlic cloves, peeled
2 egg yolks, room temperature
About 2 tablespoons strained fresh
  lemon juice

1½ cups extra-virgin olive oil,
  room temperature
Salt and freshly ground pepper
1 tablespoon luke warm water

3 hard-boiled eggs, cut into halves
  or quarters

French bread, as an accompaniment

To trim artichokes, cut off top 1 inch of large artichokes or ½ inch of small ones. Trim spikes from tips of leaves. Put artichokes in a medium-size saucepan of simmering salted water and cover with a lid of slightly smaller diameter than that of pan to keep them submerged. Cook over medium heat until a leaf can be easily pulled out; large artichokes will require about 45 to 50 minutes, and small ones about 15 to 20 minutes. Using tongs, remove artichokes from water and turn them upside down to drain thoroughly.

Cook each of the remaining vegetables separately. Start carrots and potatoes in pans of cold salted water and bring to a boil. Cover and simmer potatoes about 20 minutes and carrots about 25 minutes, or until tender. Start green beans and cauliflower in pans of boiling salted water. Cook green beans about 8 minutes and cauliflower about 7 minutes. Drain all vegetables thoroughly.

AÏOLI

Cut off brown end and any brown spots from garlic. Halve garlic cloves lengthwise and remove any green sprouts from center.

To make aïoli in food processor, drop garlic cloves through feed tube of food processor fitted with metal blade, with motor running, and process until finely chopped. Add egg yolks, 1 tablespoon lemon juice, 1 tablespoon oil, and a pinch of salt and pepper, and process until thoroughly blended, scraping bottom and sides of processor container several times. With motor running, gradually pour in ¼ cup oil in a thin trickle. After adding ¼ cup oil, remaining oil can be poured in a little faster, in a thin stream. With motor still running, gradually pour in remaining tablespoon lemon juice, 1 teaspoon at a time. Add lukewarm water, 1 teaspoon at a time, to make sauce slightly thinner. Taste and adjust seasoning.

To prepare aïoli using mixer or whisk, chop garlic as finely as possible so that it becomes almost a purée. Combine garlic, egg yolks, 1 tablespoon lemon juice, and a pinch of salt and pepper in mixer bowl or a medium-size heavy bowl set on a towel. Beat at high speed or whisk until thoroughly blended. Begin beating in oil, drop by drop. When 2 or 3 tablespoons oil have been added, continue beating in oil in very thin stream until 1 cup oil has been incorporated. Beat in 1 teaspoon of remaining lemon juice to thin sauce and make beating easier. Gradually beat in remaining oil in fine stream. Gradually beat in remaining lemon juice, 1 teaspoon at a time, then water, 1 teaspoon at a time. Taste and adjust seasoning.

Transfer aïoli to a serving bowl.

Serve vegetables warm or at room temperature, and sauce at room temperature. Arrange vegetables and eggs in separate piles on a platter or on serving plates. Serve aïoli and French bread separately.

SPINACH AÏOLI

Bring aïoli to room temperature. Remove stems from 11 ounces fresh spinach. Rinse leaves thoroughly and put in a large saucepan containing enough boiling salted water to cover them generously. Return to boil and cook, uncovered, 1 minute. Drain, rinse with cold running water until cool and drain. Squeeze spinach by handfuls to remove as much water as possible. Purée spinach in a food processor until very finely chopped. Add aïoli and process until smooth. Taste and adjust seasoning.

RED PEPPER AÏOLI

Preheat broiler. Broil 3 medium-size red bell peppers about 2 inches from heat, turning them slightly every few minutes, until their skins blister on all sides and turn black, about 15 to 20 minutes. Put peppers in a plastic bag, close bag, and let stand 10 minutes. Peel, cut in half, and remove cores. Cool completely in colander. Pat dry.

Purée peppers in food processor until as fine as possible. Whisk purée into aïoli in three portions. Stir thoroughly to blend. Taste and adjust seasoning. If a smoother sauce is desired, return to food processor and blend until smooth.

BABY VEGETABLES WITH HERB BUTTER SAUCE
Petits légumes au beurre d'herbes

This dish was inspired by a lovely first course I enjoyed at Le Pré Catalan, the beautiful restaurant in the Bois de Boulogne near Paris. The butter sauce was spooned on the plate and the baby vegetables were arranged attractively on top. In this version, each type of vegetable is cooked separately so it retains its own flavor and cooks evenly. Other miniature vegetables, such as baby corn, tiny artichokes, and small pattypan squash, can also be included.

MAKES 4 APPETIZER SERVINGS

HERB BUTTER SAUCE

2 large shallots, minced

2 tablespoons tarragon vinegar or
   white wine vinegar

3 tablespoons dry white wine

2 tablespoons heavy cream

Salt and freshly ground white
   pepper

1 cup cold unsalted butter, cut into
   16 pieces

1 tablespoon snipped chives

1 tablespoon minced tarragon

1 tablespoon minced fresh chervil or
   parsley

BABY VEGETABLES

8 baby beets (about 1 inch or less
   in diameter)

12 baby carrots with about
   ½ inch green tops

8 baby turnips with green tops

16 baby zucchini

4 cherry tomatoes

HERB BUTTER SAUCE

In a small heavy nonaluminum saucepan, simmer shallots in vinegar and wine over medium heat until liquid is reduced to about 2 tablespoons. Reduce heat, stir in cream, and simmer, whisking occasionally, until mixture is reduced to about 3 tablespoons. Season lightly with salt and white pepper. (The mixture can be kept, covered, for 1 hour at room temperature.) Keep butter and herbs in refrigerator until ready to use.

BABY VEGETABLES

Rinse beets. Put 1 inch of water in a steamer and bring to a boil. Place beets in steamer rack or in another rack or colander above boiling water. Cover tightly and steam about 15 to 20 minutes, or until just tender. Let cool slightly and slip off skins. Put in a warm bowl, cover, and keep warm.

Put carrots in a small saucepan and add water to cover and a pinch of salt. Bring to a boil, reduce heat to low, cover, and simmer about 10 minutes, or until just tender when pierced with a knife. Drain, cover, and keep warm.

Put turnips in small saucepan and add water to cover and a pinch of salt. Bring to a boil, reduce heat to low, cover, and simmer about 5 minutes, or until just tender when pierced with a knife. Drain thoroughly. Add to carrots and keep warm.

Add zucchini to a medium-size saucepan of boiling salted water and boil 2 to 5 minutes, or until just tender when pierced with a knife. Drain thoroughly and add to carrots and turnips.

Put cherry tomatoes in a small saucepan of boiling water, return to a boil, and drain, rinse, and peel. Add to pan of carrots, turnips, and zucchini. Cover and keep warm.

To Finish Sauce: Bring shallot mixture to simmer in its saucepan.

Over low heat, add one piece of butter, stirring liquid with a whisk constantly. When butter piece is nearly blended in, add another piece, still whisking. Continue adding butter pieces one or two at a time, whisking constantly. The sauce should be pleasantly warm to touch. If it becomes too hot and drops of melted butter appear, remove pan immediately from heat and whisk well; add next butter pieces off heat, whisking constantly. When temperature of sauce drops again to warm, return to low heat to continue adding remaining butter pieces. Remove from heat as soon as last butter piece is added. Strain sauce into a bowl. Stir in herbs. Taste and adjust seasoning.

Serve sauce as soon as possible. (Sauce can be kept warm for about 15 minutes in its saucepan set on a rack above warm water, but it must be whisked frequently to prevent separation.)

To serve, spoon about 3 tablespoons Herb Butter Sauce onto each of 4 appetizer plates. Arrange vegetables on plates, dividing them evenly and making sure not to add any liquid that may have accumulated as they were waiting to be served. Serve any remaining sauce separately.

CAULIFLOWER IN ROSEMARY-SCENTED TOMATO SAUCE
Chou-fleur en sauce tomate au romarin

A single sprig of rosemary adds a distinctive aroma to this dish. Pair it with roast chicken or meat, or with poached, baked, or hard-boiled eggs. MAKES 4 TO 6 SERVINGS

1 sprig of fresh rosemary
1 sprig of fresh thyme, or ¼ teaspoon dried thyme, crumbled
1 bay leaf
2 tablespoons olive or vegetable oil
½ onion, chopped

1 large garlic clove, minced
2½ pounds ripe tomatoes, peeled, seeded, and chopped
Salt and freshly ground pepper
1 large cauliflower, divided into medium-size florets

Wrap rosemary, thyme, and bay leaf in a piece of cheesecloth and tie tightly to make a bouquet garni. In a large saucepan, heat oil over low heat, add onion, and cook, stirring occasionally, until soft but not browned. Add garlic, tomatoes, bouquet garni, and salt and pepper to taste. Cook over medium heat, stirring often, about 20 minutes, or until tomatoes are soft and mixture is thick and smooth. Discard bouquet garni. Taste and adjust seasoning. (The sauce can be prepared 2 days ahead and kept in refrigerator. Reheat before continuing.)

In a large pan of boiling salted water, cook cauliflower, uncovered, over high heat about 3 to 4 minutes, or until nearly tender. Rinse with cold water and drain thoroughly.

Add cauliflower to tomato sauce, cover, and simmer, gently turning florets over occasionally, about 2 minutes, or until they are tender. Taste and adjust seasoning. Serve hot or at room temperature.

❧ FRENCH CURRIED CAULIFLOWER
Chou-fleur au curry

Curry is associated with Indian cooking, but French cooks like to use this spice mixture as well, although with a light hand. Cilantro (fresh coriander) is new to French cooking and this is due to the influence of Moroccan food and the many couscous restaurants in France.

MAKES ABOUT 4 SERVINGS

1 medium-size cauliflower, divided into medium-size florets
1 tablespoon butter
¼ cup finely chopped onion
1 teaspoon curry powder
3 tablespoons dry white wine

2 tablespoons water
Salt and freshly ground pepper
1 cup heavy cream
2 teaspoons minced cilantro or parsley (optional)

In a large pan of boiling salted water, cook cauliflower, uncovered, over high heat about 4 or 5 minutes, or until just tender. Drain, rinse with cold water, and drain thoroughly.

In a heavy sauté pan or deep skillet, heat butter over low heat, add onion, and cook until soft but not browned. Stir in curry powder and cook, stirring, about 30 seconds. Add wine, water, a pinch of salt and pepper, and simmer over medium heat until liquid is reduced to about 2 tablespoons.

Add cream and bring to a boil. Add cauliflower and simmer, uncovered, over medium heat, stirring and spooning sauce over it, about 2 minutes, or until tender. Transfer cauliflower to a shallow serving dish, using slotted spoon.

Continue to cook sauce over medium heat, stirring often, for 3 minutes, or until reduced slightly and thick enough to coat a spoon. Taste and adjust seasoning. Spoon over cauliflower. Sprinkle with cilantro or parsley, if desired. Serve hot or at room temperature.

✺ BROCCOLI WITH ROQUEFORT SAUCE
Brocolis au roquefort

Serve this flavorful combination with simply cooked chicken, veal, or beef or with rice or pasta. It makes a great brunch dish when topped with poached eggs. MAKES ABOUT 4 SERVINGS

1 tablespoon unsalted butter	Pepper
2 shallots, minced	Pinch of salt (optional)
½ cup dry white wine	2 pounds broccoli, divided into
1 cup heavy cream	fairly large florets with about
⅓ cup crumbled Roquefort cheese	1½ inches of stalks

In a heavy medium-size saucepan, melt butter over low heat, add shallots, and cook, stirring, about 2 minutes, until softened. Add wine and boil, stirring often, until only about 2 tablespoons liquid remain. Stir in cream and cook over medium heat, stirring often, until sauce is thick enough to coat a spoon, about 7 minutes. Reduce heat to low, add Roquefort cheese, and simmer, whisking, just until sauce is smooth. Add pepper to taste; salt may not be needed because Roquefort cheese is salty.

In a large saucepan of boiling salted water, cook broccoli florets, uncovered, about 7 minutes, or until just tender. Drain thoroughly in colander. Arrange on a platter with florets pointing outward from center. Reheat sauce if necessary. Spoon a little sauce over broccoli stems. Serve remaining sauce separately.

ZUCCHINI WITH CAPERS AND HAZELNUT BUTTER
Courgettes au beurre noisette

Hazelnut butter is not made of hazelnuts but rather refers to the aroma of the heated butter, which resembles that of toasted hazelnuts. It goes well with zucchini and is also delicious with cauliflower and broccoli.   MAKES 4 SERVINGS

4 small zucchini (about 1 pound)   *2 tablespoons chopped fresh parsley*
Salt and freshly ground pepper   *⅓ cup unsalted butter*
4 teaspoons capers, well drained

Cut zucchini in 1½- to 2-inch chunks. Cut each chunk in lengthwise slices about ⅜ inch thick and each slice in sticks about ⅜ inch thick.

Add zucchini sticks to a large saucepan containing enough boiling salted water to generously cover. Cook over high heat about 2 minutes, or until barely tender. Do not overcook or they will be mushy. Drain very thoroughly and transfer to a shallow heatproof serving dish. Sprinkle zucchini lightly with salt and pepper, toss gently, and sprinkle with capers and parsley.

In a small heavy saucepan, cook butter over medium heat, shaking pan occasionally, until butter is light brown and has a nutty aroma. Pour evenly over zucchini and serve immediately.

LYONNAISE GREEN BEANS
Haricots verts à la lyonnaise

Like many dishes from Lyon, these green beans are flavored with
sautéed onions. Wax beans and cooked dried white beans can also be
seasoned in this way. MAKES 4 TO 6 SERVINGS

¼ cup butter
1 onion, halved and cut in thin
   slices
1½ pounds green beans, trimmed
   and broken in half

Salt and freshly ground pepper
2 tablespoons chopped fresh parsley
2 tablespoons mild white wine
   vinegar (5 percent acidity)

In a medium-size skillet or sauté pan, melt butter over low heat,
add onion, and cook, stirring, until softened and just beginning to
turn golden.

Meanwhile, in a large pan of boiling salted water, cook green
beans, uncovered, over high heat about 8 minutes, or until just tender.
Drain thoroughly and add to skillet. Over very low heat, toss beans
lightly with onions and season to taste with salt and pepper. Transfer
to a serving dish and sprinkle with parsley.

Add vinegar to hot skillet and bring to a simmer. Immediately
pour over beans, toss well, and serve.

GREEN BEANS WITH DELICATE GARLIC BUTTER
Haricots verts au beurre gascon

Serve these beans with poached or grilled fish or with rice. The
garlic becomes surprisingly mild after being simmered. The garlic
butter is also good with other vegetables, especially grilled mushrooms, zucchini, and poached dried beans. MAKES 4 SERVINGS

6 large garlic cloves, unpeeled
6 tablespoons unsalted butter,
* softened*
Salt and freshly ground pepper

1 ½ pounds green beans, trimmed
* and broken in half, or*
* haricots verts (thin French*
* green beans), trimmed*

Add garlic cloves to a small pan of boiling water and simmer over low heat about 10 minutes, or until very tender. Peel garlic, put in a bowl, and mash pulp with a fork. The garlic should not be in large pieces but there is no need for it to be completely smooth. Add butter and salt and pepper to taste and mash together until well mixed.

In a large pan of boiling salted water, cook green beans, uncovered, over high heat about 7 minutes, or until just tender; if using thin French beans, cooking time will be about 4 minutes. Drain thoroughly and return to pan. Add garlic butter and toss lightly over very low heat just until it coats beans but does not melt completely. If beans are very hot, they can be tossed with butter off heat. Taste and adjust seasoning and serve immediately.

WAX BEANS WITH FRENCH PESTO SAUCE
Haricots beurre au pistou

Although pistou, like pesto, is best known as a zesty flavoring for soup or pasta, it is also wonderful with vegetables. Try it with cauliflower, too.   MAKES 4 TO 6 SERVINGS

3 large garlic cloves
1 ounce fresh basil (about 1 bunch)
½ cup freshly grated Parmesan
* cheese*
⅓ cup extra-virgin olive oil

1 ½ pounds wax beans or green
* beans, trimmed and broken in*
* half*
Salt and freshly ground pepper

Chop garlic in a food processor. Discard basil stems. Add basil leaves and cheese and purée until basil is chopped. Gradually add olive oil, with motor running. Scrape down sides and purée again so mixture is well blended. Transfer to a bowl.

In a large pan of boiling salted water, cook beans, uncovered, over high heat about 8 minutes, or until just tender. Drain thoroughly, reserving 2 tablespoons cooking liquid, and transfer to a serving dish.

Whisk reserved hot cooking liquid into basil sauce and add to beans. Toss until well combined. Add salt and pepper and taste and adjust seasoning. Serve immediately.

❧ BRUSSELS SPROUTS WITH CREAMY MUSTARD-SAGE SAUCE
Choux de bruxelles, sauce moutarde à la sauge

Brussels sprouts are pretty and delicious when fresh and not overcooked. To cut down on cooking time and to keep their color bright green, these brussels sprouts are cut in half before being boiled. Serve them as an appetizer or alongside roast chicken or meats.

MAKES 4 SERVINGS

1 tablespoon butter
½ medium-size onion, minced
2 tablespoons mild white wine
   vinegar (5 percent acidity)
¼ cup water
1 tablespoon chopped fresh sage, or
   1 teaspoon dried sage,
   crumbled

Salt and freshly ground pepper
1 cup heavy cream
¾ pound small Brussels sprouts
4 teaspoons Dijon mustard

In medium-size heavy saucepan, melt butter over low heat, add onion, and cook, stirring often, about 5 minutes, or until soft but not brown. Blend in vinegar, water, sage, and small pinch of salt. Increase heat to medium and boil, stirring often, until liquid is reduced to about 2 tablespoons. Stir in cream. Cook, stirring often, until sauce is slightly reduced and thick enough to coat back of spoon, about 7 minutes. (Sauce mixture can be kept, covered, 2 days in refrigerator.)

Trim Brussels sprouts, removing tough bases and any yellow leaves. Cut sprouts in half lengthwise. In a large pan of boiling salted water, cook sprouts, uncovered, over high heat about 7 minutes, or until just tender but still bright green. Drain thoroughly.

While sprouts cook, reheat sauce, if necessary, over medium heat, whisking. Reduce heat to low, and whisk in mustard and a pinch of pepper. Taste and adjust seasoning.

To serve, spoon sauce onto plates and set Brussels sprouts on top, alternating some cut side up, some cut side down.

CABBAGE WITH BUTTER AND WINE VINEGAR
La chouée

This bright green, slightly crisp cabbage dish, which originated in the Loire Valley in central France, can be served with almost any poultry, meat, or even seafood.   MAKES 4 SERVINGS

1 small green cabbage (about   ¼ cup butter
   1 ½ pounds)   Salt and freshly ground pepper
4 teaspoons white wine vinegar

Cut cabbage in half, core it, and rinse thoroughly. Cut in thin strips. In a large saucepan of boiling salted water, cook cabbage for 5 minutes, or until just tender. Rinse under cold running water and drain thoroughly. Gently squeeze dry in a colander.

In a large skillet, heat cabbage with vinegar, 2 tablespoons butter, and salt and pepper to taste over medium heat, stirring, for 3 minutes, or until butter and vinegar are absorbed. Remove from heat. Stir in remaining butter and taste for seasoning.

ARTICHOKES WITH TOMATO BÉARNAISE SAUCE
Artichauts, sauce choron

Artichokes are considered a noble vegetable and are served with hollandaise and other fine sauces. Students in my California cooking classes love this elegant first course, in which the artichokes are accompanied by the zesty, colorful tomato béarnaise.

MAKES 6 SERVINGS

6 medium-size artichokes, or 12
    small artichokes
¾ cup unsalted butter
2 tablespoons white wine vinegar
3 tablespoons dry white wine
½ teaspoon coarsely cracked
    peppercorns
2 shallots, chopped
3 fresh tarragon stems (without
    leaves), chopped

3 egg yolks
Salt
¼ cup Fresh Tomato Sauce
    (page 36), or 1 tablespoon
    tomato paste
Pinch of white pepper or cayenne
    pepper
1 tablespoon minced fresh tarragon
1 tablespoon minced fresh parsley

To trim artichokes, cut off top 1 inch of large artichokes or ½ inch of small ones. Trim spikes from tips of leaves with scissors. Put artichokes in a large saucepan of boiling salted water and cover with a lid of slightly smaller diameter than that of pan to keep them submerged. Cook over medium heat until a leaf can be easily pulled out; large artichokes will require about 45 to 50 minutes and small ones about 15 to 20 minutes. Using tongs, remove artichokes from water, turn them upside down, and drain thoroughly. Cover to keep warm.

To clarify butter, melt in a small heavy saucepan over low heat. Skim white foam from surface. Pour remaining clear butter into a bowl, leaving white sediment behind in saucepan. Let cool to lukewarm.

In a small heavy-bottomed nonaluminum saucepan, combine vinegar, wine, peppercorns, shallots, and tarragon stems. Simmer until only about 2 tablespoons liquid remain. Strain, pressing hard on shallots. Return liquid to saucepan and let cool to room temperature.

With a whisk, stir egg yolks and a pinch of salt into liquid. Set pan over low heat and cook, whisking vigorously and constantly, until mixture is creamy and thick enough so whisk leaves a clear trail on base of pan. Remove pan occasionally from heat; it should not become so hot that you can't touch sides of pan with your hands. Be careful not to let mixture become too hot or egg yolks will curdle. When yolk mixture becomes thick enough, remove it immediately from heat. Continue to whisk for about 30 seconds.

Gradually whisk in clarified butter, drop by drop. After sauce has absorbed about 2 or 3 tablespoons butter, add remaining butter in a very thin stream, whisking vigorously and constantly. (If sauce separates while you are adding butter, whisk 1 tablespoon of sauce with

1 tablespoon cold water in a bowl. Gradually whisk remaining sauce into mixture. If this doesn't work, start again by whisking 1 egg yolk and 1 tablespoon water in a small heavy-bottomed saucepan over low heat as above; then gradually whisk in separated sauce, in same manner as clarified butter was whisked in.)

If using Fresh Tomato Sauce, purée it in a food processor until it is smooth. Stir tomato sauce or tomato paste into sauce. Add a pinch of pepper and minced tarragon and parsley. Taste and adjust seasoning. Serve as soon as possible. (Sauce can be kept warm for about 15 minutes in its bowl set on a rack above warm water, but it must be stirred frequently. It can also be kept warm in a Thermos.)

If sauce is too thick, stir in 1 to 2 teaspoons water. Serve in sauceboat. Use for dipping artichoke leaves and heart.

MORELS WITH CREAM
Morilles à la crème

One of the best of culinary preparations, morels in cream are served as a festive side dish with chicken or poached eggs, or as a first course inside artichoke hearts, tartlet shells, or puff pastry cases.

MAKES ABOUT 4 SERVINGS

6 to 8 ounces fresh morels, or 1½ ounces dried morels (about 1½ cups)
1 tablespoon butter
2 medium shallots, minced
½ cup dry white wine

½ cup Chicken Stock (see recipe) or Vegetable Stock (see recipe)
Salt and freshly ground pepper
1½ cups heavy cream
1 tablespoon chopped fresh parsley (optional)

If using fresh morels, rinse thoroughly in several changes of water and brush to remove all the sand that may be in the crevices.

Soak dried morels in hot water to cover for about 30 minutes or until soft. Rinse and drain well.

Cut in half or slice any large morels.

In a medium-size saucepan, melt butter over low heat, add shallots, and cook about 2 minutes, or until they soften. Add fresh morels (but not dried ones) and sauté over medium heat about 5 minutes, or until tender. Pour in wine and bring it to a boil, stirring. Add stock, dried morels, and salt and pepper and bring to a boil. Reduce heat to medium and simmer until liquid is reduced to about ¾ cup. Stir in cream and bring mixture to a boil. Reduce heat to medium and simmer, stirring occasionally, for 7 minutes, or until cream mixture is thick enough to coat a spoon. Taste and adjust seasoning. (The morels can be kept, covered, 1 day in refrigerator.)

Serve hot. Sprinkle with chopped parsley, if desired.

WHITE BEANS WITH TOMATOES AND ONIONS
Haricots à la bretonne

This dish from Brittany is a favorite with grilled and roast meats and with eggs. It is sometimes flavored with diced bacon and can also be prepared with flageolets (light green French dried beans) instead of white beans.　　MAKES 6 SERVINGS

2½ cups (1 pound) dried white beans, such as Great Northern
1 celery stalk
1 medium-size carrot, peeled
1 medium-size onion, peeled
2 whole cloves
4 sprigs fresh thyme, or 1½ teaspoons dried thyme
2 bay leaves
5 parsley stems

Salt and freshly ground pepper
3 tablespoons butter
1 large onion, thinly sliced
2 teaspoons minced shallots
3 large garlic cloves, minced
2 pounds ripe tomatoes, peeled, seeded, and chopped
1 tablespoon tomato paste (optional)
1 tablespoon chopped fresh parsley

Soak beans 8 hours or overnight in cold water to generously cover; drain thoroughly.

Put beans, celery, carrot, and whole onion in a large pot. Wrap cloves, 2 sprigs fresh thyme or ¾ teaspoon dried thyme, 1 bay leaf, and parsley stems in a piece of cheesecloth and tie tightly to make a bouquet garni; add to pot. Add enough water to cover ingredients generously. Bring to a boil over medium heat and simmer, uncovered, adding hot water occasionally so beans remain covered, about 45 minutes. Add pinch of salt and pepper and simmer another 45 minutes, or until tender. Toward end of cooking time bean mixture should be moist but not soupy. Season to taste with salt and pepper. Reserve beans in their liquid. Discard bouquet garni.

Wrap remaining thyme and bay leaf in a piece of cheesecloth and tie tightly to make a bouquet garni. In a large saucepan, melt butter over low heat, add sliced onion, and cook, stirring occasionally, until soft but not browned. Stir in shallots and garlic. Add tomatoes, bouquet garni, and salt and pepper to taste, and bring to a boil. Add ½ cup liquid from beans and bring again to a boil. Cook over medium heat, stirring often, about 25 minutes, or until tomatoes are soft and mixture is thick and smooth. Stir in tomato paste, if desired, for brighter color. Discard bouquet garni.

Drain beans and add to tomatoes. Bring to a simmer and cook, uncovered, 2 to 3 minutes. Taste and adjust seasoning. (The beans can be prepared 2 days ahead and kept, covered, in refrigerator.) Sprinkle with parsley and serve hot.

FAVA BEANS IN GARLIC CREAM
Fèves à la crème d'ail

Lima beans or green beans are also good with this sauce, which has a delicate taste of garlic. Savory is a traditional flavoring for fava beans and often grows wild alongside them in the fields.

MAKES 4 SERVINGS

3½ pounds fresh fava beans or lima beans (weight with pods)

1 sprig of fresh savory, or pinch of dried savory, crumbled (optional)

5 garlic cloves, chopped

1 bay leaf

5 parsley stems

⅓ cup dry white wine

1 tablespoon white wine vinegar

1¼ cups heavy cream

Salt and freshly ground pepper

1 teaspoon chopped fresh savory, or ¼ teaspoon dried savory, crumbled (optional)

Pinch of cayenne pepper

1 tablespoon chopped fresh parsley (optional)

Shell beans. Put them in a large saucepan of boiling salted water, add sprig of savory, and cook, uncovered, over high heat about 15 to 20 minutes, or until tender; taste a bean to check. Drain thoroughly, reserving 2 tablespoons cooking liquid and discarding fresh savory. Peel off thick skins.

Combine garlic, bay leaf, parsley stems, wine, vinegar, and 2 tablespoons reserved cooking liquid in a large saucepan. Bring to a boil and simmer, uncovered, until reduced to about 3 tablespoons.

Add cream and a small pinch of salt and pepper. Bring to a simmer and cook over medium heat, stirring often, until sauce is thick enough to coat a spoon, about 9 minutes.

Strain sauce, add chopped savory and a pinch of cayenne pepper. Taste and adjust seasoning.

To reheat, bring sauce nearly to a boil, add fava beans, and simmer 1 or 2 minutes.

Taste and adjust seasoning, sprinkle with parsley, and serve.

NOTE: Two 10-ounce packages frozen lima beans can be substituted for the fresh beans. Cook according to the package directions, adding the sprig of savory to the water.

Baked, Grilled, Sautéed, and Fried Vegetables

Vegetables often associated with Mediterranean cooking, such as zucchini, eggplant, peppers, and tomatoes, are most often cooked by baking, grilling, sautéing, or frying. These techniques are also ideal for cooking mushrooms, both cultivated and wild, and potatoes (which are discussed in the chapter "Potatoes, Rice, and Pasta").

The cooking methods in this chapter are considered "dry-heat techniques" and are very popular for several reasons: they are quick and easy and, more important, the vegetable keeps in all its flavor rather than losing some to a liquid.

Baked and Grilled Vegetables

≈ঔ

In addition to some of the Mediterranean vegetables, root vegetables also benefit from baking, as in Baked Beets with Lemon Cream. Some vegetables are precooked in water and then baked, as in Artichokes and Baby Onions Antiboise.

For grilling vegetables, any grilling equipment can be used: an outdoor grill or barbecue, a stove-top ridged grill, or an oven broiler. The most tender vegetables, such as mushrooms, peppers, zucchini, and small eggplants, are best for grilling.

ঔ*ঔ* ZUCCHINI, EGGPLANT, AND TOMATO SLICES BAKED WITH HERBS
Courgettes, aubergines, et tomates aux herbes

This colorful dish is inspired by a creation of Master Chef Fernand Chambrette. He alternated these vegetables with sautéed monkfish slices for a recipe that appeared in *La Cuisine du Poisson,* the fish cookbook we coauthored in France.   MAKES 4 SERVINGS

2 medium-size zucchini (about
     ¾ pound)
2 slender Japanese eggplants (about
     ¾ pound), unpeeled
½ pound large ripe plum tomatoes
     or small ripe regular tomatoes
About ¼ cup all-purpose flour
6 tablespoons vegetable oil

Salt and freshly ground pepper
5 tablespoons butter
1 large garlic clove, minced
2 teaspoons fresh thyme, or
     ¾ teaspoon dried thyme,
     crumbled
1 tablespoon chopped fresh basil
1 tablespoon chopped fresh parsley

Cut zucchini in disks about ⅜ inch thick and eggplant in disks about ¼ inch thick. Core tomatoes and cut in rounds about ¼ inch thick; discard ends of tomatoes. Poke out seeds from slices. Put tomato slices on plate in one layer.

Lightly flour eggplant slices and put in one layer on plate. In a large heavy skillet, heat 2 tablespoons oil over medium-high heat. Add half the eggplant slices and sauté about 1½ minutes per side, or until lightly browned. Remove with slotted spatula to a paper towel–lined tray. Add 2 tablespoons oil to skillet, heat oil, and sauté remaining eggplant. Transfer to tray.

Add another tablespoon oil to skillet and heat. Lightly flour zucchini pieces, add half of them to skillet, and sauté about 2 minutes per side. Add another tablespoon oil and sauté second batch. Remove with slotted spatula.

Preheat oven to 400°F. Sprinkle eggplant, zucchini, and tomato slices evenly with salt and pepper on both sides.

Butter a 14-by-8-inch oval gratin dish or other large shallow baking dish. Alternate eggplant, zucchini, and tomato slices in one layer in pan, overlapping slightly. If any slices remain, arrange them in an individual gratin dish. If desired, all vegetables can be arranged in individual gratin dishes.

In a small skillet, melt butter over low heat, add garlic, and cook 10 seconds. Remove from heat and stir in thyme, basil, and parsley. Pour butter evenly over vegetables in gratin dish. Bake about 15 minutes, or until vegetables are tender. Serve hot or warm, from baking dish.

܀ BAKED MUSHROOMS WITH ESCARGOT BUTTER AND WALNUTS
Champignons au beurre d'escargots aux noix

Escargot butter is the irresistible garlic and parsley butter that is by far the most popular accompaniment for escargots, or snails. Actually, many people admit that this butter is the main reason they like snails. Whether or not you like snails, you will find that this flavored butter is wonderful with mushrooms.   MAKES 6 SERVINGS

18 medium-size mushrooms (about
    ¾ pound)
2 tablespoons walnut pieces
3 tablespoons small parsley sprigs
    (without large stems)

1 small shallot, minced
2 medium-size garlic cloves, minced
6 tablespoons butter, softened
Salt and freshly ground pepper

Preheat oven to 425°F. Remove mushroom stems and discard.

Grind walnuts in a food processor until fine and remove. Add parsley sprigs and chop fine. Combine walnuts, parsley, shallot, garlic, and butter in processor and process until well blended. (To prepare by hand: Chop walnuts and parsley as fine as possible. Combine with minced shallot, garlic, and butter and beat with wooden spoon until well blended.) Season to taste with salt and pepper.

Arrange mushrooms in a lightly buttered shallow baking dish. Sprinkle them with salt. Spoon 1 to 1½ teaspoons flavored butter into each, enough to fill it to top. Spread filling smooth. (If there is extra flavored butter, freeze it and serve it on other cooked vegetables, rice, or pasta.)

Bake about 12 minutes, or until mushrooms are just tender when pierced with a small knife and butter begins to bubble. Serve immediately.

ARTICHOKES AND BABY ONIONS ANTIBOISE
Fonds d'artichauts à l'antiboise

In this dish, named for the French Riviera town of Antibes, artichoke hearts and small onions are baked briefly in fresh tomato sauce.   MAKES 4 SERVINGS

1 lemon
4 artichokes
2 tablespoons olive oil
2 pounds ripe tomatoes, peeled,
    seeded, and finely chopped
1 teaspoon chopped fresh thyme or
    fresh oregano, or ¼ teaspoon
    dried thyme or oregano

Salt and freshly ground pepper
2 medium-size garlic cloves, minced
¼ pound pearl onions
1 tablespoon unseasoned bread
    crumbs

Prepare artichoke hearts according to directions on page 143.

Squeeze any juice remaining in lemon into medium-size saucepan of boiling salted water, add artichoke hearts, cover, and simmer over low heat about 15 minutes, or until tender when pierced with a knife. Cool to lukewarm in liquid. Using a teaspoon, scoop out choke from center of each artichoke heart. Return artichokes to liquid until ready to use. Cut each artichoke into 4 pieces.

Preheat oven to 400°F. In a skillet, heat 1 tablespoon olive oil over medium-high heat, add tomatoes, thyme or oregano, and salt and pepper to taste. Cook, stirring often, about 15 minutes, or until tomatoes are tender and liquid that comes out of them has evaporated. Stir in garlic and simmer 30 seconds. Taste and adjust seasoning.

Put pearl onions in a medium-size saucepan, cover with water, and bring to a boil. Cook 1 minute. Rinse under cold water and drain well. Peel, return to saucepan, and add water to cover and a pinch of salt. Bring to a boil and simmer over medium heat about 10 to 15 minutes, or until tender when pierced with a knife. Drain thoroughly.

Transfer artichokes and onions to a baking dish. Spoon tomato mixture over them. (Vegetables can be kept, covered, up to 1 day in refrigerator.)

Sprinkle top with bread crumbs, then with remaining tablespoon olive oil. Bake about 10 minutes, or until bubbling. Brown under broiler about 1 minute.

ᶂᶘ BAKED ONIONS WITH DILL BUTTER
Oignons au four, beurre d'aneth

Onions should be baked until they are meltingly tender inside. Baked onions are also good simply served with butter, salt, and pepper.   MAKES 4 SERVINGS

4 medium-size onions, with skins
    intact (about 2 pounds)
About 1 cup water
6 tablespoons unsalted butter, room
    temperature, cut in pieces

3 tablespoons snipped dill
Salt and freshly ground pepper

Preheat oven to 400°F. Cut off root end of onions so they can stand up. Prick skins a few times with a fork. Oil a gratin dish or other heavy baking dish just large enough to hold onions. Add ¼ cup water to dish. Put onions in dish and bake, adding more water, about ¼ cup at a time, when dish gets dry, about 1¾ hours, or until tender when squeezed and knife can pierce them easily.

Meanwhile, in small bowl cream butter with a wooden spoon until softened. Stir in dill and add salt and pepper to taste.

To serve, peel onions and cut in half. Spoon some dill butter over each one. Serve remaining dill butter separately.

❧ PROVENÇAL BAKED TOMATOES
Tomates à la provençale

This well-known dish is prepared by a combination of sautéing and baking and, for best flavor, should be made when tomatoes are at the height of their season. It is wonderful with grilled fish or meat and with eggs. The garlic flavor is quite strong; if you would like a more delicate taste, use only two cloves.   MAKES 4 SERVINGS

4 medium-size tomatoes, ripe but not too soft (about 1⅓ to 1½ pounds)
3 medium-size garlic cloves, very finely minced
3 tablespoons chopped fresh parsley
2 tablespoons unseasoned bread crumbs
Salt and freshly ground pepper
5 tablespoons olive oil

Preheat oven to 425°F. Make a shallow cut to remove green top of core of tomatoes, then cut in half horizontally. Squeeze each half gently to remove seeds. Pat dry. Lightly oil a gratin dish or other baking dish in which tomato halves can fit in single layer. In a small bowl, mix garlic, parsley, bread crumbs, and a pinch of salt and pepper.

Heat 3 tablespoons olive oil in a medium-size heavy skillet over medium-high heat. Sprinkle 4 tomato halves lightly with salt and pepper. Put them, cut side down, in hot oil. Be very careful because oil splatters. Cook 3 minutes. Turn over and sauté 1 minute. Transfer carefully with slotted spatula to prepared baking dish and place them cut side up. Repeat with remaining tomato halves.

Spoon garlic mixture over tomatoes and into their cavities. Sprinkle with remaining 2 tablespoons oil. Bake about 15 minutes, or until tender. Serve hot, warm, or at room temperature.

BAKED BEETS WITH LEMON CREAM
Betteraves au four à la crème de citron

Baking beets is one of the best ways to keep in their flavor. In France beets are usually purchased at the market already baked. Vendors pick them up with a fork and wrap them carefully to avoid stains.

MAKES 4 SERVINGS

8 small beets, about 1½ inches in
    diameter

LEMON CREAM

1 tablespoon butter

1 shallot, minced

¼ cup dry white wine

1 cup heavy cream

4 teaspoons grated or finely chopped
    lemon peel

2½ teaspoons strained fresh lemon
    juice

Salt and freshly ground white
    pepper

A few thin strips lemon peel,
    removed with lemon zester, for
    garnish

Preheat oven to 325°F. Rinse beets and trim roots and tops, leaving beets whole and skin intact. Put beets in a gratin dish or other heavy shallow baking dish, cover tightly with foil, and bake 1½ hours, or until beets are tender when pierced with a knife.

LEMON CREAM

In a small saucepan, melt butter over low heat, add shallot, and cook about 2 minutes. Stir in wine and cook until liquid is reduced to about 2 tablespoons. Stir in cream, bring to a boil, and cook, stirring, over medium heat until sauce is thick enough to coat a spoon. Just before serving, add lemon peel and juice and salt and pepper to taste.

To serve, peel beets, spoon Lemon Cream over each, and sprinkle with a little shredded lemon peel.

This dish is also delicious cold. If the chilled sauce is too thick, stir in a few teaspoons cream.

GRILLED PEPPERS WITH GARLIC AND OLIVE OIL
Poivrons grillés à l'ail et à l'huile d'olive

These Provençal peppers are wonderful as a first course with French or Italian bread or as a side dish with grilled chicken.

MAKES 4 SERVINGS

2 medium-size red bell peppers
2 medium-size green bell peppers
6 tablespoons extra-virgin olive oil
1 to 2 teaspoons strained fresh
 lemon juice

Salt and freshly ground pepper
4 large garlic cloves, cut into
 quarters

Preheat broiler. Broil peppers about 2 inches from heat source until blistered and charred, turning often, for a total of about 15 to 20 minutes. Transfer to plastic bag and close bag. Let stand 10 minutes. Peel, cut into quarters, and remove cores. Drain well in colander. Pat dry.

Put peppers in shallow serving dish. Whisk olive oil with lemon juice and salt and pepper to taste. Sprinkle peppers with olive oil mixture and garlic. Let stand at room temperature, turning occasionally, at least 2 hours; or refrigerate overnight. Remove garlic and serve at room temperature.

GRILLED EGGPLANT WITH FRESH HERBS
Aubergines grillées aux herbes

Eggplant is sometimes salted to remove any bitter juices. If the eggplant is fresh, the salting process can be omitted and the eggplant can be lightly seasoned with salt before grilling. This eggplant dish is best at room temperature. If desired, garnish it with strips of grilled red or green pepper.   MAKES 4 SERVINGS

1 medium-size eggplant (about 1¼ pounds), unpeeled
1½ teaspoons salt
About ¼ cup extra-virgin olive oil, for brushing
2 medium-size garlic cloves, finely minced

2 tablespoons minced fresh parsley
2 tablespoons coarsely chopped basil
6 tablespoons extra-virgin olive oil, for sprinkling
Freshly ground pepper
Fresh basil leaves, for garnish (optional)

Cut eggplant in ⅜-inch slices crosswise, discarding ends. Arrange slices in one layer on a rack set over a tray. Sprinkle them evenly with about ¾ teaspoon salt, turn them over, and sprinkle second side evenly with remaining salt. Let slices drain for 1 hour, turning them over after 30 minutes. Pat them dry very thoroughly with several changes of paper towels.

Preheat broiler with rack about 2 inches from heat source, or prepare grill. Brush oil on both sides of 6 eggplant slices or enough to make one layer in broiler or grill. Broil or grill for 3 minutes on each side, lightly oiling top after turning, or until eggplant is tender when pierced with a fork.

To use a ridged stove-top grill pan instead, lightly oil one side of eggplant slices and put them, oiled side down, in one layer on preheated grill pan over moderately high heat. Grill them for 3 minutes on each side until tender, lightly oiling top of each slice before turning it.

Combine garlic, parsley, and basil in a small bowl or cup. Transfer eggplant slices to a shallow dish, such as a round 8½-inch gratin dish, 1½ to 2 inches deep, so that eggplant makes three layers. Sprinkle each layer of eggplant evenly with about one-third of herb mixture, about 2 tablespoons oil, and with freshly ground pepper to taste. Cover slices and refrigerate at least 4 hours or overnight, turning them over once. (The slices can be kept up to 2 days in refrigerator.)

Serve eggplant at room temperature, garnish it with basil leaves, and accompany it with fresh bread.

GRILLED MUSHROOMS WITH GARLIC PURÉE
Champignons grillés à la purée d'ail

Mushrooms serve as cups for the flavorful garlic purée, a must for garlic lovers. They are perfect with broiled lamb chops or lamb steaks, but are also superb with beef steaks and even broiled fish. For a vegetable feast, they can be served with an assortment of stuffed vegetables.   MAKES 4 SERVINGS

2 medium-size whole heads garlic	*8 to 12 large mushroom caps*
1 tablespoon butter	*2 teaspoons vegetable oil*
Salt and freshly ground pepper	*2 teaspoons minced fresh parsley*
4 to 5 tablespoons heavy cream	

Separate garlic heads into cloves and peel them. Put them in a small heavy saucepan of cold water, bring to a boil, and cook for 5 minutes. Drain thoroughly.

In a medium-size heavy saucepan, heat butter over very low heat, add garlic and salt and pepper to taste, and cook, stirring often, about 20 minutes, or until nearly all moisture evaporates. Be careful not to let garlic burn.

Purée garlic in a food processor or blender, adding a little cream if necessary; or mash it with a fork. Return it to saucepan. (Garlic purée can be kept, covered, 1 day in refrigerator.)

Preheat broiler or prepare grill. Brush mushroom caps with oil and broil or grill, turning often, about 7 minutes, or until just tender. Sprinkle lightly with salt and pepper.

Just before serving, reheat garlic purée over low heat, stirring. Gradually stir in 3 or 4 tablespoons heavy cream to taste, and heat just until hot. Season to taste with salt and pepper. Spoon a little purée into each mushroom. Sprinkle each with a small pinch of parsley. Serve hot. Serve any remaining garlic purée separately.

Sautéed and Fried Vegetables

Both sautéing and frying are excellent for cooking vegetables because the hot oil or butter gives them a delicious, rich taste that cannot be achieved by any other cooking method.

Sautéing is one of the simplest cooking techniques and enables the cook to have many vegetables ready in a few minutes. Only a small amount of fat is required, especially if a heavy, good-quality pan is used.

Almost any vegetable can be sautéed. Those that are naturally tender, such as peppers, celery, mushrooms, and zucchini, can simply be cut in small pieces and sautéed. Others, such as green beans and carrots, are usually precooked in water so that they soften first. Colorful combinations of vegetables can also be sautéed, as in Medley of Vegetables with Fresh Thyme. Sautéing is an ideal method for heating leftover cooked vegetables and rice, because they heat quickly and do not dry out.

French cooks generally sauté vegetables in butter, oil, or a mixture of both. Olive oil is used to give them a Mediterranean flavor.

For sautéing or frying, the vegetables should be dry to prevent steam from forming when they are added to the oil. This is first and foremost a matter of safety for the cook, to prevent the hot fat from splattering in contact with moisture. But in addition, steam created by this moisture would prevent the food from being sealed by the hot oil and would diminish its flavor. To help ensure a dry surface on the vegetables, cooks often dip them in flour or in a coating, as in Batter-Fried Vegetables with Rémoulade Sauce.

Deep-fried vegetables can be light and not greasy if a few simple rules are followed. Pure, clean oil is crucial for crisp, good-tasting fried foods. Plain vegetable oil of a neutral flavor, such as corn, peanut, or soybean oil, can be used, as can shortening. The fat can be saved and used again once or twice, but it should be carefully strained after use and kept in a cool place. If it smokes during cooking, however, it should not be reused.

A deep-fryer or a deep heavy saucepan is needed for deep-frying. The pan should be large enough so that it can hold an adequate amount of oil to cover the food generously but at the same time should not be more than half full of oil. It should be very stable so that there is no danger of it tipping over. A slotted spoon or wire skimmer is best for removing the food from the pan. To maintain the fat at the correct temperature, a frying thermometer is most efficient. If the fat is too hot, the food may burn before it is cooked inside. On the other hand, if it is not hot enough, the food will absorb too much oil.

Hints

• When sautéing several batches of food, add more oil or butter to the pan between batches, if necessary, so the pan remains coated. Heat the oil before continuing. Sautéed vegetables can be reheated, although they will be less crisp.

• Give your full attention to deep-frying; do not leave in the middle to do something else.

• Do not fill the pan more than half full of oil or fat.

• If vegetables are to be coated before deep-frying, they must be completely covered with the coating material so that no moist surfaces are exposed to the hot fat.

• Be extremely careful not to let any water or vegetable juice get into the oil because it will splatter violently.

• Hold the vegetables near the surface of the oil and slide them in gently. Do not drop them in because they will splash hot oil.

• Do not crowd the pan with food because the oil can bubble up to the top and even overflow. Besides, too much food lowers the temperature of the oil.

• Regulate the heat to keep the oil at the required temperature.

• Do not move the deep-fryer when the fat in it is hot.

• To remove excess fat, drain fried foods on paper towels before serving and pat their top surfaces with paper towels.

🌿 MEDLEY OF VEGETABLES WITH FRESH THYME
Meli-melo de légumes au thym frais

Serve this colorful dish of sautéed vegetables alone as a side dish
or on a bed of rice as a main dish. The vegetables are finished with
a "persillade," or mixture of sautéed garlic and parsley, a favorite
French seasoning.   MAKES 4 SERVINGS

*2 medium-size leeks (about 1
    pound)*
1 medium-size red bell pepper
2 medium-size celery stalks
*2 small zucchini (about 6 to 8
    ounces)*
*1 medium-size eggplant (about 1
    pound)*

9 tablespoons olive oil
Salt and freshly ground pepper
*2 tablespoons minced fresh thyme,
    or 2 teaspoons dried thyme,
    crumbled*
5 medium-size garlic cloves, minced
2 tablespoons minced fresh parsley

Use white and light green parts of leeks only. Cut leeks in half
lengthwise and soak in cold water 15 minutes. Check between layers
to be sure no sand remains and rinse thoroughly. Cut in 2-inch pieces,
press with hand to flatten, and cut in ¼-inch lengthwise slices; separate
slices into strips if they remain joined at root end.

Cut pepper in half lengthwise, core, and remove ribs. Cut again
crosswise and then cut each quarter into strips ¼ inch wide. Peel
celery to remove strings. Cut into 2-by-¼-by-¼-inch strips. Cut each
zucchini in 3 pieces crosswise, then in lengthwise strips about ¼ inch
wide and ¼ inch thick. Cut peel from eggplant and discard ends. Cut
eggplant in 2-by-½-by-¼-inch strips.

In large skillet, heat 3 tablespoons olive oil over medium heat,
add eggplant, and sprinkle with salt. Sauté, tossing constantly, about
7 minutes, or until just tender. Transfer to bowl.

Heat 4 tablespoons olive oil in large skillet over medium-low
heat. Add leeks and cook, stirring often, 5 minutes. Add red pepper,
celery, salt and pepper, and thyme, and cook, tossing often, about 5
minutes, or until all vegetables are nearly tender. Add zucchini and
eggplant and cook, tossing often, about 3 minutes, or until zucchini
is crisp-tender. Remove vegetables to serving dish and keep warm.

Wipe skillet clean. Add remaining 2 tablespoons olive oil and heat over low heat. Add garlic and cook about 30 seconds, or until barely tender but not brown. Add parsley and heat 2 or 3 seconds. Pour mixture over vegetables, toss thoroughly, taste and adjust seasoning. Serve immediately.

❧ GREEN BEANS WITH SAUTÉED WALNUTS
Haricots verts aux noix

Sautéed nuts are a quick, easy, and wonderful way to add zip to vegetables. In this dish almonds can be substituted for the walnuts.

MAKES 4 TO 6 SERVINGS

1 ½ pounds green beans, ends removed, broken in half *2 tablespoons butter*	*⅓ cup walnut pieces* *Salt and freshly ground pepper*

In a large saucepan of boiling salted water, cook beans, uncovered, over high heat about 5 minutes or until just tender but still crisp. Drain and rinse under cold water until cool and drain well.

In a large skillet, melt 1 tablespoon butter over medium-low heat, add nuts, and a pinch of salt, and sauté about 2 or 3 minutes, or until lightly browned. Remove with slotted spoon.

Raise heat to medium-high and add remaining butter to skillet and melt. Add beans, and salt and pepper, and sauté until tender and hot; do not let them brown. Transfer to a serving dish and sprinkle with walnuts.

❧ CARROTS WITH RASPBERRY VINEGAR
Carottes au vinaigre de framboises

Carrots are precooked before being sautéed so they will be uniformly tender. Serve these fruit-scented carrots with poultry or lamb. Raspberry vinegar also makes a tasty vinaigrette for carrot salad.

MAKES 2 SERVINGS

½ pound long, slender carrots,
*   peeled*
2 tablespoons unsalted butter
Salt and freshly ground pepper

2 tablespoons raspberry vinegar
1 tablespoon chopped fresh parsley
*   (optional)*

Cut carrots in eighths lengthwise, then in 3-inch pieces. In a medium saucepan of boiling salted water, cook carrots 4 minutes. Drain thoroughly.

In a large skillet, melt butter over medium-low heat, add carrots and salt and pepper to taste, and sauté, stirring often, about 4 minutes, or until tender.

In a very small saucepan, heat vinegar to a simmer. Pour over carrots in skillet. Boil, tossing, until carrots are coated with vinegar. Taste and adjust seasoning. Transfer to a serving dish, sprinkle with parsley, if desired, and serve.

SAUTÉED JERUSALEM ARTICHOKES
Topinambours sautés

Sautéing is an excellent technique for cooking Jerusalem artichokes (sunchokes) because it preserves their crispness. These Jerusalem artichokes make a pleasant accompaniment for roast chicken or broiled meat. For uniform cooking, choose Jerusalem artichokes of even size and as smooth as possible.   MAKES 3 TO 4 SERVINGS

1 tablespoon fresh lemon juice or
*   white wine vinegar*
1 pound Jerusalem artichokes

3 tablespoons unsalted butter
Salt and freshly ground pepper

Add lemon juice or vinegar to a bowl of 1 quart water. Peel Jerusalem artichokes and put each into the bowl of acidulated water. Cut large ones into approximately 1-inch chunks, leaving whole those that are 1 inch in diameter or smaller. Return them to acidulated water until ready to cook. Rinse, drain in a colander, and pat them dry with paper towels.

In a medium-size heavy sauté pan, melt butter over medium heat. Add Jerusalem artichokes and a pinch of salt and pepper. Sauté about

3 minutes, tossing them with a slotted spatula. Reduce heat to low, cover, and cook, shaking pan often and turning them over occasionally, about 15 minutes, or until largest pieces are just tender when pierced with a thin-bladed knife. Serve immediately.

⚜ RED AND GREEN CABBAGE SAUTÉ WITH GOAT CHEESE
Sauté de chou rouge et vert au fromage de chèvre

Greek feta cheese or Roquefort can be used instead of the goat cheese in this colorful dish. MAKES 4 SERVINGS

¾ pound green cabbage (½ small head), cored
1 pound red cabbage (½ medium-size head), cored
6 tablespoons vegetable oil

Salt and freshly ground pepper
2 tablespoons capers, drained well
3 tablespoons mild white wine vinegar (5 percent acidity)
⅔ cup coarsely crumbled goat cheese

Shred each type of cabbage separately; a food processor fitted with shredding disk makes this easy. You will have about 4 cups shredded green cabbage and about 5 cups shredded red cabbage.

Heat 3 tablespoons oil in large heavy skillet over medium heat. Add green cabbage and salt and pepper, and sauté, tossing often, about 5 minutes, or until barely tender. Remove from heat. Add capers, taste and adjust seasoning. Cover and keep warm.

Meanwhile, heat 3 tablespoons oil in second large heavy skillet over medium heat. Add red cabbage and sauté, tossing often, about 5 minutes, or until barely tender. Remove from heat. Bring vinegar to boil in very small saucepan and pour it over sautéed red cabbage; color will change dramatically. Toss well. Add ⅓ cup cheese, pepper, and toss again. Taste and adjust seasoning.

Arrange green cabbage in a ring along outer edge of platter. Spoon red cabbage mixture into center. Make hollow in center of red cabbage and spoon in remaining ⅓ cup cheese. Serve hot or warm. When serving, spoon some of each mixture separately onto plates.

🌿 SAUTÉED CUCUMBERS WITH DILL
Concombres sautés à l'aneth

Cucumbers are used in France not only for salads, but also as a lightly cooked hot vegetable. These are perfect with broiled or sautéed fish.

MAKES 4 SERVINGS

1 large cucumber	*2 tablespoons minced fresh dill*
2 to 3 tablespoons butter	*Salt and freshly ground pepper*

Cut cucumber in half lengthwise and remove seeds. Cut in thin slices.

In a skillet, melt butter over medium heat, add cucumber slices and sauté, stirring often, about 2 minutes, or until just tender. Do not overcook or they will be mushy. Remove from heat and stir in dill. Season to taste with salt and pepper. Serve immediately.

🌿 GARLIC-SCENTED ZUCCHINI WITH CELERY
Courgettes et celeris à l'ail

Zucchini and celery cook very quickly and are ideal for sautéing. Serve this dish with entrées such as sautéed seafood, roast chicken, or grilled meats. For a vegetable dish with a more exotic character, substitute cilantro (fresh coriander) for the parsley.

MAKES 4 SERVINGS

4 small zucchini (about 1 pound)	*Salt and freshly ground pepper*
3 celery stalks, peeled	*1 large garlic clove, very finely*
1 tablespoon vegetable oil	*minced*
2 tablespoons butter or olive oil	*2 tablespoons chopped fresh parsley*

Cut zucchini in 1½-inch chunks. Cut each chunk in lengthwise slices about ¼ inch thick and each slice in sticks about ¼ inch wide. Cut peeled celery in very thin strips, about 1½ inches long and a bit thinner than the zucchini sticks.

In a large skillet, heat oil and butter over medium-high heat, add celery, and sauté about 2 minutes. Add zucchini sticks and pinch of salt and pepper and sauté, tossing often, about 2 minutes, or until nearly tender.

Reduce heat to medium, add garlic and parsley, and sauté for 1 minute. Taste and adjust seasoning. Serve immediately.

SAUTÉED SALSIFY WITH FRESH HERBS
Salsifis sautés aux fines herbes

Salsify, or oyster plant, is popular in France because of its delicate flavor, which slightly resembles that of asparagus. This long root vegetable is not easy to find in American markets but it is worth tasting if you happen to see it. Sautéing with herbs is a favorite way of preparing salsify in France, but it is also made into gratins and beignets.   MAKES 4 SERVINGS

1¼ pounds salsify	*1 tablespoon minced fresh parsley*
3 tablespoons white vinegar	*2 teaspoons chopped fresh tarragon*
3 to 4 tablespoons butter	*1 teaspoon snipped chives*
Salt and freshly ground pepper	

Rinse salsify. Prepare a bowl of cold water and add 2 tablespoons white vinegar. Put a salsify on a cutting board. Holding one end, peel it thoroughly and immediately put it in the bowl of acidulated water to prevent it from discoloring. Continue with remaining salsify.

Bring a large saucepan of water to a boil, add salt and 1 tablespoon vinegar. Cut salsify in 2- or 3-inch pieces and add to water. Cook over high heat about 10 minutes, or until tender when pierced with a knife. Drain thoroughly.

In a large skillet, melt butter over medium heat, add salsify, and sauté, tossing or turning often, until is very lightly browned. Sprinkle it with salt and pepper and add parsley, tarragon, and chives. Toss a few seconds and remove from heat. Taste and adjust seasoning and serve hot.

SPINACH, LEEK, AND PUMPKIN PANCAKES
Petites crêpes de légumes

The three vegetables combine to become colorful pancakes, which make a delicious main course for lunch or brunch or a side dish to accompany roast chicken, veal, or lamb.

MAKES 4 TO 6 SERVINGS, 22 TO 24 SMALL PANCAKES

8- to 10-ounce piece of pumpkin or winter squash, such as banana, Hubbard, or acorn squash

¾ pound fresh spinach (leaves with stems)

2 large leeks (about 1 pound)

5 tablespoons vegetable oil

Salt and freshly ground pepper

½ cup all-purpose flour

2 eggs

¼ teaspoon salt

Freshly grated nutmeg

Cut pumpkin or squash in 2 or 3 pieces. Put in a medium sauce-pan with enough salted water to cover. Bring to a boil, cover, reduce heat to low, and simmer about 15 minutes, or until tender. Drain thoroughly and cut off peel. Cut in pieces and mash with a fork. Press gently in a strainer to remove excess liquid. Transfer to a bowl.

Remove spinach stems and wash leaves thoroughly. In a large pan of boiling salted water, cook spinach, uncovered, over high heat about 3 minutes, or until tender. Rinse under cold water. Squeeze spinach to remove excess liquid. Chop finely and transfer to bowl of squash.

Discard dark green leaves and roots of leeks. Split twice length-wise and dip several times in cold water until no sand remains between layers. Cut in thin slices crosswise. In a large heavy saucepan, heat 1 tablespoon oil over low heat, add leeks, and sprinkle with salt and pepper. Cover and cook, stirring occasionally, for 5 minutes, or until tender. Transfer to bowl of vegetables.

In a medium-size bowl, mix flour, eggs, ¼ teaspoon salt, and pepper and nutmeg to taste to make a very thick batter. Add batter to bowl of vegetables and mix very well. Taste and adjust seasoning.

Preheat oven to 250°F. In a heavy skillet, heat remaining 4 table-spoons oil over medium heat until hot. Fry vegetable mixture by tablespoonfuls, flattening each after adding it, about 2 minutes, or until golden brown on each side. Turn very carefully using two pancake turners. Transfer to paper towels on an ovenproof tray. Keep warm in oven while frying rest of pancakes.

The pancakes are best if served immediately, but they can be kept warm about 30 minutes. (They can be kept 1 day in refrigerator; reheat in 1 layer on paper towels on a baking sheet in a 250°F. oven.)

❧ BATTER-FRIED VEGETABLES WITH RÉMOULADE SAUCE
Fritots de légumes, sauce rémoulade

A variety of vegetables can be dipped in this white wine batter and fried. The cauliflower and Jerusalem artichokes are partially precooked so they will not require much time in the hot oil.

MAKES 4 TO 6 SERVINGS

RÉMOULADE SAUCE

1 cup Mayonnaise (see recipe)	2 tablespoons chopped fresh parsley
1 tablespoon Dijon mustard or herb mustard	2 teaspoons chopped fresh tarragon
	1 hard-boiled egg, chopped

1 cup all-purpose flour	¾ cup dry white wine
2 large egg yolks	2 large egg whites, room temperature
½ teaspoon salt	
Pinch of cayenne pepper	Pinch of cream of tartar
1 tablespoon olive oil	

½ pound Jerusalem artichokes, scrubbed but not peeled	1 teaspoon strained fresh lemon juice (optional)
1 small cauliflower, divided into medium-size florets	½ teaspoon anchovy paste (optional)
1 tablespoon capers, drained, rinsed, and chopped	2 medium-size zucchini, cut in ¼-inch slices
1 tablespoon chopped pickle	Salt and freshly ground pepper

Vegetable oil or vegetable shortening for deep-frying (about 6 cups)	Fresh parsley sprigs, for garnish

RÉMOULADE SAUCE

Mix mayonnaise and mustard in a bowl until thoroughly blended. Stir in parsley, tarragon, egg, capers, and pickle. Taste, and add lemon juice, anchovy paste, and salt and pepper, if needed. (Sauce can be kept, covered, up to 2 days in refrigerator.)

Review the hints on deep-frying on page 207.

Sift flour into a medium-size bowl and make a well in center. Into well put egg yolks, salt, cayenne pepper, olive oil, and wine. Using a whisk, stir ingredients together in well and gradually stir in flour until mixture is smooth; do not beat it. Cover and chill for 1 hour.

In a medium-size saucepan, boil 1 quart water and add salt. Add whole Jerusalem artichokes, cover, and cook about 10 minutes, or until they are barely tender. Drain them in a colander and pat them dry. Using a paring knife, scrape off peel. (To save time, they may be left unpeeled.) Using a thin-bladed knife, carefully cut them in ¼-inch-wide slices. Use only unbroken slices.

In a large saucepan of boiling salted water to generously cover, cook cauliflower, uncovered, over high heat about 5 minutes, or until barely tender. Rinse and drain thoroughly.

Bring Rémoulade Sauce to room temperature.

Just before frying, beat egg whites with cream of tartar until they hold fairly stiff peaks. Fold them into batter.

In a deep fryer or a medium-size, deep heavy saucepan, heat oil or vegetable shortening to 375°F. Do not fill pan more than half full of fat. Heat oven to 200°F.

Dip pieces of vegetable in batter, a few at a time, coating them completely and shaking them gently so excess drips off. Carefully lower each coated slice into pan, using your fingertips, tongs, or a fork, and being careful not to splash hot fat and not to get your fingers too close to it. Handle coated food as little as possible. Fry pieces in batches, without crowding, for 2 minutes, or until golden on all sides, turning them over with a slotted skimmer. As they are done, transfer to paper towels to drain, keeping them in a single layer. Keep them warm in oven while frying remaining pieces.

Sprinkle fried vegetables with salt. Transfer to a heated platter lined with a napkin, garnish with parsley sprigs, and serve immediately. Serve sauce separately.

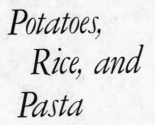

Potatoes, Rice, and Pasta

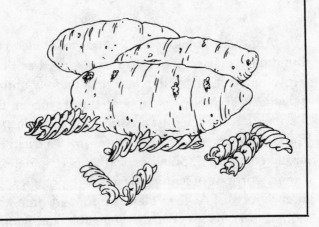

Because of their neutral flavor, potatoes, rice, and pasta are perfect accompaniments for most foods and are so versatile they can be seasoned with almost any flavoring. Although it is difficult to imagine French menus without them, all were once imports to France, potatoes originally coming from the Americas, rice from the Orient, and pasta from Italy.

A French chef, planning a menu around shellfish in a savory sauce, will frequently choose plainly cooked potatoes, rice pilaf, or pasta as a side dish to go with his creation, so their delicate flavor will harmonize with that of the sauce.

This does not mean that potatoes, rice, and pasta are good only with sauced food. They go well with grilled or roast chicken or meat and fried, sautéed, or grilled fish.

The French match a very wide range of ingredients with potatoes, rice, and pasta, including fresh herbs; some spices, especially nutmeg, saffron, and curry; and a great variety of cheeses and nuts. Cooked vegetables, such as peas, diced carrots, zucchini strips, diced artichoke hearts, broccoli florets, peeled red and green peppers, and sautéed sliced or quartered mushrooms enhance rice and pasta dishes by adding freshness and color.

Potatoes

Although potatoes are central to French cooking, up until two hundred years ago they were hardly used at all. French food writers are often baffled by the fact that their countrymen refused to eat potatoes when they first appeared in France in the sixteenth century. Parmentier, the scientist credited with popularizing the potato late in the eighteenth century, had to resort to a trick: He positioned guards around his field of potatoes, so that people realized that he had something worth protecting. Gradually, potatoes began to appear on French menus. As if to make up for lost time, the French developed hundreds of recipes for the vegetable and named many of them for Parmentier to show their gratitude.

Potatoes can be prepared by almost every vegetable cooking technique and can be made into creamy gratins, crisp sautés, and even elegant soufflés. Their natural properties make it possible for them to hold together in dishes such as Baked Potato Cakes.

One of the most popular basic dishes for preparing potatoes is as purée. Although the procedure is simple, the cooking and seasoning should be done carefully. In fact, the owner of the famous La Tour d'Argent restaurant in Paris tested prospective chefs by asking them to prepare potato purée. Some French gastronomes say you can judge the quality of a restaurant by tasting its potato purée.

Potato purée is a versatile basic recipe that can be turned into many more elaborate dishes. Adding choux pastry and frying yields Potatoes Dauphine, those puffy, delicate fritters with a light, crisp coating. Sprinkling potato purée with grated cheese and browning it in the oven produces a crusty gratin. Enriching potato purée with egg yolks and folding in egg whites gives an elegant soufflé. A delicious purée can also be made from baked potatoes and is used as a base for several dishes, such as Potato and Leek Pancakes.

POTATOES WITH VEGETABLE JULIENNE SAUCE
Pommes de terre à la julienne de légumes

The colorful sauce of carrots, leeks, and mushrooms turns simple boiled potatoes into a festive dish.　　　MAKES 4 TO 6 SERVINGS

1 small or ½ large leek
1 carrot, peeled
½ small celery stalk
6 very white large mushroom caps
¼ cup dry white wine
1 tablespoon white wine vinegar
1 tablespoon minced shallots

Salt and freshly ground white
*　pepper*
1 cup heavy cream
2 pounds red-skinned potatoes of
*　uniform size*
2 teaspoons chopped fresh parsley
*　(optional)*

Trim and discard root and top of leek, leaving white part and about 2 inches of deep green. Using sharp knife, slit leek lengthwise, starting from center and cutting toward green end (leave small section in center uncut to keep leek in one piece). Rinse leek in cold water, separating pieces to remove all dirt.

Cut leek, carrot, and celery into thin julienne about 1½ inches long. Slice mushroom caps crosswise into rounds. Cut rounds into thin strips.

Combine wine, vinegar, and shallots in a medium-size heavy saucepan and bring to a simmer over medium heat. Simmer until reduced to about 2 tablespoons, stirring occasionally to prevent burning. Add mushroom julienne and pinch of salt and pepper, and bring to a boil. Stir in cream, reduce heat to medium, and simmer, stirring occasionally, about 6 minutes, or until mushrooms are tender and sauce is thick enough to coat back of a spoon lightly. Remove sauce from heat and set aside.

Fill large saucepan with water and bring to boil. Add carrot, leek, and celery and boil 3 minutes. Drain well. (Sauce and vegetable julienne can be prepared several hours ahead and kept in separate containers in refrigerator.)

Scrub and peel potatoes. Cut in halves or quarters. Put potatoes in large saucepan, cover with water by about ½ inch, and add some salt. Bring to boil, cover, reduce heat to low, and simmer about 18 minutes, or until knife pierces center of largest potato easily and potato falls from knife when lifted. Do not overcook or potatoes will fall apart. Drain thoroughly.

Just before serving, reheat sauce, stir in vegetable julienne, and bring to simmer. Remove from heat. Taste and adjust seasoning.

Pour sauce over potatoes, sprinkle with parsley, and serve.

NOTE: Potatoes can be peeled a few hours ahead and kept in a bowl of cold water to prevent discoloring.

POTATO AND CHEESE GÂTEAU
Pommes de terre voisin

Parmesan cheese adds a lively flavor to this classic variation of potatoes Anna. Instead of being prepared the traditional way in a skillet and turned out, this version is baked in a springform pan and browned in the broiler and thus is easier to make. The starchiness of the potatoes holds them together in an attractive cake.

MAKES 4 SERVINGS

½ cup unsalted butter
2 pounds baking potatoes
Salt and freshly ground pepper

1⅓ cups plus 1 tablespoon freshly grated Parmesan cheese (about 6 ounces)

Line base and sides of an 8-inch springform pan with 2 layers of foil, each time using a single piece. Set on baking sheet. Spread 2 tablespoons butter on base and sides of lined pan. Cut remaining butter in about 15 slices and cut each piece in half.

Position rack in lower third of oven and preheat to 400°F. Peel potatoes and cut crosswise in ⅛-inch-thick round slices in food processor, with mandoline, or with knife.

Beginning at the center of bottom of pan, arrange 1 layer of potato slices so they overlap and form a spiral. (The pattern will show on finished dish.) Sprinkle with salt and pepper. Arrange a second layer of potatoes without forming a pattern. Sprinkle with ⅓ cup cheese and a little pepper. Scatter 6 butter pieces on top. Continue making layers of potatoes, cheese, and butter in same manner as the second layer, reserving 1 tablespoon cheese.

Set springform on baking sheet and bake in lower third of oven for 30 minutes, pressing twice on cake with pancake turner to make it compact. Cover with foil and continue baking another 40 minutes, or until potatoes are very tender when pierced with a paring knife or skewer. (Potato cake can be baked several hours ahead and kept at cool room temperature). Before serving, reheat in low oven, if necessary.

Cool 10 minutes. Turn over onto a platter. Release spring and remove pan. Remove first layer foil. To remove inner layer, peel off top and very carefully peel off sides, using paring knife to free any potatoes that are stuck.

Sprinkle 1 tablespoon cheese on top. Broil until lightly brown. Serve immediately.

STEAMED NEW POTATOES WITH TARRAGON BUTTER
Pommes de terre nouvelles, beurre d'estragon

Steamed potatoes or "pommes vapeur" have long been a favorite in France, especially as a partner for fish.   MAKES 4 SERVINGS

5 tablespoons butter, softened	Salt and freshly ground pepper
4 teaspoons chopped fresh tarragon leaves	1½ pounds new potatoes

Beat butter in medium-size bowl until very smooth. Stir in tarragon. Season to taste with salt and pepper. Let butter stand at room temperature.

Remove eyes from potatoes, scrub well, and peel.

Bring at least 1 inch of water to a boil in base of steamer. Boiling water should not reach holes in top part of steamer.

Set potatoes in steamer and sprinkle with salt. Cover tightly and steam over high heat about 20 minutes, or until very tender when pierced with a sharp knife but not falling apart. Remove potatoes, drain briefly on paper towels, and transfer to a serving bowl.

Add tarragon butter in spoonfuls and toss lightly with potatoes. Serve immediately.

LIGHT POTATO FRITTERS WITH PINE NUTS
Pommes dauphine aux pignons

Various versions of these fritters are served at elegant meals, especially as an accompaniment for roasted or braised meat or poultry. They are made of potato purée and choux pastry and puff slightly when deep-fried because of the eggs in the pastry. Their delicately crisp crust and creamy interior make them one of France's best-loved potato dishes.   MAKES 6 TO 8 SERVINGS

POTATO PURÉE

1½ pounds boiling potatoes   *Salt and white pepper*
⅓ cup milk   *Freshly grated nutmeg*
2 tablespoons butter

2 teaspoons butter   *⅓ cup pine nuts*

CHOUX PASTRY

½ cup plus 1 tablespoon   *¼ teaspoon salt*
   all-purpose flour   *¼ cup unsalted butter*
½ cup water   *2 eggs*

Vegetable oil for deep-frying (at least 6 cups)

Read the hints on deep-frying (page 207) before beginning.

POTATO PURÉE

Peel potatoes and cut each in 2 or 3 pieces. Put in a nonaluminum saucepan and add enough water to just cover and a pinch of salt. Cover, bring to a boil, and simmer over medium heat 20 to 25 minutes, or until potatoes are very tender. Drain thoroughly. Purée potatoes in a food mill and return to saucepan. Add milk and butter and season with salt, white pepper, and nutmeg to taste. Over low heat, stir vigorously with a wooden spoon until milk and butter are absorbed. Remove from heat, and let cool.

In a small skillet, melt 2 teaspoons butter over low heat, add pine nuts and a pinch of salt, and sauté about 2 minutes, or until lightly toasted. Set aside.

CHOUX PASTRY

Sift flour onto a piece of wax paper. Heat water, salt, and butter in a medium-size saucepan until butter melts. Raise heat to medium-high and bring to a boil. Remove from heat, add flour immediately, and stir quickly with a wooden spoon until mixture is smooth. Set pan over low heat and beat mixture for about 30 seconds. Remove and let cool for a few minutes. Add 1 egg and beat it thoroughly into mixture. Beat in second egg.

Add potatoe purée to choux pastry, stir in pine nuts, and taste for seasoning.

Preheat oven to 300°F. Heat oil in a deep-fryer or deep heavy saucepan to about 370°F. on a frying thermometer. Do not fill pan more than halfway with oil. If a thermometer is not available, test by putting a drop of potato mixture into oil; when oil is hot enough, it should bubble energetically.

Take a rounded teaspoonful of batter and use a second teaspoon to slide it gently into oil, forming a rounded fritter. Do not crowd pan because fritters need room to puff. While frying, turn them over occasionally, until they are golden brown on all sides. Remove to ovenproof trays lined with paper towels. Keep in oven with door slightly open while frying remaining fritters. Serve as soon as possible.

POTATO GRATIN WITH CREAM
Gratin dauphinois

In France people say that the potato was created in order to be made into this dish. Numerous French restaurants feature it as a side dish and many chefs count this as their favorite potato specialty. In addition to its wonderful taste, *gratin dauphinois* has the advantage of being one of the few potato dishes that is good made ahead and reheated. As in the variation, the potatoes can also be baked with wild mushrooms.   MAKES 4 SERVINGS

1½ pounds baking potatoes
Salt and white pepper
Freshly grated nutmeg
2½ cups milk
1 garlic clove, halved

1½ cups heavy cream or Crème
*   Fraîche (see recipe)*
4 to 6 tablespoons grated Gruyère
*   or Swiss cheese*

Peel potatoes and cut them in slices about ⅛ inch thick, using a food processor, mandoline cutter, or sharp knife. Season with salt, white pepper, and nutmeg, and toss to distribute seasonings.

Bring milk to a boil in a medium-size heavy saucepan, stirring occasionally. Add potatoes, reduce heat to medium, and simmer, uncovered, for 10 minutes, stirring occasionally. Drain potatoes; milk can be reserved for soup.

Rub a 4- to 5-cup gratin dish or other shallow baking dish with garlic; then butter dish. Preheat oven to 425°F.

Return potatoes to saucepan and add cream. Bring to a simmer over medium-high heat. Reduce heat to medium and simmer, stirring occasionally, about 15 minutes, or until potatoes are tender but not falling apart. Taste and add more salt, white pepper, and nutmeg if needed. Spoon potatoes and cream into baking dish. Sprinkle with cheese. (The gratin can be prepared 4 days ahead up to this point, covered, and refrigerated.)

Bake 15 to 20 minutes, or until hot and golden brown. If top is not golden brown, broil briefly to brown. Serve hot, from dish.

POTATO GRATIN WITH CÈPES

Soak 1 ounce dried cèpes or *porcini* mushrooms in hot water to cover about 20 minutes, or until tender. Lift into strainer, rinse, and drain well. Cut cèpes into ¼-inch pieces. Add to potatoes in saucepan after they have cooked 10 minutes in cream.

POTATO SOUFFLÉ IN POTATO SKINS
Pommes de terre en robe de chambre soufflées

In this easy-to-make soufflé, an elegant version of stuffed baked potatoes, the potato pulp is made into a soufflé and baked right in the skins. Freshly grated nutmeg is the favorite spice for creamy potato dishes like this and should be used liberally.   MAKES 4 SERVINGS

4 large baking potatoes (2 to 2½
    pounds)
2 tablespoons unsalted butter
2 tablespoons cream cheese
2 tablespoons heavy cream

4 eggs, separated, room temperature
Salt and freshly ground pepper
Freshly grated nutmeg
1 cup grated Gruyère cheese

Preheat oven to 425°F. Scrub potatoes but do not peel. Bake them about 50 minutes, or until tender. Leave oven on. Cut a thin slice from top of each potato. Using a teaspoon, carefully remove most of pulp, leaving only a small amount attached to potato skin so it won't fall apart.

Purée potato pulp in a food mill or mash with a potato masher and put it in a small saucepan. Gradually add butter, stirring vigorously with a wooden spoon, and remove from heat. Stir in cream cheese and cream. Then stir in egg yolks, one at a time. Add salt, pepper, and nutmeg to taste. Butter a shallow baking dish and set potato skins in it. Butter two small ramekins generously.

Beat egg whites until stiff but not dry. Fold about one-quarter of whites into potato mixture. Return this mixture to remaining whites, add about ¾ cup of grated Gruyère cheese, and fold all together as lightly but as quickly as possible.

Fill potato skins with soufflé mixture. Spoon any remaining mixture into buttered ramekins. Sprinkle remaining grated cheese on top of soufflé mixture. Bake about 15 minutes, or until puffed. Serve immediately.

BAKED POTATO CAKES
Pommes Byron

For best flavor and texture these delicate cakes are made from baked potatoes. The potato cakes are sautéed lightly, and then are baked with a luscious topping of cream and Gruyère cheese.

MAKES 10 CAKES, ABOUT 5 SERVINGS

2 pounds baking potatoes (about 3 large potatoes), scrubbed but not peeled
½ cup heavy cream or Crème Fraîche (see recipe)
Salt and freshly ground white pepper

Freshly grated nutmeg
About ¼ cup all-purpose flour
2 tablespoons vegetable oil
2 tablespoons butter
⅔ cup grated Gruyère cheese

Preheat oven to 425°F. Pierce potatoes with a fork. Bake on rack in preheated oven about 1 hour or until tender.

Cut hot potatoes in half, scoop out pulp, and transfer it to a bowl. Mash it with a fork. Stir in 3 tablespoons cream. Mix well with fork and season to taste with salt, pepper, and nutmeg.

Shape mixture into cakes, using ¼ cup for each and making them approximately ¾ inch thick and 2 inches in diameter. Put on a tray or plate in one layer.

Roll each potato cake in flour and pat so all sides are lightly coated.

In a medium-size heavy skillet, melt oil and butter over medium heat. Add half of potato cakes and sauté lightly on both sides, turning very carefully with two spatulas.

Using spatula, transfer to gratin dish or shallow baking dish of about 9 inches in diameter or any baking dish in which all of potato cakes will fit in one layer. Sauté remaining potato cakes. (Potato cakes can be prepared about 4 hours ahead and kept at room temperature.)

Preheat oven to 450°F. Pour remaining 5 tablespoons cream over cakes and sprinkle with grated cheese.

Bake about 8 minutes or until bubbling. If necessary, place in broiler to brown lightly. Serve immediately.

❧ SAUTÉED POTATOES WITH PEPPERS AND THYME
Pommes sautées aux poivrons et au thym

Although potatoes can be sautéed raw, they are much easier to handle when they are partially cooked first, as in this recipe. These potatoes are a perfect accompaniment for fish, eggs, or meat and can be varied in many ways. Yellow peppers can be substituted for the red or green, or they can be omitted and only the onions added. Oregano or marjoram can replace the thyme.   MAKES 6 SERVINGS

2 pounds boiling potatoes
¼ cup olive or vegetable oil
2 tablespoons butter
3 medium-size onions, halved and
*   thinly sliced*
1 red bell pepper, cored, seeded, and
*   cut in thin strips*
1 green bell pepper, cored, seeded,
*   and cut in thin strips*

Salt and freshly ground pepper
2 teaspoons minced fresh thyme, or
*   ¾ teaspoon dried thyme,*
*   crumbled*
2 tablespoons chopped fresh parsley
*   (optional)*

Put potatoes in a large saucepan, cover with water, and add salt. Cover, bring to a boil, and cook over medium heat 15 to 20 minutes, or until softened but not completely cooked. Drain thoroughly. Peel potatoes and cut in thick slices.

In a large heavy skillet, heat 2 tablespoons oil and the butter over low heat, add onions, and cook 3 minutes. Add peppers, salt, pepper, and thyme, and sauté, stirring, until vegetables are tender. Raise heat to medium and continue sautéing until onions brown very slightly. Remove from skillet.

Add another tablespoon oil to skillet and heat over medium-high heat. Add about half the potatoes and sauté, carefully turning them over occasionally, until browned and tender. Remove from skillet. Add remaining oil and sauté remaining potatoes in same way.

Return all of potatoes and pepper mixture to skillet. Sauté together over medium heat about 2 minutes, tossing carefully. Taste and adjust seasoning, transfer to a serving dish, sprinkle with parsley, and serve.

❧ CREAMY POTATO PURÉE
Pommes purée

When the French speak of "purée" without specifying the vegetable, it is understood that they mean potato. Prepared the French way, potato purée is light, smooth, fluffy, and rich. It is soft, because cooks like to beat in plenty of milk or cream. This exquisite purée is sometimes called potatoes "mousseline," a reference to its creaminess and richness.

Because the starch of mature potatoes is needed to make a good purée, any type of potato can be used, except new potatoes.

Old-fashioned methods are best when it comes to puréeing the potatoes. French chefs prefer to push them through a large drum sieve called a *tamis.* Home cooks often use a hand-operated food mill instead; a potato masher also works well. If none of these is available, the potatoes can be drained very well and crushed with a wooden spoon against the sides of the saucepan in which they were cooked. The texture of the potatoes can become unpleasantly elastic if they are puréed in a blender or food processor.

The neutral taste of potato purée makes it a good partner for most foods, whether delicate or strong-flavored. It is a favorite French accompaniment to all meats, chicken, and sausages.

MAKES 6 SERVINGS

2 pounds white boiling potatoes
Salt and white pepper
¾ cup heavy cream or milk, or a
    mixture of both

¼ cup butter
Freshly grated nutmeg
A few tablespoons milk (optional)

Peel potatoes and cut each in 2 or 3 pieces. Put in a nonaluminum saucepan and add enough water to just cover and a pinch of salt. Cover, bring to a boil, and simmer over medium heat 20 to 25 minutes, or until potatoes are very tender. Drain thoroughly. Purée potatoes and return to saucepan.

In a small saucepan, bring cream, milk, or mixture of cream and milk to a simmer. Add butter and a little hot cream or milk to potatoes and season with salt, pepper, and nutmeg. Over low heat, stir vigorously with a wooden spoon until purée is light and smooth.

Add remaining cream gradually, still stirring vigorously. The purée should be soft but not soupy; if it is too stiff, beat in a few tablespoons milk. Add more salt, pepper, and nutmeg, if desired. (The purée can be prepared 30 minutes ahead. To keep it hot, pour a few tablespoons cold milk over purée without stirring it in to prevent a skin from forming on surface; set saucepan of purée in a pan of hot water over low heat. Before serving, stir in milk.) Serve hot.

POTATO AND LEEK PANCAKES
Crêpes aux pommes de terre et aux poireaux

Potatoes and leeks are a favorite French pair, not only for soup, but also for these rich pancakes. Originally developed to use up extra baked potatoes, these have gained prestige and are often served in restaurants as a savory side dish with many main courses.

MAKES 4 TO 5 SERVINGS, ABOUT 16 SMALL PANCAKES

1¼ pounds baking potatoes (2 large potatoes), scrubbed but not peeled	1½ teaspoons salt
	Freshly ground pepper
	Freshly grated nutmeg
1 pound large leeks	3 eggs
2 tablespoons unsalted butter	2 tablespoons all-purpose flour
½ cup plus 1 tablespoon milk	⅓ cup vegetable oil

Preheat oven to 425°F. Pierce potatoes with a fork. Bake about 1 hour, or until tender.

Use only white and light green parts of leeks. Cut leeks in half lengthwise, rinse well, and cut in ¼-inch slices. Soak sliced leeks in cold water to cover for 5 minutes to remove any sand. Lift into colander or large strainer, rinse, and drain well.

In medium-size heavy skillet, melt butter over medium heat, add leeks, and cook, stirring very often, about 10 minutes, or until leeks are very soft but not brown. If any liquid remains in pan, cook leeks over medium-high heat, stirring, until it evaporates. Transfer leeks to bowl and cool.

Remove pulp of hot potatoes and purée in a food mill or push through a sieve into a bowl. Stir in milk, salt, pepper, and nutmeg. Let cool. Stir in leeks. Add eggs, one by one, stirring well after each addition, then flour. Taste and adjust seasoning if necessary.

Preheat oven to 250°F. In a large heavy skillet, heat ¼ cup oil over medium heat. Using a large tablespoon, add a spoonful of batter to oil and flatten slightly to make a small pancake of 2 to 2½ inches in diameter. Mixture should spread but pancake does not need to be very thin. If mixture is too thick to spread at all, add a little milk to batter. (The amount of milk to add varies according to the absorbing power of the potatoes.) If pancakes do not hold together, add 1 tablespoon more flour to batter.

Make more pancakes of same size and fry until golden brown on both sides, about 5 minutes, turning carefully with two pancake turners. Transfer to paper towels on an ovenproof tray. Keep warm in oven while frying rest of pancakes.

The pancakes are best if served immediately, but they can be kept warm about 30 minutes. (They can be kept 1 day in refrigerator; reheat in one layer on paper towels on a baking sheet in a 250°F. oven.)

FRENCH FRIED SWEET POTATOES
Patates douces frites

Sweet potatoes can be treated like regular potatoes to produce special, sweet french fries.   MAKES 4 SERVINGS

2 pounds sweet potatoes, peeled   *Salt*
About 2 quarts vegetable oil, for
*   deep-frying*

Read the hints on deep-frying (page 207) before beginning.

If potatoes are over 4 inches long, cut them in half crosswise, then cut in lengthwise slices about ½ inch wide. Cut each slice in strips about ¼ inch wide. Trim irregular edges.

With paper towels, thoroughly pat potatoes dry in small batches. This step is very important because if they are even slightly wet, fat will bubble up violently.

Line trays with two layers of paper towels. Heat oil in a deep-fryer or deep, heavy saucepan to about 350°F. on a frying thermometer. If no thermometer is available, test oil with a piece of potato; oil should foam up around it.

Dip a frying basket or a large skimmer into hot oil to prevent potatoes from sticking. Put about one-third to one-half of potatoes in basket or skimmer and carefully lower into hot oil. Do not overfill because fat bubbles up vigorously when potatoes are added and can be dangerous. Leave basket in oil during frying.

Fry potatoes about 4 to 5 minutes, or until tender and light brown. Check by pressing one; it should crush easily. Use slotted skimmer to remove potatoes to towel-lined trays. Reheat oil before adding next batch.

Sprinkle potatoes with salt and toss gently. Serve immediately.

Rice

In France there are two basic methods for preparing rice. In the first, rice is cooked like pasta, in a large pan of boiling salted water, then drained well. This method is often used for salads and stuffings. The second technique for cooking rice is pilaf.

Rice pilaf is among the best-traveled recipes. It originated in Persia and spread to the Middle East and the Mediterranean area. In France, many classic recipes are called *à la turque* when they are accompanied by pilaf, because Europe probably learned about rice pilaf from the Turks during the Crusades. Pilaf is a favorite formula for preparing rice in France and appears in the finest as well as the simplest restaurants.

Most people think they are familiar with rice pilaf because the name frequently appears on restaurant menus. Unfortunately, the rice that passes for pilaf is a far cry from the buttery, delicate grain dish it should be. There is no excuse for this because rice pilaf is extremely simple to make.

Pilaf has more flavor than boiled or steamed rice due to the preliminary sautéing of the rice with an onion in oil or butter. This sautéing is a key step in preparing pilaf, because the oil or butter coats the grains and helps keep them from sticking. Next the rice is simmered in stock or water over low heat or in the oven. The rice is fluffy and each grain is distinct. It is easy to prepare, reheats well, and can be kept warm, which makes it convenient for both professional and home menu planning.

Vegetables are generally cooked separately and mixed with the cooked rice. This permits each ingredient to cook evenly. Stocks give the richest-tasting rice pilaf, while water yields the whitest rice with the most delicate flavor.

Whether they boil rice or cook it as pilaf, French cooks like to enrich it with a little fresh butter as a final touch. When moistened with vinaigrette instead and accented by the addition of a few fresh vegetables, rice can become a refreshing luncheon salad.

Pilaf is perfect for pairing with grilled foods, roasts, and quick sautés and is the classic partner for brochettes of lamb, beef, or seafood, which are often set on a bed of the rice. It also makes a savory stuffing for poultry and vegetables.

An elegant presentation for rice prepared by either method is molded rice. It can be presented as a ring, with sauced or sautéed food in the center, as in Rice Ring with Curried Eggplant, or as individual cakes formed by unmolding the rice from ramekins.

Hints

• A sauté pan or deep skillet is best for preparing pilaf because the wide surface area makes sautéing easier and encourages even cooking. Use a heavy pan so the rice will not stick to it. Packaged rice is clean and there is no need to rinse it. Rinsing would interfere with the sautéing.

• Use a fork for stirring butter or any other ingredients, such as vegetables, meats, or seafood, into cooked rice. Be sure any additions to the pilaf are in small pieces, and always stir by tossing the rice as lightly as possible to avoid crushing the grains.

RICE WITH PEAS AND BASIL
Riz aux petits pois au basilic

Rice is often cooked like pasta—in a very large pan of boiling salted water, a method that keeps the grains separate and is known in France as Creole rice. At least four times as much water as rice should be used. It is a favorite technique for preparing rice to use in both hot dishes and salads.   MAKES 4 SERVINGS

1 cup long-grain white rice
1 pound fresh peas (about 1 cup shelled), or 1 cup frozen peas
¼ cup butter
2 medium-size garlic cloves, finely chopped

Salt and freshly ground pepper
2 tablespoons chopped fresh basil
Fresh basil leaves, for garnish (optional)

In a large saucepan, bring about 6 cups water to a boil and add a pinch of salt. Add rice, stir once, and cook, uncovered, about 12 to 14 minutes, or until tender; check by tasting. Drain in strainer, rinse with cold water until cool, and let sit for 5 minutes.

In a medium-size saucepan, bring enough water to generously cover peas to a boil and add a pinch of salt. Add peas and cook, uncovered, until just tender, about 7 minutes for fresh peas and about 3 minutes for frozen. Drain thoroughly.

Melt 2 tablespoons butter in a large skillet over low heat. Stir in garlic and cook about 30 seconds. Add peas, rice, and salt and pepper to taste. Heat mixture over low heat, tossing lightly with a fork, until hot.

Add remaining butter. Cover pan and let rice stand about 2 minutes, or until butter melts. Add chopped basil; toss again lightly. Taste and adjust seasoning. Garnish, if desired, with fresh basil leaves.

RICE WITH SAUTÉED VEGETABLES AND WALNUT OIL
Riz aux légumes sautés à l'huile de noix

Serve this colorful dish for a light main course or as an accompaniment to fish or chicken.   MAKES 4 SERVINGS

1 cup long-grain white rice
6 to 8 ounces Swiss chard, rinsed
   thoroughly
2 medium-size carrots, trimmed,
   peeled, and cut in matchsticks
2 medium-size green onions,
   trimmed
2 tablespoons butter

2 medium-size shallots, minced
Salt and freshly ground pepper
¼ cup walnut oil
2 medium-size celery stalks,
   trimmed, peeled, and cut in
   matchsticks
2 tablespoons coarsely chopped fresh
   flat-leaf or curly-leaf parsley

In a large saucepan, bring about 6 cups water to a boil and add a pinch of salt. Add rice, stir once, and cook, uncovered, about 12 to 14 minutes, or until tender; check by tasting. Drain in strainer, rinse with cold water until cool, and let sit for 5 minutes.

Cut chard leaves from ribs. Peel stringy side of ribs and cut crosswise into ¼-inch slices. Pile chard leaves, cut them in half lengthwise and cut crosswise in strips ½ inch wide. In medium-size saucepan of boiling salted water, cook chard ribs, uncovered, about 5 minutes, or until just tender. Drain thoroughly.

Put carrots in medium-size saucepan and add enough water to cover and a pinch of salt. Bring to boil, reduce heat to low, cover, and simmer about 4 minutes, or until tender. Drain thoroughly.

Keep white and light green parts of green onions separate from dark parts. Cut each in thin slices.

In saucepan used to cook rice, melt butter over low heat, add shallots, and cook 1 minute. Add rice and salt and pepper to taste. Heat mixture, tossing lightly with a fork, cover partially, and keep warm.

In large skillet, heat 2 tablespoons walnut oil over medium heat, stir in celery and white and light parts of green onions, then chard leaves, and sauté for 3 minutes. Add chard ribs, carrots, dark parts of green onions, and salt and pepper. Sauté mixture, tossing lightly, about 1½ minutes, or until hot.

With a fork, gently stir vegetable mixture into rice; add remaining walnut oil and parsley. Taste and adjust seasoning. Transfer to serving dish and serve immediately.

SAVORY RICE PILAF WITH EGGPLANT
Pilaf aux aubergines

Sautéed mushrooms or cubes of zucchini are other good additions to this pilaf.   MAKES 6 TO 8 SERVINGS

5 *parsley stems (without leaves)*	*Salt and freshly ground pepper*
2 *fresh thyme sprigs, or ½ teaspoon*	4 *or 5 Japanese eggplants, or 2*
dried thyme	*relatively small or medium-size*
1 *bay leaf*	*regular eggplants*
5 *tablespoons unsalted butter*	¼ *cup olive or vegetable oil*
2 *medium-size onions, chopped*	3 *tablespoons minced fresh flat-leaf*
1 *large garlic clove, minced*	*or curly-leaf parsley*
2 *cups long-grain white rice*	
4 *cups hot Vegetable Stock (see*	
recipe) or water	

Position rack in lower third of oven and preheat to 350°F. Wrap parsley stems, thyme, and bay leaf in a piece of cheesecloth and tie tightly to make a bouquet garni. Cut a piece of parchment paper to fit pan to be used for cooking rice (8 to 9½ inches) and butter it.

In a large ovenproof sauté pan or deep skillet, heat 3 tablespoons butter over low heat, add onions, and cook, stirring, about 10 minutes, or until soft but not brown. Add garlic and sauté 30 seconds. Raise heat to medium, add rice, and sauté, stirring, about 4 minutes, or until grains begin to turn milky white.

Bring stock or water to boil over high heat. Pour hot stock or water over rice and stir once. Add bouquet garni and submerge it in liquid. Add pinch of salt and pepper. Raise heat to high and bring mixture to boil. Set buttered paper, buttered side down, on rice, and cover with tight lid. Bake, without stirring, for 18 minutes.

Meanwhile, rinse and wipe eggplants. Do not peel Japanese eggplants; peel regular eggplants only if their skins are tough. Cut eggplants in small dice. In a large skillet, heat 2 tablespoons oil over medium heat, add half of eggplant cubes and pinch of salt and pepper, and sauté about 7 minutes, or until eggplant is tender. Remove to a bowl. Repeat with remaining oil and remaining eggplant.

Taste rice; if it is too chewy or if liquid is not absorbed, bake 2 more minutes. Discard bouquet garni.

(Rice can be kept up to 2 days in refrigerator and reheated in a little melted butter or heated oil in a large skillet; eggplant can be prepared 4 hours ahead and kept at room temperature.)

When rice is cooked, cut remaining butter in small pieces and scatter them on top. Cover and let stand 4 minutes for slightly chewy rice, or up to 10 minutes if more tender rice is preferred.

Meanwhile, reheat eggplant cubes in skillet. Taste and adjust seasoning.

Use fork to fluff rice and to gently stir in minced parsley and eggplant. Taste and adjust seasoning.

MEDITERRANEAN SAFFRON RICE PILAF WITH VEGETABLES
Pilaf safrané aux légumes

Among the spices that go well with pilaf, saffron is the most honored by tradition and has long been a favorite in France and in other Mediterranean countries. This pilaf can be a main course for a light meal. If you like, instead of sprinkling the rice with almonds, serve a bowl of grated Gruyère or Parmesan cheese on the side.

MAKES 4 TO 6 SERVINGS

1 lemon
4 medium-size artichokes
1 tablespoon strained fresh lemon
    juice
2 cups boiling water
¼ teaspoon crushed saffron threads
    (2 pinches)

5 parsley stems (without leaves)
1 fresh thyme sprig, or ¼ teaspoon
    dried thyme
1 bay leaf
5 tablespoons olive oil
½ cup minced onion
1 cup long-grain white rice

Salt and freshly ground pepper
2 medium-size ripe tomatoes, peeled,
   seeded, and cut in about
   ⅜-inch dice
⅓ cup slivered almonds

1 medium-size zucchini (about
   ¼ pound)
1½ teaspoons minced flat-leaf or
   curly-leaf parsley

Prepare artichoke hearts according to directions on page 143.

Add 1 tablespoon lemon juice to medium-size saucepan of boiling salted water. Add artichoke hearts, cover, and cook over low heat about 15 minutes, or until they are just tender when pierced with knife. Cool to lukewarm in liquid. Using teaspoon, scoop out choke from center of each artichoke. Cut each in ½-inch dice and drain on paper towels.

Combine boiling water and saffron in small saucepan. Cover and keep warm over low heat.

Position rack in lower third of oven and preheat to 350°F. Wrap parsley stems, thyme, and bay leaf in a piece of cheesecloth and tie tightly to make a bouquet garni. Cut a piece of parchment paper to fit pan to be used for cooking rice and butter it.

In 8- to 9½-inch-diameter ovenproof sauté pan or deep skillet, heat 3 tablespoons oil over low heat, add onion, and cook, stirring, about 7 minutes, or until soft but not brown. Raise heat to medium, add rice, and sauté, stirring, about 4 minutes, or until grains begin to turn milky white.

While rice is sautéing, bring saffron water to boil over high heat. Pour over rice and stir once. Add bouquet garni and submerge it in liquid. Add ¼ teaspoon salt and pinch of pepper. Raise heat to high and bring mixture to boil. Set buttered paper, buttered side down, on rice, and cover with tight lid. Bake, without stirring, for 18 minutes. Taste rice; if it is too chewy or if liquid is not absorbed, bake 2 more minutes. Discard bouquet garni. (Rice can be prepared 2 days ahead and refrigerated. Reheat in skillet with 1 tablespoon oil, stirring gently with fork, until just warm.)

While rice cooks, put tomatoes in strainer and leave to drain. Toast almonds in small baking dish in oven alongside pilaf about 4 minutes, or until they are light brown. Transfer almonds to a plate and reserve at room temperature.

Cut zucchini in 3 chunks, each about 1½ inches long. Cut each chunk in lengthwise slices about ¼ inch thick, and each slice in lengthwise strips about ¼ inch thick. In a medium-size skillet, warm 2 tablespoons olive oil over medium heat, add zucchini and salt and pepper to taste, and sauté about 1½ minutes, or until barely tender. Transfer zucchini pieces with their oil to a plate.

When rice is cooked, scatter tomatoes and artichokes on top. Cover and let stand 4 minutes for slightly chewy rice, or up to 10 minutes if more tender rice is preferred. Use fork to fluff rice and to gently stir in tomatoes and artichokes. Add minced parsley and zucchini and its oil, stir in gently, taste and adjust seasoning.

Transfer rice gently to a serving dish. Sprinkle with half of almonds. Serve remaining almonds in a small dish.

❧ CREAMY RICE PILAF WITH ASPARAGUS
Riz pilaf à la crème et aux asperges

Cream can be used to enrich rice pilaf, as in this elegant dish. Serve it on its own or with lobster, shrimp, or chicken.

MAKES 4 TO 6 SERVINGS

10 to 12 ounces thin asparagus
5 parsley stems (without leaves)
1 fresh thyme sprig, or ¼ teaspoon
dried thyme
1 bay leaf
¼ cup butter
½ cup minced onion
1 cup long-grain white rice
2 cups hot Chicken Stock (see
recipe), Vegetable Stock (see
recipe), or water

¼ teaspoon salt
Freshly ground pepper
¼ cup heavy cream, room
temperature
2 tablespoons minced fresh tarragon
or parsley

Peel asparagus and cut 2½-inch-long asparagus tips from stems. Cut stems in pieces about 1½ inches long, discarding tough ends.

Position rack in lower third of oven and preheat to 350°F. Wrap parsley stems, thyme, and bay leaf in a piece of cheesecloth and tie tightly to make a bouquet garni. Cut a piece of parchment paper to fit pan to be used for cooking rice and butter it.

In an ovenproof sauté pan or deep skillet 8 to 9½ inches in diameter, melt 3 tablespoons butter over low heat, add onion, and cook, stirring, about 7 minutes, or until soft but not brown. Raise heat to medium, add rice, and sauté, stirring, about 4 minutes, or until grains begin to turn milky white.

While rice is sautéing, bring stock or water to boil over high heat, pour over rice, and stir once. Add bouquet garni and submerge it in liquid. Add salt and pepper to taste, raise heat to high, and bring mixture to boil. Set buttered paper, buttered side down, on rice, and cover with tight lid. Bake, without stirring, 18 minutes. Taste rice; if it is too chewy or if liquid is not absorbed, bake 2 more minutes. Discard bouquet garni. (Rice can be prepared 2 days ahead and refrigerated. Reheat in skillet with 1 additional tablespoon butter, stirring gently with fork, until just warm.)

Meanwhile, put asparagus pieces into large saucepan containing enough boiling salted water to cover them generously. Return to boil. Cook, uncovered, about 1 minute, or until asparagus is just tender when pierced with a small sharp knife. Drain, rinse with cold running water until cool, and drain thoroughly.

When rice is cooked, pour cream quickly and evenly over it; do not stir. Cover rice with its buttered paper and lid and for slightly chewy rice, let stand 4 minutes, or just until cream is absorbed; for more tender rice, let stand up to 10 minutes.

In large skillet, melt remaining tablespoon butter over medium heat, add asparagus, and sauté about 1 minute, or just until hot. Reserve 8 to 12 asparagus tips for garnish.

Use fork to fluff rice and to gently stir in minced tarragon and remaining asparagus. Taste and adjust seasoning. Transfer pilaf gently to serving dish, garnish with reserved asparagus tips, and serve.

MULTICOLORED PILAF WITH SWEET RED PEPPERS AND WALNUTS
Pilaf multicolore aux poivrons rouges et aux noix

Nuts and pilaf make a wonderful pair; the crunchiness of sautéed nuts provide a perfect complement to the tender rice.

MAKES 4 SERVINGS

4 tablespoons butter
¾ cup walnut halves
About ½ teaspoon salt
2 tablespoons vegetable oil
1 medium-size onion, finely chopped
1 red bell pepper, cored and cut in
    small dice

2 celery stalks, peeled and cut in
    thin slices
1½ cups long-grain rice
3 cups boiling water
Pinch of black pepper

In a small heavy skillet, melt 1 tablespoon butter over medium-low heat, add walnut halves and a pinch of salt, and sauté about 2 minutes, or until lightly browned. Set aside and reserve at room temperature.

In a sauté pan or large skillet, heat oil and 1 tablespoon butter over low heat, add onion, red bell pepper, and celery, and cook, stirring, about 10 minutes, or until soft but not brown. Add rice and sauté, stirring, about 4 minutes.

Add boiling water, ½ teaspoon salt, and a pinch of black pepper. Stir once, cover, and cook over low heat, without stirring, 18 minutes. Taste rice; if not yet tender, simmer 2 more minutes. (Rice can be prepared 2 days ahead and refrigerated. Reheat in skillet with 1 additional tablespoon butter, stirring gently with fork, until just warm.) Remove from heat and dot with remaining 2 tablespoons butter. Cover and let stand for 10 minutes. Gently stir with a fork to distribute butter. Taste and adjust seasoning.

Transfer rice to a serving dish and sprinkle with sautéed walnuts.

RICE PILAF WITH ARTICHOKE HEARTS, CARROTS, AND TOASTED ALMONDS
Pilaf aux coeurs d'artichauts, aux carottes, et aux amandes grillées

Although rice pilaf frequently accompanies meat or fish in sauces —whether creamy or spicy—it is rich enough to be paired with plainer dishes as well, such as grilled foods, roasts, and quick sautés.

MAKES 4 SERVINGS

1 lemon (for fresh artichokes)

2 fresh artichokes, or 8 frozen
    artichoke heart pieces, cooked

¾ cup slivered almonds

2 tablespoons vegetable oil

3 tablespoons unsalted butter

1 medium-size onion, finely chopped

2 medium-size carrots, cut in small
    dice

1½ cups long-grain white rice

3 cups boiling water

About ½ teaspoon salt

Pinch of pepper

If using fresh artichokes, prepare hearts according to instructions on page 143.

Preheat oven to 400°F. In a shallow baking dish, toast almonds in oven about 5 minutes, or until lightly browned. Transfer to a plate and leave at room temperature.

In a sauté pan or large skillet, warm oil and 1 tablespoon butter over low heat, add onion and carrots, and cook, stirring, about 10 minutes, or until onion is soft but not brown. Add rice and sauté, stirring, about 2 minutes.

Add boiling water, ½ teaspoon salt, and a pinch of pepper. Stir once, cover and cook over low heat, without stirring, for 18 minutes. Taste rice; if not yet tender, simmer 2 more minutes. Remove from heat and dot with remaining 2 tablespoons butter. Cover and let stand for 10 minutes. (Rice can be prepared 2 days ahead and refrigerated. Reheat in skillet with 1 additional tablespoon butter, stirring gently with fork, until just warm.)

Cut artichoke hearts into quarters if using fresh. With a fork, gently stir into rice. Taste and adjust seasoning. Transfer rice to a serving dish and sprinkle with toasted almonds.

❧ BROWN RICE PILAF WITH TARRAGON
Pilaf de riz complet à l'estragon

Brown rice is rarely used in France, and so I was amazed to find it on the menu at Paul Bocuse's world-famous restaurant. The brown rice was from the Camargue, the area in southern France where rice is cultivated, and was served with casserole-roasted guinea hen, tarragon cream sauce, and an assortment of vegetables. Brown rice is very good when cooked as pilaf and can be substituted for white rice in the other pilafs in this chapter.   MAKES 4 TO 6 SERVINGS

5 parsley stems (without leaves)

5 tarragon stems (without leaves)

1 fresh thyme sprig, or ¼ teaspoon dried thyme, crumbled

1 bay leaf

2 tablespoons butter, for enrichment (optional)

2 cups hot Chicken Stock (see recipe), Vegetable Stock (see recipe), or water

3 tablespoons unsalted butter, vegetable oil, or olive oil

½ cup minced onion

1 cup long-grain brown rice

¼ teaspoon salt

Freshly ground pepper

2 tablespoons chopped fresh tarragon

Position rack in lower third of oven and preheat to 350°F. Wrap parsley stems, tarragon stems, thyme, and bay leaf in a piece of cheese-cloth and tie tightly to make a bouquet garni. Cut a piece of parchment paper to fit pan to be used for cooking rice, and butter it.

Cut 2 tablespoons optional butter into small pieces and let stand at room temperature while preparing pilaf.

If using stock, keep it hot in small saucepan over low heat, covered; if using water, keep it hot in kettle over low heat.

In ovenproof sauté pan or deep skillet 8 or 9½ inches in diameter, warm 3 tablespoons butter or oil over low heat, add onion, and cook, stirring, until soft but not brown, about 7 minutes. Raise heat to medium, add rice, and sauté, stirring, until grains begin to turn milky white, about 4 minutes.

Bring stock or water to boil over high heat, pour over rice, and stir once. Add bouquet garni and submerge it in liquid. Add salt and pepper to taste. Raise heat to high and bring mixture to boil. Press buttered paper, buttered side down, onto rice, and cover with tight lid. Bake, without stirring, 35 minutes. Taste rice; if it is too chewy or if liquid is not absorbed, bake 5 more minutes and check again. Discard bouquet garni. (Rice can be prepared 2 days ahead and refrigerated. Reheat in skillet with 1 additional tablespoon butter or oil, stirring gently with fork, until just warm.)

When rice is cooked, scatter reserved butter pieces over it. For slightly chewy rice, fluff by tossing with fork; if more tender rice is preferred, cover rice with its buttered paper and lid, let stand up to

10 minutes, and then fluff with fork. Continue tossing until butter is evenly blended into rice. Add fresh tarragon. Taste and adjust seasoning.

❧ RICE RING WITH CURRIED EGGPLANT
Couronne de riz aux aubergines, sauce curry

Since rice can be easily molded into an attractive ring, it is a popular presentation of pilaf in France because a rich mixture can be spooned into the center. If desired, add other vegetables such as zucchini, cauliflower, mushrooms, or peas to the sauce.

MAKES 4 SERVINGS

RICE PILAF WITH PEPPERS

¼ cup butter

1 large onion, finely chopped

1 large red bell pepper, cored, ribs removed, finely diced

1 cup long-grain white rice

2 cups hot water

¼ teaspoon salt

Freshly ground pepper

CURRIED EGGPLANT

2 tablespoons butter

2 tablespoons minced shallots

1 tablespoon minced fresh ginger

2 teaspoons minced garlic

2 teaspoons curry powder

1 cup Chicken Stock (see recipe) or Vegetable Stock (see recipe)

1 bay leaf

Salt and freshly ground pepper

1½ cups heavy cream

1 pound Japanese eggplants, unpeeled

1 tablespoon vegetable oil

RICE PILAF WITH PEPPERS

Preheat oven to 300°F. In large heavy skillet, melt 2 tablespoons butter over low heat, add onion, and cook 3 minutes. Add red pepper and cook, stirring occasionally, about 5 minutes, or until softened. Add rice and cook, stirring, about 4 minutes, or until evenly coated. Add water, salt and pepper to taste, stir once, and bring to boil. Cover and cook over low heat, without stirring, about 18 minutes, or until liquid is absorbed. Let stand, covered, 5 minutes.

Cut remaining 2 tablespoons butter in cubes. Fluff rice with fork. Using fork, gently stir in butter cubes. Taste and adjust seasoning. (Rice can be prepared 2 days ahead and refrigerated.)

CURRIED EGGPLANT

In medium-size heavy saucepan, melt 1 tablespoon butter over low heat, add shallots, and cook, stirring, about 2 minutes, or until soft but not browned. Add ginger and garlic and cook 1 minute. Add curry powder and cook, stirring, 30 seconds. Add stock, bay leaf, and a little salt and pepper. Stir well and bring to boil. Simmer, uncovered, over medium-high heat, stirring occasionally, until mixture is reduced to about ¼ cup. Discard bay leaf. Add cream and bring to boil, stirring. Reduce heat to medium and simmer until sauce is thick enough to coat a spoon. (Sauce can be prepared 4 hours ahead and refrigerated.)

Cut eggplant in ¾-inch dice and season lightly with salt. In large skillet, heat oil and remaining tablespoon butter over medium heat, add eggplant, and sauté, tossing often, about 5 minutes, or until lightly browned. Reduce heat to low, cover, and cook, stirring occasionally, about 5 minutes, or until tender. Transfer to bowl and keep warm. (Eggplant can be prepared 2 hours ahead and kept at room temperature. Reheat in covered skillet.)

Preheat oven to 300°F. If rice was prepared ahead, reheat it in skillet with 1 additional tablespoon butter, stirring gently with fork, until just warm. Butter 4- to 5-cup ring mold. Spoon rice into mold and press it in gently so there are no holes; do not crush grains. Cover with foil and warm in oven 10 minutes.

Reheat sauce to simmer in medium-size heavy saucepan, stirring. Taste and adjust seasoning. Sauce should be quite sharply flavored. Cover and keep warm.

Unmold pilaf ring onto round platter, put a layer of eggplant in center, and spoon enough sauce over it to coat it. Top with a layer of eggplant. Repeat layering, arranging eggplant pieces decoratively on top. Filling should be mounded above level of rice ring. With slotted spoon, transfer any remaining eggplant pieces to sauce, mix gently, and spoon into separate dish. Serve immediately.

NOTE: To make individual portions of molded rice, spoon cooked pilaf into 4 to 6 buttered 4- or 5-ounce ramekins. Press with a spoon so the rice is lightly packed, but do not crush grains. Put molds in a roasting pan and add enough simmering water to come halfway up the molds. Cover with buttered parchment paper. Bake in a preheated 350°F. oven for 10 minutes. Unmold the ramekins onto plates. Serve with any sauced mixture. To serve with eggplant dish above, mix eggplant cubes with curry sauce and spoon them around rice molds.

Pasta

During the five years we lived in Paris, my husband and I enjoyed taking trips throughout France and Italy and sampling a variety of pasta dishes. We discovered to our surprise that the pasta dishes in the best French restaurants were on the whole even better than those on the other side of the border. It was difficult to find pasta dishes in Italy that could match such French creations as ragoût of fresh pasta with black truffles, sole fillets with white wine butter sauce on a bed of pasta, or the unparalleled noodle gratin with foie gras that we savored at L'Auberge de l'Ill, the world-famous restaurant in Alsace.

When we considered it further, we realized that actually this is not a new phenomenon. The French have adopted and refined Italian dishes for centuries. Important ingredients such as spinach and fresh peas and basic preparations such as genoise all came to France from Italy and were then used by the French in their own way. Following the same tradition, French cooks have recently created marvelous dishes with their neighbor's pasta by adding their special touches—delicious sauces, inspired combinations, and unique presentation.

Up until modern times, pasta lovers who wanted to enjoy their favorite food in France had to travel to Provence and Alsace, but now chefs all over France are giving pasta a place of honor on their menus. They have realized that the incomparable crème fraîche and the delicate French sauces—exquisite butter sauces, cream-based sauces, and traditional velouté sauces prepared from concentrated seafood and chicken stocks—are perfect with pasta. Like the Italians, the French also enjoy pasta with tomato sauce made from ripe tomatoes and cooked briefly to preserve their fresh flavor. The smoothness and richness of the sauces are balanced in France by such zesty flavorings as Dijon mustard, fresh tarragon, sorrel, shallots, morels, smoked salmon, and Roquefort, Gruyère, and goat cheeses.

Rather than confining pasta to first courses, the French prefer to broaden its role and serve it as part of the main course or as a side dish, because it is a wonderful complement to seafood, poultry, and meats. A favorite French presentation is topping a bed of pasta with a portion of seafood or meat.

The French are careful to cook their pasta only until it is al dente, or slightly firm to the bite, and they too use this Italian term to refer to properly cooked pasta. To check whether the pasta is done, a strand is removed from the pot and tasted; tongs are a convenient tool for doing this.

Hints

- Whether buying fresh or dried pasta, be sure it is thin.
- A wooden pasta fork or other large fork is best for mixing the pasta gently but efficiently with the sauce and the other ingredients.
- Always season sauces well before adding them to pasta, so that they provide a flavorful contrast to its subtle taste.

TOMATO PASTA WITH GOAT CHEESE AND GARLIC
Pâtes rouges au fromage de chèvre et à l'ail

In this very quick, easy, and flavorful pasta dish, the garlic provides just the right complement for the goat cheese. The sauce is also delicious with spinach noodles.

MAKES 4 SERVINGS AS A SIDE DISH OR FIRST COURSE OR
2 SERVINGS AS A MAIN COURSE

1 to 1¼ cups heavy cream

8 medium-size garlic cloves, lightly
  crushed and peeled

2 ounces creamy French goat cheese,
  such as Montrachet

8 ounces fresh tomato pasta, or 6
  ounces dried

2 tablespoons minced fresh parsley

Freshly ground pepper

Salt (optional)

In a small saucepan, bring 1 cup cream to a boil, add garlic, reduce heat to low, and simmer about 8 minutes, or until garlic is just tender.

If using a goat cheese with a dark rind, remove rind. Cut cheese in a few pieces. Transfer garlic with a slotted spoon to a food processor or blender, add goat cheese and ½ cup hot cream, and purée mixture. Gradually add remaining cream and process until smooth.

Return sauce to pan and heat it gently. If sauce is thin, simmer until thick enough to coat a spoon; if it is too thick, stir in enough of remaining cream to obtain desired consistency. (The sauce can be kept, covered, for 4 hours in refrigerator; thin it out with 1 to 2 tablespoons more cream when reheating.)

In a large pan of boiling salted water, cook pasta over high heat, stirring occasionally, about 3 minutes for fresh pasta or 7 minutes for dried, or until it is al dente, and drain it well. While pasta is cooking, reheat sauce over moderate heat, stirring.

Transfer pasta to a heated serving dish and toss it with sauce. Add parsley and pepper to taste. Add salt if desired; it may not be needed because of cheese. Serve immediately.

PASTA WITH FRESH PEAS AND SAFFRON BUTTER SAUCE
Pâtes aux petits pois, beurre au safran

Unlike the Italians, the French often serve pasta as a side dish. This pasta dish is wonderful with scallops, shrimp, lobster, or other seafood.   MAKES 6 SERVINGS AS A SIDE DISH

SAFFRON BUTTER SAUCE

¼ teaspoon crumbled saffron
   threads
2 tablespoons minced shallots
2 tablespoons white wine vinegar
3 tablespoons dry white wine

3 tablespoons heavy cream
Salt and freshly ground pepper
1 cup cold unsalted butter, cut into
   16 pieces

2 cups shelled fresh peas (about 2
   pounds in pods) or frozen peas

1 pound fresh fettucine, or 12
   ounces dried
2 tablespoons butter, cut into pieces

2 large ripe tomatoes, peeled, seeded,
   well-drained, and diced
Salt and freshly ground pepper

SAFFRON BUTTER SAUCE

In a small heavy nonaluminum saucepan, simmer saffron and shallots in vinegar and wine over medium heat until liquid is reduced to about 2 tablespoons. Reduce heat to low, stir in cream, and simmer, whisking occasionally, until mixture is reduced to about 2 tablespoons. Season lightly with salt and pepper. Cover and reserve. (The mixture can be kept, covered, for 1 hour at room temperature.) Keep butter in refrigerator until ready to use.

In a saucepan of boiling salted water, cook peas for 7 minutes if using fresh peas, or 3 minutes if using frozen peas, or until they are just tender. Drain well.

In a large pan of boiling salted water, cook pasta over high heat, stirring occasionally, about 3 minutes for fresh pasta or 7 minutes for dried, or until it is al dente, and drain it well. Transfer it to a large skillet. Add 2 tablespoons butter, peas, tomatoes, and pinch of salt and pepper, and toss mixture over low heat just until it is hot.

To finish sauce, bring saffron mixture to a simmer in its saucepan. Reduce heat to low. Add one piece of butter, whisking liquid constantly. When butter piece is nearly blended into liquid, add another piece, still whisking. Continue adding butter pieces one or two at a time, whisking constantly. The sauce should be pleasantly warm to touch. If it becomes too hot and drops of melted butter appear, remove pan immediately from heat and whisk well; add next butter pieces off heat, whisking constantly. When temperature of sauce drops again to warm, return to low heat to continue adding remaining butter pieces. Remove from heat as soon as last butter piece is added. Taste and adjust seasoning and serve sauce as soon as possible. (Sauce can be kept warm for about 15 minutes in its saucepan set on a rack above warm water, but it must be whisked frequently to prevent separation.)

Transfer pasta mixture to a platter and toss with sauce. Taste and adjust seasoning. Serve immediately.

PASTA WITH CREAMY BROCCOLI PURÉE
Pâtes à la crème de brocolis

By adding cream to vegetable purées, it is easy to prepare delicious sauces for pasta, as in this colorful dish.   MAKES 4 SERVINGS

2 pounds broccoli, divided into
   medium-size florets
1½ cups heavy cream
3 tablespoons butter, room
   temperature
2 medium-size shallots, minced

Salt and freshly ground pepper
Freshly grated nutmeg
8 ounces fresh fettucine or
   medium-width egg noodles, or
   6 ounces dried

Reserve 16 relatively small florets for garnish. Peel large stalk of each head of broccoli. Cut peeled stalk in slices ¾ inch thick. In a large saucepan of boiling salted water, cook broccoli slices 2 minutes. Add florets (except those reserved for garnish) and cook, uncovered, over high heat for about 5 minutes, or until stems of florets are tender when pierced with a sharp knife. Drain, rinse under cold running water, and drain thoroughly.

Purée cooked broccoli in a food processor, or in batches in a blender, adding a total of ¼ cup cream, a little at a time. Purée until very smooth.

In a medium-size saucepan, melt 1 tablespoon butter over low heat, add shallots, and cook about 7 minutes, stirring often, until soft but not browned. Add broccoli purée and gradually stir in remaining cream. Bring to simmer. Season to taste with salt, pepper, and nutmeg.

Keep warm over low heat. (Sauce can be kept, covered, up to 2 days in refrigerator.)

In a large pan of boiling salted water, cook pasta over high heat, stirring occasionally, about 3 minutes for fresh pasta or 7 minutes for dried, or until it is al dente, and drain it well. Put in a serving dish.

Meanwhile, in a separate saucepan of boiling salted water, cook reserved broccoli florets over high heat about 2 minutes, or until flower ends are just tender. Drain thoroughly.

Stir remaining 2 tablespoons butter into broccoli sauce and toss pasta with two-thirds of sauce. Garnish with florets. Serve remaining sauce separately.

❧ FETTUCINE WITH MORELS AND ASPARAGUS
Fettucine aux morilles et aux asperges

Morels are one of the most flavorful of mushrooms; a small amount of morels can add a wonderfully rich taste to a sauce. This creamy pasta dish is great on its own and makes a delectable accompaniment for veal or chicken.

MAKES 2 TO 3 SERVINGS AS A MAIN COURSE, OR
4 TO 6 SERVINGS AS A FIRST COURSE OR SIDE DISH

*¾ ounce dried morels (about
    ¾ cup)*
½ pound thin asparagus
¼ cup unsalted butter
4 teaspoons minced shallots
½ cup dry white wine

*½ cup Chicken Stock (see recipe) or
    Vegetable Stock (see recipe)*
Salt and freshly ground pepper
1 cup heavy cream
*8 ounces fresh fettucine, or 6 ounces
    dried*

Soak morels in hot water to cover for about 30 minutes, or until soft. Rinse and drain well. Cut any large morels in half. Remove asparagus tips and cut stalks in 1-inch pieces, discarding any thick, white bases. Refrigerate 2 tablespoons butter.

In a medium-size saucepan, melt 1 tablespoon of remaining butter over low heat, add shallots, and cook about 2 minutes, or until softened. Pour in wine and bring to a boil, stirring. Add stock, morels, and salt and pepper to taste. Bring to a boil, reduce heat to medium, and simmer until liquid is reduced to about ¾ cup. Stir in cream and bring mixture to a boil. Simmer, stirring occasionally, over medium heat for 7 minutes, or until mixture is thick enough to coat a spoon. (The sauce can be kept, covered, 1 day in refrigerator.)

In a saucepan of boiling salted water, cook asparagus for 2 minutes. Drain, rinse under cold water, and drain thoroughly. In a skillet over medium-low heat, melt remaining 1 tablespoon butter, add asparagus and salt and pepper to taste, and sauté for 2 minutes, or until tender. Reserve some tips for garnish.

In a large pan of boiling salted water, cook pasta over high heat, stirring occasionally, about 3 minutes for fresh pasta or 7 minutes for dried, or until it is al dente, and drain it well. Transfer to a bowl. While pasta is cooking, reheat sauce over medium heat, stirring. Add 2 tablespoons cold butter to sauce and stir over low heat just until blended. Taste and adjust seasoning.

To serve, toss pasta with sauce and asparagus and transfer to a heated platter. Garnish edge of platter with reserved asparagus tips.

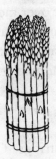

SPAGHETTI WITH FALL VEGETABLES AND TOMATO-TARRAGON SAUCE
Spaghetti aux légumes d'automne, sauce tomate à l'estragon

Any vegetable in season can be used in this dish. Tarragon adds a pleasant accent to both the sauce and the vegetables.

MAKES 3 TO 4 SERVINGS

TOMATO-TARRAGON SAUCE

5 tarragon stems (optional)

1 bay leaf

1 tablespoon olive oil

1 tablespoon butter

3 ½ pounds ripe tomatoes, peeled, seeded, and chopped

Pinch of thyme

Salt and freshly ground pepper

2 tablespoons chopped fresh tarragon, or 2 teaspoons dried tarragon, crumbled

1 celery stalk

1 small Japanese eggplant (about 3 ounces), unpeeled

1 medium-size carrot, peeled

1 tablespoon olive oil

¼ cup butter

1 tablespoon chopped fresh tarragon, or 1 teaspoon dried tarragon, crumbled

Salt and freshly ground pepper

1 small or ½ large cauliflower (about 1 pound), divided into small florets

8 ounces spaghetti

TOMATO-TARRAGON SAUCE

Tie tarragon stems and bay leaf in a piece of cheesecloth to make a bouquet garni. (If using dried tarragon, cheesecloth is not needed.) In a large skillet, heat oil and butter over medium heat, add tomatoes, thyme, bouquet garni or bay leaf, and salt and pepper. Cook, stirring often, about 25 minutes, or until tomatoes are soft and mixture is thick and smooth. Discard bouquet garni or bay leaf. (Sauce can be kept, covered, 3 days in refrigerator.)

Add chopped tarragon leaves, taste and adjust seasoning.

Peel celery stalk to remove strings. Cut celery, eggplant, and carrot into thin strips about 1½ inches long. Put vegetable strips in a large pan of boiling salted water and cook, uncovered, about 3 minutes. Drain, rinse under cold running water and drain thoroughly. Return to pan and add olive oil, 1 tablespoon butter, and tarragon. Heat, stirring gently, about 2 minutes, or until just tender. Season to taste with salt and pepper.

In a large pan of boiling salted water, cook cauliflower, uncovered, about 5 minutes, or until just tender. Drain thoroughly.

In a large pan of boiling salted water, cook spaghetti uncovered, over high heat about 7 minutes, or until just tender but still al dente, or slightly firm to bite; check by tasting. Drain thoroughly and add to pan of vegetable strips. Add remaining 3 tablespoons butter and half of cauliflower and toss gently over low heat, using pasta spoons or two forks, just until hot. Taste and adjust seasoning.

Reheat tomato sauce if necessary. Transfer spaghetti mixture to a platter or to plates and spoon tomato sauce over center. Set remaining cauliflower pieces on tomato sauce and serve.

PASTA WITH VEGETABLE "NOODLES"
Pâtes aux "nouilles" de légumes

French cooks like to cut colorful vegetables, such as the carrots and zucchini here, in strips and toss them with white noodles, giving the illusion of mixing different colored noodles. For a delicious main course, serve these surrounded by sautéed shrimp.

MAKES 2 TO 3 SERVINGS

About ½ pound carrots, preferably large, peeled
8 ounces fresh medium-width noodles, or 6 ounces dried
1 medium-size zucchini (about 5 ounces)

2 tablespoons plus 2 teaspoons minced shallots
½ cup dry white wine
1 cup heavy cream
Salt and freshly ground pepper
2 tablespoons snipped fresh dill

Cut carrots in thin strips about 1½ to 2 inches long and of same width as noodles. Cut zucchini in strips of same size as carrot strips.

In a saucepan, combine shallots and wine and bring to a boil. Cook over low heat about 5 minutes, or until liquid is reduced to about 2 tablespoons. Stir in cream, add a pinch of salt and pepper, and bring sauce to a boil. Cook it over medium heat for 6 minutes, or until it is thick enough to coat a spoon.

In a large pan of boiling salted water, cook pasta over high heat, stirring occasionally, about 3 minutes for fresh pasta or 7 minutes for dried, or until it is al dente, and drain it well. Transfer it to a heated platter.

In another saucepan of boiling salted water, cook carrots about 3 minutes, or until just tender. Add zucchini and cook 1 minute. Rinse and drain thoroughly.

Bring sauce to a boil, remove it from heat, and stir in dill, zucchini, and carrots. Pour mixture over noodles and toss gently, using
a large fork or tongs. Taste and adjust seasoning.

❧ CREAMY PASTA GRATIN WITH CHEESE
Gratin de pâtes à la crème et au fromage

This dish is inspired by potato gratin dauphinois. French chefs
also make pasta gratins with black truffles and even with foie gras.

MAKES 6 SERVINGS AS SIDE DISH

8 ounces dried fettucine
2 cups Crème Fraîche (see recipe)
¼ teaspoon freshly grated nutmeg
Salt and freshly ground white
  pepper

1 cup grated imported Gruyère
  cheese
1 cut garlic clove (optional)

Preheat oven to 400°F. In a large pan of boiling salted water,
cook fettucine over high heat, stirring occasionally, about 7 minutes,
or until it is al dente, and drain it well.

In a large bowl, mix crème fraîche with nutmeg and salt and
white pepper to taste. Add pasta and ½ cup grated cheese and toss.
Taste and adjust seasoning, if necessary, so mixture is well-flavored.

Rub a shallow 5- or 6-cup gratin dish or other baking dish with
cut garlic clove. Butter dish, transfer pasta mixture to it, and sprinkle
with remaining Gruyère. Bake about 10 minutes, or until pasta absorbs cream. If necessary, place in broiler to brown lightly.

❧ BAKED PASTA WITH EGGPLANT
Macaronis aux aubergines au four

This vegetable and pasta dish is hearty enough to be served as a
main course. A fresh tomato sauce like the one served with Eggplant
Savarin (see recipe) is a good complement and provides both color
and flavor. Or serve with Provençal Baked Tomatoes (see recipe).

MAKES 4 TO 6 SERVINGS

1 pound eggplant
6 tablespoons vegetable oil
Salt
2 tablespoons butter
1 small onion, minced
2 ½ tablespoons all-purpose flour
1 ½ cups milk

Freshly ground white pepper
Freshly grated nutmeg
1 ½ cups elbow macaroni
2 eggs, beaten
1 cup grated Gruyère or Swiss
  cheese
Fresh Tomato Sauce (page 36)

Peel eggplant and cut in approximately ½-inch cubes. Preheat oven to 375°F. Generously butter a 5- to 6-cup soufflé dish or deep baking dish.

In a medium-size skillet, heat 3 tablespoons oil over medium heat, add half of eggplant cubes, sprinkle them with salt, and sauté about 7 minutes, or until tender; since oil is absorbed quickly, reduce heat and stir constantly so eggplant doesn't burn. Remove cubes and repeat with remaining oil and eggplant cubes.

In a medium-size heavy saucepan, melt butter over low heat, add onion, and cook about 5 minutes, or until soft but not brown. Sprinkle with flour and cook, stirring, about 2 minutes. Remove from heat. Gradually whisk in milk. Bring to a boil over medium-high heat, stirring constantly with a whisk, add a small pinch of salt, white pepper, and nutmeg, and reduce heat to low. Cook, whisking often, for 5 minutes. Transfer to a bowl.

In a large pan of boiling salted water, cook macaroni over high heat, stirring occasionally, about 9 minutes, or until it is al dente. Rinse with cold water and drain well.

Add macaroni and eggplant to sauce and mix gently. Gently stir in eggs and cheese. Add more salt, pepper, and nutmeg, if needed. (Mixture can be prepared 1 day ahead; in this case dab surface with a small piece of butter to prevent a skin from forming. Cover and keep in refrigerator.) Transfer to buttered dish. Set in a shallow pan and put in oven. Add enough very hot water to pan to come halfway up sides of dish. Bake about 40 minutes, or until mixture sets.

Remove from pan of water. Serve hot with Fresh Tomato Sauce.

✤ PASTA WITH BROCCOLI, CAULIFLOWER, AND ROQUEFORT SAUCE
Pâtes aux brocoli et chou-fleur, sauce roquefort

Serve this pasta dish on its own or to accompany chicken or veal.

MAKES 4 TO 6 SERVINGS

2 tablespoons unsalted butter
2 medium-size shallots, minced
½ cup dry white wine
1 ½ cups heavy cream
½ cup crumbled Roquefort cheese
Freshly ground pepper
½ medium-size head cauliflower,
*   divided into medium-size florets*

¾ pound broccoli, divided into
*   medium-size florets*
1 pound fresh good-quality
*   fettucine, or 12 ounces dried*
Salt (if needed)

In a large heavy saucepan, melt 1 tablespoon butter over low heat, add shallots, and cook, stirring, 2 minutes. Add wine and simmer, stirring often, until liquid is reduced to about 2 tablespoons. Stir in cream and cook over medium-high heat, stirring often, about 7 minutes, or until sauce is thick enough to coat a spoon. Reduce heat to low, whisk in Roquefort cheese, and cook sauce, stirring, just until smooth. Add pepper to taste.

In a large pan of boiling salted water, cook cauliflower, uncovered, about 7 minutes, or until just tender. Drain thoroughly. In a pan of boiling salted water, cook broccoli about 5 minutes, or until just tender. Drain thoroughly.

In a large pan of boiling salted water, cook pasta over high heat, stirring occasionally, about 3 minutes for fresh pasta or 7 minutes for dried, or until it is al dente, and drain it well. Transfer to bowl, add remaining butter and ¼ cup sauce, toss, and season to taste with pepper; salt may not be needed.

Transfer pasta to a heated platter and set broccoli and cauliflower florets on top. Coat them partially with sauce. Serve any remaining sauce separately.

COUSCOUS WITH CHANTERELLES
Couscous aux chanterelles

There are many Moroccan and Tunisian couscous restaurants in France, and they are very popular. French chefs now use couscous combined with their favorite flavorings, in this case wild mushrooms, butter, and a touch of Parmesan cheese, to create a totally different effect from the North African couscous dishes.

MAKES 4 SERVINGS

*5 ounces fresh chanterelle
    mushrooms
1 tablespoon vegetable oil
½ cup unsalted butter, room
    temperature, cut into 16 pieces
Salt and freshly ground pepper*

*2 tablespoons minced shallots
1 cup couscous
1 cup Chicken Stock (see recipe) or
    Vegetable Stock (see recipe)
¼ cup freshly grated Parmesan
    cheese*

Gently rinse mushrooms and dry them on paper towels. If they are large, cut them lengthwise into pieces about ½ inch thick. In a skillet, heat oil and 4 pieces (2 tablespoons) of butter over medium heat, add mushrooms and salt and pepper, and sauté about 3 minutes, or until mushrooms render their liquid. Add shallots and sauté over medium-high heat, tossing often, about 3 more minutes, or until mushrooms are browned and tender and liquid has evaporated.

In a saucepan, combine couscous with pinch of salt and pepper. Shake pan to spread couscous in an even layer. Scatter 4 pieces (2 tablespoons) of butter over couscous. In a small saucepan, bring stock to a boil, pour it evenly over couscous, immediately cover saucepan tightly, and let mixture stand for 5 minutes. Scatter remaining butter pieces over couscous and let it stand, covered, for 1 minute. Reheat mushrooms, if necessary.

Fluff couscous mixture with a fork to break up any lumps, tossing until butter is blended in. Add cheese and two-thirds of sautéed chanterelles, toss, and taste it for seasoning. Transfer to a serving dish and garnish with remaining chanterelles.

❧ COUSCOUS PILAF WITH CARROTS, PEAS, AND SAUTÉED MUSHROOMS
Pilaf de couscous aux carottes, aux petits pois et aux champignons sautés

Although a Tunisian woman in Israel taught me to prepare couscous the traditional way, my first taste of couscous pilaf was in Paris, where it was cooked by a French chef. He quickly poured hot stock over the couscous and enriched it with butter. The couscous was ready in 5 minutes and was delicious.   MAKES 5 TO 6 SERVINGS

¾ cup blanched almonds
2 medium-size carrots
1 cup Chicken Stock (see recipe), Vegetable Stock (see recipe), or water
Salt and freshly ground pepper
1¼ cups shelled fresh peas (about 1¼ pounds in the pod), or 1¼ cups frozen peas

7 tablespoons unsalted butter, room temperature
¼ pound mushrooms, halved and thinly sliced
1 large onion, minced
1 cup couscous

Preheat oven to 400°F. Toast almonds in small baking pan or baking dish in oven, stirring occasionally, for 8 minutes, or until they are golden brown. Transfer to plate and reserve at room temperature.

Cut carrots in half lengthwise and then into slices ⅛ inch thick. In a medium-size saucepan, combine carrots with 1 cup stock or water and bring to a boil. Add salt to taste and cook over medium heat about 7 minutes, or until they are just tender. Drain, reserving cooking liquid. Measure liquid from carrots, add enough hot water to make 1 cup, and pour it into a small saucepan.

In a second saucepan of boiling salted water, cook fresh peas for 7 minutes, or frozen peas for 3 minutes, or until they are just tender. Drain well.

In a medium-size skillet, melt 2 tablespoons butter over medium heat, add mushrooms and salt and pepper, and sauté, stirring, for 3 minutes, or until lightly browned. Add carrots and peas and cook over low heat, stirring, for 1 minute. Cover and keep warm.

In a large skillet, melt 2 tablespoons butter over low heat, add onion, and cook, stirring, for 10 minutes, or until it is soft but not brown. Add 1 tablespoon butter and heat until butter melts. Add couscous and stir with a fork until blended. Remove skillet from heat and shake to spread couscous in an even layer. Bring measured carrot cooking liquid to a boil, pour it evenly over couscous, immediately cover skillet tightly, and let mixture stand for 5 minutes. Cut remaining butter into 4 pieces. Scatter butter pieces over couscous and let it stand, covered, 1 minute. Fluff with a fork to break up any lumps in couscous, tossing until butter is blended in. Add vegetables, toss, and taste it for seasoning. Transfer couscous to a serving dish or mound it on a platter and garnish it with almonds.

Vegetable Soups

Vegetable soup is one of the most appealing first courses, whether it is a warm, comforting bowl of soup on a cold day or a cool, refreshing one on a hot day.

French cooks prepare soups from nearly every vegetable. These soups can contain chunks of vegetables or can be smooth purées. Generally the smooth type is made of a single vegetable but sometimes several vegetables are combined harmoniously. I particularly remember a lovely cream of asparagus and broccoli soup at Alain Chapel restaurant near Lyon.

Although vegetables do not need to be as crisp for soups as for salads, the flavor of the soup will be best if all ingredients are fresh. This does not mean that leftovers have no place in soups. Yesterday's cooked cauliflower, spinach, peas, or carrots, for example, can certainly be added to today's vegetable soup. To save time, frozen vegetables can also be simmered in soups. In this case, however, it is important that some of the ingredients be fresh to give the soup zest.

Soups can play different roles in a meal. A chunky soup, such as Southwestern Vegetable Soup with Vegetable Croutons, makes a lovely light lunch and is best served in larger bowls. Cream soups, however, are so rich they should be presented in small, dainty bowls. Many soups, such as Country Spinach Soup, are equally good hot or cold.

Some of the following soups are thickened. Only a small quantity of potato, rice, or flour is required in soups to help produce a smooth, creamy consistency. The right amount of properly cooked flour does not make soups pasty. Without one of these thickeners, large quantities of cream are often needed to achieve the same degree of smoothness. When these soups are brought to the right consistency with stock or milk, so that they barely coat a spoon, they are never heavy.

Soups that are served cold require more seasoning than those served hot and should be tasted again before they are served. They should not be enriched with butter because it would congeal when chilled and mar their consistency.

Whether a soup is brought to the table in an elegant tureen or ladled into bowls in the kitchen, it is a good idea to warm or chill the tureen or bowls first, depending of course on the type of soup and the weather.

Hearty Vegetable Soups

Hearty soups are the symbol of simple, wholesome country cooking. They can contain a variety of vegetables, as well as rice and pasta, and are served as a satisfying first course or main dish.

These soups can be varied infinitely, gaining liveliness from almost any herb, from many spices, and from seasonal vegetables. Sauces such as aïoli, rouille, and pistou, the French version of pesto, can enrich a vegetable soup.

❧ VEGETABLE BOUILLABAISSE
Bouillabaisse de légumes

Provençal cooks make vegetable bouillabaisse seasoned like its cousin, fish bouillabaisse. This sumptuous vegetable soup is flavored with saffron, garlic, and thyme and is served with rouille sauce. Other vegetables, such as zucchini and green beans, can be added instead of or in addition to the peas.   MAKES 4 TO 6 SERVINGS

ROUILLE SAUCE

½ jalapeño pepper or other hot pepper
3 medium-size garlic cloves, peeled
1 egg yolk, room temperature
Salt
2 to 3 teaspoons strained fresh lemon juice

¾ cup extra-virgin olive oil, room temperature
1 to 2 tablespoons tomato paste
Freshly ground pepper
Pinch of cayenne pepper (optional)

SAFFRON-VEGETABLE SOUP

½ pound boiling potatoes, peeled
¼ cup extra-virgin olive oil
1 large onion, halved and thinly sliced
6 large garlic cloves, chopped
1 quart water
Salt and freshly ground pepper
¾ teaspoon minced fresh thyme, or ¼ teaspoon dried thyme

1 bay leaf
½ teaspoon fennel seed
Scant ½ teaspoon saffron threads (1 small vial of 0.2 grams)
1½ pounds fresh peas, shelled and rinsed
2 small zucchini (about ¼ pound), diced

Slices of French baguette, left whole, or 8 slices of Italian bread, about ¼ inch thick, cut in half

ROUILLE SAUCE

Wear rubber gloves if you are sensitive to hot peppers. Discard seeds and ribs from hot pepper. Handle hot pepper carefully and be sure to wash your hands, the knife, and the board immediately after they come in contact with the pepper. Chop garlic and pepper as finely as possible so that they become almost a purée.

In a medium-size heavy bowl set on a towel, whisk egg yolk with garlic, hot pepper, a pinch of salt, and 2 teaspoons lemon juice. Using a whisk or hand mixer, begin stirring or beating in the oil, drop by drop. When 2 or 3 tablespoons oil have been incorporated, whisk in remaining oil in a very thin stream. After adding ½ cup oil, whisk in ½ teaspoon lemon juice to thin sauce and make stirring easier. When all of oil is added, gradually stir in tomato paste. Add salt, pepper, cayenne pepper, and more lemon juice, if desired. (The sauce can be made 2 days ahead and kept, covered, in refrigerator.) Serve it at room temperature.

SAFFRON-VEGETABLE SOUP

Cut potatoes lengthwise into quarters if they are round. If using long, oval potatoes, cut them lengthwise in half. Cut potato quarters or halves in ¼-inch slices.

In a medium-size saucepan, warm oil over low heat, add onion, and cook, stirring often, about 15 minutes, or until soft but not brown. Add garlic and cook, stirring, 30 seconds.

Add potatoes and stir. Add water and salt and pepper to taste. Wrap thyme, bay leaf, and fennel seed in a piece of cheesecloth and tie tightly to make a bouquet garni; add to soup. Bring to a simmer, crumble in saffron, and stir. Bring to a boil, reduce heat to low, cover, and cook for 10 minutes. Stir in peas and zucchini, cover, and cook about 25 to 30 minutes or until vegetables are tender. Discard bouquet garni. Taste soup and adjust seasoning. (Soup can be kept, covered, 1 day in refrigerator. Reheat over low heat.)

Toast bread and spread a little rouille sauce on 4 to 6 slices. Serve separately. Pass remaining toast and sauce separately. Toast spread with rouille can be floated in soup or eaten separately.

RICH ONION SOUP WITH PORT
Soupe à l'oignon au porto

Although onion soup is a restoring midnight snack to enjoy at cafés or small restaurants in Paris, it is also a favorite for lunch or supper and makes a wonderful light meal at home. The secrets of delicious onion soup are cooking the onions slowly in butter and using a good homemade stock and a good cheese; French or Swiss Gruyère yield the best results.   MAKES 6 SERVINGS

¼ cup unsalted butter
1 ½ pounds onions, thinly sliced
Salt and freshly ground pepper
5 cups Chicken Stock (see recipe),
   Vegetable Stock (see recipe), or
   a mixture of stocks
1 bay leaf

3 sprigs fresh thyme
6 thick slices French or Italian
   bread (about ¾ inch thick
   and 3 inches in diameter)
2 egg yolks, room temperature
⅓ cup port
1 ½ cups grated Gruyère cheese

Prepare 6 ovenproof soup bowls or large ramekins.

In a large heavy saucepan melt butter over low heat, add onions and pinch of salt and pepper. Cover with buttered parchment paper or foil and with a lid and cook, stirring occasionally, about 20 minutes, or until onions are tender. Uncover and continue cooking over medium heat until onions are golden brown. Add stock. Wrap bay leaf and thyme in a piece of cheesecloth and tie tightly to make a bouquet garni; add to soup. Bring to a boil, cover, reduce heat to low, and simmer for at least 30 minutes, or up to 1 hour, until well flavored. Discard bouquet garni and taste and adjust seasoning. (Soup can be kept, covered, up to 2 days in refrigerator. Reheat, covered, over medium heat.)

Meanwhile, preheat oven to 325°F. Put sliced bread on a baking sheet and bake about 5 minutes on each side, or until dry. Beat egg yolks with port and put in a sauceboat.

To serve, put 1 slice bread in each ovenproof soup bowl. Ladle soup over bread. Sprinkle with cheese. Broil until cheese is lightly browned. Serve immediately. (If you do not have ovenproof soup bowls, you can sprinkle the cheese on the bread slices, set them on a baking sheet, brown them in the broiler, and pass them separately.) Serve port mixture separately so that those who wish can stir it into their soup under the topping.

CREAMY ONION SOUP WITH PASTA
Potage thourins Roumanille

This easy-to-prepare soup requires no stock. Simmering the onions in milk and adding thin pasta to cook directly in the mixture give it a creamy texture and a delicious flavor.   MAKES 6 SERVINGS

3 to 4 tablespoons butter
5 medium-size onions, halved and
  cut in very thin slices
2 sprigs fresh thyme
1 bay leaf
5 parsley stems
1 large garlic clove, minced

1 tablespoon all-purpose flour
2 cups water
About 3 cups milk
Salt and white pepper
½ cup very thin short noodles
Freshly grated Parmesan cheese, as
  an accompaniment

In a medium-size heavy saucepan, melt butter over low heat, add onions, and cook, stirring often, about 30 minutes, without letting onions brown. If onions seem to be beginning to brown, cover pan after 10 minutes of cooking so that steam will help prevent browning, but continue stirring often. Wrap thyme, bay leaf, and parsley stems in a piece of cheesecloth and tie tightly to make a bouquet garni.

Add garlic to onions and cook 1 minute. Sprinkle flour over mixture and cook over low heat, stirring, for 2 minutes.

Gradually add water to mixture, stirring. Pour in 3 cups milk, stirring. Add bouquet garni and a little salt and white pepper. Bring to a boil, reduce heat to low, and cook, stirring often, for 10 minutes.

Add noodles and continue cooking 5 minutes, or until they are just tender. Add more pepper, taste, and adjust seasoning. Discard bouquet garni. If soup is too thick, stir in a little more milk.

When serving, pass grated cheese for sprinkling on soup.

COUNTRY SPINACH SOUP
Potage campagnard aux épinards

For this rustic soup, the ingredients are not puréed and thus retain their texture. The soup can be served hot or cold. For a vegetable feast, follow it with Spaghetti with Fall Vegetables and Tomato-Tarragon Sauce (see recipe) and a fresh green salad.

MAKES 4 SERVINGS

1 pound fresh spinach (leaves with
    stems)
3 ½ tablespoons butter
½ onion, finely chopped
1 ½ cups water
2 tablespoons uncooked long-grain
    white rice

Salt and freshly ground pepper
1 cup milk
Freshly grated nutmeg
2 egg yolks, room temperature
⅓ cup heavy cream

Discard spinach stems and rinse leaves thoroughly. Hold a handful of leaves on cutting board and cut them crosswise in thin strips. Continue with remaining leaves.

In a medium-size saucepan, heat 2½ tablespoons butter over low heat, add onion, and cook, stirring, about 5 minutes, until softened but not browned. Add spinach and stir until coated with butter. Add water, rice, and salt and pepper, and bring to a boil over high heat. Reduce heat to low, cover, and simmer about 15 minutes, or until rice is tender. Stir in milk, add nutmeg, and simmer, uncovered, for 5 minutes. Remove from heat.

Whisk egg yolks and cream in a bowl until blended. Gradually pour about ½ cup soup into egg yolk mixture. Stir this mixture into soup remaining in saucepan. Warm over low heat, stirring, about 2 minutes, or until slightly thickened; do not boil. Remove from heat, stir in remaining tablespoon butter, and add more salt, pepper, and nutmeg, if needed. Serve immediately.

❧ PROVENÇAL VEGETABLE SOUP WITH PASTA AND PISTOU
Soupe au pistou

Pistou, the French version of the Italian pesto, gives zest to this popular Provençal soup. Basil is the essential ingredient in pistou and thus makes this soup primarily a summer treat. The soup is so well loved in Provence, however, that pistou is often made in large quantities, covered with olive oil, and kept for use in a winter version of the soup as well. Traditionally a mortar and pestle were used to blend the ingredients for the sauce. Today pistou is prepared in seconds with the aid of a food processor.

In addition to or instead of some of the vegetables below, the soup can include spinach, Swiss chard, potatoes, pumpkin, or a small amount of turnip. Although traditional recipes call for cooking all the vegetables together, modern cooks prefer to add the most tender ones last so that they retain their character.   MAKES 8 SERVINGS

*½ cup dried white beans, such as
    Great Northern*
3 quarts water
¼ cup olive oil
2 garlic cloves, chopped
*2 large leeks (white and green
    parts), cleaned and chopped*
*¾ pound ripe tomatoes, peeled,
    seeded, and chopped*
*1 medium-size carrot, peeled and
    diced*

*2 ounces wax beans or green beans,
    ends removed, cut in 3 pieces*
Salt and freshly ground pepper
*4 small zucchini (about 1 pound),
    cut in cubes*
*⅓ cup shelled fresh peas (6 ounces
    in pods)*
1 cup medium-width noodles
*Freshly grated Parmesan cheese, as
    an accompaniment*

PISTOU
6 large garlic cloves
About 2 ounces basil, leaves only
*1 cup freshly grated Parmesan
    cheese*

⅔ cup extra-virgin olive oil

Soak beans overnight in cold water to generously cover; drain thoroughly. Put beans in a large saucepan with 6 cups water. Bring to a boil over medium heat. Simmer, uncovered, for 1 hour, adding hot water occasionally so beans remain covered. Reserve beans in ¾ cup of their liquid.

In saucepan, warm 2 tablespoons olive oil over medium heat, add garlic and leeks, and stir briefly. Add tomatoes and cook, stirring, about 5 minutes. Add carrot, wax or green beans, white beans in their reserved liquid, remaining 6 cups water, remaining 2 tablespoons olive oil, and a pinch of salt and pepper and bring to a boil. Cover and simmer 20 minutes. Add zucchini and simmer about 20 minutes longer, or until vegetables are very tender.

PISTOU

Chop garlic in a food processor. Add basil and cheese and purée with garlic until basil is chopped. Gradually add olive oil, with motor running. Scrape down sides and purée again so mixture is well blended.

Add peas and noodles to soup and simmer about 10 minutes or until just tender. Remove from heat, stir in pistou, taste and adjust seasoning; serve immediately. Serve grated Parmesan cheese separately. (It is best not to reheat this soup because pistou loses its fresh flavor, but any leftovers are very good cold.)

NOTE: Frozen peas (⅓ cup) can be substituted for fresh; add them 5 minutes after adding noodles.

❧ MUSHROOM CREAM SOUP WITH FRESH HERBS
Crème de champignons aux fines herbes

Like a velouté soup, this soup is made with a light velouté sauce but is chunky with slices of mushrooms rather than being puréed. Cultivation of white mushrooms, which are known as "champignons de Paris" in French, began in France about two hundred years ago, and with it came the development of numerous recipes. What a contribution they have made to Western menus!   MAKES 4 SERVINGS

2 medium sprigs fresh thyme, or ½
 teaspoon dried thyme
3 tarragon stems (optional)
1 bay leaf
3 tablespoons butter
2 medium-size shallots, minced
¾ pound small white mushrooms,
 halved and thinly sliced
Salt and freshly ground pepper
3 tablespoons all-purpose flour

1 cup Chicken Stock (see recipe),
 Vegetable Stock (see recipe), or
 water
2 cups milk
¾ cup heavy cream
1 tablespoon chopped fresh tarragon
 (optional)
1 tablespoon minced fresh parsley
Freshly grated nutmeg

Wrap thyme sprigs, tarragon stems, and bay leaf in a piece of cheesecloth and tie tightly to make a bouquet garni.

In large heavy saucepan, melt butter over medium heat, stir in shallots, and cook 1 minute. Stir in mushrooms and add salt and pepper to taste. Cover and cook, shaking pan occasionally, about 5 minutes, or until tender. Uncover and cook over medium heat, stirring, until liquid rendered by mushrooms evaporates.

Reduce heat to low, stir in flour, and cook, stirring constantly, about 3 minutes, or until mixture is well-blended and bubbly.

Remove from heat and gradually pour stock and milk into mushroom mixture, stirring and scraping bottom of saucepan thoroughly. Add bouquet garni and bring to a boil over medium-high heat, stirring constantly. Stir in cream and bring to a simmer, stirring. Reduce heat to low and simmer, uncovered, stirring often, until thickened to taste, about 10 minutes. Discard bouquet garni. (Soup can be kept, covered, up to 2 days in refrigerator. Reheat, uncovered, over low heat.)

Stir in 2 teaspoons tarragon, 2 teaspoons parsley, and nutmeg to taste. Add salt and pepper, if needed. Serve hot, sprinkled with remaining tarragon and parsley.

❧ VEGETABLE BOURRIDE WITH AÏOLI
Bourride de légumes

Traditionally bourride is prepared with fish, but it is also superb when made with vegetables. It has a zesty flavor and a creamy consistency because of the addition of äioli, or garlic sauce, at the end. Broccoli or cauliflower florets can be added instead of or in addition to the other vegetables.   MAKES 5 TO 6 SERVINGS

AÏOLI
4 large garlic cloves, chopped
4 egg yolks
1 teaspoon strained fresh lemon
    juice

½ cup extra-virgin olive oil
Salt and freshly ground pepper

¼ pound small zucchini
½ pound carrots
½ pound leeks, light green and
    white parts only
2 celery stalks, peeled
2-inch sprig fresh rosemary
2 sprigs fresh thyme
1 tablespoon olive oil

⅓ cup chopped onion
1 garlic clove, finely chopped
1 quart Vegetable Stock (see recipe),
    Chicken Stock (see recipe), or
    unsalted vegetable stock powder
    mixed with water
Salt and freshly ground pepper

AÏOLI

Drop garlic cloves through feed tube of a food processor fitted with metal blade, with motor running, and process until finely chopped. Add egg yolks, lemon juice, 1 tablespoon oil and a little salt and pepper and process until very thoroughly blended, scraping bottom and sides of container several times. With motor running, gradually pour in oil in a thin trickle. After adding ¼ cup, oil can be poured in a little faster, in a fine stream.

Cut zucchini into pieces 1½ inches long, then into ¼-inch lengthwise slices. Cut each slice lengthwise into sticks ¼ inch wide. Cut carrots, leeks, and celery in pieces of same size as zucchini. Wrap rosemary and thyme in a piece of cheesecloth and tie tightly to make a bouquet garni.

In a medium-size heavy saucepan, heat oil over low heat, add onion, and cook, stirring often, about 5 minutes, or until soft but not brown. Add garlic and cook 30 seconds, stirring.

Add stock, bouquet garni, and salt and pepper to taste. Stir and bring to a boil. Add carrots, reduce heat to low, and simmer, uncovered, 5 minutes. Add celery and leeks, cover, and return to a simmer. Cook over low heat for 15 minutes, or until carrots are just tender. Add zucchini and cook 8 minutes, or until just tender.

Remove soup from heat. Discard bouquet garni. Using slotted spoon, transfer vegetables to medium-size bowl, letting as much soup as possible drain back into pan. Holding solids back with large slotted spoon, drain any liquid from bottom of bowl back into pan.

Spoon aïoli into a medium-size heavy bowl, gradually whisk about 2 cups of soup into aïoli. With saucepan of soup off heat, gradually whisk mixture into remaining soup. Return soup to low heat and warm, whisking constantly, for 4 or 5 minutes; be careful not to let it come near a boil.

Remove from heat and gently add vegetable mixture with a slotted spoon, leaving behind any liquid in bowl. Taste and adjust seasoning. Serve hot. (Leftover bourride can be reheated in a double boiler, very carefully and with constant stirring, until just warm; or it can be served at room temperature but not cold.)

SOUTHWESTERN VEGETABLE SOUP WITH VEGETABLE CROUTONS
Potage garbure

This soup originated in the Pyrenees area of southwest France and is made from a variety of vegetables. Fresh peas, zucchini, green beans, or other vegetables in season can be added. The soup is sometimes flavored with goose fat and meat and used to be made thick enough so a spoon could stand up in it, but today many prefer this lighter version. Vegetable croutons, made of vegetable purée spread on bread, sprinkled with grated Gruyère, and browned in the oven, are the special accompaniment. They involve very little extra work because their topping is made from vegetables that cook in the soup.

⅓ cup dried white beans, such as Great Northern

1 whole onion

2 cloves

2 sprigs fresh thyme, or ½ teaspoon dried thyme

1 bay leaf

3 to 4 tablespoons butter

2 leeks, white part only, cleaned and cut in thin slices

3 medium-size celery stalks, peeled and cut in thin slices; or 1 small celery root, peeled and cut in small dice

¾ pound carrots, peeled and cut in thin slices

1 medium-size turnip, peeled and cut in thin slices

¼ small cabbage, cut in thin slices (optional)

2 medium-size potatoes, peeled, halved and cut in thin slices

2 garlic cloves, chopped

About 6 cups Vegetable Stock (see recipe) or water

Salt and freshly ground pepper

1 thin French bread (baguette), or 4 long French rolls, cut in thin slices

½ cup grated Gruyère cheese

Pinch of cayenne pepper

2 tablespoons chopped fresh parsley

Soak beans about 8 hours or overnight in cold water to generously cover; drain thoroughly. Put beans and onion in a large saucepan and add enough water to cover by about 1 inch. Wrap cloves, thyme, and bay leaf in a piece of cheesecloth and tie tightly to make a bouquet garni, and add to pan. Bring to a boil over medium heat and simmer, uncovered, for 1½ hours, adding hot water occasionally so beans remain covered. Discard bouquet garni. Reserve beans in ¾ cup of their liquid.

In a large saucepan, melt 2 tablespoons butter over low heat. Add leeks, celery, carrots, turnip, and cabbage. Cook, stirring often, 15 minutes.

Add potatoes, garlic, 6 cups stock, beans in their liquid, and pinch of salt and pepper. Bring to a boil, reduce heat to low, cover, and cook about 30 minutes, or until all vegetables are very tender.

Meanwhile, preheat oven to 375°F. Put sliced bread on a lightly buttered baking sheet and bake about 3 minutes on each side or until lightly toasted.

Remove about one-quarter of vegetables from saucepan with a

slotted spoon. Purée them in a blender or food processor until very smooth. Transfer to a small saucepan and cook over low heat, stirring, until mixture is very thick. Taste and adjust seasoning. Spread mixture generously on bread slices and sprinkle with grated cheese. Bake about 10 minutes or until cheese melts and browns lightly; if necessary, broil briefly to brown. (Soup and topping for croutons can be prepared 2 days ahead and kept, covered, in refrigerator; but croutons should be baked a short time before serving.)

Reheat soup before serving. If soup is too thick, stir in a little more stock. Stir in remaining 1 or 2 tablespoons butter, if desired, add a pinch of cayenne pepper, taste and adjust seasoning. Sprinkle with chopped parsley and serve. Serve croutons separately.

NOTE: After croutons are made, remaining vegetables can also be puréed until smooth and served as a purée soup.

Vegetable Purée Soups

Puréed vegetables are what give these quick, easy soups their characteristic flavor and thickness. The vegetables are cooked in stock or water before being puréed with their cooking liquid. There are French cooks who prefer to use water rather than stock to emphasize the natural flavor of the vegetables.

Most vegetables require the addition of a small amount of rice or potatoes to give the soup enough body. For vegetables that contain a relatively high proportion of starch, such as green peas, chestnuts, or dried beans, the thickener can be omitted. A light version of purée soups can be made from nonstarchy vegetables by simply increasing the amount of vegetable purée, as in Light Cauliflower Soup. Whichever technique is chosen, a little cream or fresh butter provide the ideal final enrichment.

Hints

• A food processor, blender, or food mill with a fine disk can be used to purée vegetables for soups. When using a food processor, it is best to add the vegetables and a few tablespoons of the liquid. In a blender, the soup can be puréed most efficiently if all the liquid is added along with the cooked vegetables. A food mill is useful for puréeing fibrous vegetables such as watercress, so that the strings do not go through into the soup. Another way to eliminate the fibers is to purée the soup in a blender or food processor and then strain it.

• If substituting canned broth or broth made from powder for homemade stock in soups, use volume of regular-strength broth equal to amount of stock called for in the recipe.

• Fresh herbs, especially tarragon, dill, basil, parsley, chives, and chervil, can be added to purée, cream, and velouté soups for extra flavor and color. Stir 2 to 3 tablespoons minced herb into the soup just before serving; or after ladling the bowl into a tureen or into bowls, sprinkle with about 1 tablespoon minced herb for garnish.

• Purée, cream, and velouté soups thicken on standing. After reheating them or when serving them cold, gradually add 1 or 2 tablespoons heavy cream, milk, stock, or water to the soup to bring it back to the desired consistency.

FRESH PEA SOUP WITH MINT CREAM
Purée de petits pois à la crème de menthe

Serve this rich, bright-green soup in small portions, either hot or cold.   MAKES 4 SERVINGS

½ cup Crème Fraîche (see recipe)
or purchased crème fraîche or
sour cream
1 tablespoon chopped fresh mint
4 cups shelled fresh peas (about 4
pounds in pods)
2 cups Vegetable Stock (see recipe)
or water

Salt and freshly ground pepper
1 cup milk
1 cup heavy cream
Small sprigs of mint, for garnish
(optional)

To make mint cream, mix crème fraîche or sour cream with chopped mint. Let stand for 30 minutes at room temperature if serving soup hot, or in refrigerator if serving it cold.

In a medium-size saucepan, combine peas with stock or water and salt and pepper to taste. Bring to a boil, reduce heat to medium-low, cover, and simmer about 7 minutes, or until barely tender. Remove 2 tablespoons peas with a slotted spoon and reserve for garnish. Continue cooking remaining peas about 10 minutes, or until very tender.

Transfer peas and their cooking liquid to a blender or food processor. Purée peas until very fine. With machine running, gradually pour in 1 cup milk. Continue to purée until very smooth. Return to saucepan and simmer over low heat 2 minutes, stirring often.

Stir in heavy cream. Bring to a boil, stirring, and simmer soup to desired consistency, about 5 minutes. Taste and adjust seasoning. (The soup may be kept, covered, up to 1 day in refrigerator.)

Just before serving, reheat soup over medium-low heat, stirring. To reheat reserved peas, put them in a pan of boiling water and heat 30 seconds; drain well. Ladle soup into shallow bowls. Spoon mint cream into center of each bowl. Garnish with reserved peas and sprigs of mint.

NOTE: Four cups (20 to 21 ounces or two 10-ounce packages) frozen peas can be substituted for fresh. Cook peas for garnish about 5 minutes; continue cooking remaining peas about 3 minutes more.

TOURAINE CHESTNUT SOUP
Potage aux marrons à la tourangelle

This soup from the Loire Valley south of Paris makes a rich, elegant first course. Fresh herbs are added to the finished soup to balance the delicate, naturally sweet taste of the chestnuts.

MAKES 4 SMALL SERVINGS

1 pound fresh chestnuts

1 tablespoon butter

1 medium-size leek, white part
  only, chopped

1½ cups Chicken Stock (see recipe),
  Vegetable Stock (see recipe), or
  water

1 small celery stalk, broken in two
  pieces

1 bay leaf

Salt and freshly ground pepper

3 cups milk, plus a little more if
  needed

⅓ cup heavy cream or Crème
  Fraîche (see recipe)

2 teaspoons sliced or snipped chives

2 teaspoons minced fresh tarragon

1 tablespoon plus 2 teaspoons
  minced fresh parsley

In a medium-size saucepan, combine half the chestnuts with enough water to cover them by about 1 inch. Bring to full boil and cook 1 minute. Remove one nut with slotted spoon and peel: first cut base and pull off outer skin, and then pull and scrape off inner skin. Continue with remaining nuts, removing from water one by one.

In a medium-size saucepan, melt butter over low heat, add leek, and cook, stirring, about 5 minutes, or until soft but not brown. Add chestnuts, 1½ cups stock or water, celery, bay leaf, and salt and pepper to taste. Bring to a boil, reduce heat to low, cover, and simmer until chestnuts are just tender when pierced with point of knife, about 15 minutes.

Bring milk to a boil in a separate saucepan. Stir 2 cups hot milk into soup. (Cover remaining milk and reserve.) Simmer soup, uncovered, over medium heat, about 20 minutes, or until chestnuts are very tender. Discard celery pieces and bay leaf. Purée soup in blender or purée chestnuts in a food processor and add rest of soup liquid to food processor with motor running. Return puréed soup to clean saucepan.

Bring soup to a boil, stirring, add remaining milk, and return to a boil. Add cream and return to a boil. Remove from heat. If preparing soup ahead, stir as it cools. (Soup can be kept, covered, up to 2 days in refrigerator.)

Soup thickens on standing. If soup was cold, reheat it, whisking. If soup is too thick after reheating, stir in 1 or 2 tablespoons milk to bring it to desired consistency.

Stir in chives, tarragon, and 1 tablespoon parsley. Taste and adjust seasoning; be generous with the seasoning so soup will not be bland. Serve hot. Sprinkle remaining parsley on each serving.

ASPARAGUS SOUP WITH OLIVE OIL
Soupe d'asperges à la languedocienne

Asparagus is delicious both in a cream soup in the style of northern France (as in the variation) and in this southern version, from Languedoc.   MAKES 3 TO 4 SERVINGS

2 egg yolks, room temperature
1 teaspoon strained fresh lemon
   juice
Salt
6 tablespoons extra-virgin olive oil

2 pounds medium-size asparagus
   spears
4 cups water
White pepper

CROUTONS (OPTIONAL)
4 slices white bread, crusts removed   *1 egg yolk*
4 to 6 tablespoons vegetable oil
⅓ cup heavy cream or Crème
   Fraîche (see recipe)

In a medium-size heavy bowl set on a towel, whisk egg yolks with lemon juice and a pinch of salt. Begin whisking or beating in oil, drop by drop. When 2 or 3 tablespoons oil have been added, whisk in remaining oil in a very thin stream. Transfer to a large bowl.

Peel asparagus spears and cut in 2-inch pieces, discarding tough ends. Reserve 16 to 20 tips for garnish.

In medium-size saucepan, bring 4 cups water to boil and add salt. Add asparagus pieces (except tips reserved for garnish) and return to a boil. Simmer, uncovered, over medium heat about 15 minutes, or until stalks are very tender when pierced with a small sharp knife. Drain, reserving 2 cups cooking liquid.

Purée asparagus in food processor until very smooth. Gradually add 2 cups reserved cooking liquid, with machine running. (If using blender, combine asparagus with reserved liquid and purée.) Strain into a medium-size heavy saucepan, pushing and stirring hard and repeatedly and using rubber spatula to scrape mixture from underside of strainer.

In a medium-size saucepan of boiling salted water, cook asparagus tips, uncovered, over high heat about 2 minutes, or until barely tender. Rinse and drain well.

Bring soup to a boil and remove from heat. Gradually whisk soup into egg yolk mixture. Return to saucepan and cook over low heat, stirring, about 2 minutes, or until slightly thickened; do not let soup come near boil or it will curdle. Add white pepper and taste and adjust seasoning. Stir in asparagus tips. Serve immediately in shallow bowls; pass croutons separately.

CREAMY ASPARAGUS SOUP
Beat the 2 egg yolks with ½ cup heavy cream. Omit oil, lemon juice, and croutons. Finish soup as above, thickening it with the cream mixture.

CROUTONS
Cut bread in ½-inch squares.

In a large heavy skillet, heat 4 tablespoons oil. Test oil by adding a bread square; if oil is hot enough, it should bubble vigorously around bread. Remove bread piece with slotted spatula.

Add enough of remaining bread squares to hot oil to make one layer in skillet. Toss them frequently to turn them over so they will brown evenly. Alternately, turn them over frequently using a slotted spatula. Fry them until they are golden brown.

Transfer to paper towels to drain. If pan is dry, add another 2 tablespoons oil and heat thoroughly. Repeat frying remaining bread squares. (The croutons can be made 2 hours ahead and kept at room temperature.)

LIGHT CAULIFLOWER SOUP
Potage léger au chou-fleur

This soup is light in texture because no thickening ingredients are added. It is good hot or cold. If you like, serve it with Cheese Puffs (see recipe).   MAKES 4 TO 6 SERVINGS

1 small cauliflower (about 1¼ pounds)

2 tablespoons butter

1 onion, thinly sliced

¼ teaspoon fresh thyme, or pinch of dried thyme

1 bay leaf

Salt and freshly ground pepper

1½ cups water

1 cup milk

Freshly grated nutmeg

½ cup heavy cream

1½ to 2 tablespoons thinly sliced or snipped chives

Divide cauliflower into medium-size florets. Reserve a few small florets for garnish. Peel and slice cauliflower stalk. In a medium-size saucepan, melt butter over low heat, add onion, and cook, stirring occasionally, about 10 minutes, or until tender. Add cauliflower (except florets reserved for garnish), thyme, bay leaf, and salt and pepper to taste. Stir briefly over low heat, cover, and cook 2 to 3 minutes. Add water, cover, bring to a boil, reduce heat to low, and simmer, stirring often so all cauliflower pieces come in contact with water, about 20 minutes, or until cauliflower is very tender.

Discard bay leaf. Transfer cauliflower and onion pieces to a food processor; reserve cooking liquid. Purée cauliflower and onion until smooth and return purée to saucepan of cooking liquid. (If using a blender, purée cauliflower and onion with cooking liquid and return to pan.) Bring to a boil, stirring, add milk and nutmeg to taste, and bring to a boil. Stir in cream and bring again to a boil. Simmer, stirring, about 3 minutes, or until soup thickens to desired consistency. Add half of chives and more salt, pepper, and nutmeg, if needed. (The soup can be kept, covered, up to 1 day in refrigerator.)

A short time before serving, cook reserved florets in a pan of boiling salted water about 4 minutes, or until just tender. Reheat soup if necessary. To serve, set 1 or 2 florets in center of each soup bowl. Sprinkle remaining chives around florets.

PUMPKIN AND PASTA SOUP
Purée de potiron à la bourgeoise

While American cooks have been stimulated by the sweet flavor and smooth texture of pumpkin to make pie fillings, the French find those same characteristics perfect for making savory dishes, including a soup with the poetic name of *creme d'or* or "golden cream." In this recipe the short-seasoned pumpkin can be replaced by winter squash, such as Hubbard or banana squash, which are available most of the year.   MAKES 4 SERVINGS

2½ pounds fresh pumpkin or
     winter squash
1½ cups water
4 teaspoons sugar
Salt and freshly ground pepper

1½ cups milk
½ cup thin noodles or vermicelli,
     broken in 1½- to 2-inch
     lengths
¼ cup butter

Cut pumpkin or squash in pieces and cut off peel. Remove any seeds or stringy flesh. Cut pumpkin or squash in about 1½-inch cubes and rinse them. In a saucepan, combine pumpkin or squash with water, sugar, and salt and pepper. Cover and bring to a boil, reduce heat to medium-low, and simmer, turning pieces over often, about 20 minutes, or until tender.

With a slotted spoon, transfer pumpkin or squash pieces to a food processor or blender and purée until smooth. Return purée to pan of cooking liquid and bring to a boil. Cook, uncovered, over low heat for 5 minutes, stirring often. Add milk and bring to a simmer. Cook over low heat, stirring often, 5 more minutes. (The soup can be prepared 1 day ahead up to this point and kept, covered, in refrigerator.)

Reheat soup if necessary. Add noodles, stir gently, and cook over low heat about 7 minutes, or until they are just tender; do not overcook or they will lose their texture. Taste and adjust seasoning. Remove from heat and add butter, 1 tablespoon at a time. Stir and serve immediately.

PUMPKIN, POTATO, AND LEEK SOUP
Potage de potiron aux poireaux et aux pommes de terre

This light, delicate soup is more colorful than its famous cousin, potato and leek soup. The green part of the leek should not be used because it gives the soup an odd color.   MAKES 4 SERVINGS

1 pound fresh pumpkin or winter
   squash
2 leeks, white part only, rinsed
   thoroughly
2 medium-size potatoes
1 ½ cups water

Salt
1 cup milk
½ cup heavy cream
White pepper
Freshly grated nutmeg
1 tablespoon chopped fresh parsley

Cut pumpkin or squash in pieces and cut off peel. Remove any seeds or stringy flesh. Cut pumpkin or squash in cubes. Thoroughly rinse and slice leeks. Peel potatoes and cut them in pieces.

In a saucepan, combine pumpkin, leeks, potatoes, water, and a pinch of salt. Cover and bring to a boil, reduce heat to low, and simmer about 30 minutes, or until vegetables are very tender.

With a slotted spoon, transfer vegetables to a food processor and add a few tablespoons of their cooking liquid; purée until smooth and return to saucepan containing remaining cooking liquid. If using a blender, purée vegetables together with their liquid.

Bring soup to a boil and simmer 5 minutes. Stir in milk, reduce heat to low, and simmer 2 minutes. Stir in cream and bring to a simmer. Add white pepper and nutmeg to taste. Add more salt, pepper, and nutmeg, if needed. (Soup can be kept, covered, 1 day in refrigerator.)

Reheat soup over low heat if necessary. Sprinkle each serving with chopped parsley.

PROVENÇAL TOMATO SOUP
Soupe de tomates à la provençale

This soup is made with the favorite ingredients of Provence: tomatoes, garlic, basil, and olive oil. It is important to use very ripe tomatoes at the peak of their season. The pestolike herb oil added just before the soup is served gives it extra zest.   MAKES 4 SERVINGS

2 tablespoons extra-virgin olive oil
1 large onion, thinly sliced
3 small garlic cloves, minced
4 pounds very ripe soft tomatoes,
     cored and cut in eighths
Salt
½ to ¾ teaspoon sugar

2 tablespoons coarsely chopped fresh
     basil
¾ teaspoon minced fresh thyme, or
     ¼ teaspoon dried thyme
Freshly ground pepper
1 clove
1 bay leaf

HERB OIL

1 large garlic clove
⅓ cup loosely packed fresh parsley

⅓ cup loosely packed fresh basil
3 tablespoons extra-virgin olive oil

1 tablespoon thin strips of fresh
     basil, or a few small whole
     basil leaves, for garnish
     (optional)

In a large heavy saucepan, heat oil over low heat, add onion, and cook, stirring often, about 20 minutes, or until soft and just beginning to brown. Add garlic and cook, stirring, 1 minute.

Add tomatoes, sprinkle them with salt, and stir. Add ½ teaspoon sugar, basil, thyme, and a pinch of pepper. Tie clove and bay leaf in cheesecloth, add to saucepan, and push into tomatoes. Bring to a boil, cover, and simmer over medium heat, stirring often, for 20 minutes, or until very soft. Discard cheesecloth bag.

Purée tomato mixture in a food mill, using fine disk. Push as much as possible through until pulp remaining in food mill is dry. Scrape off any mixture remaining on underside of disk. Rinse saucepan. Return purée to pan and bring to a boil, reduce heat to low, and simmer, uncovered, stirring often, about 15 minutes, or until soup is of desired thickness. (Soup can be kept, covered, 1 day in refrigerator.)

HERB OIL

In a food processor, chop garlic clove, add basil and parsley, and process until finely minced. Add oil and purée until blended. The mixture will not be smooth and emulsified. Transfer to a bowl and stir briefly to blend in oil.

Just before serving, reheat soup if necessary. Remove from heat and stir in herb oil. Taste and adjust seasoning, adding remaining sugar if desired. Serve garnished with basil.

❧ LIGHT ZUCCHINI SOUP WITH CURRY PUFFS
Purée de courgettes aux gnocchis

This light soup is thickened by a generous amount of zucchini purée. The curry puffs are made of a mixture similar to a rich *pâte à choux* and can be flavored with paprika or herbs (added to finished dough) instead of curry powder. These types of puffs can be used to garnish other vegetable purée soups, especially cauliflower, broccoli, and spinach soups.   MAKES 4 TO 6 SERVINGS

CURRY PUFFS

⅔ cup all-purpose flour

½ cup milk

¼ teaspoon salt

½ teaspoon curry powder

3 tablespoons unsalted butter, cut in cubes

1 egg

1 egg yolk

LIGHT ZUCCHINI SOUP

1 ½ pounds small zucchini

2 tablespoons butter

1 onion, thinly sliced

1 sprig of fresh thyme, or ¼ teaspoon dried thyme

1 bay leaf

Salt and freshly ground pepper

1 ½ cups water

½ cup milk

⅓ to ½ cup heavy cream

Pinch of cayenne pepper

CURRY PUFFS

Sift flour onto a piece of wax paper.

Combine milk, salt, curry powder, and butter in a small heavy saucepan. Cook over low heat, stirring constantly, until butter melts. Raise heat to medium-high and bring to a boil. Remove from heat, immediately add flour all at once, and stir quickly with a wooden spoon until mixture is smooth. Set pan over low heat and beat mixture about 30 seconds.

Remove from heat and cool about 3 minutes. Beat egg and yolk in a small bowl. Gradually beat egg mixture into dough. Beat with a wooden spoon until mixture is very smooth. (The mixture can be kept, covered, up to 4 hours in refrigerator.)

LIGHT ZUCCHINI SOUP

Cut zucchini in medium-size slices. In a medium-size saucepan, melt butter over low heat, add onion, and cook, stirring occasionally, about 10 minutes, or until soft. Add zucchini, thyme, bay leaf, and salt and pepper to taste. Stir briefly over low heat so zucchini absorbs flavor from butter, add water, and bring to a boil. Reduce heat to low, cover, and simmer 7 to 10 minutes, or until zucchini is tender.

Discard bay leaf and fresh thyme sprig, if using fresh. Transfer zucchini and onion pieces to blender or food processor, reserving cooking liquid. Purée until smooth. Return purée to saucepan of cooking liquid; bring to boil, stirring. Stir in milk and bring to boil. Stir in 1/3 cup cream and bring again to boil. Add cayenne pepper, taste and adjust seasoning. (Soup can be kept, covered, 1 day in refrigerator.)

A short time before serving, boil a generous amount of salted water in a large wide saucepan. Reduce heat to medium so water simmers. Take a half teaspoonful of curry dough on a teaspoon; dip a second teaspoon in simmering water and use it to push mixture from first spoon into water. Continue making puffs in this way; try to give them a fairly even oval shape. Do not crowd; they need room to puff.

Reduce heat to low and cook puffs, uncovered, about 10 to 15 minutes. To check whether they are done, remove one and cut it; if dough sticks to knife, they are not cooked enough.

Remove with a slotted spoon and drain on paper towels.

To serve, bring soup to a boil, stirring. Ladle it into bowls and put two or three puffs in each.

NORMAN POTATO-SHALLOT SOUP
Potage de pommes de terre aux échalotes à la normande

This simple country potato soup is accented by a delicate shallot flavor and enriched with cream.　　　　MAKES 3 TO 4 SERVINGS

2 thyme sprigs, or ½ teaspoon dried
    thyme
1 bay leaf
2 tablespoons butter
10 medium-size shallots, chopped
    (about ½ pound)
2 medium-size potatoes, peeled and
    diced (about 13 ounces)

3 cups water
Salt and white pepper
½ cup Crème Fraîche (see recipe)
    or purchased crème fraîche or
    heavy cream
1 or 2 tablespoons milk or heavy
    cream (optional)

Wrap bay leaf and thyme sprigs in a piece of cheesecloth and tie tightly to make a bouquet garni.

In a large saucepan, melt butter over low heat, add shallots, and cook, stirring often, about 3 minutes, or until they soften. Add potatoes, water, bouquet garni, and salt and white pepper to taste, and bring to a boil. Reduce heat to low, cover, and cook about 25 minutes, or until potatoes are tender.

Discard bouquet garni. Stir cream into soup and bring to a simmer. With a slotted spoon, transfer vegetables to a food processor and add a few tablespoons of their cooking liquid; purée them until smooth and gradually add remaining cooking liquid. If using a blender, purée vegetables together with all their cooking liquid.

Return soup to saucepan and bring to a boil, add more pepper, taste and adjust seasoning. (Soup can be kept, covered, 1 day in refrigerator.)

Reheat soup over medium heat, stirring often. If soup is too thick, stir in a few tablespoons milk or cream.

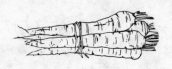

CARROT SOUP WITH CHIVES
Purée de carottes à la ciboulette

This sensational soup has a great flavor and superb color. A small amount of cooked rice puréed with the carrots imparts a velvety texture to the soup.
    MAKES 4 SERVINGS

2 tablespoons butter
1 pound carrots, finely diced
2 cups water or Vegetable Stock (see recipe)
2 tablespoons uncooked rice
Salt and freshly ground pepper
Pinch of sugar

1/4 teaspoon dried thyme
1 bay leaf
About 1 cup milk
1/3 cup heavy cream
4 teaspoons thinly sliced or snipped chives

In a medium-size heavy saucepan, melt butter over low heat, add carrots, and cook, stirring often, about 3 minutes.

Add water or stock, rice, salt, pepper, sugar, thyme, and bay leaf to saucepan and bring to a boil. Reduce heat to low, cover, and cook about 30 minutes, or until carrots and rice are very tender. Discard bay leaf.

Using a slotted spoon, transfer carrots and rice to a blender or food processor, reserving their cooking liquid. Purée carrots until fine. With machine running, gradually pour in carrot cooking liquid. Purée until very smooth. Return to saucepan and simmer over low heat 5 minutes, stirring often.

Add enough of milk to bring soup to desired consistency. Bring to a boil, stirring. Add cream and bring again to a boil, stirring. Taste and adjust seasoning. (Soup can be kept, covered, 2 days in refrigerator.)

Just before serving, reheat soup over medium-low heat, stirring. Ladle soup into bowls and garnish with chives.

Vegetable Cream and Velouté Soups

Velouté in French means velvety and is the perfect description of the texture of cream and velouté soups. They acquire a smooth, silky texture from a roux made of butter and flour cooked together, which also thickens them. These delicious festive soups are a French culinary treasure.

The traditional technique for preparing cream soups calls for a thin béchamel sauce, made from milk and a roux, combined with a puréed vegetable, as in Swiss Chard Soup with Toasted Hazelnuts. This method can be used to create a cream soup from almost any vegetable, but the favorites are asparagus, broccoli, cauliflower, carrots, leeks, lettuce, mushrooms, spinach, tomatoes, turnips, watercress, and zucchini.

Velouté soups are based on a light version of velouté sauce, which is composed of stock thickened with a small amount of roux. For vegetable veloutés, either chicken stock or vegetable stock can be used. Like cream soups, veloutés can be prepared from a purée of nearly any vegetable. In classic cuisine, velouté soups are enriched with a mixture of cream and egg yolks, which gives them a wonderful flavor and a beautiful light yellow color. Many contemporary cooks omit the egg yolks because of their tendency to curdle during reheating.

Delicacy of taste is characteristic of these soups and extra flavorings are usually avoided so the flavor of the major ingredient will remain pure.

The favorite decoration for cream and velouté soups is a small quantity of the main element, which is left in pieces instead of being puréed or strained. In Red Pepper Velouté Soup, for example, a little diced red pepper is added at the last moment. To highlight the garnish and prevent it from sinking, shallow bowls are preferred for serving this kind of soup.

"Soup is to a dinner what the entrance portico is to a building," wrote Grimod de la Reynière, a noted French gastronomic writer. Because cream and velouté soups are rich, they should be served in rather small portions. They are not meant to play the role of a main course, but rather of an elegant beginning that should stimulate the appetite for the rest of a fine meal.

Hints

• Soups that contain flour should be cooked in a heavy saucepan to prevent sticking. A whisk is most practical for stirring soups that do not contain any chunks; otherwise use a wooden spoon. These soups should be stirred often while they simmer, by moving the whisk or spoon over the entire surface of the saucepan and around the edges, to prevent the flour from causing lumps.

- To ensure complete smoothness, cream and velouté soups can be strained.
- Cream and velouté soups should be delicately flavored but not bland. Season them well.
- Reheat soups gently over low heat, whisking or stirring. If a soup containing egg yolks must be reheated, set it over low heat in a double boiler or a pan above hot, not boiling, water and heat it carefully, stirring constantly. Remove the soup from the heat as soon as it is warm. It should not boil.

SWISS CHARD SOUP WITH TOASTED HAZELNUTS
Crème de blettes aux noisettes

A sprinkling of toasted hazelnuts on each serving contributes elegance, flavor, and a crunchy contrast to this smooth and creamy pale green soup.   MAKES 4 SERVINGS

1 ¼ pounds Swiss chard
3 cups water
¼ cup butter
¼ cup all-purpose flour
2 cups milk, plus a few tablespoons
    more if needed

Salt and freshly ground pepper
Freshly grated nutmeg
¼ cup hazelnuts
⅓ cup heavy cream

Discard chard stems and rinse leaves thoroughly. In a medium-size saucepan, bring 3 cups water to a boil and add chard. Boil 3 minutes or until just tender. Drain, reserving liquid. Rinse chard under cold water and drain thoroughly. Squeeze out excess liquid. Measure 2 cups chard cooking liquid.

In medium-size saucepan, melt 1 tablespoon butter over low heat, add chard, and cook, stirring, about 2 minutes to dry.

In a medium-size heavy saucepan, melt remaining 3 tablespoons butter over low heat, add flour, and cook over low heat, whisking constantly, for 2 minutes. Remove from heat, gradually whisk in milk and reserved 2 cups chard cooking liquid, and cook over medium-high heat, whisking constantly, until mixture comes to boil. Add chard and season with salt, pepper, and nutmeg to taste. Reduce heat to low and cook, stirring often, about 10 minutes.

Preheat oven to 350°F. In a shallow baking pan, toast hazelnuts in oven about 8 minutes, or until skins begin to split. Transfer to a large strainer. Rub hot nuts against strainer with terry-cloth towel to remove most of skins. Cool nuts completely. Chop coarsely with a knife.

Purée soup in a blender, food processor, or food mill with a fine disk. Return soup to saucepan. Bring to a boil, stirring. Add cream and return to boil. Simmer, stirring often, about 6 minutes, or until thickened slightly; it should be slightly thick so the hazelnuts will not sink. (Soup can be kept, covered, 2 days in refrigerator; keep toasted hazelnuts separately in covered container at room temperature.)

Reheat soup if serving hot. Stir in a few tablespoons milk if soup is too thick. Taste and add more salt, pepper and nutmeg if needed. Serve hot or cold. Spoon into bowls and sprinkle hazelnuts over each serving.

❧ LEEK CREAM SOUP WITH DICED TOMATOES
Crème de poireaux aux dés de tomates

Ripe tomatoes add bright flecks of red to this delicate, rich soup.

MAKES 4 SERVINGS

2 medium sprigs fresh thyme, or ½ teaspoon dried thyme
1 bay leaf
3 tablespoons butter
8 medium or 4 large leeks, white and light green parts only, split and cleaned
Salt and freshly ground pepper
2 tablespoons all-purpose flour

1 cup Chicken Stock (see recipe), Vegetable Stock (see recipe), or water
2½ to 3 cups milk
½ cup heavy cream
1 large ripe tomato, peeled, seeded, drained well, and diced
Freshly grated nutmeg
1 tablespoon minced fresh parsley

Wrap thyme sprigs or dried thyme and bay leaf in a piece of cheesecloth and tie tightly to make a bouquet garni.

In a large heavy saucepan, melt butter over medium heat, stir in leeks, and add salt and pepper. Reduce heat to low and cook, stirring often, about 10 minutes, or until leeks are softened but not brown.

Stir in flour and cook, stirring constantly, about 2 minutes, or until mixture is well blended and bubbly.

Remove from heat; gradually pour stock and 2½ cups milk into leek mixture, stirring and scraping bottom of saucepan thoroughly. Add bouquet garni and bring to a boil over medium-high heat, stirring constantly. Reduce heat to low and simmer, uncovered, stirring often, about 15 minutes, or until leeks are tender.

Discard bouquet garni. Purée soup in a blender or food processor until smooth. If soup is too thick, stir in enough of remaining milk to thin it so it lightly coats a spoon. Stir in cream and bring to a boil. Simmer, if necessary, to desired consistency. (Soup can be kept, covered, 2 days in refrigerator.)

Reheat soup, if necessary, over medium heat, reduce heat to low, add tomato, and simmer 1 minute.

Stir in nutmeg to taste and 2 teaspoons parsley. Add more salt, pepper, and nutmeg if needed. Serve hot; sprinkle each serving with a little of remaining parsley.

ᕫ SORREL VELOUTÉ SOUP
Velouté d'oseille

Creamy, tangy, refreshing sorrel soup is a favorite throughout northern France, from Brittany to Alsace and south to the Loire Valley.   MAKES 4 SERVINGS

¼ pound fresh sorrel (leaves with stems)

3 tablespoons unsalted butter

3 tablespoons all-purpose flour

2 cups Vegetable Stock (see recipe), Chicken Stock (see recipe), or water

Salt and freshly ground pepper

1½ cups milk, plus a few tablespoons more if needed

⅓ cup heavy cream or Creme Fraîche (see recipe) or purchased crème fraîche

1 egg yolk

Croutons, sautéed in oil, if desired (see page 277)

Remove sorrel stems and wash leaves thoroughly. Chop leaves coarsely.

In a medium-size saucepan, melt butter over low heat, add sorrel, and cook, stirring often, about 10 minutes, or until sorrel is wilted and most of liquid has evaporated. Sprinkle with flour and cook, stirring, until flour is absorbed. Remove from heat.

Gradually stir in stock or water with a whisk. Add a little salt and pepper to taste. Return to medium-high heat and bring to a boil, whisking constantly. Reduce heat to low and simmer, uncovered, whisking often, 20 minutes, or until well flavored. Add milk and bring to a boil, whisking. Remove from heat. (Soup can be kept, covered, 1 day in refrigerator.)

Reheat soup if necessary; if it has become too thick, stir in a few tablespoons milk.

In a medium-size bowl, beat cream with egg yolk. Gradually add about 1 cup of soup. Pour this mixture in a thin stream into remaining soup. Return to low heat and cook, stirring, about 2 minutes, or until hot; do not boil or yolks will curdle. Add more pepper and taste and adjust seasoning.

Ladle into bowls and serve hot. Pass croutons separately.

✤ WATERCRESS VELOUTÉ SOUP WITH CHEESE PUFFS
Velouté de cresson, petits choux au fromage

Watercress becomes delicate when made into a creamy soup in this way, and cheese puffs provide a perfect flavor complement. The watercress purée is strained to remove the stems and stringy parts. Be sure to use very fresh watercress.   MAKES 3 TO 4 SERVINGS

CHEESE PUFFS

1 1/2 ounces imported Gruyère cheese

1/2 cup plus 1 tablespoon
    all-purpose flour

1/2 cup water

1/4 teaspoon salt

1/4 cup unsalted butter, cut in pieces

3 eggs

1 egg, beaten with a pinch of salt,
    for glaze

WATERCRESS SOUP

About 10 to 12 ounces watercress

1/4 cup butter

1 large onion, thinly sliced

1 3/4 cups Chicken Stock (see recipe),
    Vegetable Stock (see recipe), or
    water

Salt and white pepper

3 tablespoons all-purpose flour

1 1/2 to 1 3/4 cups milk

Freshly grated nutmeg

1/4 to 1/2 cup heavy cream

BAKED CHEESE PUFFS

Preheat oven to 400°F. Lightly butter two baking sheets. Use food processor fitted with shredding disk to shred cheese, or grate it by hand. Sift flour onto a piece of wax paper.

In a small heavy saucepan, heat water, salt, and butter until butter melts. Raise heat to medium-high and bring to a boil. Remove from heat, add flour immediately and stir quickly with a wooden spoon until mixture is smooth. Set pan over low heat and beat mixture for about 30 seconds. Remove from heat and let cool for a few minutes.

Add 1 egg and beat it thoroughly into mixture. Add second egg and beat mixture until it is smooth. Reserve 2 tablespoons of shredded cheese for sprinkling on top. Add remaining cheese to dough and beat until blended.

In a small bowl beat third egg with a fork. Gradually beat enough of this egg into dough until dough becomes very shiny and is soft enough so it just falls from spoon.

Using a pastry bag and small plain tip, or using two teaspoons, shape small mounds of dough, spacing them about 1 1/2 inches apart on baking sheets. Brush them with egg glaze. Sprinkle them with remaining cheese. Bake in preheated oven about 15 minutes, or until dough is puffed and browned.

Transfer puffs to a rack to cool. (They can be baked 1 day ahead and kept in an airtight container, but taste best on day they are baked.)

WATERCRESS SOUP

Thoroughly rinse watercress, discard large stems and reserve only upper, leafy third of each bunch. Reserve a few attractive watercress leaves for garnish.

Plunge watercress into a large pan of boiling water. Bring back to a boil, drain, and rinse under cold running water. Squeeze dry in handfuls.

In a medium-size heavy saucepan, melt 1 tablespoon butter over low heat, add onion, and cook, stirring often, until soft but not brown. Add watercress and cook, stirring, 2 more minutes. Add stock and a pinch of salt and pepper and bring to a boil. Cover, reduce heat to low, and simmer, stirring occasionally, about 20 minutes, or until onion is very tender.

Purée soup in a food mill. Alternatively, purée it in a blender or food processor, then strain to remove stringy parts of watercress.

In a medium-size heavy saucepan, melt remaining 3 tablespoons butter over low heat, add flour, and stir it into butter. Cook over low heat, whisking constantly, 2 minutes. Remove from heat and gradually add watercress mixture, followed by 1½ cups milk. Cook over medium-high heat, whisking constantly, until soup comes to boil. Adjust seasoning and add nutmeg to taste. Reduce heat to low and cook, stirring often, about 10 minutes.

Stir in ¼ cup cream and bring again to a boil. If soup is too thin, simmer until it reaches desired consistency; it should lightly coat a spoon. If soup is too thick, stir in ¼ cup cream or milk. Add nutmeg; taste and add more salt, pepper and nutmeg if needed. (The soup can be kept, covered, 1 day in refrigerator.)

If desired, reheat cheese puffs in a 300°F. oven. Reheat soup over low heat, stirring. Stir in 1 to 2 tablespoons milk if needed.

For garnish, put reserved watercress leaves in a small strainer and dip in a small pan of boiling water for 30 seconds. Rinse and drain.

To serve, ladle soup into bowls and garnish with watercress leaves. Serve cheese puffs, hot or at room temperature, separately.

CAULIFLOWER VELOUTÉ SOUP WITH BROCCOLI
Velouté de chou-fleur aux brocolis

Bright green, briefly cooked broccoli florets garnish this rich, creamy cauliflower soup. This soup can also be done in reverse: the broccoli can be made into a velouté soup and garnished with cauliflower florets. Each soup can instead be garnished by florets of the same vegetable.   MAKES 4 TO 5 SERVINGS

2 small heads cauliflower (about
    2½ pounds total), cut into
    medium-size florets
2 to 4 tablespoons butter
2 tablespoons all-purpose flour
1½ cups Vegetable Stock (see
    recipe) or Chicken Stock (see
    recipe)

Salt and white pepper
Freshly grated nutmeg
About 1½ cups milk
⅓ cup heavy cream
About 20 small broccoli florets

Peel cauliflower stalks and slice. Fill large saucepan with water and bring to boil. Add salt, cauliflower florets, and stalks and return to boil. Remove to a colander and rinse under cold water.

In medium-size heavy saucepan, melt 2 tablespoons butter over low heat, add flour, and combine it with butter. Cook over low heat, whisking constantly, for 2 minutes. Remove from heat and gradually whisk in stock. Cook over medium-high heat, whisking constantly, until mixture thickens and comes to boil. Add a pinch of salt, pepper, and nutmeg to taste.

Add cauliflower florets to stock mixture. Add ½ cup milk; liquid will not cover cauliflower. Bring to boil, stirring. Reduce heat to low, cover, and simmer, stirring often so that all pieces come in contact with liquid and so flour does not stick to bottom of pan. As cauliflower becomes more tender, crush slightly with spoon while stirring. Simmer about 25 minutes, or until cauliflower is very tender.

Using a slotted spoon, remove cauliflower and purée it (in batches if necessary) in a blender, food processor, or food mill with a fine disk. If using blender or food processor, gradually add rest of soup to purée, while machine is running. Purée until very smooth. Return soup to saucepan and bring to a boil, stirring.

Add enough of remaining milk to bring soup to desired consistency; it should lightly coat a spoon. Bring to a boil, stirring, add cream, and bring again to a boil, stirring. Simmer 1 or 2 minutes to thicken slightly. Taste and adjust seasoning; soup should be generously flavored with salt, pepper, and nutmeg. (Soup can be kept, covered, 2 days in refrigerator.)

Just before serving, in a medium-size saucepan of boiling salted water, boil broccoli florets, uncovered, over high heat about 3 minutes, or until just tender. Drain thoroughly.

If soup was made ahead, reheat it over medium-low heat, stirring. Remove soup from heat and stir in remaining 2 tablespoons butter, if desired. Ladle soup into a tureen or into bowls and garnish with broccoli florets.

COLD CAULIFLOWER VELOUTÉ SOUP WITH BROCCOLI
Omit optional 2 tablespoons butter. If soup is too thick, stir in a few tablespoons cream. Taste for seasoning before serving. Garnish with broccoli as above.

❧ RED PEPPER VELOUTÉ SOUP
Velouté de poivrons rouges

Red peppers are a fashionable ingredient today. Yet their vibrant color and sweet taste have long been loved in the French kitchen. This classic soup is made of peppers simmered in stock and is garnished with rice. MAKES 4 SERVINGS

3 medium-size red bell peppers (about 1 ¼ pounds), cut in half, cored, and seeded
6 tablespoons unsalted butter
3 ¾ cups Chicken Stock (see recipe) or Vegetable Stock (see recipe)

2 tablespoons uncooked long-grain rice
Salt and freshly ground pepper
3 tablespoons all-purpose flour
2 tablespoons heavy cream
Pinch of cayenne pepper

Cut peppers in thin strips, about ⅜ inch wide. In a large skillet, melt 3 tablespoons butter over low heat and stir in pepper strips. Cover and cook, stirring occasionally, about 7 minutes, or until softened. Remove 8 pepper strips with slotted spoon and reserve for garnish. Add ¾ cup stock to skillet, cover, and bring to simmer. Reduce heat to low and cook until peppers are very tender, about 15 minutes.

Put 1½ cups boiling salted water in a small saucepan, add rice, and cook, uncovered, over medium-high heat about 12 minutes, or until just tender; taste to check. Drain thoroughly, rinse, and reserve for garnish.

Transfer peppers and their cooking liquid to a blender or food processor. Purée for 2 minutes, or until very smooth.

In a medium-size heavy saucepan, melt remaining 3 tablespoons butter over low heat, add flour, and cook, whisking constantly, until mixture turns a light beige color, 2 to 3 minutes. Remove from heat.

Gradually ladle 3 cups of stock into flour mixture, whisking. Bring to a boil, whisking constantly, over medium-high heat. Add a pinch of salt and pepper. Reduce heat to medium-low and simmer, uncovered, whisking often, for 5 minutes. Add puréed peppers and simmer, stirring often, for 5 minutes.

Stir in cream and bring to a boil, add cayenne pepper, and simmer, stirring, about 1 minute, or until soup thickens slightly. Taste and adjust seasoning.

Gently peel skin off pepper strips reserved for garnish. Dice peppers. (Soup can be prepared ahead up to this point and kept, covered, up to 1 day in refrigerator; refrigerate pepper strips and rice in separate containers.)

Bring pepper dice to room temperature and reheat soup, if necessary, over medium-low heat, stirring. Stir rice into hot soup and heat briefly. Ladle soup into bowls and garnish with pepper dice.

VEGETABLE STOCK
Fond de légumes

Vegetable stock is made of aromatic vegetables and mild herbs. Because it is a base for a great number of dishes and should not clash with the taste of other ingredients, it should have a relatively neutral taste. Salt is not added, because often stock is used in a dish that already contains salty ingredients. Rather, the dishes using the stock are seasoned to taste.

The purpose of stock is to provide depth of flavor to dishes; vegetables with an assertive flavor, such as cauliflower, cabbage, and turnips, should not be used.

Small pieces of onion, carrot, leeks, mushrooms, and celery can be frozen in bags or containers and saved for stock.

The cook who is in a great hurry can substitute stock powder or cubes, diluted with water according to the package directions, or frozen stocks, for homemade stocks.   MAKES ABOUT 1 QUART

2 tablespoons unsalted butter

3 medium-size onions, coarsely chopped

1 medium-size carrot, scraped and diced

2 celery stalks, chopped

Dark green part of 1 leek, rinsed thoroughly and sliced (optional)

6 cups water

1 bay leaf

2 sprigs fresh thyme, or ½ teaspoon dried thyme

3 medium-size garlic cloves, peeled and crushed

5 parsley stems (optional)

½ teaspoon black peppercorns

1½ to 2 cups sliced mushrooms or mushroom stems (optional)

In a large saucepan, melt butter over low heat, add onions, carrot, celery, and leek, and cook, stirring, about 10 minutes. Add water, bay leaf, thyme, garlic, parsley stems, peppercorns, and mushrooms and mix well. Bring to a boil.

Reduce heat to low and simmer, uncovered, 1 hour. Strain, pressing on ingredients in strainer; discard these ingredients. (Stock can be kept up to 3 days in refrigerator, or it can be frozen.)

❦ CHICKEN STOCK
Fond de volaille

Chicken stock is a useful, all-purpose light stock that adds a good flavor to a great variety of French soups and sauces. With just a little salt, pepper, chopped fresh herbs, and perhaps a few cooked vegetables added, homemade chicken stock is a very good soup on its own.

It is convenient to prepare a large quantity of chicken stock and keep it in the freezer in small or medium-size containers.

MAKES ABOUT 2½ QUARTS

3 pounds chicken wings and backs, or a mixture of wings, backs, necks, and giblets (except livers)

2 medium-size onions, cut into quarters

Green part of 1 leek, cleaned (optional)

2 medium-size carrots, cut into quarters

2 bay leaves

10 parsley stems

About 4 quarts water

2 sprigs fresh thyme, or ½ teaspoon dried thyme

½ teaspoon black peppercorns

Combine chicken, onions, leek, carrots, bay leaves, and parsley stems in a stockpot or other large pot. Add enough water to cover ingredients. Bring to a boil, skimming foam that collects on top. Add thyme and peppercorns.

Reduce heat to very low so that stock bubbles very gently. Partially cover and cook, skimming foam and fat occasionally, for at least 2 or up to 3 hours.

Strain stock into large bowl; discard ingredients in strainer. If not using immediately, cool to lukewarm. Refrigerate until cold and skim fat off top. (Stock can be kept, covered, 3 days in refrigerator, or it can be frozen.)

Vegetable Salads

In France in the past decade, the role of salads has become much more central. With the growing interest in light foods and the beginning of nouvelle cuisine, salads became very popular when they gained an important place on the menus of the finest restaurants.

While the starred restaurants compete with each other to invent new and original salads, including warm salads that feature meat or seafood, the small bistros and cafés still serve simple salads, such as crudités. A wide variety of freshly prepared salads can be found at the charcuteries as well. These are mainly traditional salads that have long been favorites, such as French potato salad, corn and pepper salad, and "macédoine," a salad of diced cooked vegetables with mayonnaise. Often a few exotic newcomers are included as well, such as the Lebanese tabbouleh.

There are two basic types of salads: simple salads, consisting of one major ingredient, and composed salads, made up of two or more main components. Generally, a composed salad is more substantial than a simple one.

Serving Salads

Salads are not served very cold in France, but rather at cool room temperature, because cold vegetables have less flavor.

Fresh French bread, especially the long, thin baguette, is an important accompaniment for salads and is nearly always on the table. At cafés in France, a popular light lunch is a colorful salad served with fresh bread.

Traditionally, the time to serve a green salad is after the main course in order to refresh the palate before the cheese course or dessert. Today's menus, however, are more flexible. Green salads often accompany the main course, especially one of grilled meat or fish. Other salads, depending on their size, can be a first course or even a main course.

Salad Dressings

The favorite salad dressing in France is the simplest, a vinaigrette made of only four ingredients: oil, vinegar, salt, and pepper. Vinaigrette is always the choice when a light dressing is desired, and it serves to show off the colorful ingredients.

The oil and vinegar can be varied to your taste. The traditional dressing in France is a neutral-flavored vegetable oil and a wine vinegar, but often olive oil is used and sometimes the more exotic walnut or hazelnut oils. Herb or garlic vinegars or sometimes fruit vinegars can also add zip to salads. Many variations on the basic vinaigrette are given in the following chapter.

Homemade mayonnaise is the second most important salad dressing, for richer, more substantial salads. Crème fraîche is another popular salad enhancer. Both recipes are given in this chapter for your reference.

Dijon mustard is a good addition to both mayonnaise and vinaigrette for its flavor and because it helps thicken them. Fresh herbs are also popular additions. It is important to remember, however, that the purpose of the dressing is to enhance the flavors of the salad ingredients and not to overpower them. The French almost never add sugar to salad dressings and are horrified when they hear of such an idea.

Hints

• When preparing cooked vegetables for salad, cook them until they are tender but still retain a touch of crunchiness. Rinse green vegetables with cold water immediately after cooking until they are cold.

• After cooking vegetables or rinsing raw salad ingredients, be sure to drain and dry them very thoroughly. If any water remains, it dilutes the dressing, makes it run off the vegetables, and results in a watery, flavorless salad.

• Add enough dressing to coat the salad ingredients; do not drench them.

• Always taste a salad after tossing with the dressing to be sure it is well seasoned. Even if the dressing itself is seasoned, after the addition of a generous amount of vegetables the salad might be bland.

• For elegant meals, toss the salad in a mixing bowl and then transfer it to a serving bowl so that the edges of the bowl remain clean.

Simple Vegetable Salads

These salads can be made of raw or cooked vegetables. A favorite way of presenting raw vegetables for a first course is as a plate of crudités, a combination of several colorful vegetable salads. Which vegetables to include depends on the season and on personal taste. Of course, vegetables served raw should be absolutely fresh; some say that a favorite way for restaurant reviewers to judge small restaurants is by the freshness of their crudités platter.

For salads of cooked vegetables, the vegetables are generally steamed or cooked in water, then drained and mixed with the dressing.

❧ WATERCRESS SALAD WITH GOAT CHEESE AND WALNUTS
Salade de cresson au fromage de chèvre et aux noix

Creamy goat cheese is a popular addition to green salads. Often the cheese is warmed in the oven or sautéed, but it is also very good at room temperature. Do not purchase watercress more than one day in advance; it quickly turns yellow.   MAKES 4 SERVINGS

WALNUT OIL VINAIGRETTE
2 tablespoons white wine vinegar   *6 tablespoons walnut oil*
Salt and freshly ground pepper

6 ounces very fresh watercress   *½ cup walnut pieces, coarsely*
1 small head tender lettuce, such as   *chopped*
butter or Boston
½ pound Montrachet or other
creamy French goat cheese
(about 1 cup)

WALNUT OIL VINAIGRETTE
Put vinegar with salt and pepper in a small bowl; stir in walnut oil with a whisk. Taste and adjust seasoning and set aside.

Stir vinaigrette again and add enough to greens to moisten them and then toss. Taste and adjust seasoning. When serving, sprinkle each serving with goat cheese and walnuts.

Use upper part of watercress—tiny sprigs and leaves only—and discard large stems. Thoroughly rinse and dry watercress and lettuce. Put both greens in a bowl.

If goat cheese has a dark rind, cut it off, then crumble cheese.

GREEN SALAD WITH PINE NUTS AND SHERRY VINAIGRETTE
Salade verte aux pignons

The traditional green salad served in France after the main course is now often embellished with nuts and with vinaigrettes made of exotic vinegars and oils. This salad can also be served as an accompaniment for roast chicken or grilled steak. MAKES 6 SERVINGS

SHERRY VINAIGRETTE

2 tablespoons sherry vinegar or white wine vinegar

Salt and freshly ground pepper

1 teaspoon Dijon-style mustard (optional)

6 tablespoons vegetable oil

2 heads butter lettuce, or 1 head romaine lettuce

½ head radicchio (optional)

2 teaspoons vegetable oil

⅓ cup pine nuts

Salt

1 tablespoon chopped fresh parsley (optional)

SHERRY VINAIGRETTE

Stir vinegar, salt, pepper, and mustard in a small bowl until blended. Gradually add oil, stirring with a whisk. Taste and adjust seasoning; vinaigrette should be highly seasoned to flavor lettuce. (Vinaigrette can be kept 2 weeks in covered jar in refrigerator.)

Discard any yellow lettuce leaves and any tough bases of lettuce leaves. Rinse lettuce leaves and radicchio well in a sinkful of water. Remove leaves from water so that any sand sinks to bottom. Dry well in a salad spinner or in a towel. The leaves can be kept in a towel 1 to 2 hours in refrigerator.

In a small skillet, heat 2 teaspoons oil over low heat, add pine nuts and a pinch of salt, and sauté about 2 minutes, or until lightly toasted. Transfer to a bowl and cool.

Leave small lettuce leaves whole; tear large leaves in a few pieces. Put in a bowl.

Stir vinaigrette with a whisk. Add parsley, if desired. Add enough vinaigrette to lettuce leaves, tossing them, to coat. Taste and adjust seasoning. Do not add so much vinaigrette that a pool of it remains at bottom of bowl. When serving, sprinkle pine nuts over each serving.

NOTE: Other lettuces in season can be added. *Mâche* (also called lamb's lettuce) will add a festive note and wonderfully delicate flavor to green salad, but remember to rinse it very thoroughly.

CELERY ROOT SALAD WITH MUSTARD DRESSING
Celeri-rave rémoulade

Celery root salad is often served as part of crudités, a selection of colorful salads. When garnished with walnuts and eggs, as in this version, it can make a first course on its own. For further color, surround it with a ring of cherry tomato halves.

MAKES 4 TO 6 SERVINGS

1 cup Mayonnaise (see recipe)
2 to 3 teaspoons Dijon mustard
About 1 pound celery root
½ lemon
Salt and freshly ground pepper

3 tablespoons chopped fresh parsley
2 hard-boiled eggs, quartered
  (optional)
½ cup walnut halves (optional)

To make dressing, mix mayonnaise with 2 teaspoons mustard. Taste and adjust seasoning and add another teaspoon mustard if desired.

Use a sharp knife to peel celery root, removing all brown parts. Rub peeled celery root with cut side of lemon half to prevent it from discoloring. Cut peeled celery root in thin strips, using a sharp knife or julienne blade of a food processor.

Put celery root in a pan of water and bring to a boil. Cook, uncovered, for 1 to 2 minutes, or until slightly softened so celery root is crisp but not unpleasantly hard. Drain thoroughly and dry on paper towels. Put in a bowl.

Add enough dressing to moisten celery root and 2 tablespoons parsley. Taste and adjust seasoning. Serve at room temperature or cold. (Salad can be kept up to 2 days in refrigerator.) Garnish with quartered hard-boiled eggs, remaining parsley, and walnut halves, if desired.

❧ FENNEL SALAD WITH HERBED CRÈME FRAÎCHE
Fenouil à la crème

Salting fennel slightly softens it so that it is good in salad. Cream is a good match for fennel's distinctive flavor, but fennel salad can also be seasoned with vinaigrette or mayonnaise. This salad is white and is best served with a selection of other colorful salads.

MAKES 4 TO 6 SERVINGS

2 medium-size fennel bulbs
Salt
1 cup Crème Fraîche (see recipe) or
  purchased crème fraîche, or ⅔
  cup sour cream mixed with ⅓
  cup heavy cream

Freshly ground pepper
3 to 4 teaspoons strained fresh
  lemon juice
1 tablespoon chopped fresh parsley
1 tablespoon snipped chives

Remove stalks and tough outer layers of fennel bulbs. Slice lengthwise, then cut in sticks about ¼ inch thick and place in a colander or on a rack. Sprinkle with salt on both sides and let stand 30 minutes. Rinse well and pat dry with paper towels.

To make dressing, mix cream with salt, pepper, lemon juice to taste, parsley, and 2 teaspoons chives in a medium-size bowl.

Put fennel in a bowl and add enough dressing to moisten it. Fold until blended. Taste and adjust seasoning. Refrigerate at least 30 minutes or as long as overnight. Sprinkle with remaining chives and serve.

✤ CUCUMBER SALAD WITH YOGURT HERB DRESSING
Salade de concombres au yaourt

This refreshing salad is a summer favorite. The long European cucumbers are best because they have few or no seeds.

MAKES 6 SERVINGS

1 small garlic clove, crushed and
  finely chopped
1 teaspoon salt
½ cup plain yogurt
½ cup sour cream
¼ cup heavy cream

2 tablespoons minced fresh parsley,
  snipped chives, or dill
1 large seedless cucumber (about 1
  pound)
Small sprigs of parsley or dill, for
  garnish (optional)

In a bowl, mash garlic with salt, using back of a spoon. Add yogurt, sour cream, and heavy cream and blend well. Stir in minced parsley, chives, or dill.

Peel cucumber and cut it in half lengthwise. Cut it in thin slices and add to yogurt mixture. Fold in gently. Taste and adjust seasoning. Refrigerate at least 15 minutes or up to 4 hours before serving.

To serve, garnish with small sprigs of parsley or dill.

✤ ESCAROLE SALAD WITH ROQUEFORT CHEESE
Salade de scarole au roquefort

Unlike other green salads, this one is made ahead so that the escarole leaves become tenderized by the dressing. If desired, bleu d'auvergne or other French blue cheese can be used instead of Roquefort.

MAKES 4 TO 6 SERVINGS

1 head escarole
Walnut Oil Vinaigrette (page
  302), using 3 tablespoons
  white wine vinegar to 9
  tablespoons walnut oil

½ cup crumbled Roquefort cheese
½ cup walnut pieces (optional)

Rinse and dry escarole leaves thoroughly. Tear large leaves in half but leave small ones whole.

Prepare Walnut Oil Vinaigrette according to the instructions in recipe for Watercress Salad with Goat Cheese and Walnuts.

Mix escarole leaves with vinaigrette, add most of cheese and walnuts, leaving a little of each for garnish, and toss. Taste and adjust seasoning. Cover and refrigerate 30 minutes to wilt slightly.

Just before serving, garnish with remaining Roquefort cheese and walnuts.

SUMMER TOMATO SALAD WITH FRESH HERBS
Salade de tomates aux herbes

When tomatoes are at the peak of their season, this salad is made at many homes and small restaurants in France. If desired, the vinaigrette can be made with less vinegar or lemon juice than usual because the tomatoes have their own natural acidity.

MAKES 6 TO 8 SERVINGS

6 medium-size ripe tomatoes   *2 green onions*

FRESH HERB VINAIGRETTE
1 to 2 tablespoons strained fresh   *1 garlic clove, minced*
*   lemon juice or white wine*   *1 tablespoon finely chopped fresh*
*   vinegar*   *   parsley*
Salt and freshly ground pepper   *1 tablespoon chopped fresh basil or*
6 tablespoons extra-virgin olive oil   *   oregano (optional)*

Slice tomatoes and arrange overlapping in a shallow dish.

Slice white part of green onions and sprinkle over tomatoes. Chop green part of onions.

FRESH HERB VINAIGRETTE

In a small bowl, stir lemon juice with salt and pepper and add oil, using a whisk. Add green part of onions, garlic, parsley, and basil, and taste and adjust seasoning.

Pour enough vinaigrette over tomatoes to moisten them.

This salad can be kept, covered, 4 hours in refrigerator but is best served immediately and at cool room temperature. Serve any remaining vinaigrette separately.

TOMATO AND EGG SALAD
Arrange tomato slices alternating with slices of hard-boiled egg.

LEEKS MIMOSA WITH HAZELNUTS
Poireaux mimosa aux noisettes

This dish is a new, nut-flavored version of the classic leeks mimosa, in which "mimosa" refers to the yellow and white decoration of chopped eggs. Leeks are sometimes called in France "asparagus of the poor" because they are delicious but inexpensive and, indeed, this salad is also made with asparagus, as in the variation.

MAKES 4 SERVINGS

¼ cup hazelnuts
2 pounds small leeks

Salt
2 hard-boiled eggs

PARSLEY VINAIGRETTE
2 tablespoons white wine vinegar
Salt and freshly ground pepper
3 tablespoons hazelnut oil and 3
*   tablespoons vegetable oil, or 6*
*   tablespoons vegetable oil*

2 tablespoons chopped fresh parsley

Preheat oven to 350°F. In a shallow baking pan, toast hazelnuts in oven about 8 minutes, or until skins begin to split. Transfer to a large strainer. Rub hot nuts against strainer with terry-cloth towel to remove most of skins. Cool nuts completely. Chop coarsely with a knife.

Remove dark green ends of leeks and discard. Slit each leek lengthwise twice, beginning halfway through center of white part and slitting upward in direction of green tops. Dip repeatedly in a sinkful of cold water to remove any sand. Cut off roots.

In a large saucepan of boiling salted water, cook leeks, uncovered, over medium heat about 10 minutes, or until tender. Drain thoroughly. Cut in 2 or 3 pieces crosswise. Arrange on a platter, reconstructing each leek and arranging so all point in same direction.

Cut hard-boiled eggs in half and remove yolks. Chop egg whites separately from yolks.

PARSLEY VINAIGRETTE

In a small bowl, stir vinegar with salt and pepper, and whisk in oil. Add parsley, taste and adjust seasoning.

To serve, spoon enough dressing over leeks to moisten them. Sprinkle egg whites in a row across their bases, then a row of hazelnuts next to whites, then a row of chopped yolks. Leave top ends of leeks showing. Serve at room temperature. Serve remaining dressing separately.

ASPARAGUS MIMOSA WITH HAZELNUTS

Substitute asparagus for leeks. Peel asparagus stems and cut off bases. Rinse well. Put asparagus in a sauté pan or deep skillet with enough boiling salted water to cover. Cook, uncovered, over high heat about 5 minutes, or until just tender when pierced with a sharp knife. With a slotted spatula transfer asparagus carefully to a plate lined with paper towels and let cool to room temperature.

To serve, arrange asparagus on a platter, with tips all pointing in same direction. Dress as above. When sprinkling nuts and eggs, leave asparagus tips showing.

MARINATED GREEN BEAN SALAD WITH GREEN ONIONS
Salade de haricots verts marinés aux oignons nouveaux

For a colorful assortment, serve this salad together with Grilled Peppers with Garlic and Olive Oil (see recipe) and with a rice, pasta, or potato salad.   MAKES 4 SERVINGS

1 ¼ pounds green beans or mixed
   green beans and wax beans,
   ends discarded
1 small garlic clove, crushed
Salt and freshly ground pepper
2 tablespoons strained fresh lemon
   juice

¼ cup extra-virgin olive oil
1 to 2 tablespoons chopped fresh
   parsley
2 green onions, white part and a
   little of green, chopped

Break beans in approximately 2-inch pieces. In a medium-size saucepan of boiling salted water, cook, uncovered, over high heat about 5 minutes, or until just tender but still slightly crisp. Drain and rinse under cold water until cool.

In a small bowl, mash garlic with salt until very fine, stir in lemon juice, olive oil, parsley, and chopped onions. Toss with green beans. Taste and adjust seasoning. Let stand about 30 minutes to marinate. Serve at room temperature.

❧ WARM DANDELION SALAD WITH MUSHROOMS AND POACHED EGGS
Salade de pissenlits aux champignons et à l'oeuf poché

Dandelion greens are an acquired taste, but those who like them find their characteristic bitterness refreshing. Warm dandelion salads are generally topped with sautéed bacon; in this recipe mushrooms are used instead, but diced sautéed bacon can be added as well. Poached eggs are a favorite finishing touch among some French cooks and turn the salad into a richer dish.   MAKES 3 TO 4 SERVINGS

½ pound dandelion greens
6 tablespoons vegetable oil
2 tablespoons very finely minced
   onion

½ pound small mushrooms, cut
   into quarters
Salt and freshly ground pepper
¼ cup white wine vinegar

POACHED EGGS
6 cups water   4 or 5 very fresh eggs
¼ cup vinegar

French bread, for accompaniment

Remove stalks of dandelion from bases and discard bases. Thoroughly rinse and drain dandelion greens. Break each stalk in 2-inch pieces. Put them in a large heatproof bowl.

Heat 3 tablespoons vegetable oil in a heavy medium-size skillet, over medium heat. Add onion and sauté over low heat until soft but not browned. Add mushrooms and salt and pepper to taste and sauté until tender and light brown. Transfer mushrooms and their oil to bowl with greens. With pan off heat, pour in vinegar, then bring to a boil, stirring. Pour over greens, add remaining oil, and mix thoroughly. Return greens to pan and toss over medium heat for 1 minute, or until just wilted. Return to bowl and taste and adjust seasoning. Keep warm while poaching eggs.

POACHED EGGS
Prepare a bowl of cold water for cooling poached eggs.

Combine 6 cups water and vinegar in a large nonaluminum sauté pan or shallow saucepan and bring to a boil. Reduce heat to medium-low so that water just simmers. Break an egg into a small cup or ramekin and slide egg into water where it is bubbling. With a spoon, bring white over yolk. Repeat with another egg. Reduce heat to low and poach eggs, uncovered, for 2½ minutes. Lift each egg carefully with slotted spoon and touch it; white should be firm and yolk still soft. Transfer egg to bowl of cold water. Continue poaching remaining eggs.

Transfer eggs to paper towels and trim off uneven parts.

To serve, quickly divide salad among 3 or 4 small plates. Carefully set one egg in center of each salad. Serve immediately, with French bread.

NOTE: One or two extra eggs should be poached in case a yolk breaks or in case some of the eggs do not have an attractive shape.

BABY ARTICHOKES WITH HAZELNUT OIL VINAIGRETTE
Petits artichauts, vinaigrette à l'huile de noisettes

Large artichokes, broccoli, and tender lettuce are also good with the nut-flavored dressing. It contains less vinegar than usual so that it will best complement the delicate baby artichokes.

MAKES 4 SERVINGS

*8 to 12 baby artichokes (about 1½
   inches in diameter at their
   widest part)*

HAZELNUT OIL VINAIGRETTE
2 tablespoons white wine vinegar   ½ cup hazelnut oil
Salt and freshly ground pepper

There is no need to trim baby artichokes. Rinse them and put them in a medium-size saucepan of boiling salted water. Cover and cook over medium heat about 18 minutes, or until a leaf can be pulled out easily. Remove them and drain them thoroughly, upside down.

HAZELNUT OIL VINAIGRETTE
   In a medium-size bowl, stir vinegar with salt and pepper and whisk in oil. Taste and adjust seasoning.
   Serve artichokes warm or at room temperature, accompanied by the vinaigrette.

Composed Vegetable Salads

There are no fixed rules for creating these salads. The flavors and textures can be either complementary or contrasting. Often a great combination will be discovered by chance, by mixing ingredients that happen to be at hand. Salads of ingredients of similar shape and different color, such as cauliflower with broccoli, are attractive, and so are green and wax beans; red, yellow, and green peppers; and even chick-peas and white beans.

Fine-quality cheese such as Roquefort, goat cheese, and Gruyère add richness and flavor to contemporary French salads, while peppers, cucumbers, celery, walnuts, and almonds add crispness. When lettuce is part of a composed salad, or arranged as a bed for the other ingredients, it is combined with the rest of the salad at the last minute to avoid wilting.

Many French salads have a regional theme, mixing the typical ingredients of a certain French province. Provençal potato salad, for example, includes peppers and olives. A bean salad from Brittany in northwestern France combines cold-weather vegetables—cooked white beans, cubes of beets, mixed greens, and parsley vinaigrette.

BRETON VEGETABLE SALAD WITH CHIVE MAYONNAISE
Salade bretonne de légumes, mayonnaise à la ciboulette

Artichokes, cauliflower, and peas flourish in the western French province of Brittany and are used to make this salad. To turn this into a main course salad, hard-boiled eggs or poached shrimp or lobster can be added to the platter. MAKES 4 SERVINGS

1 large lemon (if using fresh
artichokes)
2 large artichokes, or 8 pieces
frozen artichoke hearts
Salt and freshly ground pepper
½ pound green beans, ends
removed, broken in half
1 medium-size cauliflower (about
1 ½ pounds), divided into
medium-size florets

12 baby carrots, peeled
1 ½ cups cooked peas (fresh or
frozen)
⅓ cup Mayonnaise (see recipe)
1 tablespoon snipped chives

VINAIGRETTE
1 tablespoon white wine vinegar
Salt and freshly ground pepper

3 tablespoons vegetable oil

1 head romaine lettuce, leaves
rinsed and dried thoroughly

If using fresh artichokes, prepare hearts according to directions on page 143.

Squeeze any juice remaining in lemon into medium-size saucepan of boiling salted water, add artichoke hearts, cover, and simmer over low heat until tender when pierced with a knife, about 15 minutes for fresh ones, and about 7 minutes for frozen ones. Cool to lukewarm in liquid. Using a teaspoon, scoop out choke from center of each fresh artichoke heart. Cut each fresh artichoke into 8 pieces and each piece frozen artichoke heart into 2 pieces. Return artichokes to liquid until ready to use.

In a medium-size saucepan of boiling salted water, cook green beans, uncovered, over high heat about 5 minutes, or until just tender but still slightly crisp. Drain, rinse under cold water until cool, and drain thoroughly.

In a large saucepan of boiling salted water, cook cauliflower, uncovered, over high heat about 5 minutes, or until just tender but still slightly crisp. Drain, rinse under cold water until cool, and drain thoroughly. Divide half the cauliflower florets into smaller florets.

Put baby carrots in a saucepan, cover with water, and add salt. Bring to a boil, cover, and simmer over medium heat about 5 minutes, or until just tender when pierced with a knife; size of baby carrots varies greatly and this affects cooking time. Drain thoroughly.

Combine cooked artichokes, peas, and small cauliflower florets in a bowl. Mix mayonnaise with 1 teaspoon chives. Add enough mayonnaise to vegetables to moisten them. Mix gently, taste and adjust seasoning. (Salad can be kept, covered, 1 day in refrigerator.)

VINAIGRETTE
In a small bowl, whisk vinegar with salt and pepper; whisk in oil. Taste and adjust seasoning.

Make a bed of romaine lettuce on a large platter. Spoon artichoke and pea mixture into center. Arrange green beans, baby carrots, and remaining cauliflower florets in piles around mixture and sprinkle them with vinaigrette. Sprinkle remaining chives over artichoke and pea mixture and over separate cauliflower florets.

CORN SALAD WITH PEPPERS
Salade de maïs aux poivrons

This quick, colorful salad can be found displayed in the windows of many charcuteries throughout Paris under the name *salade mexicaine* or *salade américaine*, a tribute to the origin of its major ingredients. Sometimes black olives or tuna in olive oil is added.

MAKES 6 SERVINGS

2½ to 3 cups corn kernels, either
   cut from fresh cobs or frozen

VINAIGRETTE

3 tablespoons white wine vinegar or   9 tablespoons vegetable oil or olive
   fresh strained lemon juice   oil
Salt and freshly ground pepper

1 medium-size or large red bell   ¼ pound Gruyère cheese, finely
   pepper, cored, seeded, and   diced
   finely diced   12 lettuce leaves, rinsed, dried well,
1 medium-size or large green bell   and cut in thin strips
   pepper, cored, seeded, and   (optional)
   finely diced
2 celery stalks, peeled and finely
   diced (optional)

Add corn to a large saucepan of boiling water and simmer, uncovered, about 5 minutes, or until just tender. Drain thoroughly.

VINAIGRETTE

In small bowl, whisk vinegar with salt and pepper; whisk in oil. Taste and adjust seasoning.

A short time before serving, combine corn, peppers, celery, and cheese in a bowl and add enough vinaigrette to moisten. Toss well and taste and adjust seasoning. (Salad can be kept, covered, up to 1 day in refrigerator.) Just before serving, add lettuce and toss salad again.

TOMATOES STUFFED WITH MUSHROOM SALAD
Tomates farcies salade de champignons

The contrast of colors between the red tomatoes and the white mushroom salad makes this an attractive first course. It is essential to use very white fresh mushrooms.

MAKES 6 SERVINGS

MUSHROOM SALAD

1½ tablespoons white wine vinegar or strained fresh lemon juice	7 tablespoons sour cream or Crème Fraîche (see recipe)
1 garlic clove, very finely minced	5 ounces white mushrooms, cleaned
Salt and freshly ground white pepper	
3 large ripe tomatoes	1 tablespoon minced fresh parsley

MUSHROOM SALAD

In a medium-size bowl, whisk vinegar with garlic and salt and pepper to taste. Add sour cream. Cut mushrooms in very thin slices. Add immediately to dressing and mix well. Taste and adjust seasoning; add a few drops more vinegar or lemon juice if needed. Cover and refrigerate at least 2 hours so mushrooms absorb flavor from dressing. (Salad can be kept, covered, 8 hours in refrigerator.)

If necessary, cut a thin slice from each end of each tomato so it can stand up without rolling. Cut each tomato in half horizontally. Using a small spoon, carefully remove pulp from tomatoes. Sprinkle tomatoes with salt and pepper. Turn them upside down on a plate and let stand 30 minutes so the excess juices can drain off.

Spoon mushroom salad into tomatoes to fill them generously. Just before serving, sprinkle with parsley.

ENDIVE AND BEET SALAD
Salade d'endives aux betteraves

The sweetness of the beets is a perfect complement for the slight bitterness of the Belgian endive in this salad. If desired, other greens, such as pieces of romaine lettuce, can be added as well. Because beets have a tendency to color everything near them purple, they are added to the salad at the last minute so that the other ingredients keep their color. MAKES 6 SERVINGS

5 small beets (about 1½ inches in
    diameter)
¾ pound Belgian endive

2 celery stalks, peeled and cut in
    thin slices

CHAMPAGNE VINAIGRETTE
2 tablespoons champagne vinegar or
    white wine vinegar
Salt and freshly ground pepper

2 teaspoons champagne mustard or
    Dijon mustard
6 tablespoons vegetable oil

½ cup walnut pieces

Rinse beets, put 1 inch of water in a steamer, and bring to a boil.
Place beets on steamer rack or on another rack or in a colander above
boiling water. Cover tightly and steam 50 to 60 minutes, or until
tender, adding boiling water occasionally if water evaporates. Let
cool. Run them under cold water and slip off skins.

Wipe endives and trim their bases. Cut leaves in fairly thin slices
crosswise. Combine with celery in a bowl.

CHAMPAGNE VINAIGRETTE
In a small bowl, whisk vinegar with salt, pepper, and mustard
until blended. Stir in oil, taste, and adjust seasoning.

Toss endives and celery with vinaigrette. Leave to marinate for
5 to 10 minutes. Just before serving, dice beets, add to salad, and toss
gently. Adjust seasoning, sprinkle with walnuts, and serve.

CHICK-PEA AND BEAN SALAD WITH TOMATOES AND BASIL
Salade de pois chiches et haricots aux tomates et au basilic

This colorful salad, dressed with sautéed onions and an olive oil
and lemon dressing, is best served warm.   MAKES 4 SERVINGS

½ cup Great Northern beans,
    rinsed and sorted
½ cup dried chick-peas (also called
    garbanzo beans), rinsed and
    sorted
1 quart water
Salt and freshly ground pepper
1 bay leaf
½ pound green beans, ends
    removed, broken in half
½ cup extra-virgin olive oil

1 large onion, halved and cut in
    thin slices
½ pound ripe tomatoes, diced
½ cup Niçoise olives or other
    oil-cured black olives, cut in
    half and pitted
3 tablespoons coarsely chopped fresh
    basil
1 tablespoon plus 1 teaspoon
    strained fresh lemon juice

Soak Great Northern beans in a bowl of 1½ cups cold water in a cool place for 8 hours, or overnight. Soak chick-peas in 1½ cups cold water in another bowl for 8 hours, or overnight.

Drain and rinse Great Northern beans. Put them in a medium-size saucepan and add 2 cups water and bay leaf. Bring to boil, reduce heat to low, cover, and simmer 45 minutes. Add pinch of salt and simmer about 45 minutes more, or until tender.

At the same time as Great Northern beans are cooking, drain and rinse chick-peas. Put them in medium-size saucepan and add 2 cups water. Bring to boil, reduce heat to low, cover, and simmer 45 minutes. Add pinch of salt and simmer about 30 minutes more, or until tender. (Both types beans can be kept in their cooking liquid for 1 day in refrigerator.) Reheat both types beans together to simmer before serving. Drain beans, discarding bay leaf. Cover and keep warm.

Meanwhile, in medium-size saucepan of boiling salted water, cook green beans, uncovered, over high heat about 7 minutes, or until just tender. Drain thoroughly.

In medium-size skillet, heat 3 tablespoons olive oil over low heat, add onion, and cook, stirring often, about 12 minutes, or until soft but not brown.

Combine chick-peas, Great Northern beans, green beans, cooked onion with its oil, tomatoes, olives, and basil in a glass bowl and toss lightly. Whisk lemon juice with 5 tablespoons olive oil and salt and pepper to taste; use salt lightly because olives are salty. Add to bowl and toss until ingredients are coated. Taste and adjust seasoning. Serve warm or at room temperature. (Leftover salad can be kept, covered, 1 day in refrigerator; serve at room temperature.)

NOTE: Substitute 1½ cups canned chick-peas for dried, if desired. Drain them well, add them to cooked Great Northern beans, and heat gently.

❧ AVOCADO AND MUSHROOM SALAD WITH SWISS CHARD
Salade d'avocats et de champignons aux blettes

This beautiful salad makes a wonderful main course for a warm day. It consists of a bed of greens topped with sautéed mushrooms and Swiss chard, slices of avocado and egg and halved cherry tomatoes, all moistened with a creamy chive dressing.   MAKES 4 SERVINGS

8 to 10 leaves of green leaf lettuce
　(also called salad bowl lettuce)
About 10 ounces Swiss chard
3 tablespoons vegetable oil

Salt and freshly ground pepper
¼ pound small mushrooms, cut in
　quarters

CREAMY CHIVE VINAIGRETTE
½ teaspoon Dijon mustard
1 tablespoon white wine vinegar
Salt and freshly ground pepper

3 tablespoons vegetable oil
3 tablespoons heavy cream
2 tablespoons thinly sliced chives

1 medium-size avocado
3 hard-boiled eggs, sliced

4 to 8 cherry tomatoes, cut in half,
　for garnish

Wash lettuce and dry thoroughly. Tear each leaf in 3 or 4 pieces. Chill until ready to use.

Remove chard stalks from leaves and discard. Rinse leaves thoroughly. Pile chard leaves, cut them in half lengthwise and then crosswise into ½-inch-wide strips.

In a large skillet, heat 2 tablespoons oil over low heat, add about half the chard and a pinch of salt and pepper, and cook, stirring often, about 6 minutes, or until tender. Remove with tongs, add remaining chard and a little salt and pepper, and cook it also until tender. Return all of chard to pan and heat, stirring, 1 minute. Transfer to a plate and cool to room temperature.

In a large skillet, heat 1 tablespoon oil over medium-high heat, add mushrooms, salt, and pepper, and sauté, tossing often, about 3 minutes, or until tender and light brown. Remove with a slotted spoon and reserve at room temperature. (Chard and mushrooms can be kept about 4 hours at room temperature.)

CREAMY CHIVE VINAIGRETTE

In a small bowl, whisk together mustard, vinegar, and salt and pepper to taste. Gradually stir in oil; dressing will thicken slightly. Using a fork, mix 2 tablespoons of dressing into chard. Taste and adjust seasoning.

Gradually whisk cream into remaining dressing, stir in chives, and taste and adjust seasoning.

Cut avocado in half and remove pit by hitting it with heel of a heavy knife. Peel avocado and slice it crosswise.

Arrange lettuce leaves on a platter. Set chard in center. Arrange avocado slices and egg slices in a ring around chard. Arrange mushrooms around them, discarding any liquid. Whisk dressing and spoon it over avocado and egg. Garnish with cherry tomato halves. Serve immediately.

CAULIFLOWER AND TOMATO SALAD WITH GARLIC AND WALNUT DRESSING
Salade de chou-fleur et tomates, sauce aillade

The garlic and walnut dressing, or sauce aillade, is adapted from a cookbook that is very special to me—*French Regional Cooking* by Anne Willan and La Varenne. The dressing always reminds me of a garlic fair my husband and I visited near Toulouse, where the sauce originated. The wreaths of purple, pink, and white garlic were huge, beautiful, and impressive. Many people were buying them as their garlic supply for the next few months.　MAKES 6 TO 8 SERVINGS

GARLIC AND WALNUT DRESSING

2 large garlic cloves, peeled and cut
   in half
⅓ cup parsley sprigs
⅔ cup walnut halves
Salt and freshly ground pepper

2 tablespoons cold water
¾ cup walnut oil
1 to 2 teaspoons strained fresh
   lemon juice, or to taste
   (optional)

1 medium-size cauliflower, divided
   into medium-size florets
1 red bell pepper
1 green bell pepper

1 head butter lettuce
4 medium-size ripe tomatoes, cut in
   wedges

GARLIC AND WALNUT DRESSING

Drop garlic cloves into food processor one at a time, with blades turning, and process until finely chopped. Add parsley sprigs and continue to process until fine. Add walnuts, salt, and pepper, and process until walnuts are finely ground. Add water and process to a smooth paste.

With blades turning, add walnut oil in a very thin stream. Stop occasionally to scrape down sides and bottom of work bowl. Transfer to a bowl, whisk in lemon juice, if desired, taste and adjust seasoning. Transfer to a jar and keep in refrigerator. (Sauce can be kept up to 2 weeks.) Bring to room temperature before using.

In a large saucepan of boiling salted water, cook cauliflower, uncovered, over high heat about 5 minutes, or until just tender. Drain, rinse, and drain thoroughly.

Preheat broiler. Broil peppers about 2 inches from heat source, turning often, about 20 minutes, or until blistered and charred. Transfer to plastic bag and close bag. Let stand 10 minutes. Peel, cut in half, and remove cores. Drain well in colander, pat dry, and cut them in about ¾-inch strips.

Arrange a bed of butter lettuce leaves on one large or two medium-size platters. Stir dressing. Pour about ⅓ cup dressing over lettuce. Arrange cauliflower, tomato wedges, and peppers decoratively on top; cauliflower in center, tomato wedges around it, and pepper strips around them, radiating outward. Pour a ring of dressing around outer edge of ring of tomatoes and serve. Serve remaining dressing separately.

❦ ARTICHOKE, ASPARAGUS, GREEN BEAN, AND FRESH PEA SALAD WITH TARRAGON MAYONNAISE
Salade Saint-Jean

For this springtime salad, use freshly cooked vegetables and homemade mayonnaise to obtain the best results.

MAKES 4 TO 6 SERVINGS

FRESH TARRAGON MAYONNAISE

1 egg yolk, room temperature
Salt and white pepper
½ teaspoon Dijon mustard
1 tablespoon strained fresh lemon juice or tarragon vinegar

½ cup vegetable oil
1 tablespoon warm water (optional)
1 tablespoon chopped fresh tarragon

1 lemon (if using fresh artichokes)
4 small fresh artichoke hearts, cut into quarters, or 12 pieces frozen artichoke hearts
8 medium-size asparagus spears, peeled and cut in 1½- to 2-inch pieces, or 2 cups asparagus tips

2 cups green beans, cut in thirds
1 cup green peas
2 hard-boiled eggs, sliced
1 or 2 cornichons (tiny French pickles) or small gherkins, sliced
A few tarragon leaves, for garnish

FRESH TARRAGON MAYONNAISE

Stir egg yolk in a medium-size heavy bowl with a pinch of salt, white pepper, mustard, and 1 teaspoon lemon juice. With a whisk, begin beating in oil, drop by drop. When 2 or 3 tablespoons oil have been added, beat in remaining oil in a very thin stream. Whisk in remaining lemon juice. If mayonnaise is very thick, whisk in about 1 tablespoon warm water. Stir in chopped tarragon and taste and adjust seasoning. Let stand 1 hour at room temperature, or refrigerate up to overnight to blend flavors.

If using fresh artichokes, prepare hearts according to the directions on page 143.

Squeeze any juice remaining in lemon into medium-size saucepan of boiling salted water, add artichoke hearts, cover, and simmer over low heat until tender when pierced with a knife, about 15 minutes for fresh ones, and about 7 minutes for frozen ones. Cool to lukewarm in liquid. Using a teaspoon, scoop out choke from center of each fresh artichoke heart. Cut each fresh artichoke into 4 pieces. Return artichokes to liquid until ready to use.

In a medium-size saucepan of boiling salted water, cook each of the remaining vegetables separately, uncovered, until just tender; asparagus will require about 3 minutes, green beans about 7 minutes, fresh peas about 7 minutes, and frozen peas about 3 minutes. Rinse and drain thoroughly. Cool completely.

Combine vegetables in a bowl and toss with mayonnaise. Spoon into a serving dish. Garnish with egg slices alternating with slices of cornichon. Put tarragon leaves on egg slices for garnish. Serve at room temperature.

NOTE: If you have homemade mayonnaise already prepared, flavor ½ cup mayonnaise with the tarragon. Whisk in a little water to thin it out if necessary.

PROVENÇAL MARINATED VEGETABLES
Légumes marinés à la provençale

Delicately sweet and sour, this colorful dish is made of vegetables that cook directly in their dressing of tomatoes, olive oil, white wine, and lemon juice, along with a few raisins. If you prefer, the raisins can be omitted.   MAKES 4 SERVINGS

¼ pound pearl onions
1 cup small cauliflower florets
2 ounces wax beans, ends removed, broken in 2 or 3 pieces
¾ cup mild olive oil
1 medium-size onion, minced
3 large ripe tomatoes, peeled, seeded, and chopped (about 1⅓ to 1½ pounds)
¼ cup dark raisins (optional)
Salt and freshly ground pepper

¼ pound small mushrooms, cut into quarters
1 celery stalk, peeled and thinly sliced
⅓ cup diced fennel (optional)
2 teaspoons fresh thyme leaves, or ½ teaspoon dried thyme
¾ cup dry white wine
3 tablespoons strained fresh lemon juice

Put pearl onions in a medium-size saucepan, cover with water, and bring to a boil. Cook 1 minute, rinse under cold water, drain well, and peel.

In a medium-size saucepan of boiling salted water, cook cauliflower and beans, uncovered, over high heat for 2 minutes. Rinse with cold water and drain thoroughly.

In a medium-size sauté pan, warm 1 tablespoon olive oil over low heat, add minced onion, and cook about 7 minutes, or until soft but not brown. Add tomatoes, raisins, and salt and pepper to taste, and cook over medium heat, stirring often, about 12 minutes, or until tomatoes are soft and most of their liquid has evaporated.

Add 7 tablespoons oil to tomato mixture and bring to a boil, stirring. Stir in mushrooms, pearl onions, celery, fennel, and thyme, and cook over high heat for 2 minutes. Stir in wine and bring to a boil. Add cauliflower, beans, and 2 tablespoons lemon juice.

Reduce heat to low, cover, and cook about 25 minutes, or until vegetables are very tender; check by piercing pearl onion with knife.

Add remaining 4 tablespoons oil and 1 tablespoon lemon juice and bring to a boil. Remove from heat. Taste and adjust seasoning. Let cool completely. (Vegetables can be kept, covered, up to 3 days in refrigerator.) Serve cold or at room temperature.

NOTE: Green beans can be substituted for wax beans.

Potato, Rice, and Pasta Salads

In France, potato and rice salads are a standard item at charcuteries, but pasta salads are gaining favor among home cooks. Both home cooks and professional chefs vary the salads to suit their own taste and produce a great array of salads with many different flavors.

The simplest form of potato, rice, or pasta salad is composed of the main ingredient, dressing, and often chopped onions or shallots. An infinite number of combinations can be created from this basic formula because the neutral taste of potatoes, rice, and pasta enables them to harmonize with nearly all foods, whether of mild or strong flavor. Colorful cooked vegetables such as beets, carrots, and peas are a welcome addition. Zesty condiments such as pickled cucumbers, capers, black olives, or chopped anchovies add zip to all types of salads.

Whether the salad is plain or elaborate, it is the dressing that determines its character. For potato salad, vinaigrette is preferred, although mayonnaise is sometimes used to make a creamy salad similar to American-style potato salad. Potato salad is often served cold but is best at room temperature.

Besides occupying the center of a salad buffet table or accompanying cold meats or hot sausages, a potato, rice, or pasta salad can play the role of a light main course if it contains meat, fish, cheese, or eggs.

Rice is so associated with the cuisines of the East that some people might find it surprising that Escoffier, author of the "bible" of French cuisine, devotes a major section of his chapter on first courses to rice salads. He even wrote a whole book of recipes for cooking rice. His salads often combine just a few ingredients to make a lovely balance. For example, Salade Andalouse combines rice flavored with vinaigrette, garlic, onion, and parsley with julienne of sweet red peppers and small tomato wedges; Salade des Moines is of rice, asparagus tips, strips of chicken, and mustard vinaigrette, and sprinkled with black truffles.

Hints

• For potato salads, be sure the potatoes are cooked just right. Undercooked potatoes do not taste good; if potatoes are overcooked, they fall apart when cut and tossed with the dressing. If the potatoes are not all of one size, check each with a knife to see if it is tender and remove the smaller ones first.

• Potatoes, rice, and pasta should be freshly cooked for salad but other vegetables can be cooked one day ahead.

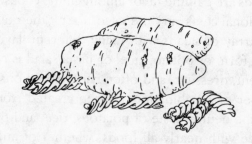

POTATO AND BEET SALAD
Salade de pommes de terre aux betteraves

The most suitable potatoes for salad are relatively small, preferably new, boiling potatoes. These have firm, waxy flesh, unlike mealy
baking potatoes, and therefore do not fall apart in the water during
cooking and do not crumble when cut. The potatoes are cooked whole
in their skins to keep in their taste. This potato and beet salad is
colorful, light, and perfect for any season.   MAKES 4 SERVINGS

4 beets, about 1 ½ inches in
    diameter
2 tablespoons dry white wine
1 tablespoon mild white wine
    vinegar (5 percent acidity)
1 tablespoon vegetable oil

Salt and freshly ground pepper
2 pounds red-skinned potatoes of
    uniform size, scrubbed but not
    peeled
2 tablespoons minced green onion or
    chives

VINAIGRETTE
3 tablespoons white wine vinegar
Salt and freshly ground pepper

9 tablespoons vegetable oil

Put beets in medium-size saucepan, cover with water, and bring
to boil. Cover, reduce heat to low, and cook about 35 minutes, or until
just tender when pierced with knife. Drain beets and slip off skins.

Combine wine, vinegar, oil, and salt and pepper to taste in small
bowl and whisk until blended.

Put potatoes in large saucepan, cover with water by about ½ inch,
and add salt. Bring to boil, cover, reduce heat to low, and simmer
about 25 minutes, or until knife pierces center of largest potato easily
and potato falls from knife when lifted; to be sure potato is cooked
enough, check by cutting largest potato in half at widest point, cut a
slice from center of potato and taste. Do not overcook, or potatoes
will fall apart when cut.

Drain potatoes in colander and peel while hot. To peel, set potato
on board rather than holding it so it is easy to peel while still hot. Slit
potato skin with paring knife, peel strip of skin around center of
potato, and pull off skin in large pieces. Use knife to gently scrape off

any remaining bits of peel. Cut off any dark parts of potato. Cut potatoes into medium dice.

Put potatoes in large bowl. Stir wine mixture until blended and pour it over potatoes. Toss or fold gently to mix, separating any potato pieces that are stuck together. Fold in green onion. Cool to room temperature.

VINAIGRETTE
In a small bowl, whisk vinegar with salt and pepper; whisk in oil. Taste and adjust seasoning.

Add ½ cup vinaigrette to potato mixture and fold it in gently, using a rubber spatula. Add more vinaigrette if needed. (Salad tastes best on day it is made but it can be prepared 1 day ahead, covered, and refrigerated.) If salad was prepared ahead and absorbed all of dressing, add about 2 tablespoons more vinaigrette, or enough to moisten.

Just before serving, dice beets and fold into salad. Taste and adjust seasoning. Transfer salad to serving dish and serve at room temperature.

SUMMER POTATO AND GREEN BEAN SALAD
Salade de pommes de terre aux haricots verts

In French potato salads, the potatoes are sliced and tossed with a simple white wine marinade immediately after cooking, because they absorb seasonings best when they are still warm.

MAKES 4 SERVINGS

2 tablespoons dry white wine
1 tablespoon vegetable oil
Salt and freshly ground pepper
2 pounds red-skinned or other
    boiling potatoes of uniform
    size, scrubbed but not peeled

2 tablespoons minced green onion

VINAIGRETTE

3 tablespoons tarragon vinegar or
   white wine vinegar

Salt and freshly ground pepper
9 tablespoons vegetable oil

½ pound green beans, ends
   trimmed, broken in thirds
2 tablespoons minced fresh tarragon
   (optional)

1 tablespoon capers, rinsed and
   drained
2 small ripe tomatoes, cut into
   quarters

Combine wine, oil, and salt and pepper in small bowl and whisk until blended.

Put potatoes in large saucepan, cover with water by about ½ inch, and add salt. Bring to boil, cover, reduce heat to low, and simmer about 25 minutes, or until knife pierces center of largest potato easily and potato falls from knife when lifted.

Drain potatoes in colander and peel while hot. Cut off any dark parts of potato. Cut potatoes into medium dice.

Put potatoes in large bowl. Stir wine mixture until blended and pour it over potatoes. Toss or fold gently to mix, separating any potato pieces that are stuck together. Fold in green onion. Cool to room temperature.

VINAIGRETTE

In a small bowl, whisk vinegar with salt and pepper; whisk in oil. Taste and adjust seasoning.

Add ½ cup vinaigrette to potato mixture and fold it in gently, using a rubber spatula. Taste and adjust seasoning.

In a medium-size saucepan of boiling salted water, cook green beans, uncovered, over high heat about 5 minutes, or until just tender. Rinse with cold water and drain thoroughly.

Fold beans, tarragon, and capers into salad. If salad was prepared ahead and absorbed all of dressing, add about 2 tablespoons more vinaigrette, or enough to moisten. Taste and adjust seasoning and transfer salad to serving dish. Garnish with tomato quarters and sprinkle them with a little vinaigrette. Serve salad at room temperature. (Salad tastes best on day it is made but it can be prepared 1 day ahead, covered, and refrigerated.)

CLASSIC SALADE NIÇOISE
Omit tarragon and garnish salad with black olives and anchovy fillets.

❧ POTATO-PEPPER SALAD À LA PROVENÇALE
Salade de pommes de terre et poivrons à la provençale

Peppers of three hues make this one of the most colorful of potato salads. It is flavored with three favorites of southern France— olive oil, black olives, and anchovies.   MAKES 4 SERVINGS

2 tablespoons dry white wine
1 tablespoon extra-virgin olive oil
Salt and freshly ground pepper
2 pounds red-skinned potatoes of
    uniform size, scrubbed but not
    peeled

2 tablespoons minced green onion
1 medium-size red bell pepper
1 medium-size green bell pepper
1 medium-size yellow bell pepper

VINAIGRETTE
3 tablespoons white wine vinegar
9 tablespoons extra-virgin olive oil

4 anchovy fillets in olive oil
    (optional)

1 cup black olives, preferably
    Niçoise olives, pitted and cut
    in half lengthwise

Combine wine, olive oil, and salt and pepper to taste in small bowl and whisk until blended.

Put potatoes in large saucepan, cover with water by about ½ inch, and add salt. Bring to boil, cover, reduce heat to low, and simmer about 25 minutes, or until knife pierces center of largest potato easily and potato falls from knife when lifted.

Drain potatoes in colander and peel while hot. Cut off any dark parts of potato. Cut potatoes into medium dice.

Put potatoes in large bowl. Stir wine mixture until blended and pour it over potatoes. Toss or fold gently to mix, separating any potato pieces that are stuck together. Fold in green onion. Cool to room temperature.

Preheat broiler. Broil peppers about 2 inches from heat source, turning often with tongs, about 15 to 20 minutes, or until they are blistered and charred. Transfer to plastic bag and close bag. Let stand

10 minutes. Peel, cut in half, remove cores, and pat dry. Cut pepper halves crosswise in half. Cut each half lengthwise into strips about ½ inch wide.

Make vinaigrette according to the instructions given in recipe for Breton Vegetable Salad with Chive Mayonnaise. Put anchovy fillets in small bowl, cover with warm water, and soak 5 minutes. Drain, pat them dry, and chop very finely. Add to ½ cup vinaigrette and taste and adjust seasoning.

Fold the anchovy-flavored vinaigrette into potato mixture. Reserve 6 olive halves for garnish. Fold peppers and remaining olives gently into salad and adjust seasoning. (Salad can be kept, covered, 1 day in refrigerator.)

If salad was prepared ahead and absorbed all of dressing, add about 2 tablespoons more vinaigrette, or enough to moisten salad. Taste and adjust seasoning and transfer salad to serving dish. Garnish with reserved olives. Serve salad at room temperature.

AUVERGNE POTATO SALAD WITH CANTAL CHEESE
Salade auvergnate

This is a favorite lunchtime salad in French cafés. Walnuts are often used in salads in the region of Auvergne in central France, but pecans or other nuts are just fine. If Cantal cheese is not available, it can be replaced by good-quality Gruyère.

MAKES 4 TO 6 SERVINGS

2 pounds red-skinned potatoes   *Salt*

VINAIGRETTE
¼ cup white wine vinegar   *¾ cup olive oil, walnut oil, or*
Salt and freshly ground pepper   *vegetable oil*

½ pound Cantal cheese, cut in thin   *1 head green leaf lettuce*
strips   *⅔ cup walnut pieces*

Scrub potatoes but do not peel them. Put them in a saucepan, cover them generously with water, and add a pinch of salt. Cover, bring to a boil, and simmer for 25 minutes, or until tender when pierced with a sharp knife.

VINAIGRETTE
In a medium bowl, whisk vinegar with salt and pepper; whisk in oil. Taste and adjust seasoning.

When potatoes are tender, drain them and leave until cool enough to handle. Peel potatoes, cut them in half lengthwise, and slice. Put them in a large bowl. Whisk dressing briskly, spoon ⅓ cup dressing over potatoes, and mix gently. Let cool to room temperature. Add cheese. (Salad tastes best on day it is made but it can be prepared 1 day ahead, covered, and refrigerated.)

Rinse and dry lettuce leaves thoroughly. Tear large leaves in half but leave small ones whole.

A short time before serving, toss lettuce leaves with ¼ cup vinaigrette and taste and adjust seasoning. Arrange on a platter.

Add enough of remaining dressing to potato mixture to lightly coat ingredients. Add all but 2 tablespoons of walnuts. Mix gently, taste and adjust seasoning.

To serve, spoon potato salad onto bed of lettuce. Garnish with remaining walnuts.

POTATO SALAD WITH WATERCRESS
Salade de pommes de terre au cresson

A generous amount of fresh watercress accents this potato salad with a bright green color and a lively flavor.   MAKES 4 SERVINGS

2 tablespoons dry white wine
1 tablespoon vegetable oil
Salt and freshly ground
    pepper

2 pounds red-skinned potatoes of
    uniform size, scrubbed but not
    peeled
2 tablespoons minced green onion

VINAIGRETTE
3 tablespoons white wine vinegar   *9 tablespoons vegetable oil*
Salt and freshly ground pepper

1 ⅓ cups snipped watercress leaves

Combine wine, oil, salt, and pepper in small bowl and whisk until blended.

Put potatoes in large saucepan, cover with water by about ½ inch, and add salt. Bring to boil, cover, reduce heat to low, and simmer about 25 minutes, or until knife pierces center of largest potato easily and potato falls from knife when lifted.

Drain potatoes in colander and peel while hot. Cut potatoes into medium dice.

Put potatoes in large bowl. Stir wine mixture until blended and pour it over potatoes. Toss or fold gently to mix, separating any potato pieces that are stuck together. Fold in green onion. Cool to room temperature.

VINAIGRETTE
In a small bowl, whisk vinegar with salt and pepper; whisk in oil. Taste and adjust seasoning.

Add ½ cup vinaigrette to potato mixture and fold it in gently, using a rubber spatula. Taste and adjust seasoning. (Salad tastes best on day it is made but it can be prepared 1 day ahead, covered, and refrigerated.) If salad was prepared ahead and absorbed all of dressing, add about 2 tablespoons more vinaigrette, or enough to moisten salad.

Just before serving, fold in watercress, taste and adjust seasoning. Transfer salad to serving dish and serve at room temperature.

POTATO, ASPARAGUS, AND ARTICHOKE SALAD
Salade Rachel

Classic versions of this salad also add as many truffles as potatoes, but here they are obviously optional.

MAKES 4 SERVINGS

2 tablespoons dry white wine
1 tablespoon mild white wine
vinegar (5 percent acidity)
1 tablespoon vegetable oil
Salt and freshly ground pepper
2 pounds red-skinned or other
boiling potatoes of uniform
size, scrubbed but not peeled
1 lemon (if using fresh artichokes)

4 fresh artichokes, or 16 frozen
artichoke heart pieces
2 cups cooked fresh or frozen
asparagus tips
2 celery stalks, peeled and very
thinly sliced
1⅓ cups Mayonnaise (see recipe)
2 tablespoons minced fresh
tarragon, chives, or parsley

Combine wine, vinegar, oil, and salt and pepper in small bowl and whisk until blended.

Put potatoes in a large saucepan, cover with water by about ½ inch, and add salt. Bring to a boil, cover, reduce heat to low, and simmer about 25 minutes, or until knife pierces center of largest potato easily.

Drain potatoes in colander and peel while hot. Cut potatoes into medium dice.

Put potatoes in large bowl. Whisk wine mixture until blended and pour it over potatoes. Toss or fold gently to mix, separating any potato pieces that are stuck together. Cool to room temperature.

If using fresh artichokes, prepare hearts according to the directions on page 143.

Squeeze any juice remaining in lemon into medium-size saucepan of boiling salted water, add artichoke hearts, cover, and simmer over low heat until tender when pierced with a knife, about 15 minutes for fresh ones, and about 7 minutes for frozen ones. Cool to lukewarm in liquid. Using a teaspoon, scoop out choke from center of each fresh artichoke heart. Cut each fresh artichoke into 4 pieces. Return artichokes to liquid until ready to use.

Reserve 8 asparagus tips for garnish. Add artichokes, celery, and remaining asparagus tips to potato salad. Add mayonnaise and tarragon and fold them in gently, using a rubber spatula. Taste and adjust seasoning. (Salad tastes best on day it is made but it can be prepared 1 day ahead, covered, and refrigerated.) Transfer salad to serving dish, garnish with reserved asparagus tips, and serve at room temperature.

RICE SALAD WITH PEAS AND PEPPERS
Salade de riz aux petits pois et aux poivrons

This is one of the prettiest of salads—the snowy white rice is dotted with green peas, diced grilled red peppers, and pieces of black olives.   MAKES 6 TO 8 SERVINGS

2 red bell peppers (about ¾ pound)
Salt
1½ cups long-grain white rice
¼ cup thinly sliced green onion,
   green and white parts
1½ cups cooked shelled fresh or
   frozen peas

¾ cup pitted black olives, cut
   lengthwise in 4 pieces
1 tablespoon chopped fresh parsley
2 teaspoons drained capers

VINAIGRETTE
3 tablespoons white wine vinegar
Salt and freshly ground pepper

9 tablespoons extra-virgin olive oil

Preheat broiler. Broil peppers about 2 inches from heat source, turning often, about 15 to 20 minutes, or until blistered and charred. Transfer to plastic bag and close. Let stand 10 minutes. Peel, cut peppers in half, and remove cores. Drain well in colander, pat dry, and dice.

In a large saucepan, boil about 2 quarts water and add a pinch of salt. Add rice, stir once, and cook, uncovered, about 12 to 14 minutes, or until tender; check by tasting. Drain, rinse with cold water, and leave in strainer for about 15 minutes.

Combine rice, onion, peas, peppers, olives, parsley, and capers in a large bowl; mix well.

Make vinaigrette according to the instructions in recipe for Breton Vegetable Salad with Chive Mayonnaise.

Add vinaigrette to rice mixture, stir gently, taste and adjust seasoning. Cover and refrigerate at least 1 hour. (Salad can be kept, covered, 2 days in refrigerator.) Serve at room temperature.

❧ RICE SALAD WITH PYRENEES CHEESE, MUSHROOMS, AND TOMATOES
Salade de riz au fromage des Pyrénées, aux champignons, et aux tomates

Use a fine-quality cheese, very fresh mushrooms, and ripe tomatoes for best results.   MAKES 6 TO 8 SERVINGS

Salt

1½ cups long-grain white rice

2 celery stalks

VINAIGRETTE

3 tablespoons white wine vinegar

Salt and freshly ground pepper

1 teaspoon Dijon mustard (optional)

9 tablespoons vegetable oil

3 ounces small white mushrooms

2 hard-boiled eggs, chopped (optional)

3 to 4 ounces Pyrenees, Cantal, or Gruyère cheese, cut in thin strips

2 large ripe tomatoes, diced

2 tablespoons chopped fresh parsley

In a large saucepan, boil about 2 quarts water and add a pinch of salt. Add rice, stir once, and cook, uncovered, about 12 to 14 minutes, or until tender; check by tasting. Drain, rinse with cold water, and leave in strainer for about 15 minutes.

Peel strings from celery and cut in ¼-inch dice.

VINAIGRETTE

Whisk vinegar with mustard, salt and pepper in a bowl. Gradually whisk in oil. Taste and adjust seasoning.

Cut mushrooms in half and thinly slice, transfer to a small bowl, and sprinkle immediately with about 1 tablespoon vinaigrette to prevent them from discoloring. Toss gently.

Combine rice, celery, eggs, cheese, and mushrooms in a large bowl and mix well.

Whisk vinaigrette, add to rice mixture, and fold gently. Fold in tomatoes and parsley and mix. Taste and adjust seasoning, cover, and refrigerate at least 1 hour. (Salad can be kept, covered, 1 day in refrigerator.) Serve at room temperature.

🦐 PASTA SALAD WITH RED PEPPERS, BROCCOLI, AND GARLIC DRESSING
Salade de pâtes aux poivrons rouges et aux brocolis, sauce à l'ail

Pasta salads are not as popular in France as they are here but can be found occasionally in Alsace and Provence, the areas known for their pasta dishes. The dressing in this salad resembles a light mayonnaise flavored with garlic, and is also good with cooked vegetables.

GARLIC DRESSING
2 large garlic cloves
1 egg, room temperature
Salt and freshly ground pepper
¼ cup olive oil
¼ cup vegetable oil
2 tablespoons white wine vinegar

1 bunch broccoli (about 1½ pounds)
1 red bell pepper
½ pound wide egg noodles
½ to 1 cup black olives

GARLIC DRESSING
In a food processor, chop garlic until very fine. Add egg, salt and pepper to taste, and 1 tablespoon olive oil and process until blended. With blades of processor turning, pour in remaining olive oil and vegetable oil in a very thin stream. Pour in vinegar gradually. Taste and adjust seasoning. (To prepare dressing using a blender, first chop garlic with a knife, then combine with egg, salt, pepper, and 1 tablespoon oil and proceed as above.)

Divide broccoli into small florets. Peel large stem, removing all woody parts and leaving only tender core. Slice peeled stem, put in a pan of boiling salted water, and cook for 1 minute. Add broccoli florets and boil about 4 minutes, or until just tender. Drain, rinse, under cold running water, and drain thoroughly.

Cut pepper in half lengthwise, remove core and thick ribs, and cut again crosswise. Cut pepper in short strips. Put pepper strips in a medium-size saucepan of boiling salted water and cook for 1 minute. Drain, rinse, and drain thoroughly.

Add noodles to a large pan of boiling salted water and cook, uncovered, over high heat 6 to 7 minutes, or until just tender but still al dente, or slightly firm to bite; check by tasting. Rinse under cold running water and drain thoroughly.

Reserve about ¼ cup red pepper strips for garnish. In a large bowl, toss noodles with broccoli and remaining pepper strips. Add dressing, taste and adjust seasoning. Transfer to a serving bowl and garnish center with reserved pepper strips and edges with olives. Serve at room temperature or cool, but not chilled.

MAYONNAISE
Mayonnaise

Homemade mayonnaise is delicious with a great variety of cooked and raw vegetables and is the base of many dressings and cold sauces.　　　　　　MAKES ABOUT 1 ⅓ CUPS

2 egg yolks, room temperature
Salt and white pepper
1 teaspoon Dijon mustard, or more
　to taste (optional)
2 tablespoons plus 2 teaspoons mild
　white wine vinegar (5 percent
　acidity), or strained fresh
　lemon juice, or more to taste

1 ¼ cups vegetable oil, or ½ cup
　vegetable oil mixed with ¾
　cup olive oil, room temperature
1 tablespoon plus 1 teaspoon
　lukewarm water

To prepare mayonnaise in a blender or food processor, combine egg yolks, pinch of salt, white pepper, mustard, 1 tablespoon vinegar and 1 tablespoon oil in blender or food processor fitted with metal blade. Process mixture until well blended. With motor running, pour in about ¼ cup oil in thin trickle. After ¼ cup oil has been added, remaining oil can be poured in a little faster, in thin stream. With motor still running, gradually add remaining 1 tablespoon plus 2 teaspoons vinegar. Taste and adjust seasoning; gradually add a little more vinegar if desired. Gradually add enough water to thin mayonnaise so that it holds soft, not stiff, peaks.

To prepare mayonnaise in a bowl with a whisk or a mixer, beat egg yolks with a pinch of salt, white pepper, mustard, and 1 tablespoon vinegar. Begin beating in oil, drop by drop. When 2 or 3 tablespoons oil have been added, beat in remaining oil in a very thin stream. Stir in remaining vinegar and taste and adjust seasoning. Gradually add enough water to thin mayonnaise so that it holds soft, not stiff, peaks.

(Mayonnaise can be kept, covered, about 4 days in refrigerator.) Bring to room temperature before using. If mayonnaise thickened on standing, gradually add a few drops more water.

NOTES

• If mayonnaise separates during preparation, whisk the separated mixture very gradually into 1 teaspoon Dijon mustard or 1 egg yolk; then continue adding any remaining oil according to the recipe.
• If preparing mayonnaise in a large food processor, do not try to make half a recipe.
• If preparing mayonnaise in a blender or food processor, egg yolks can be replaced by 1 whole large egg. This mayonnaise will be slightly less rich and a bit thinner than that made with egg yolks.

CRÈME FRAÎCHE
Crème fraîche

Thick, slightly tangy crème fraîche is a wonderful French ingredient. Fortunately it is becoming more and more available at fine cheese shops and other specialty shops in America. It is quite simple and less expensive to make your own, however. MAKES ABOUT 2 CUPS

2 cups heavy cream, preferably not   ¼ cup whole-milk yogurt
    ultrapasteurized

    Stir cream and yogurt together in a medium-size saucepan. Heat over very low heat, stirring constantly, for 1 minute. Pour into a jar, partially cover, and leave overnight, or at least 8 hours, at room temperature or until thickened. Stir gently, cover, and refrigerate. (Crème fraîche keeps about 2 weeks in refrigerator.)

Index

Aïoli. *See* Sauces
Almonds, Toasted, Artichoke
    Hearts, Carrots, and,
    Rice Pilaf with,
    240–41
Alsatian Onion and Cream Cheese
    Tart, 89–90
Appetizers
    Baked Broccoli Gnocchi with
        Parmesan Cheese Sauce,
        75–77
    Brie Beignets, 73–74
    Cèpe Turnovers, 101–102
    Country Leek Tart, 85–87
    Green Onion and Parmesan
        Croissants, 90–91

Mushroom and Olive Pastry
    Rolls, 92–93
    See also Canapés
Apples and Cider, Cabbage with,
    164–65
Artichoke(s)
Asparagus, Green Bean, and Fresh
    Pea Salad with Tarragon
    Mayonnaise, 323–24
Baby, with Hazelnut Oil
    Vinaigrette, 312
and Baby Onions Antiboise,
    199–200
in Breton Vegetable Salad
    with Chive Mayonnaise,
    313–15

Artichoke(s) *(cont'd)*
  in Colorful Vegetable
    Blanquette, 169–70
  Filled with Peas, 145
  hearts
    Carrots and, Toasted Almonds,
      Rice Pilaf with, 240–41
    to cook, 3
    to shape, 3
  Jerusalem. *See* Jerusalem
    artichokes
  in Mediterranean Saffron Rice
    Pilaf with Vegetables,
    236–38
  with Onion Compote, 143–44
  Potato, Asparagus, and, Salad,
    333–34
  in Provençal Vegetable and
    Garlic Feast, 179–81
  and Rice Salad, Tomatoes Filled
    with, 151–52
  with Tomato Béarnaise Sauce,
    190–91
Asparagus
  Artichoke, Green Bean, and
    Fresh Pea Salad with
    Tarragon Mayonnaise,
    323–24
  with Beurre Blanc, 174–76
  and Carrots with Madeira,
    166–67
  Cheese Puff Crown with, 69–71
  Creamy Rice Pilaf with, 238–39
  -filled Pastry Cases with
    Watercress Sauce, 94–96
  Mimosa with Hazelnuts, 309
  Morels and, Fettucine with,
    250–51
  to peel, 3
  Potato, and Artichoke Salad,
    333–34
  and Roquefort Canapés, 116–17
  Soup(s)
    Creamy, 278
    with Olive Oil, 277–78

    Timbales with Hollandaise
      Sauce, 13–15
  in Vegetable Terrine with
    Mushroom Mousse and
    Fresh Tomato Vinaigrette,
    32–35
Auvergne Potato Salad with Cantal
  Cheese, 331–32
Avocado
  Mousse, 43–44
  and Mushroom Salad with Swiss
    Chard, 320–21

Baby Vegetables
  with Herb Butter Sauce, 181–83
  See also Names of vegetables
Baked Beets with Lemon Cream,
  202–203
Baked Broccoli Gnocchi with
  Parmesan Cheese Sauce,
  75–77
Baked Mushrooms with Escargot
  Butter and Walnuts, 198–99
Baked Onions with Dill Butter,
  200–201
Baked Pasta with Eggplant,
  254–55
Baked Potato Cakes, 226
Baking vegetables, notes on,
  197
Basil
  -Garlic Sauce, Creamy,
    Tricolored Vegetable
    Terrine with, 29–32
  Peas and, Rice with, 233
  Tomatoes and, Chick-pea and
    Bean Salad with, 318–20
  Zucchini Purée with, 135–36
Batter-fried Vegetables with
  Rémoulade Sauce, 215–16
Bavarian, Broccoli, 44–46
Bean(s)
  Chick-pea and, with Tomatoes
    and Basil, 318–20
  Fava, in Garlic Cream, 194–95

Bean(s) *(cont'd)*
  Flageolets with Green and
      Yellow Beans and Green
      Onion Butter, 167–69
  green. *See* Green beans
  wax. *See* Wax beans
  white
    in Southwestern Vegetable
        Soup with Vegetable
        Croutons, 271–73
    with Tomatoes and Onions,
        193–94
Beet(s)
  baby, *in* Baby Vegetables with
      Herb Butter Sauce, 181–83
  Baked, with Lemon Cream,
      202–203
  Endive and, Salad, 317–18
  with Orange Hollandaise,
      176–78
  Potato and, Salad, 327–28
  Timbales, 11–13
Beignets, Brie, 73–74
Belgian endives. *See* Endives
Beurre Blanc, Asparagus with,
    174–76
Blanquette, Vegetable, Colorful,
    169–70
Boiling vegetables, notes on, 178
Bouillabaisse, Vegetable, 262–63
Bourride, Vegetable, with Aïoli,
    270–71
Braised Chestnuts, 162–63
Braised Fennel with Peppers and
    Olives, 166
Braising vegetables, notes on, 162
Breton Vegetable Salad with Chive
    Mayonnaise, 313–15
Brie Beignets, 73–74
Bright Green Spinach Tart, 58–60
Broccoli
  Bavarian, 44–46
  in Buckwheat Crêpes with
      Creamy Vegetables,
      105–106

Cauliflower
  and Roquefort Sauce, Pasta
      with, 256
  Velouté Soup with, 294–95
  Velouté Soup with, Cold, 295
Gnocchi, Baked, with Parmesan
    Cheese Sauce, 75–77
Gratin
  with Light Cheese Sauce,
      128
  Quick, with Celery and Nuts,
      129–30
  and Mushroom Soufflé with
      Chives, 43–54
  Purée, Creamy, Pasta with,
      249–50
  Red Peppers, and Garlic
      Dressing, Pasta Salad with,
      337–38
  with Roquefort Sauce, 185–86
  Timbales with Garlic Butter
      Sauce, 16–18
Brown Rice Pilaf with Tarragon,
    241–42
Brussels sprouts
  Baked in Mornay Sauce, 130–31
  with Creamy Mustard-Sage Sauce,
      189–90
Buckwheat Crêpes with Creamy
    Vegetables, 105–106
Butter(s)
  -braised endives, 165
  Dill, Baked Onions with,
      200–201
  Escargot, and Walnuts, Baked
      Mushrooms with, 198–99
  Garlic
    Delicate, Green Beans with,
        187–88
    -glazed Carrots, 160–61
    Sauce, Broccoli Timbales with,
        16–18
  Green Onion, Green and
      Yellow Beans and,
      Flageolets with, 167–69

Butter(s) *(cont'd)*
  Hazelnut, Capers and, Zucchini
      with, 186
  Mint
      Green Pea Purée with,
          140–41
      Zucchini with, 173–74
  Pistachio, Steamed Carrots with,
      176
  salted vs. unsalted, 6
  Tarragon, Steamed New
      Potatoes with, 221–22
  Tomato, Sauce, Cauliflower
      Timbales with, 23–25
  and Wine Vinegar, Cabbage
      with, 190

Cabbage
  with Apples and Cider, 164–65
  with Butter and Wine Vinegar,
      190
  Cream-braised, with Leeks,
      163–64
  Gratin with Light Cheese Sauce,
      128
  and Mushroom Gratin, Layered,
      128–29
  Red and Green, Sauté with Goat
      Cheese, 211
  in Southwestern Vegetable Soup
      with Croutons, 271–73
  Tart with Caraway Seeds, 63–64
Cakes, Baked Potato, 226
Canapés
  Asparagus and Roquefort,
      116–17
  Cucumber and Herbed Goat
      Cheese, 117
  Radish Flower, 118
  Roasted Pepper, 119
Cantal Cheese, Auvergne Potato
      Salad with, 331–32
Capers and Hazelnut Butter,
      Zucchini with, 186
Caraway Seeds, Cabbage Tart with,
      63–64

Carrot(s)
  Artichoke Hearts, and Toasted
      Almonds,
      Rice Pilaf with, 240–41
  Asparagus and, with Madeira,
      166–67
  baby
      in Baby Vegetables with Herb
          Butter Sauce, 181–83
      in Colorful Vegetable
          Blanquette, 169–70
      in Breton Vegetable Salad
          with Chive Mayonnaise,
          313–15
      Butter-glazed, 160–61
      in Chanterelle Feuilletés with
          Vegetable Julienne, 96–98
      in Festive Vegetable Tart, 87–88
      in Pasta with Vegetable
          "Noodles," 253–54
  Peas, and Sautéed Mushrooms,
      Couscous Pilaf with, 258–59
  in Provençal Vegetable and
      Garlic Feast, 179–81
  Purée(s)
      Cream Puffs with, 71–73
      Creamy, 140
  with Raspberry Vinegar,
      209–210
  in Rice with Sautéed Vegetables
      and Walnut Oil, 234–35
  Soufflé, Cold, with Peas, 46–48
  Soup with Chives, 285–86
  in Southwestern Vegetable Soup
      with Vegetable Croutons,
      271–73
  Steamed, with Pistachio Butter,
      176
  Timbales, 15–16
  in Tricolored Vegetable Terrine
      with Creamy Basil Garlic
      Sauce, 29–32
  and Turnips, Ginger-glazed,
      159–60
  in Vegetable Bourride with
      Aïoli, 270–71

Carrot(s) *(cont'd)*
  in Vegetable Terrine with
      Mushroom Mousse and
      Fresh Tomato Vinaigrette,
      32–35
Cauliflower
  in Batter-fried Vegetables with
      Rémoulade Sauce, 215–16
  in Breton Vegetable Salad with
      Chive Mayonnaise, 313–15
  Broccoli, and Roquefort Sauce,
      Pasta with, 256
  in Buckwheat Crêpes with
      Creamy Vegetables,
      105–106
  Curried, French, 184–85
  Gratin with Light Cheese Sauce,
      126–28
  and Potato Purée, 136–37
  in Provençal Marinated
      Vegetables, 324–25
  in Provençal Vegetable and
      Garlic Feast, 179–81
  Quiche with Onion and Gruyère
      Cheese, 66–67
  in Rosemary-scented Tomato
      Sauce, 183–84
  Soufflé Pudding with Gruyère
      Cheese, 55–56
  Soup, Light, 278–79
  Timbales with Tomato Butter
      Sauce, 23–25
  and Tomato Salad with Garlic
      and Walnut Dressing,
      321–22
  Velouté Soup with Broccoli,
      294–95
    Cold, 295
Celery
  in Chanterelle Feuilletés with
      Vegetable Julienne, 96–98
  Garlic-scented Zucchini with,
      212–13
  Gratin with Tomato Sauce, 126
  in Medley of Vegetables with
      Fresh Thyme, 208–209

  in Provençal Marinated
      Vegetables, 324–25
  in Rice with Sautéed Vegetables
      and Walnut Oil, 234–35
  root. *See* Celery root
  in Southwestern Vegetable Soup
      with Vegetable Croutons,
      271–73
  in Vegetable Bourride with
      Aïoli, 270–71
Celery root
  Purée, 139
  Salad with Mustard Dressing,
      304–305
  in Southwestern Vegetable Soup
      with Vegetable Croutons,
      271–73
Cèpe(s)
  in Mixed Mushroom Ragoût,
      171
  Potato Gratin with, 224
  Tartlets, 63
  Turnovers, 101–102
Champagne Vinaigrette, 318
Chanterelle(s)
  Couscous with, 257
  Feuilletés with Vegetable
      Julienne, 96–98
Chard. *See* Swiss chard
Cheese
  Creamy Pasta Gratin with,
      254
  Potato and, Gâteau, 220–21
  Puff(s)
    Crown with Asparagus,
        69–71
    Watercress Velouté Soup with,
        291–93
  sauces. *See* Sauces
  See also Names of cheese
Cherry tomatoes, *in* Baby
      Vegetables with Herb
      Butter Sauce, 181–83
Chestnut(s)
  Braised, 162–63
  Soup, Touraine, 275–76

Chick-pea
  and Bean Salad with Tomatoes
    and Basil, 318–20
  Pancake, Baked, Niçoise, 115
Chicken Stock, 297–98
Chive(s)
  Broccoli and Mushroom Soufflé
    with, 53–54
  Carrot Soup with, 285–86
  Creamy Mushroom Tart with,
    64–66
  Mayonnaise, Breton Vegetable
    Salad with, 313–15
  to snip, 4
  Vinaigrette, Creamy, 320–21
Cider, Apples and, Cabbage with,
    164–65
Classic Salade Niçoise, 329
Cold Carrot Soufflé with Peas,
    46–48
Cold Cauliflower Velouté Soup
    with Broccoli, 295
Colorful Vegetable Blanquette,
    169–70
Compote, Onion, Artichokes with,
    143–44
Corn
  oil, to use, 7
  Salad with Peppers, 315–16
Country Leek Tart, 85–87
Country Spinach Soup, 266
Couscous
  with Chanterelles, 257
  Pilaf with Carrots, Peas, and
    Sautéed Mushrooms,
    258–59
Cream(s)
  -braised Cabbage with Leeks,
    163–64
  Morels with, 192–93
  Potato Gratin with, 223–24
  Sauce
    Spinach Gratin with, 124–25
    and Walnuts, Belgian Endive
      Gratin with, 124
  soups. See Soups

Garlic, Fava Beans in, 194–95
  Lemon, Baked Beets with,
    202–203
  Mint, Fresh Pea Soup with,
    274–75
  Mushroom, Green Vegetable
    Quenelles with, 77–79
  Paprika, Pattypan Squash with,
    174
Cream Cheese, Onion and, Tart,
    Alsatian, 89–90
Cream Puffs with Carrot Purée,
    71–73
Creamy Asparagus Soup, 278
Creamy Basil-Garlic Sauce,
    Tricolored Vegetable
    Terrine with, 29–32
Creamy Carrot Purée, 140
Creamy Chive Vinaigrette, 320–21
Creamy Mushroom Sauce,
    Spinach-Cauliflower Gâteau
    with, 39–41
Creamy Mushroom Tart with
    Chives, 64–65
Creamy Mustard-Sage Sauce,
    Brussels Sprouts with,
    189–90
Creamy Onion Soup with Pasta,
    265
Creamy Pasta Gratin with Cheese,
    254
Creamy Potato Purée, 228–29
Creamy Rice Pilaf with Asparagus,
    238–39
Crème Fraîche, 339–40
  Herbed, Fennel Salad with,
    305
  Spinach-filled Crêpes with,
    106–108
Crêpe(s)
  Buckwheat, with Creamy
    Vegetables, 105–106
  Eggplant Soufflé-filled, with Red
    Pepper Sauce, 112–15
  Leek and Mushrooms, 109–10
  notes on, 103–104

Crêpe(s) *(cont'd)*
  pan(s)
    to clean, 104
    to season, 104
    types of, 104
  with Peppers, Onions, and Peas
      in Curry Sauce, 110–12
  Spinach-filled, with Crème
      Fraîche, 106–108
Croissants, Green Onion and
    Parmesan, 90–91
Croûtes, Spinach Purée on, 137–38
Croutons, Vegetable, Southwestern
    Vegetable Soup with,
    271–73
Cucumber(s)
  and Herbed Goat Cheese
      Canapés, 117
  Salad with Yogurt Herb
      Dressing, 306
  Sautéed, with Dill, 212
Cumin, Hollandaise Sauce, Quick,
    Spinach Timbales with,
    21–23
Curry
  Puffs, Light Zucchini Soup with,
      283–84
  Sauce, Crêpes with Peppers,
      Onions, and Peas in,
      110–12
  Tomato, Sauce, Pine Nut Pilaf
      and, Stuffed Eggplant with,
      145–47

Dandelion Salad, Warm, with
    Mushrooms and Poached
    Eggs, 310–11
Deep-frying vegetables, notes on,
    206–207
Delicate Garlic Butter, Green
    Beans with, 187–88
Dill
  Butter, Baked Onions with,
      200–201
  Sauce, Squash Timbales with,
      26–28

Sautéed Cucumbers with, 212
  to snip, 4
Dressing(s)
  Garlic
    Red Peppers, Broccoli, Pasta
        Salad with, 337–38
    and Walnut, Cauliflower and
        Tomato Salad with, 321–22
  Mustard, Celery Root Salad
      with, 304–305
  notes on, 300
  Yogurt Herb, Cucumber Salad
      with, 306
  See also Mayonnaise; Vinaigrettes
Duxelles
  Eggplant Stuffed with, 149–50
  Leek and, Gratin, 122–23

Egg(s)
  large, to use, 6
  Poached, Mushrooms and, Warm
      Dandelion Salad with, 310–11
  Tomato
    and, Canapés, 118–19
    Salad, 308
Eggplant
  Baked Pasta with, 254–55
  Curried, Rice Ring with, 243–45
  with Fresh Herbs, Grilled,
      204–205
  in Medley of Vegetables with
      Fresh Thyme, 208–209
  Savarin with Fresh Tomato
      Sauce, 36–38
  Savory Rice Pilaf with, 235–36
  Soufflé-filled Crêpes with Red
      Pepper Sauce, 112–15
  Stuffed
    with Duxelles, 149–50
    with Pine Nut Pilaf and
        Tomato Curry Sauce,
        145–47
    with Tomatoes, Saffron and
        Garlic, 147–48
  Zucchini, and Tomato Slices
      Baked with Herbs, 197–98

Endive(s) (Belgian)
  and Beet Salad, 317–18
  Butter-braised, 165
  Gratin with Cream Sauce and
    Walnuts, 124
Escargot Butter and Walnuts,
    Baked Mushrooms with,
    198–99
Escarole Salad with Roquefort
    Dressing, 306–307

Fat for deep frying, notes on,
    207–208
Fava Beans in Garlic Cream,
    194–95
Fennel
  Braised, with Peppers and
    Olives, 166
  in Provençal Marinated
    Vegetables, 324–25
  Salad with Herbed Crème
    Fraîche, 405
Festive Vegetable Tart, 87–88
Fettucine with Morels and
    Asparagus, 250–51
Feuilletés, Chanterelle, with
    Vegetable Julienne, 96–98
Flageolets with Green and Yellow
    Beans and Green Onion
    Butter, 167–69
Flour, as soup thickener, 261,
    287
French Curried Cauliflower,
    184–85
French-fried Sweet Potatoes,
    230–31
Fresh Pea Soup with Mint Cream,
    274–75
Fritters, Potato, Light, with Pine
    Nuts, 222–23

Garlic
  Basil-, Sauce, Creamy,
    Tricolored Vegetable
    Terrine, 29–32

Butter
  Delicate, Green Beans with,
    187–88
  Sauce, Broccoli Timbales with,
    16–18
  to chop or mince, 4
  Cream, Fava Beans in, 194–95
  Dressing, Red Peppers, Broccoli,
    and, Pasta Salad with,
    337–38
  Goat Cheese and, Tomato Pasta
    with, 246–47
  and Olive Oil, Grilled Peppers
    with, 203
  to peel, 3
  Purée, Grilled Mushrooms with,
    205–206
  -scented Zucchini with Celery,
    212–13
  Tomatoes, Saffron, and, Eggplant
    with, 147–48
  Vegetable and, Feast, Provençal,
    179–81
  and Walnut Dressing,
    Cauliflower and Tomato
    Salad with, 321–22
Gâteau
  Cheese and Potato, 220–21
  Spinach-Cauliflower, with
    Creamy Mushroom Sauce,
    39–41
Ginger-glazed Carrots and Turnips,
    159–60
Glazed Baby Onions and Zucchini,
    161–62
Glazing vegetables, notes on,
    159
Gnocchi, Broccoli, Baked, with
    Parmesan Cheese Sauce,
    75–77
Goat cheese
  and Garlic, Tomato Pasta with,
    246–47
  Herbed, Cucumber and,
    Canapés, 117

Goat cheese *(cont'd)*
  Red and Green Cabbage Sauté
    with, 211
  Spinach and, Soufflé, 49–50
  Tomato and, Tartlets, with Fresh
    Thyme, 61–63
  and Walnuts, Watercress Salad
    with, 302
Gratin(s)
  Belgian Endive, with Cream
    Sauce and Walnuts, 124
  Broccoli, with Light Cheese
    Sauce, 128
  Brussels Sprouts Baked in
    Mornay Sauce, 130–31
  Cabbage
    with Light Cheese Sauce, 128
    and Mushroom, Layered,
      128–29
  Cauliflower, with Light Cheese
    Sauce, 126–28
  Celery, with Tomato Sauce, 126
  dishes, notes on, 122
  Leek and Duxelles, 122–23
  notes on, 121–22
  Pasta, Creamy, with Cheese, 254
  Potato
    with Cèpes, 224
    with Cream, 223–24
  Spinach, with Cream Sauce,
    124–25
  Swiss Chard and Pepper, with
    Tomatoes, 131–32
  Turnip and Onion, with
    Parmesan, 133
  Winter Squash, with Fresh
    Tomato Sauce, 125–26
  Zucchini Baked in Mornay
    Sauce, 131
Green bean(s)
  Artichoke, Asparagus, and Fresh
    Pea Salad with Tarragon
    Mayonnaise, 323–24
  in Breton Vegetable Salad with
    Olive Mayonnaise, 313–15

  with Delicate Garlic Butter,
    187–88
  Lyonnaise, 187
  Potato and, Salad, Summer,
    328–29
  in Provençal Vegetable and
    Garlic Feast, 179–81
  Salad, Marinated, with Green
    Onions, 309–10
  with Sautéed Walnuts, 209
  in Vegetable Terrine with
    Mushroom Mousse and
    Fresh Tomato Vinaigrette,
    32–35
  and Yellow Beans and Green
    Onion Butter, Flageolets
    with, 167–69
Green (bell) pepper(s)
  in Corn Salad with Peppers,
    315–16
  in Grilled Peppers with Garlic
    and Olive Oil, 203
  in Peppers Stuffed with Rice,
    Mushrooms, and Olives,
    153–54
  in Potato-Pepper Salad à la
    Provençale, 330–31
  in Sautéed Potatoes with
    Peppers and Thyme, 227
  in Swiss Chard and Pepper
    Gratin with Tomatoes,
    131–32
Green onion(s)
  Butter, Green and Yellow Beans
    and Flageolets with, 167–69
  Marinated Green Bean Salad
    with, 309–10
  and Parmesan Croissants, 90–91
  in Rice with Sautéed Vegetables
    and Walnut Oil, 234–35
Green Pea Purée with Mint
    Butter, 140–41
Green Salad with Pine Nuts and
    Sherry Vinaigrette, 303–304
Green vegetables. *See* Vegetables

Grilled Eggplant with Fresh Herbs, 204–205
Grilled Mushrooms with Garlic Purée, 205–206
Grilled Peppers with Garlic and Olive Oil, 203
Grilling vegetables, notes on, 197
Gruyère (cheese)
Cauliflower Soufflé Pudding with, 55–56
in Creamy Pasta Gratin with Cheese, 254
and Nuts, Quick Broccoli Gratin with, 129–30
Onion and, Cauliflower Quiche with, 66–67

Hazelnut(s)
Asparagus Mimosa with, 309
Butter, Capers and, Zucchini with, 186
Leeks Mimosa with, 309
Oil, Vinaigrette, Baby Artichokes with, 312
Toasted, Swiss Chard Soup with, 288–89
Herb(s)
Butter Sauce, Baby Vegetables with, 181–83
fresh
to chop or mince, 4
Grilled Eggplant with, 204–205
Mushroom Cream Soup with, 268–69
Sautéed Salsify with, 213
as seasoning for soups, 274
Summer Tomato Salad with, 307–308
Vinaigrette, 307
Oil, 282
Yogurt, Dressing, Cucumber Salad with, 306
Zucchini, Eggplant, and Tomato Slices Baked with, 197–98
See also Names of herbs
Hollandaise sauce. See Sauces

Individual Onion Soufflés, 52–53

Jerusalem artichoke(s)
in Batter-fried Vegetables with Rémoulade Sauce, 215–16
Sautéed, 210–11

Layered Cabbage and Mushroom Gratin, 128–29
Layered Vegetable Tourte, 98–101
Leek(s)
Cabbage with, Cream-braised, 163–64
in Chanterelle Feuilletés with Vegetable Julienne, 96–98
to clean, 4
Cream Soup with Diced Tomatoes, 289–90
and Duxelles Gratin, 122–23
in Festive Vegetable Tart, 87–88
in Medley of Vegetables with Fresh Thyme, 208–209
Mimosa with Hazelnuts, 308–309
and Mushroom Crêpes, 109–10
Potato and, Pancakes, 229–30
Pumpkin, Potato, and, Soup, 280–81
in Southwestern Vegetable Soup with Vegetable Croutons, 271–73
Spinach, and Pumpkin Pancakes, 214–15
Tart, Country, 85–87
in Vegetable Bourride with Aïoli, 270–71
Lemon Cream, Baked Beets with, 202–203
Light Cauliflower Soup, 278–79
Light Potato Fritters with Pine Nuts, 222–23
Light Zucchini Soup with Curry Puffs, 283–84
Lyonnaise Green Beans, 187

Madeira, Asparagus and Carrots with, 166–67
Marinated Green Bean Salad with Green Onions, 309–10
Mayonnaise, 338–39
    Chive, Breton Vegetable Salad with, 313–15
    separated, to correct, 339
    Tarragon, Artichoke, Asparagus, Green Bean, and Fresh Pea Salad with, 323–24
    See also Dressings
Mediterranean Saffron Rice Pilaf with Vegetables, 236–38
Medley of Vegetables with Fresh Thyme, 208–209
Milk, whole, to use, 7
Mint
    Butter
        Green Pea Purée with, 140–41
        Zucchini with, 173–74
    Cream, Fresh Pea Soup with, 274
Mixed Mushroom Ragoût, 171
Morels
    and Asparagus, Fettucine with, 250–51
    with Cream, 192–93
Mornay sauce. *See* Sauces
Mousse(s)
    Avocado, 43–44
    Broccoli Bavarian, 44–46
    Mushroom, and Fresh Tomato Vinaigrette, Vegetable Terrine with, 32–35
    Tomato, Two-Tone, 42–43
    See also Soufflés
Multicolored Pilaf with Sweet Red Peppers and Walnuts, 239–40
Mushroom(s)
    Avocado and, Salad with Swiss Chard, 320–21
    Baked, with Escargot Butter and Walnuts, 198–99

Broccoli and, Soufflé with Chives, 53–54
in Buckwheat Crêpes with Creamy Vegetables, 105–106
Cabbage and, Gratin, Layered, 128–29
Chanterelle(s)
    Couscous with, 257
    Feuilletés with Vegetable Julienne, 96–98
    to clean, 4
in Colorful Vegetable Blanquette, 169–70
Cream
    Green Vegetable Quenelles with, 77–79
    Soup with Fresh Herbs, 268–69
in Festive Vegetable Tart, 87–88
Grilled, with Garlic Purée, 205–206
in Layered Vegetable Tourte, 98–101
Leek and, Crêpes, 109–110
Morels
    and Asparagus, Fettucine with, 250–51
    with Cream, 192–93
Mousse and Fresh Tomato Vinaigrette, Vegetable Terrine with, 32–35
and Olive Pastry Rolls, 92–93
and Poached Eggs, Warm Dandelion Salad with, 310–11
in Provençal Marinated Vegetables, 324–25
Pyrenees Cheese, and Tomatoes, Rice Salad with, 336–37
Salad, Tomatoes Stuffed with, 316–17
Sauce, Cream, Spinach-Cauliflower Gâteau with, 39–41
Sautéed, Carrots, Peas, and, Couscous Pilaf with, 258–59

Mushroom(s) *(cont'd)*
  Shiitake, *in* Mixed Mushroom
    Ragoût, 171
  to slice, 4
  Stuffed with Fresh Tomato
    Purée, 142–43
  Tart, Creamy, with Chives,
    64–66
  See also Duxelles
Mustard
  Dressing, Celery Root Salad
    with, 304–305
  -Sage Sauce, Creamy, Brussels
    Sprouts with, 189–90
  Sauce, 11–13

Niçoise Baked Chick-pea Pancake,
  115
"Noodles," Vegetable, Pasta with,
  253–54
Norman Potato-Shallot Soup,
  284–85
Nuts, Gruyère and, Quick Broccoli
  Gratin with, 129–30

Oil(s)
  Hazelnut, Vinaigrette, Baby
    Artichokes with, 312
  Herb, 282
  Olive
    Asparagus Soup with, 277–78
    Garlic and, Grilled Peppers
      with, 203
  peanut, to use, 7
  safflower, to use, 7
  Walnut
    Sautéed Vegetables and, Rice
      with, 234–35
    Vinaigrette, 302
Olive(s)
  Mushroom and, Pastry Rolls,
    92–93
  Oil
    Asparagus Soup with, 277–78
    Garlic and, Grilled Peppers
      with, 203

Peppers and, Braised Fennel
    with, 166
Onion(s)
  Baby
    Artichokes and, Antiboise,
      199–200
    and Zucchini, Glazed, 161–62
  Baked, with Dill Butter,
    200–201
  to chop or mince, 5
  Compote, Artichokes with,
    143–44
  and Cream Cheese Tart,
    Alsatian, 89–90
  and Gruyère Cheese, Cauliflower
    Quiche with, 66–67
  pearl, *in* Provençal Marinated
    Vegetables, 324–25
  to peel, 5
  Peppers, and Peas, Crêpes with,
    in Curry Sauce, 110–12
  to slice, 5
  Soufflés, Individual, 52–53
  Soup
    Creamy, with Pasta, 265
    Rich, with Port, 264–65
  Stuffed with Spinach, 155–56
  Tomatoes and, White Beans
    with, 193–94
  Turnip and, Gratin with
    Parmesan, 133
Orange Hollandaise, Beets with,
  176–78

Pancake(s)
  Chick-pea, Baked, Niçoise, 115
  Potato and Leek, 229–30
  Spinach, Leek, and Pumpkin,
    214–15
Paprika Cream, Pattypan Squash
  with, 174
Parmesan (cheese)
  Green Onion and, Croissants,
    90–91
  in Potato and Cheese Gâteau,
    220–21

Parmesan (cheese) *(cont'd)*
and Rice, Stuffed Pattypan
Squash with, 156–57
Sauce, Baked Broccoli Gnocchi
with, 75–77
Turnip and Onion Gratin with,
133
Parsley
Purée, 138
Sauce, Parsnip Timbales with,
19–20
Vinaigrette, 308–309
Parsnip Timbales with Parsley
Sauce, 19–20
Pasta
Baked, with Eggplant, 254–55
with Broccoli, Cauliflower, and
Roquefort Sauce, 256
with Creamy Broccoli Purée,
249–50
Creamy Onion Soup with, 265
Fettucine with Morels and
Asparagus, 250–51
with Fresh Peas and Saffron
Butter Sauce, 247–49
Gratin, Creamy, with Cheese,
254
notes on, 245–46
and Pistou, Provençal Vegetable
Soup with, 267–68
Pumpkin and, Soup, 279–80
salad(s)
notes on, 325–26
with Red Peppers, Broccoli,
and Garlic Dressing,
337–38
Spaghetti with Fall Vegetables
and Tomato-Tarragon Sauce,
251–53
Tomato, with Goat Cheese and
Garlic, 246–47
with Vegetable "Noodles,"
253–54
Pastry(ies)
Cases, Asparagus-filled, with
Watercress Sauce, 94–96

Cèpe Turnovers, 101–102
Chanterelle Feuilletés with
Vegetable Julienne, 96–98
Green Onion and Parmesan
Croissants, 90–91
Layered Vegetable Tourte,
98–101
for quiches and tarts, notes on,
58
Rolls, Mushroom and Olive,
92–93
See also Puffs
Pâté(s)
Spinach, Quick, 35–36
See also Terrines
Pattypan squash
with Paprika Cream, 174
Stuffed, with Parmesan and Rice,
156–57
Pea(s)
Artichokes Filled with, 145
and Basil, Rice with, 233
in Breton Vegetable Salad with
Chive Mayonnaise, 313–15
Carrots, and Sautéed
Mushrooms, Couscous Pilaf
with, 258–59
Cold Carrot Soufflé with, 46–48
Fresh
Artichoke, Asparagus, Green
Bean, and, Salad with
Tarragon Mayonnaise,
323–24
and Saffron Butter Sauce,
Pasta with, 247–49
Soup, with Mint Cream,
274–75
Green, Purée with Mint Butter,
140–41
Peppers, Onions, and, Crêpes
with, in Curry Sauce,
110–12
and Peppers, Rice Salad with,
335
in Vegetable Bouillabaisse,
262–63

Pea(s) *(cont'd)*
  in Vegetable Terrine with
    Mushroom Mousse and
    Fresh Tomato Vinaigrette,
    32–35
Peanut oil, to use, 7
Pearl onions, *in* Provençal
    Marinated Vegetables,
    324–25
Peppers. *See* Red, green, yellow
    bell peppers
Pesto Sauce, French, Wax Beans
    with, 188–89
Pilaf(s)
  Couscous with Carrots, Peas, and
    Sautéed Mushrooms,
    258–59
  rice. *See* Rice
Pine nuts
  Light Potato Fritters with,
    222–23
  Pilaf and Tomato Curry Sauce,
    Stuffed Eggplant with,
    145–47
  and Sherry Vinaigrette, Green
    Salad with, 303–304
Pipérade Pizza, 84–85
Pistachio Butter, Steamed Carrots
    with, 176
Pistou, Pasta and, Provençal
    Vegetable Soup with,
    267–68
Pizza(s)
  Pipérade, 84–85
  Provençal, 79–81
  Ratatouille, 81–83
Plum Tomatoes with Shallot Purée,
    152–53
Poaching vegetables, notes on,
    178
Port, Rich Onion Soup with,
    264–65
Potato(es)
  Baked, Cakes, 226
  Cauliflower and, Purée, 136–37

and Cheese Gâteau, 220–21
Fritters, Light, with Pine Nuts,
    222–23
Gratin
  with Cèpes, 224
  with Cream, 223–24
and Leek Pancakes, 229–30
New, Steamed, with Tarragon
    Butter, 221–22
notes on, 218–19
in Provençal Vegetable and
    Garlic Feast, 179–81
Pumpkin, and Leek Soup,
    280–81
purée(s)
  Creamy, 228–29
  uses for, 218–19
salads. *See* Salads
for salads, to cook, 326
Sautéed, with Peppers and
    Thyme, 227
-Shallot Soup, Norman, 284–85
Skins, Potato Soufflé in, 225
as soup thickener, 261, 273
in Southwestern Vegetable Soup
    with Vegetable Croutons,
    271–73
Sweet, French-fried, 230–31
in Vegetable Bouillabaisse,
    262–63
with Vegetable Julienne Sauce,
    219–20
Provençal Baked Tomatoes,
    201–202
Provençal Marinated Vegetables,
    324–25
Provençal Pizza, 79–81
Provençal Tomato Soup,
    281–83
Provençal Vegetable and Garlic
    Feast, 179–81
Provençal Vegetable Soup with
    Pasta and Pistou, 267–68
Pudding, Soufflé, Cauliflower, with
    Gruyère Cheese, 55–56

Puffs
Cheese, Watercress Velouté
Soup with, 291–93
Cream, with Carrot Purée,
71–73
Curry, Light Zucchini Soup with,
283–84
Pumpkin
and Pasta Soup, 279–80
Potato, and Leek Soup, 280–81
Spinach, Leek, and, Pancakes,
214–15
Purée(s)
Broccoli, Creamy, Pasta with,
249–50
Carrot
Cream Puffs with, 71–73
Creamy, 140
Cauliflower and Potato, 136–37
Celery Root, 139
Fresh Tomato, Mushrooms
Stuffed with, 142–43
Garlic, Grilled Mushrooms with,
205–206
Green Pea, with Mint Butter,
140–41
methods for, 135
notes on, 134–35
Parsley, 138
Potato, Creamy, 228–29
uses for, 218–19
Red Pepper, Zucchini Stuffed
with, 150–51
to season, 135
Shallot, Plum Tomatoes with,
152–53
soups, notes on, 273–74
Spinach, on Croûtes, 137–38
Zucchini, with Basil, 135–36
Pyrenees Cheese, Mushrooms, and
Tomatoes, Rice Salad with,
336–37

Quenelles, Green Vegetable, with
Mushroom Cream, 77–79

Cauliflower, with Onion and
Gruyère Cheese, 66–67
pastry for, notes on, 58
See also Tarts
Quick Broccoli Gratin with
Gruyère and Nuts, 129–30
Quick Hollandaise Sauce, 13–15
Quick Spinach Pâté, 35–36

Radish Flower Canapés, 118
Ragoût, Mixed Mushroom, 171
Raspberry Vinegar, Carrots with,
209–210
Ratatouille Pizza, 81–83
Red and Green Cabbage Sauté
with Goat Cheese, 211
Red (bell) pepper(s)
Aïoli, 181
in Braised Fennel with Peppers
and Olives, 166
Broccoli, and Garlic Dressing,
Pasta Salad with, 337–38
in Corn Salad with Peppers,
315–16
in Crêpes with Peppers, Onions,
and Peas in Curry Sauce,
110–12
in Festive Vegetable Tart, 87–88
in Grilled Peppers with Garlic
and Olive Oil, 203
in Layered Vegetable Tourte,
98–101
in Medley of Vegetables with
Fresh Thyme, 208–209
in Peppers Stuffed with Rice,
Mushrooms, and Olives,
153–54
in Potato-Pepper Salad à la
Provençale, 330–31
Purée, Zucchini Stuffed with,
150–51
in Rice Salad with Peas and
Peppers, 335
in Roasted Pepper Canapés,
119

Red (bell) pepper(s) *(cont'd)*
  Sauce, Eggplant Soufflé-filled
    Crêpes with, 112–15
  in Sautéed Potatoes with
    Peppers and Thyme, 227
  Sweet, and Walnuts,
    Multicolored Pilaf with,
    239–40
  in Swiss Chard and Pepper
    Gratin with Tomatoes,
    131–32
  Velouté Soup, 295–96
"Refreshing" vegetables, notes on,
    178
Rémoulade Sauce, Batter-fried
    Vegetables with, 215–16
Rice
  Brown, Pilaf, with Tarragon,
    241–42
  with Peas and Basil, 233
  Pilaf(s)
    with Artichoke Hearts,
      Carrots, and Toasted
      Almonds, 240–41
    Creamy, with Asparagus,
      238–39
    Multicolored, with Sweet Red
      Peppers and Walnuts,
      239–40
    notes on, 231–32
    Pine Nut, and Tomato Curry
      Sauce, Stuffed Eggplant
      with, 145–47
    Saffron, with Vegetables,
      Mediterranean, 236–38
    Savory, with Eggplant, 235–36
  Ring with Curried Eggplant,
    243–45
  salads. *See* Salads
  with Sautéed Vegetables and
    Walnut Oil, 234–35
  as soup thickener, 261, 273
Rich Onion Soup with Port,
    264–65
Root vegetables, to purée, 134

Roquefort (cheese)
  Asparagus and, Canapés, 116–17
  Escarole Salad with, 306–307
  Sauce
    Broccoli with, 185–86
    Broccoli, Cauliflower, and,
      Pasta with, 256
  Rosemary-scented Tomato Sauce,
    Cauliflower in, 183–84
Rouille Sauce, 262–63

Safflower oil, to use, 7
Saffron
  Butter Sauce, Fresh Peas and,
    Pasta with, 247–49
  Rice Pilaf with Vegetables,
    Mediterranean, 236–38
  Tomatoes, and Garlic, Eggplant
    with, 147–48
Sage, Mustard-, Sauce, Creamy,
  Brussels Sprouts with,
    189–90
Salad(s)
  Artichoke
    Asparagus, Green Bean, and
      Fresh Pea Salad with
      Tarragon Mayonnaise,
      323–24
    Baby, with Hazelnut Oil
      Vinaigrette, 312
    and Rice, Tomatoes Filled
      with, 151–52
  Asparagus Mimosa with
    Hazelnuts, 309
  Avocado and Mushroom, with
    Swiss Chard, 320–21
  Cauliflower and Tomato, with
    Garlic and Walnut Dressing,
    321–22
  Celery Root, with Mustard
    Dressing, 304–305
  Chick-pea and Bean, with
    Tomatoes and Basil,
    318–20
  Classic Salade Niçoise, 329

Salad(s) *(cont'd)*
  composed, notes on, 299–300,
    313
  Corn, with Peppers, 315–16
  Cucumber, with Yogurt Herb
    Dressing, 306
  Dandelion, Warm, with
    Mushrooms and Poached
    Eggs, 310–11
  dressings
    notes on, 300
    See also Dressings
  Endive and Beet, 317–18
  Escarole, with Roquefort Cheese,
    306–307
  Fennel, with Herbed Crème
    Fraîche, 305
  Green, with Pine Nuts and
    Sherry Vinaigrette, 303–304
  Green Bean, Marinated, with
    Green Onions, 309–10
  Leeks Mimosa with Hazelnuts,
    308–309
  Mushroom, Tomatoes Stuffed
    with, 316–17
  notes on, 299–301
  pasta, notes on, 325–26
  Potato
    Asparagus, and Artichoke,
      333–34
    Auvergne, with Cantal Cheese,
      331–32
    and Beet, 327–28
    and Green Bean, Summer,
      328–29
    notes on, 325–26
    -Pepper à la Provençale,
      330–31
    with Watercress, 332–33
  Rice
    notes on, 325–26
    with Peas and Peppers, 335
    with Pyrenees Cheese,
      Mushrooms, and Tomatoes,
      336–37

  to season, 301
  to serve, 300
  simple, notes on, 299, 301
  Tomato
    and Egg, 308
    Summer, with Fresh Herbs,
      307–308
  Vegetable, Breton, with Chive
    Mayonnaise, 313–15
  Watercress, with Goat Cheese
    and Walnuts, 302
Salsify, Sautéed, with Fresh Herbs,
  213
Sauce(s)
  Aïoli, 179–81
    Red Pepper, 181
    Spinach, 181
  Basil-Garlic, Creamy, Tricolored
    Vegetable Terrine with,
    29–32
  Beurre Blanc, Asparagus with,
    174–76
  Cheese, Light
    Broccoli Gratin with, 128
    Cabbage with, 128
    Cauliflower Gratin with,
      126–28
  Cream
    Spinach Gratin with, 124–25
    and Walnuts, Belgian Endive
      Gratin, 124–25
  Curry, Crêpes with Peppers,
    Onions, and Peas in,
    110–12
  Dill, Squash Timbales with,
    26–28
  Garlic Butter, Broccoli Timbales
    with, 16–18
  Herb Butter, Baby Vegetables
    with, 181–83
  Hollandaise
    Asparagus Timbales with,
      13–15
    Cumin, Quick, Spinach
      Timbales with, 21–23

Sauce(s), Hollandaise *(cont'd)*
    Orange, Beets with, 176–78
    Quick, 13–15
  Mornay
    Brussels Sprouts Baked in,
      130–31
    Zucchini Baked in, 131
  Mushroom, Creamy,
    Spinach-Cauliflower Gâteau
      with, 39–41
  Mustard, 11–13
    -Sage, Creamy, Brussels
      Sprouts with, 189–90
  Parmesan Cheese, Baked
    Broccoli Gnocchi, 75–77
  Parsley, Parsnip Timbales with,
    19–20
  Pesto, French, Wax Beans with,
    188–89
  Remoulade, Batter-fried
    Vegetables with, 215–16
  Roquefort
    Broccoli, Cauliflower, and,
      Pasta with, 256
    Broccoli with, 185–86
  Rouille, 262–63
  Saffron Butter, Fresh Peas and,
    Pasta with, 247–49
  Tomato
    Béarnaise, Artichokes with,
      190–92
    Butter, Cauliflower Timbales
      with, 23–25
    Celery Gratin with, 126
    Curry, Pine Nut Pilaf, Stuffed
      Eggplant with, 145–47
    Fresh, Eggplant Savarin with,
      36–38
    Fresh, Winter Squash Gratin
      with, 125–26
    Rosemary-scented, Cauliflower
      in, 183–84
    Tarragon, Fall Vegetables and,
      Spaghetti with, 251–53
  Vegetable Julienne, Potatoes
    with, 219–20

  Watercress, Asparagus-filled
    Pastry Cases with, 94–96
  See also Butters; Dressings
Sauté, Red and Green Cabbage,
  with Goat Cheese, 211
Sautéed Cucumbers with Dill, 212
Sautéed Jerusalem Artichokes,
  210–11
Sautéed Potatoes with Peppers,
  227
Sautéed Salsify with Fresh Herbs,
  213
Sautéing vegetables, notes on, 206,
  207
Savarin, Eggplant, with Fresh
  Tomato Sauce, 36–38
Savory Rice Pilaf with Eggplant,
  235–36
Shallot(s)
  to peel, slice, and chop or
    mince, 5
  Potato-, Soup, Norman, 284–85
  Purée, Plum Tomatoes with,
    152–53
Sherry Vinaigrette, Pine Nuts and,
  Green Salad with, 303–304
Shiitake mushrooms, *in* Mixed
  Mushroom Ragoût, 171
Sorrel Velouté Soup, 290–91
Soufflé(s)
  Broccoli and Mushroom, with
    Chives, 53–55
  Eggplant, -filled Crêpes with Red
    Pepper Sauce, 112–15
  notes on, 49
  Onion, Individual, 52–53
  Potato, in Potato Skins, 225
  Pudding, Cauliflower, with
    Gruyère Cheese, 55–56
  Spinach and Goat Cheese, 49–50
  Winter Squash, 50–52
  See also Mousses
Soup(s)
  Asparagus
    Creamy, 278
    with Olive Oil, 277–78

Soup(s) *(cont'd)*
Carrot, with Chives, 285–86
Cauliflower, Light, 278–79
Chestnut, Touraine, 275–76
cold, to season, 261
cream
to garnish, 287
Leek, with Diced Tomatoes,
289–90
Mushroom, with Fresh Herbs,
268–69
to reheat, 288
to season, 274, 288
to thicken, 286–87
Fresh Pea, with Mint Cream,
274–75
Onion
Creamy, with Pasta, 265
Rich, with Port, 264–65
Potato-Shallot, Norman, 284–85
Pumpkin
and Pasta, 279–80
Potato, and Leek Soup,
280–81
purée
notes on, 273–74
to season, 274
Spinach, Country, 266
Swiss Chard, with Toasted
Hazelnuts, 288–89
to thicken, 261, 273
Tomato, Provençal, 281–83
Vegetable
Bouillabaisse, 262–63
Bourride with Aïoli, 270–71
Provençal, with Pasta and
Pistou, 267–68
Southwestern, with Vegetable
Croutons, 271–73
vegetables for, 260–61
Velouté
Cauliflower, with Broccoli,
294–95
Cauliflower, with Broccoli,
Cold, 295
to garnish, 287

notes on, 286–87
Red Pepper, 295–96
to reheat, 288
to season, 274, 288
Sorrel, 290–91
to thicken, 286–87
Watercress, with Cheese Puffs,
291–93
Zucchini, Light, with Curry
Puffs, 283–84
Southwestern Vegetable Soup with
Vegetable Croutons, 271–73
Spaghetti with Fall Vegetables and
Tomato-Tarragon Sauce,
251–53
Spinach
Aïoli, 181
in Buckwheat Crêpes with
Creamy Vegetables,
105–106
-Cauliflower Gâteau with Creamy
Mushroom Sauce, 39–41
to clean, 5
-filled Crêpes with Crème
Fraîche, 106–108
and Goat Cheese Soufflé, 49–50
Gratin with Cream Sauce,
124–25
in Green Vegetable Quenelles
with Mushroom Cream,
77–79
in Layered Vegetable Tourte,
98–101
Leek, and Pumpkin Pancakes,
213–15
Onions Stuffed with, 155–56
Purée on Croûtes, 137–38
Soup, Country, 266
to substitute frozen for fresh,
5–6
Tart, Bright Green, 58–60
Timbales with Quick Cumin
Hollandaise Sauce, 21–23
in Tricolored Vegetable Terrine
with Creamy Basil-Garlic
Sauce, 29–32

Squash
  Pattypan
    with Paprika Cream, 174
    Stuffed, with Parmesan and
      Rice, 156–57
    Timbales with Dill Sauce,
      26–28
  Winter
    Gratin with Fresh Tomato
      Sauce, 125–26
    Soufflé, 50–52
  See also Zucchini
Steamed Carrots with Pistachio
  Butter, 176
Steamed New Potatoes with
  Tarragon Butter, 221–22
Steaming vegetables, notes on,
  158, 172–73
Stewing vegetables, notes on,
  162
Stock(s)
  Chicken, 297–98
  Vegetable, 296–97
Stuffed Eggplant with Pine Nut
  Pilaf and Tomato Curry
  Sauce, 145–47
Stuffed Pattypan Squash with
  Parmesan and Rice, 156–57
Stuffed vegetables, notes on,
  141–42
Summer Potato and Green Bean
  Salad, 328–29
Summer Tomato Salad with Fresh
  Herbs, 307–308
Sunflower oil, to use, 7
Sweet Potatoes, French-fried,
  230–31
Swiss chard
  Avocado and Mushroom Salad
    with, 320–21
  in Buckwheat Crêpes with
    Creamy Vegetables,
    105–106
  in Colorful Vegetable
    Blanquette, 169–70

  and Pepper Gratin with
    Tomatoes, 131–32
  in Rice with Sautéed Vegetables
    and Walnut Oil, 234–35
  Soup with Toasted Hazelnuts,
    288–89
  and Tomato Tart, 67–69

Tarragon
  Brown Rice Pilaf with, 241–42
  Butter, Steamed New Potatoes
    with, 221–22
  Mayonnaise, Artichoke,
    Asparagus, Green Bean, and
    Fresh Pea Salad with,
    323–24
  Tomato-, Sauce, Fall Vegetables
    and, Spaghetti with,
    251–53
Tart(s)
  Caraway, Cabbage Tart with,
    63–64
  Leek, Country, 85–87
  Mushroom, Creamy, with
    Chives, 64–66
  Onion and Cream Cheese,
    Alsatian, 98–99
  pastry for, notes on, 58
  Spinach, Bright Green, 58–60
  Vegetable, Festive, 87–88
  See also Pastries; Pizza; Quiches;
    Tartlets
Tartlets
  Cèpe, 63
  Tomato and Goat Cheese, with
    Fresh Thyme, 61–63
  See also Tarts
Terrine(s)
  Eggplant Savarin with Fresh
    Tomato Sauce, 36–38
  Spinach-Cauliflower Gâteau with
    Creamy Mushroom Sauce,
    39–41
  Vegetable
    with Mushroom Mousse and

Terrine(s), Vegetable *(cont'd)*
  Fresh Tomato Vinaigrette,
    32–35
  Tricolored, with Creamy
    Basil-Garlic Sauce, 29–32
  See also Pâtés
Thyme
  Fresh
    Medley of Vegetables with,
      208–209
    Tomato and Goat Cheese
      Tartlets with, 61–63
    Peppers and, Sautéed Potatoes
      with, 227
Timbales
  Asparagus, with Hollandaise
    Sauce, 113–15
  Beet, 11–13
  Broccoli, with Garlic Butter
    Sauce, 16–18
  Carrot, 15–16
  Cauliflower, with Tomato Butter
    Sauce, 23–25
  to check for doneness, 10
  as main course, 9
  notes on, 8–9
  Parsnip, with Parsley Sauce,
    19–20
  sauces for, 9
  Spinach, with Quick Cumin
    Hollandaise Sauce, 21–23
  Squash, with Dill Sauce, 26–28
  Turnip, 25–26
  to unmold, 10
  water bath for, 10
Tomato(es)
  Baked, Provençal, 201–202
  and Basil, Chick-pea and Bean
    Salad with, 318–20
  Cauliflower and, Salad with
    Garlic and Walnut Dressing,
    321–22
  Chard and, Tart, 67–69
  cherry, *in* Baby Vegetables with
    Herb Butter Sauce, 181–83

  Curry Sauce, Pine Nut Pilaf and,
    Stuffed Eggplant with,
    145–47
  Diced, Leek Cream Soup with,
    289–90
  and Egg
    Canapés, 118–19
    Salad, 208
  Filled with Artichoke and Rice
    Salad, 151–52
  Fresh
    Purée, Mushrooms Stuffed
      with, 142–43 sauces. *See*
      Sauces
    Vinaigrette, Mushroom
      Mousse and, Vegetable
      Terrine with, 32–35
  and Goat Cheese Tartlets with
    Fresh Thyme, 61–63
  in Mediterranean Saffron Rice
    Pilaf with Vegetables,
    236–38
  Mousse, Two-Tone, 42–43
  and Onions, White Beans with,
    193–94
  Pasta with Goat Cheese and
    Garlic, 246–47
  to peel, seed, and chop, 6
  Plum, with Shallot Purée,
    152–53
  in Provençal Marinated
    Vegetables, 324–25
  Pyrenees Cheese, Mushrooms,
    and, Rice Salad with,
    336–37
  Saffron, and Garlic, Eggplant
    with, 147–48
  salads. *See* Salads
  sauces. *See* Sauces
  Slices, Zucchini, Eggplant,
    and, Baked with Herbs,
    197–98
  Soup, Provençal, 281–83
  Stuffed with Mushroom Salad,
    316–17

Tomato(es) *(cont'd)*
  Swiss Chard and Pepper Gratin
      with, 131–32
  -Tarragon Sauce, Fall Vegetables
      and, Spaghetti with, 251–53
Touraine Chestnut Soup, 275–76
Tourte, Vegetable, Layered,
      98–101
Tricolored Vegetable Terrine with
      Creamy Basil-Garlic Sauce,
      29–32
Turnip(s)
  baby, *in* Baby Vegetables with
      Herb Butter Sauce, 181–83
  Carrots and, Ginger-glazed,
      159–60
  and Onion Gratin with Parmesan,
      133
  in Southwestern Vegetable Soup
      with Vegetable Croutons,
      271–73
  Timbales, 25–26
  in Tricolored Vegetable Terrine
      with Creamy Basil-Garlic
      Sauce, 29–32
Turnovers, Cèpe, 101–102
Two-Tone Tomato Mousse, 42–43

Vegetable(s)
  Baby, with Herb Butter Sauce,
      181–83
  baked, notes on, 197
  Batter-fried, with Rémoulade
      Sauce, 215–16
  Blanquette, Colorful, 169–70
  boiled, notes on, 178
  Bouillabaisse, 262–63
  Bourride with Aïoli, 270–71
  cooked, to season, 159
  Creamy, Buckwheat Crêpes with,
      105–106
  Croutons, Southwestern
      Vegetable Soup with,
      271–73
  deep-fried, notes on, 206–207

Fall, and Tomato-Tarragon
      Sauce, Spaghetti with,
      251–53
  and Garlic Feast Provençal,
      179–81
  glazed, notes on, 159
  green
    to purée, 134
    Quenelles with Mushroom
        Cream, 77–79
    to "refresh," 178
  grilled, notes on, 197
  Julienne
    Chanterelle Feuilletés with,
        96–98
    Sauce, Potatoes with, 219–20
  Marinated, Provençal, 324–25
  Medley of, with Fresh Thyme,
      208–209
  "Noodles," Pasta with, 253–54
  oil, types of, to use, 7
  root, to purée, 134
  Saffron Rice Pilaf with,
      Mediterranean, 236–38
  Salad, Breton, with Chive
      Mayonnaise, 313–15
  for salads, to cook, 301
  Sautéed
    notes on, 206, 207
    and Walnut Oil, Rice with,
        234–35
  Soup
    Provençal, with Pasta and
        Pistou, 267–68
    Southwestern, with Vegetable
        Croutons, 271–72
  for soups, 260–61
  to purée, 274
  steamed, notes on, 158, 172–73
  Stock, 296–97
  stuffed, notes on, 141–42
  Tart, Festive, 87–88
  Tourte, Layered, 98–101
  See also Names of vegetables
Velouté soups. *See* Soups

Vinaigrette(s)
  Champagne, 318
  Chive, Creamy, 320–21
  Fresh Herb, 307
  Fresh Tomato, Mushroom
      Mousse and, Vegetable
      Terrine with, 32–35
  Hazelnut Oil, Baby Artichokes
      with, 312
  Parsley, 308–309
  Sherry, Pine Nuts and, Green
      Salad with, 303–304
  Walnut Oil, 302
  See also Dressings
Vinegar(s)
  Raspberry, Carrots with, 209–10
  Wine, Butter and, Cabbage with,
      190

Walnut(s)
  Cream Sauce and, Belgian
      Endive Gratin with, 124
  Escargot Butter and, Baked
      Mushrooms with, 198–99
  Garlic and, Dressing, Cauliflower
      and Tomato Salad with,
      321–22
  Goat Cheese and, Watercress
      Salad with, 302
  Oil
    Sautéed Vegetables and, Rice
        with, 234–35
    Vinaigrette, 302
  Sautéed, Green Beans with, 209
  Sweet Red Peppers and,
      Multicolored Pilaf with,
      239–40
Warm Dandelion Salad with
    Mushrooms and Poached
    Eggs, 310–11
Water bath, for timbales, 10
Watercress
  in Green Vegetable Quenelles
      with Mushroom Cream,
      77–79

Potato Salad with, 332–33
  Salad with Goat Cheese and
      Walnuts, 302
  Sauce, Asparagus-filled Pastry
      Cases with, 94–96
  Velouté Soup with Cheese Puffs,
      291–93
Wax beans
  in Flageolets with Green and
      Yellow Beans and Green
      Onion Butter, 167–69
  with French Pesto Sauce, 188–89
  in Provençal Marinated
      Vegetables, 324–25
  in Vegetable Terrine with
      Mushroom Mousse and
      Fresh Tomato Vinaigrette,
      32–35
White beans. *See* Beans
Wine
  for cooking, 7
  Vinegar, Butter and, Cabbage
      with, 190
Winter squash
  Gratin with Fresh Tomato Sauce,
      125–26
  Soufflé, 50–52

Yellow beans. See Wax beans
Yellow bell peppers, *in* Potato
      Pepper Salad à la
      Provençale, 330–31
Yogurt Herb Dressing, Cucumber
      Salad with, 306

Zucchini
  baby, *in* Baby Vegetables with
      Herb Butter Sauce, 181–83
  Baby Onions and, Glazed,
      161–62
  Baked in Mornay Sauce, 131
  in Batter-fried Vegetables with
      Rémoulade Sauce, 215–16
  with Capers and Hazelnut
      Butter, 186

Zucchini (cont'd)
  in Colorful Vegetable
      Blanquette, 169–70
  Eggplant, and Tomato Slices
      Baked with Herbs, 197–98
  in Festive Vegetable Tart, 87–88
  Garlic-scented, with Celery,
      212–13
  in Green Vegetable Quenelles
      with Mushroom Cream,
      77–79
  in Mediterranean Saffron Rice
      Pilaf with Vegetables,
      236–37
  in Medley of Vegetables with
      Fresh Thyme, 208–209
  with Mint Butter, 173–74
  in Pasta with Vegetable
      "Noodles," 253–54
  Purée with Basil, 135–36
  Soup, Light, with Curry Puffs,
      283–84
  Stuffed with Red Pepper Purée,
      150–51
  in Vegetable Bouillabaisse,
      262–63
  in Vegetable Bourride with
      Aïoli, 270–71

A NOTE ABOUT THE AUTHOR

Faye Levy, an internationally published cookbook author and certified cooking teacher, has been described by the food editor of *Gourmet* magazine as "one of the finest cooks in the country."

Born and brought up in Washington, D.C., Faye has the distinction of being the first American ever to have been commissioned to write a cookbook by Flammarion, the most prestigious cookbook publisher in France, the original publisher of Escoffier, Bocuse, and Lenotre. *La Cuisine du Poisson,* the seafood cookbook Faye co-authored with Fernand Chambrette, was published in 1984.

Faye holds the "Grand Diplome" of the first graduating class of the famous Parisian cooking school La Varenne, where she spent five years. She is the author of the school's first cookbook, *The La Varenne Tour Book.* As La Varenne's editor, Faye planned the school's curriculum and developed and drafted the recipes for the award-winning cookbooks, *French Regional Cooking, The La Varenne Cooking Course,* and *Basic French Cookery.*

Faye has been writing "The Basics" column for *Bon Appétit* magazine since 1982. Her creative dishes have been featured on the covers of *Bon Appétit* and *Gourmet,* America's top cooking magazines. Faye is the only person to have contributed to the finest collections of both magazines; her recipes appear in *The Best of Gourmet* and *The Best of Bon Appétit* series. Articles by Faye have also been published in other national magazines, as well as in *The Washington Post,* the *Chicago Tribune,* the *Boston Globe,* the *New York Post,* the *Los Angeles Herald Examiner* and in numerous other major newspapers.

Faye now lives in Santa Monica, California, with her husband/associate Yakir Levy.